T0133680

Secure Data Provenance and Inference Control with Semantic Web

OTHER BOOKS BY BHAVANI THURAISINGHAM
FROM AUERBACH PUBLICATIONS

Building Trustworthy Semantic Webs
ISBN: 978-0-8493-5080-1

Database and Applications Security: Integrating Information Security and Data Management
ISBN: 978-0-8493-2224-2

Data Management Systems: Evolution and Interoperation
ISBN: 978-0-8493-9493-5

Data Mining: Technologies, Techniques, Tools, and Trends
ISBN: 978-0-8493-1815-3

Data Mining Tools for Malware Detection
with Mehedy Masud and Latifur Khan
ISBN: 978-1-4398-5454-9

Design and Implementation of Data Mining Tools
with Lei Wang, Latifur Khan, and M. Awad
ISBN: 978-1-4200-4590-1

Developing and Securing the Cloud
ISBN: 978-1-4398-6291-9

Managing and Mining Multimedia Databases
ISBN: 978-0-8493-0037-0

Secure Semantic Service-Oriented Systems
ISBN: 978-1-4200-7331-7

Web Data Mining and Applications in Business Intelligence and Counter-Terrorism
ISBN: 978-0-8493-1460-5

XML Databases and the Semantic Web
ISBN: 978-1-4200-7331-7

AUERBACH PUBLICATIONS
www.auerbach-publications.com
To Order Call: 1-800-272-7737 • Fax: 1-800-374-3401
E-mail: orders@crcpress.com

Secure Data Provenance and Inference Control with Semantic Web

Bhavani Thuraisingham • Tyrone Cadenhead

Murat Kantarcioglu • Vaibhav Khadilkar

CRC Press
Taylor & Francis Group
Boca Raton London New York

CRC Press is an imprint of the
Taylor & Francis Group, an **informa** business

To Our Colleague and Friend

The late Dr. Steve Barker

Kings College, University of London

Thank you for the fruitful collaboration we have
had on data and applications security.

Contents

SECTION I   Conclusion

SECTION II   SECURE DATA PROVENANCE

SECTION II   Introduction

SECTION II　Conclusion

SECTION III　INFERENCE CONTROL

SECTION III　Introduction

SECTION III   Conclusion

SECTION IV   UNIFYING FRAMEWORK

SECTION IV   Introduction

SECTION IV   Conclusion

Preface

Securing Provenance Data

Provenance means the origin of a source, the history of ownership of a valued object or a work of art or literature. Information about provenance is especially important for works of arts, as it directly determines the value of the artwork. This also applies to both digital artifacts and results that are generated by applications. Therefore, data provenance is one kind of metadata that pertains to the derivation history of a product starting from its original sources. The provenance of a result or data object can be regarded as important as the data itself; therefore, the quality or trust one places on the data is important to the value and usage of the data.

Using provenance, one can ascertain the quality of data based on its ancestral data and derivations, track back to sources of errors, allow automatic re-enactment of derivations to update data, and provide attribution of the data source. Provenance is also essential to the medical domain. Provenance can be used to drill down to the source of record, track the creation of a new version of a record, and provide an audit trail for regulatory processes.

A framework for evaluating the utility and security aspects of provenance is a critical need in multiple domains. For instance, in health care, the provenance associated with a patient's medical record can be used for postdiagnosis and for verifying regulatory and health-care guidelines. Also, the provenance plays a critical part in an emergency room, since it is used to provide step-by-step transparent details of the patient's entire history. On one side of the coin, the risks of unintentional disclosure of sensitive contents of an electronic patient record (EPR) document can be severe and costly. On the other side, we need to share provenance data to verify the quality of information exchanged among mutual parties. In e-science, for example, the provenance is used to verify experiments and processes, validate data quality, and associate trust values with scientific results. Also, in intelligence, the provenance can be used to determine the quality of information on which decisions are based. Therefore, the more provenance that is associated with the information, the more useful that information is to the strategic decisions of a party.

Different security criteria have been formulated to ensure that documents are not improperly released. These include access control and redaction policies, anonymization and sanitization techniques, and cryptographic techniques. In this book, we focus on two approaches: access control and redaction policies. On the one hand, access control encompasses a list of techniques for protecting a document. These include policies that specify contextual conditions in the form of rules and those that hide the real data by distortion (e.g., cryptography, scrambling, and noise techniques). Therefore, analyzing access control policies and mechanisms are an important topic with respect to the protection of sensitive provenance information. On the other hand, redaction encourages the sharing and continued transactions among organizations and their stakeholders, but the emphasis is on removing the sensitive and proprietary components of a document before releasing it. In other words, redaction is used to eliminate the threats associated with releasing proprietary or competitive information, trade secrets, and financial records.

Motivation

The primary motivation of this book is to provide a unifying framework for securing provenance. We formulate this motivation in order to address different criteria of current information systems:

1. *Sharing Meaningful Information.* Any useful system should provide meaningful information that is relevant, accurate, and timely. A user poses queries to gather relevant information for day-to-day activities. The information may be in the same format or different formats, and the activities may vary from domain to domain. For example, in intelligence, the information is for strategic planning; in industry, it is for gaining market share; and in health care, it is for providing treatments to patients. These queries could be answered with the use of traditional systems which are already equipped with their own security mechanisms. However, for these domains, the information retrieved may be both incorrect or outdated.

2. *Verifying the Shared Information.* Each domain should be able to share meaningful information among different domains, as well as within a domain. In order to share meaningful information, a provenance information system should be in place to provide metadata describing the accuracy and currency of the domain information that is retrieved and shared. However, domains often collect and store sensitive information. For example, in intelligence, the FBI may collect, classify, and preserve records related to criminal identification and tracking for the official use by authorized officials of the government. In industry, a company may collect customers' information and transactions in order to target prospective customers effectively, tailor to their individual needs, and improve customer satisfaction and retention. In health

care, a hospital may keep a log of all activities, including patient visits to a hospital, diagnoses and treatments for diseases, and processes performed by health care professionals.

3. *Secured Provenance Framework.* There is a need to provide a framework for addressing the above two criteria. This framework will use Semantic Web technologies to integrate the different provenance information retrieved from the different domains, therefore unifying and solving any interoperability among the information formats provided by the systems. In addition, the framework will address the concerns about the security of provenance information for these systems.

In this book we examine a typical distributed health-care system for hospitals, but any discussion in this book can be applied equally to other domains. The hospitals are divided into several autonomous wards and ancillary units, which are visited by the patients for treatments and examinations during hospitalization in accordance with their illness. The treatment process is dynamic; the new information about a patient results in new treatments. The patient may visit different wards in the same physical hospital or different wards in different hospitals (in case the tests can only be done at specific hospital sites). Also, each hospital is running different health care applications. Therefore, the data (a single patient's health care history), the workflow (procedures carried out on that patient), and the logs (a recording of meaningful procedural events) are distributed among several heterogeneous and autonomous information systems.

This health care system is suitable for exploring why we need a secure provenance framework. It contains heterogeneous information and applications, which will determine our choice of a Semantic Web framework. Our reference to information here and throughout this book is for both traditional data and its provenance, unless otherwise noted. This system contains many hospitals and large distributed systems which will motivate our need to handle the scalability of our framework. Accurate and current information is critical for emergency operations in a hospital, which will in turn motivate our need for a framework with reasonable performances.

Our Approach

Provenance information contains entities and the relationships between them. The entities are the agents, processes, algorithms, and inputs and outputs to tasks; these entities are similar to the single data items in traditional systems. Our framework should be able to handle the single-data-item view of provenance as well as the more involved case of when the relationships between the entities are a part of the provenance. We will address each of these cases in turn.

We develop two broad approaches that support provenance in order to protect the sensitive components and still share it. Our first approach is based on a representation of the provenance document. When provenance is both viewed and represented as a directed labeled graph (e.g., resource description framework [RDF], web ontology language [OWL]), a rich set of graph-related techniques can be applied to a provenance graph so that access control policies and redaction policies can be used to protect provenance. The second approach is based on a utility measure of provenance. This second approach is a new formal model for determining when we should release provenance. We need to release provenance to enable the advancement of science; the inputs to a new scientific discovery must be verifiable and accurate. The accuracy of information as inputs to a decision-making tool for intelligence must be established before actions are taken based on the available information. This formal model is used to find a comparable trade-off for releasing both data and its associated provenance and hiding provenance in case of intolerable losses. We propose a special application of this model, which is to build an inference controller that emulates humanlike reasoning for the purpose of countering known inference attacks.

Our general architecture consists of a provenance management system whose role is to ensure that we provide high-quality information to a querying user while ensuring the confidentiality of the underlying data. This provenance management system is domain-neutral; for example, it is designed to protect any domain data that could be in different data formats, describing both the data and its provenance. Therefore, we can build domain-independent modules, which are closely integrated to make policy decisions related to the context of input queries and the querying user.

The user interface layer hides the actual internal representation of a query and policy from a user. This allows a user to submit both high-level queries and specification of policies without any knowledge of the underlying logic used to implement the solution. This layer also allows a user to retrieve information irrespective of the underlying data representation. The query-processing module translates a user query to one that is compatible with the underlying data representation. The policy layer module interacts with the query-processing module and is responsible for ensuring that a query conforms to a set of high-level policies. Any high-level policy language can be used to write the security policies as long as there is a compatible parser that translates these policies to a low-level representation. The redaction module is used to circumvent any sensitive contents from the result before it is returned to the user.

It is also important to note that the query-processing module, the policy-layer module, and the redaction module can all be used to enforce security policies. The query-processing module can be used to rewrite a user query according to a set of security policies. The policy layer can be used to provide advanced security features and is usually the main component for enforcing the policies. The redaction module can be used to remove (circumvent or filter) sensitive information from the results before returning a final answer to the user's query. Our solution is based on building a unified and effective policy management framework that enforces the following policies: access-control policies, redaction policies, and inference policies.

Contributions and Organization of This Book

The main highlights of this book are

- Flexible policies that are independent of our implementation. A domain user may use any policy language that describes the security policies of the domain. A suitable parser will produce a correct low-level policy.
- Definition of an access-control policy language for provenance. We can now protect provenance not only comprised of single data items, but also as paths in a connected directed graph.
- Performing redaction over a provenance graph. This is accomplished using the application of a graph-grammar technique to circumvent parts of a provenance graph.
- Semantic Web-based inference attacks. A risk-based inference approach is taken to decide suitable trade-offs for hiding and sharing provenance.

This book consists of 24 chapters and four appendices. It starts with an introduction (Chapter 1) and ends with a summary and directions chapter (Chapter 24). Chapters 2–23 are divided into four sections. Section I describes supporting technologies and consists of six chapters. Chapter 2 reviews the existing literature on access control and provenance. Chapter 3 briefly presents the background information required to follow the theory we use in this book and describes Semantic Web technologies. Chapter 4 discusses the inference problem. The various types of inference engines are discussed in Chapter 5. An overview of inference strategies is presented in Chapter 6. Aspects of cloud computing that are needed for implementing our policy engine on the cloud are discussed in Chapter 7.

Section II consists of three chapters. Chapter 8 discusses how we create flexible and scalable access-control policies by extending role-based access control (RBAC) using key Semantic Web technologies. We also implement a prototype which shows that we can scale and reason over a set of access-control policies efficiently. Chapter 9 provides a definition of an access-control policy language for provenance. This language retains the properties of traditional access-control to gain access to data. Furthermore, the language provides an additional advantage whereby we can write one policy that is a pattern for several policies, thus contracting the policy set. We also build a prototype using Semantic Web technologies that allows a user to query for data and provenance based on access-control policies defined using our policy language. Chapter 10 discusses the application of a graph-grammar technique that can be used to perform redaction over provenance. In addition, we provide an architectural design that allows a high-level specification of policies, thus separating the business layer from a specific software implementation. We also implement a prototype of the architecture based on open source Semantic Web technologies.

Section III consists of seven chapters and addresses the very important notion of inference control within the context of provenance and Semantic Web. Chapter 11 gives an overview of our inference architecture, which uses a risk-based model to determine whether provenance can be released. Chapter 12 describes inference control with two users. Chapter 13 describes provenance data representation for inference control. Chapter 14 describes query specification for inference control. Query modification for inference control is discussed in Chapter 15. Inference control with provenance data including examples is discussed in Chapter 16. Chapter 17 describes our implementation.

Section IV consists of six chapters and discusses a unifying framwork. Risk-based inference control models are discussed in Chapter 18. Some novel approaches including probabilistic deduction and mathematical programming for inference control are discussed in Chapter 19. Implementing our policy engine in the cloud for information sharing is discussed in Chapter 20. Security, privacy, and trust with respect to inference control is discussed in Chapter 21. Inference control for big data is discussed in Chapter 22. Finally, our unifying framework that takes into consideration inference control for data access and sharing is discussed in Chapter 23.

The book concludes with Chapter 24. The book is also augmented with multiple appendices. Appendix A describes data management and the relationship between our texts. This appendix is included in all of our books. Appendix B describes database management and security. A perspective of the inference problem is discussed in Appendix C. Appendix D describes one of the earliest inference controllers that was designed and developed in the 1990s and has influenced our current research and development efforts.

Data, Information, and Knowledge

As in our previous books, we give a short overview of data, information, and knowledge. In general, data management includes managing databases, interoperability, migration, warehousing, and mining. For example, data on the web has to be managed and mined to extract information and patterns and trends. Data could be in files, relational databases, or other types of databases such as multimedia databases. Data may be structured or unstructured. We use the terms data, data management, database systems, and database management systems in this book. We elaborate on these terms in the appendices. We define data management systems to be systems that manage the data, extract meaningful information from the data, and make use of the information extracted. Therefore, data management systems include database systems, data warehouses, and data mining systems. Data could be structured data such as that found in relational databases, or it could be unstructured such as text, voice, imagery, and video.

There have been numerous discussions in the past to distinguish among data, information, and knowledge. In some of our previous books on data management and mining, we did not attempt to clarify these terms. We simply stated that data could be just bits and bytes or it could convey some meaningful information to the user. However, with the advent of the web and also with increasing interest in data, information, and knowledge management as separate areas, in this book we take a different approach to data, information, and knowledge by differentiating among these terms. For us, data is usually some value like numbers, integers, and strings. Information is obtained when some meaning or semantics is associated with the data, such as "John's salary is $20,000." Knowledge is something that you acquire through reading and learning, and as a result you understand the data and information and take action. That is, data and information can be transferred into knowledge when uncertainty about the data and information is removed.

It is rather difficult to give strict definitions of data, information, and knowledge. Sometimes we will use these terms interchangeably. Our framework for data management discussed in the appendix helps clarify some of the differences. To be consistent with the terminology in our previous books, we will also distinguish between database systems and database management systems. A database management system is that component that manages the database containing persistent data. A database system consists of both the database and the database management system.

Final Thoughts

The goal of this book is to explore security issues for provenance data represented with Semantic Web technologies. In particular, we discuss access control as well as inference control for provenance data. By representing data with Semantic Web technologies, we can reason about the data. We discuss concepts, technologies, and solutions. In particular, we describe an inference controller we have developed for provenance data at The University of Texas at Dallas. While our focus is on inference control, the concepts discussed can be applied for certain aspects of privacy control.

We have used the material in this book together with the numerous references listed in each chapter for multiple graduate level courses on data and applications security, secure web services, and cloud computing, building trustworthy Semantic Webs, cyber security essentials, and analyzing and securing social networks at The University of Texas at Dallas.

The field is expanding very rapidly with emerging standards, tools, and systems. Therefore, it is important for the reader to keep up with the developments of the prototypes, products, tools, and standards for secure data management, secure Semantic Web, secure web services, and secure cloud computing.

Acknowledgments

We would like to thank the administration at the Erik Jonsson School of Engineering and Computer Science at The University of Texas at Dallas for the opportunity to direct the Cyber Security Research and Education Institute. We thank our colleagues and students for giving us many insights. We thank Ms. Rhonda Walls, our project coordinator, for proofreading and editing the chapters.

We would also like to thank the many people who have supported us in secure cloud computing:

- Dr. Robert Herklotz from the Air Force Office of Scientific Research for funding our research on secure cloud computing and inference control. Without this support we would never have been able to gain the knowledge to write this book.
- Our respective families for their encouragement and support that enabled us to write this book.
- The data and applications security community as well as the Semantic Web community for their comments and feedback on our research.

Authors

Dr. Bhavani Thuraisingham is the Louis A. Beecherl, Jr. Distinguished Professor of Computer Science and the Executive Director of the Cyber Security Research and Education Institute (CSI) at The University of Texas at Dallas (UTD). She is an elected fellow of multiple organizations including the Institute for Electrical and Electronics Engineers (IEEE) and the American Association for the Advancement of Science (AAAS). She received several prestigious awards including the IEEE Computer Society's 1997 Technical Achievement, the 2010 Association for Computing Machinery, Special Interest Group on Security, Audit and Control (ACM SIGSAC) Outstanding Contributions Award, and the Society for Design and Process Science (SDPS) Transformative Achievement Medal. Her work has resulted in over 100 journal articles, over 200 conference papers, and over 100 keynote addresses. She has a PhD in theory of computation from the University of Wales, UK, and received the prestigious higher doctorate degree for her published research in secure dependable data management from the University of Bristol in England.

Dr. Tyrone Cadenhead worked in the computer industry for many years before joining UTD for graduate school. His thesis research was on secure data provenance and inference control, and he completed his PhD in 2011. He was a postdoctoral research associate at UTD for two years, conducting research in data security and privacy, and is currently a lead developer with Blue Cross Blue Shield working on semantic web technologies.

Dr. Murat Kantarcioglu is an associate professor in the Computer Science Department and the director of the Data Security and Privacy Lab at UTD. He is also a visiting scholar at the Data Privacy Lab at Harvard University. Dr. Kantarcioglu's research focuses on creating technologies that can efficiently extract useful information from any data without sacrificing privacy or security. He has published over 100 papers in peer-reviewed journals and conferences and has received two best paper awards. He is a recipient of the prestigious NSF CAREER award, and his research has been reported in the media, including the *Boston Globe* and *ABC News*. He holds MS and PhD degrees in computer science from Purdue University. He is a senior member of both the IEEE and the ACM.

Dr. Vaibhav Khadilkar completed his MS degree at Lamar University and, after working as a systems administrator for a few years, joined UTD for his PhD. He conducted research in secure semantic web, assured information sharing, and secure social networking and completed his PhD in 2013. He received a scholarship from the CSI for his outstanding contributions. He has published numerous papers in top tier venues and is currently employed at NutraSpace in Dallas.

Permissions

Chapter 8

Scalable and Efficient Reasoning for Enforcing Role-Based Access Control. Tyrone Cadenhead, Murat Kantarcioglu, Bhavani M. Thuraisingham. Lecture Notes in Computer Science Volume 6166, Data and Applications Security and Privacy XXIV, 2010. 24th Annual IFIP WG 11.3 Working Conference, Rome, Italy, June 21–23, 2010. Proceedings, Editors: Sara Foresti, Sushil Jajodia. ISBN: 978-3-642-13738-9, pp. 209–224. © 2010. *Published with kind permission of Springer Science+Business Media.*

Chapter 9

A language for provenance access control. Tyrone Cadenhead, Vaibhav Khadilkar, Murat Kantarcioglu, Bhavani M. Thuraisingham. Proceedings of the First ACM Conference on Data and Application Security and Privacy (CODASPY), San Antonio, Tx, pp. 133–144. © 2011, ACM Inc. http://doi.acm.org/10.1145/1943513.1943532

Chapters 9 and 10

Transforming provenance using redaction. Tyrone Cadenhead, Vaibhav Khadilkar, Murat Kantarcioglu, Bhavani M. Thuraisingham. Proceedings of the 15th ACM Symposium on Access Control Models and Technologies (SACMAT), pp. 93–102. © 2011, ACM Inc. http://doi.acm.org/10.1145/1998441.1998456

Chapter 20

Design and Implementation of a Cloud-Based Assured Information Sharing System. Tyrone Cadenhead, Murat Kantarcioglu, Vaibhav Khadilkar, Bhavani M. Thuraisingham. Lecture Notes in Computer Science Volume 7531, Computer

Network Security, 2012. 6th International Conference on Mathematical Methods, Models and Architectures for Computer Network Security, MMM-ACNS 2012, St. Petersburg, Russia, October 17–19, 2012. Proceedings, pp. 36–50, ISBN 978-3-642-33703-1, Igor V. Kotenko, Victor A. Skormin (Eds.). © 2012. *Published with kind permission of Springer Science+Business Media.*

Chapter 21

Administering the Semantic Web: Confidentiality, Privacy and Trust Management. Bhavani Thuraisingham, Natasha Tsybulnik, Ashraful Alam. International Journal of Information Security and Privacy, Volume 1, No. 1, pp. 18–34. Copyright 2007, IGI Global, www.igi-global.com. Posted by permission of the publisher.

Chapter 1

Introduction

1.1 Overview

Inference is the process of forming conclusions from premises. Inferred knowledge is harmful when a user is not authorized to acquire such information from legitimate responses that he or she receives. Providing a solution to the inference problem where users issue multiple requests and consequently infer unauthorized knowledge is an open problem. An inference controller is a device that is used to detect or prevent the occurrence of the inference problem. However, an inference controller will never know in full the inferences possible from the answers to a query request since there is always some prior knowledge available to the querying user. This prior knowledge could be any subset of all possible knowledge available from other external sources. The inference problem is complex and therefore an integrated and/or incremental domain specific approach is necessary for its management. For a particular domain, one could take several approaches, such as building inference controllers that (1) act during query processing, (2) enforce constraints (i.e., policies) during the data/knowledge base design, (3) handle constraints when updating the database, and (4) provide explanations to a system security officer (Thuraisingham et al. 1993). This book discusses the implementation of these incremental approaches for a prototype inference controller for provenance in a medical domain.

Provenance is metadata that captures the origin of a data source—the history or ownership of a valued object or a work of art or literature (Moreau 2010). It allows us to verify the quality of information in a data store, to repeat manipulation steps, and to discover dependencies among data items in a data store. In addition, provenance can be used to determine the usefulness and trustworthiness of shared information. The utility of shared information relies on (1) the quality of the source of information and (2) the reliability and accuracy of the mechanisms (i.e., procedures and algorithms) used at each step of the modification (or transformation) of the underlying data items. Furthermore, provenance is a key component for the verification and correctness of a data item, which is usually stored and then shared with information users.

This book describes the design and implementation of an inference controller that operates over provenance. This controller protects the sensitive information in a provenance database from unauthorized users. The provenance is represented as a directed acyclic graph. This graphical representation of provenance can be represented and stored using Semantic Web technologies. We have built

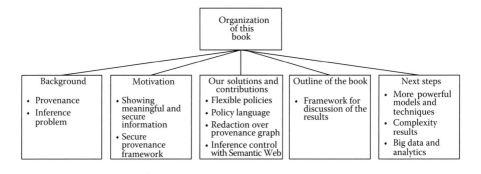

Figure 1.1   Organization of this book.

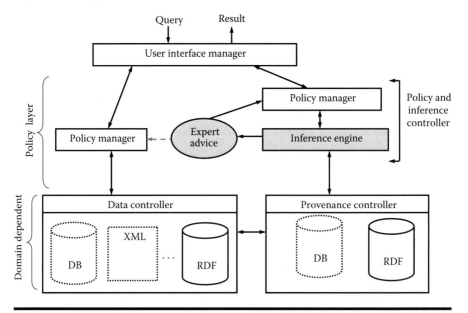

Figure 1.2   Framework for secure data provenance and inference control.

a prototype to evaluate the effectiveness of our inference controller. We store the provenance in a Semantic Web-based knowledge base and use Semantic Web reasoners to draw inferences from the explicit information in a provenance graph. We enforce constraints, also known as security policies, at the design phase as well as at runtime.

The organization of this chapter is as follows: Background information on data provenance and the inference problem will be given in Section 1.2. The motivation for our work is discussed in Section 1.3. Our solutions and contributions are given in Section 1.4. Organization of this book is discussed in Section 1.5. Figure 1.1 illustrates the contents of this chapter. The framework for our approach is illustrated in Figure 1.2.

1.2 Background

As stated in Section 1.1, provenance means the origin of a source—the history of ownership of a valued object or a work of art or literature. It allows us to share and verify data, to repeat experiments, and to discover dependencies. The utility of the information shared relies on (1) quality of the information and (2) mechanisms that verify the correctness of the data and thereby determine the trustworthiness of the shared information. Organizations rely on information sharing as a way of conducting their day-to-day activities, but with this ease of information sharing comes a risk of information misuse. An electronic patient record (EPR) is a log of all activities including patient visits to a hospital, diagnoses, and treatments for diseases and processes performed by health care professionals on a patient. This EPR is often shared among several stakeholders (for example researchers and insurance and pharmaceutical companies). Before this information can be made available to these third parties, the sensitive information in an EPR must be circumvented or hidden from the released information. This can be addressed by applying policies that completely or partially hide sensitive attributes of the information being shared. The protection of sensitive information is often required by regulations that are mandated by a company or by laws such as the Health Insurance Portability and Accountability Act (HIPAA; http://en.wikipedia.org/wiki/Health_Insurance_Portability_and_Accountability_Act). The risks of unintentional disclosure of sensitive contents of an EPR document can be severe and costly (Heath 1997). Such risks may include litigation proceedings related to noncompliance of HIPAA regulations (Heath 1997).

Traditionally, we protect documents using policies such as access control policies and sanitization-based policies. However, current mechanisms for enforcing these policies do not operate over provenance data that take the form of a directed graph (Braun et al. 2008). Additionally, users can infer sensitive information from the results returned from performing frequent queries over a provenance graph. When inferred information is something unauthorized for the user to see, we say we have an instance of an inference problem. This problem is always present in systems that contain both public and private information. The inferred knowledge could depend on data obtained from a knowledge base or it could depend on some prior knowledge possessed by the user in addition to the information obtained from the knowledge base. The inferred knowledge obtained from a knowledge base alone could be used to reveal what is and what is not in a knowledge base. For example, if a user asks information about a patient's x-ray procedure, any response could indicate whether the patient had an x-ray or not. In general, a positive answer to a query discloses what is in a knowledge base, while a negative answer could have more than one interpretation. For example, a user could interpret a negative answer to mean that the answer is not in the knowledge base, or the user could interpret that it is in the knowledge base but the knowledge base chooses not to reveal the answer to the query. These two interpretations could depend on whether the knowledge base uses a closed-world or an open-world assumption. Normally, an open-world assumption indicates that data are incomplete or it could be somewhere else in the system and is not restricted to a particular file or location.

A knowledge-based inference controller should be able to detect the inference strategies that users utilize to draw unwanted inferences and consequently protect the knowledge base from security violations. Different approaches can be employed for building an inference controller. For example, we can use state-of-the-art machine learning techniques to build a learner that automatically learns to recognize complex patterns and make intelligent decisions based on some explicit data. We can also build an inference controller that uses Semantic Web technologies equipped with reasoners that perform inferences over the data in the knowledge base. In this book, we will build an inference controller that is based on the use of Semantic Web technologies. The Semantic Web is ideal for representing provenance due to its data representation and reasoning capabilities. For example, the graph-based structure of languages such as Resource Description Framework (RDF) and Web Ontology Language (OWL) facilitate the representation of data provenance that includes the history of data values. Furthermore, due to the reasoning capabilities of RDF and OWL, one can reason about data provenance in the midst of uncertainty and incomplete data.

We urgently need a framework to represent, manage, and reason about provenance. Such a framework has applications in numerous areas including healthcare and medicine. For example, medical records may store provenance data. Such data can be used to evaluate the patients and make diagnosis. Furthermore, there are risks involved with disclosing sensitive electronic patient records (EPR) (Heath 1997). On the other hand, we need to share provenance data to determine the history of a patient. In areas such as e-science, provenance is used to validate scientific results (Greenwood et al. 2003; Simmhan et al. 2005). Provenance is also useful for intelligence applications where such data is used to make decisions (Cirincione et al. 2010).

Different security criteria have been formulated to ensure that documents are not improperly released. These include access control and redaction policies, anonymization, and sanitization and cryptographic techniques, among others. In this book, we focus on two approaches: access control and redaction policies. On the one hand, access control encompasses a list of techniques for protecting a document. These include policies that specify contextual conditions in the form of rules and those that hide the real data by distortion (e.g., cryptography, scrambling, and noise techniques). Therefore, analyzing access control policies and mechanisms are an important topic with respect to the protection of sensitive provenance information. On the other hand, redaction encourages the sharing and continued transactions among organizations and their stakeholders, but the emphasis is on removing the sensitive and proprietary components of a document before releasing it. In other words, redaction is used to eliminate the threats associated with releasing proprietary or competitive information, trade secrets, and financial records, among others.

1.3 Motivation

The primary motivation behind this book is to provide a unifying framework for securing provenance. We formulate this motivation in order to address different criteria of current information systems:

1. *Sharing meaningful information.* Any useful system should provide meaningful information that is relevant, accurate, and timely. A user poses queries to gather relevant information for the day-to-day activities. The information may be in the same format or different formats and the activities may vary from domain to domain. For example, in intelligence, the information is for strategic planning; in industry, it is for gaining market share; and in health care, it is for providing treatments to patients. These queries could be answered with the use of traditional systems that are already equipped with their own security mechanisms. However, for these domains, the information retrieved may be both incorrect or outdated.

2. *Verifying the shared information.* Each domain should be able to share meaningful information among different domains as well as within a domain. In order to share meaningful information, a provenance information system should be in place to verify and provide metadata describing the accuracy and currency of the domain information that is retrieved and shared. However, domains often collect and store sensitive information. For example, in intelligence, the Federal Bureau of Investigation (FBI) may collect, classify, and

preserve records related to criminal identification and tracking for the official use by authorized officials of the government. In industry, a company may collect customers' information and transactions in order to target prospective customers effectively, tailor to their individual needs, and improve customer satisfaction and retention. In health care, a hospital may keep a log of all activities, including patient visits to a hospital, diagnoses and treatments for diseases, and processes performed by health care professionals.

3. *Secured provenance framework.* There is a need to provide a framework for addressing the above two criteria. This framework will use Semantic Web technologies to integrate the different provenance information retrieved from the different domains, therefore unifying and solving any interoperability among the information formats provided by the systems. In addition, the framework will address the concerns about the security of provenance information for these systems.

In this book we examine a typical distributed health care system for hospitals, but any discussion in this book can be applied equally to other domains. The hospitals are divided into several autonomous wards and ancillary units, which are visited by the patients for treatments and examinations during hospitalization in accordance with their illness. The treatment process is dynamic; the new information about a patient results in new treatments. The patient may visit different wards in the same physical hospital or different wards in different hospitals (in case the tests can only be done at specific hospital sites). Also, each hospital is running different health care applications. Therefore, the data (a single patient's health care history), the workflow (procedures carried out on that patient), and the logs (a recording of meaningful procedural events) are distributed among several heterogeneous and autonomous information systems.

This health care system is suitable for exploring why we need a secure provenance framework. It contains heterogeneous information and applications that will motivate our choice of a Semantic Web framework. Our reference to information here and throughout this book is for both the traditional data and its provenance, unless otherwise noted. This system contains many hospitals and large distributed systems that will motivate our need to handle the scalability of our framework. Accurate and current information is critical for emergency operations in a hospital, which will in turn motivate our need for a framework with reasonable performance.

The provenance information contains both the entities and the relationships between them. The entities are the agents, processes, algorithms, inputs and outputs to tasks; these entities are similar to the single data items in traditional systems. Our framework should be able to handle the single-data-item view of provenance as well as the more involved case of when the relationships between the entities are a part of the provenance. We will address each of these cases in turn for this book. We will first explore the simple case where both the traditional data and provenance are treated as single data items. In the case where we consider the relationships among the provenance entities, we will extend the framework to handle new policies that are based on graph queries and graph transformation systems. We will also consider further extensions to our framework.

1.4 Our Solutions and Contributions

We develop two broad approaches that support provenance in order to protect the sensitive components and still share it. Our first approach is based on a representation of the provenance document. When provenance is both viewed and represented as a directed labeled graph, a rich set of graph-related techniques can be applied to a provenance graph so that access control policies and redaction policies can be used to protect provenance. The second approach is based on a utility measure of provenance. This second approach is a new formal model for determining when we should release provenance. We need to release provenance to enable the advancement of science; the inputs to a new scientific discovery must be verifiable and accurate. The accuracy of information as inputs to decision making for intelligence must be established before actions are taken based on the available information. This formal model is used to find a comparable trade-off for releasing both data and its associated provenance and hiding provenance in case of intolerable losses. We propose a special application of this model, which is to build an inference controller that emulates human-like reasoning for the purpose of countering known inference attacks. A discussion to this formal model is presented in this book.

Our general architecture, illustrated in Figure 1.3, consists of a provenance management system whose role is to ensure that we provide high-quality information to a querying user while ensuring the confidentiality of the underlying data.

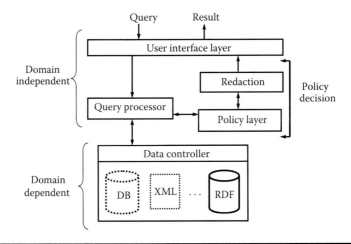

Figure 1.3   A unified provenance management system.

This provenance management system is domain neutral; for example, it is designed to protect any domain data that could be in different data formats describing both the data and its provenance. Therefore, we can build domain-independent modules that are closely integrated to make policy decisions related to the context of input queries and the querying user. Next, we provide a high-level overview of the modules of our provenance management system.

The *User Interface Layer* hides the actual internal representation of a query and policy from a user. This allows a user to submit both high-level queries and specification of policies without any knowledge of the underlying logic used to implement the solution. This layer also allows a user to retrieve information irrespective of the underlying data representation.

The *Query Processing* module translates a user query to one that is compatible with the underlying data representation.

The *Policy Layer* module interacts with the query processing module and is responsible for ensuring that a query conforms to a set of high-level policies. Any high-level policy language can be used to write the security policies as long as there is a compatible parser that translates these policies to a low-level representation.

The *Redaction* module is used to circumvent any sensitive contents from the result before it is returned to the user.

It is also important to note that the query processing module, the policy layer module, and the redaction module can all be used to enforce the security policies. The query processing module can be used to rewrite a user query according to a set of security policies. The policy layer can be used to provide advanced security features and is usually the main component for enforcing the policies. The redaction module can be used to remove (circumvent or filter) sensitive information from the results before returning a final answer to the user. Our solution is based on building a unified and effective policy management framework that enforces the following policies: access control policies, redaction policies, and inference policies.

The main contributions of this book are as follows:

- Flexible policies that are independent of our implementation. A domain user may use any policy language that describes the security policies of the domain. A suitable parser will produce a correct low-level policy.
- Definition of an access control policy language for provenance. We can now protect provenance not only as being comprised of single data items but also as paths in a connected directed graph.
- Perform redaction over a provenance graph. This is accomplished using the application of a graph grammar technique to circumvent parts of a provenance graph.
- Semantic Web-based inference attacks. A risk-based inference approach is taken to decide suitable trade-offs for hiding and sharing provenance.

1.5 Outline of the Book

This book is divided into four sections as illustrated in Figure 1.4. Section I describes supporting technologies and consists of six chapters. Chapter 2 reviews the existing literature on security and provenance. Chapter 3 presents the background information required to follow the concepts discussed in this book and also describes Semantic Web technologies. Chapter 4 discusses the notion of the inference problem. An overview of various inference engines is presented is Chapter 5. Examples of the inference problem including strategies are provided in Chapter 6. Aspects of cloud computing that are needed for implementing our policy engine on the cloud are discussed in Chapter 7.

Section II consists of three chapters. Chapter 8 discusses how we create flexible and scalable access control policies by extending role-based access control (RBAC) using key Semantic Web technologies. We also implement a prototype that shows

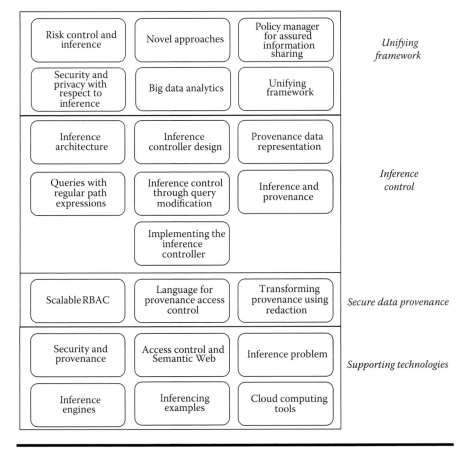

Figure 1.4   Framework for the book.

that we can scale and reason over a set of access control policies efficiently. Chapter 9 provides a definition of an access control policy language for provenance. This language retains the properties of traditional access control to gain access to data. Furthermore, the language provides an additional advantage whereby we can write one policy that is a pattern for several policies, thus contracting the policy set. We also describe our prototype that utilizes Semantic Web technologies that allows a user to query for data and provenance based on access control policies defined using our policy language. Chapter 10 discusses the application of a graph grammar technique that can be used to perform redaction over provenance. In addition, we provide an architectural design that allows a high-level specification of policies thus separating the business layer from a specific software implementation. We also implement a prototype of the architecture based on open-source Semantic Web technologies.

Section III consists of seven chapters and addresses the very important notion of inference control within the context of provenance and Semantic Web. Chapter 11 gives an overview of the architecture of our controller. Chapter 12 describes the design of the inference controller. Chapter 13 describes provenance data representation for inference control. Chapter 14 describes query specification for inference control. Query modification for inference control is discussed in Chapter 15. Inference control with provenance data with examples is discussed in Chapter 16. Implementation of the system is discussed in Chapter 17.

Section IV consists of five chapters and discusses a unifying framework. Risk and game-based models are discussed in Chapter 18, while novel approaches including game theoretic approaches as well as those based on probabilistic deduction and mathematical programming are discussed in Chapter 19. Cloud-based implementation of our policy engine for information sharing is discussed in Chapter 20. While much of the discussion in this book focuses on confidentiality aspects of the inference problem, the relationship of confidentiality to privacy and trust are discussed in Chapter 21. The inference problem for big data is the subject of Chapter 22. Finally, a unified framework for inference control that integrates policies for confidentiality, privacy, trust, redaction, and information sharing with respect to inference is discussed in Chapter 23.

The book is concluded in Chapter 24. The book is also augmented with multiple appendices. Appendix A describes data management and the relationship between our texts. We have included a version of this appendix in all of our books to provide the context. Appendix B describes database management and security technologies that includes a discussion of both discretionary and multilevel security for database management. Appendix C provides a perspective of the inference problem. Appendix D describes one of the earliest inference controllers that was designed and developed in the 1990s and which has motivated our current research. Mapping of the chapters to the framework is illustrated in Figure 1.5.

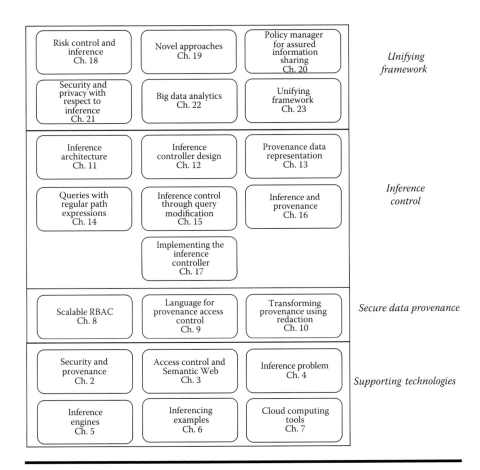

Figure 1.5   Chapters mapped to the framework.

1.6 Next Steps

This chapter has provided an introduction to the book. We first provided a brief overview of the supporting technologies for secure data provenance and inference control. Then we discussed our motivation, contributions, and approaches for securing provenance data. We also discussed inference control with respect to data provenance. This was followed by a discussion of the contents of this book.

The inference problem has been studied since the 1980s, starting with statistical databases followed by multilevel databases and more recently for health care databases. Some of the developments made on the inference problem have contributed to the more recent research on privacy. Essentially, the inference problem is about drawing unauthorized conclusions from legitimate responses received for the queries posed.

While the prior approaches have focused mainly on the inference problem occurring in relational databases, this book describes the inference problem in Semantic Web-based databases. With such databases, the data as well as policies are represented using Semantic Web technologies. The reasoning strategies inherent in Semantic Web technologies are used to reason about the data and the policies to detect unauthorized conclusions drawn via inference. Initial ideas on inference control for Semantic Web databases were presented at the United States–European Union (US-EU) workshop on Semantic Web held in Sophia Antipolis, France, in October 2001 (Thuraisingham 2001). Since then, some early efforts were reported on the inference problem based on Semantic Web technologies (Stoica and Farkas 2004; Thuraisingham 2005). However, the contents of this book are the first effort that combines access control, redaction, inference control, data provenance, and Semantic Web technologies to provide a comprehensive solution for secure data provenance and inference control.

As proved in Thuraisingham (1990), the general inference problem is unsolvable. Therefore, solutions proposed do have limitations. However, we have shown that Semantic Web technologies support reasoning and can handle certain forms of inferences. In addition, we have also provided solutions for access control for provenance data. In particular, we have discussed the need for efficient solutions for handling the inference problem and have discussed how cloud computing could be utilized for this purpose.

Due to the fact that massive amounts of data have to be managed and analyzed, there is also an opportunity to make unauthorized inferences. This is because data are often shared among individuals as we migrate from a need to know to a need to share paradigm, and furthermore, there are numerous data analytics tools that are emerging that can make associations between different pieces of data. Such associations could be highly sensitive. Therefore, as progress is made on big data analytics, we also need to be aware of the potential problems that can occur due to violations of security and privacy. We believe that the results presented in this book provide insights toward handling security and privacy for big data.

References

Braun, U., Shinnar, A. and Seltzer, M., Securing provenance, Proceedings of the 3rd Conference on Hot Topics in Security, USENIX Association, 2008.

Cirincione, G., Govindan, R., Krishnamurthy, S., Porta, T. F. L. and Mohapatra, P., Impact of security properties on the quality of information in tactical military networks, Proceedings Military Communications Conference, MILCOM, 2010.

Greenwood, M., Goble, C., Stevens, R., Zhao, J., Addis, M., Marvin, D., Moreau, L. and Oinn, T., Provenance of e-science experiments-experience from bioinformatics, Proceedings of the UK OST e-Science Second All Hands Meeting, 2003.

Heath, G., Redaction defined, Informative Graphics Corp. White Paper, http://www.infograph.com/sites/default/files/IGC_Content_Security_WhitePaper.pdf, 1997.

http://en.wikipedia.org/wiki/Health_Insurance_Portability_and_Accountability_Act.

Moreau, L., The foundations for provenance on the Web, *Foundations and Trends in Web Science,* Vol. 2, Nos. 2–3, 2010.

Simmhan, Y. L., Plale, B. and Gannon, D., A survey of data provenance in e-science, *ACM SIGMOD Record,* Vol. 34, No. 3, 2005.

Stoica, A. and Farkas, C., Ontology guided XML security engine, *Journal of Intelligent Information Systems,* Vol. 23, 2004.

Thuraisingham, B., Recursion theoretic properties of the inference problem, Computer Security Foundations Workshop, Franconia, NH, June 1990 (also available as MITRE Report MTP 291, June 1990).

Thuraisingham, B. M., Ford, W., Collins, M. and O'Keeffe, J., Design and implementation of a database inference controller, *Data and Knowledge Engineering,* Vol. 11, 1993.

Thuraisingham, B., Security for the Semantic Web, US-EU Workshop on Semantic Web, Sophia Antipolis, France, October 2001.

Thuraisingham, B. M., Security standards for the Semantic Web, *Computer Standards & Interfaces,* Vol. 27, 2005.

SUPPORTING TECHNOLOGIES

INTRODUCTION　1

As stated in the introduction, this book describes the design and implementation of an inference controller that operates over provenance. This controller protects the sensitive information in a provenance database from unauthorized users. The provenance is represented as a directed acyclic graph that can be represented and stored using Semantic Web technologies. We have built a prototype to evaluate the effectiveness of our inference controller. We store the provenance in a Semantic-Web-based knowledge base and use Semantic Web reasoners to draw inferences from the explicit information in a provenance graph.

In order to understand the main concepts discussed in this book such as secure data provenance and inference control, we need to have some knowledge of access control, provenance, Semantic Web, and inference control. We discuss these supporting technologies in Section I.

Section I describes supporting technologies and consists of six chapters. Chapter 2 reviews the existing literature on security and provenance. Chapter 3 presents the background information required to follow the concepts discussed in this book and also describes Semantic Web technologies. Chapter 4 discusses the notion of the inference problem. An overview of various inference engines is presented in Chapter 5. Examples of the inference problem are provided in Chapter 6. Aspects of cloud computing that are needed for implementing a scalable policy engine are discussed in Chapter 7.

Chapter 2

Security and Provenance

2.1 Overview

There are many opportunities for research in data provenance (Davidson and Freire 2008; Gil et al. 2007; Moreau 2009). These include (1) information management infrastructure to efficiently and effectively manage the growing volume of provenance information, (2) provenance analytics and visualization for mining and extracting knowledge from provenance data, which has been largely unexplored, and (3) interoperability of different provenance systems and tools to aid in the integration of provenance. Also, recently there have been a series of challenges for provenance (Moreau et al. 2011). The first provenance challenge aimed at establishing an understanding of the capabilities of available provenance-related systems (Moreau et al. 2008). The second challenge aimed at allowing disparate groups to gain a better understanding of the similarities, differences, core concepts, and common issues across systems. The third challenge aimed at exchanging provenance information encoded in the Open Provenance Model (OPM) and providing additional profiles. The fourth challenge was to apply OPM to scenarios and demonstrate novel functionality that can only be achieved by the presence of an interoperable solution for provenance. Some of the approaches to address these challenges use Semantic Web technologies (Golbeck and Hendler 2008). Our research has been influenced by these Semantic Web-based approaches.

We believe that a very important challenge for provenance is building a scalable and secured framework for provenance. In fact, we found some existing works in the literature relating to the scalability and security of provenance (Braun et al. 2008; Groth et al. 2006; Hasan et al. 2007; Tan et al. 2006). Furthermore, recording complete provenance would result in extremely large amounts of documentation, which presents problems for recording, querying, managing, and storing provenance information. Also, despite the importance of security issues in provenance, it has not been fully explored in the research community (Hasan et al. 2007), especially with respect to access control (Ni et al. 2009). The research community has raised many concerns about securing provenance information (Blaustein et al. 2008; Braun et al. 2008; Ni et al. 2009). In Braun et al. (2008), it is suggested that provenance needs its own security model and that existing access control models do not operate over provenance, which takes the form of a directed graph. It was then suggested in Ni et al. (2009) that a generalized access control language model for protecting provenance is needed. Some approaches also recognize that a system that handles both the security and provenance together is needed (Blaustein et al. 2008; Braun et al. 2008; Seltzer et al. 2005; Tan et al. 2006), while other works suggest that scalable access control mechanisms for provenance are needed (Rosenthal et al. 2009; Simmhan et al. 2005; Simmhan et al.).

There are several challenges in the area of securing provenance. These include providing scalable systems for handling provenance information, exploring the potential for different languages that support provenance, and representing and storing provenance as a directed graph to support visualization and graph operations over provenance. We explore these challenges and our solutions in this book. Specifically, we have developed a unifying framework for securing provenance that addresses some of the challenges. The organization of this chapter is as follows. In Section 2.2 we present relevant works related to the scalability of our secured provenance framework. In Section 2.3, we present relevant works related to our support for an access control language for provenance. Finally, in Section 2.4 we provide relevant related works on graph operations, which form the underlying theory behind the redaction module in our framework. Section 2.5 presents a summary and future directions. The concepts discussed in this chapter are illustrated in Figure 2.1. Note that we will be using some Semantic Web technologies such as OWL and Description Logic (DL) in this chapter, which will become clearer when we discuss Semantic Web in Chapter 3.

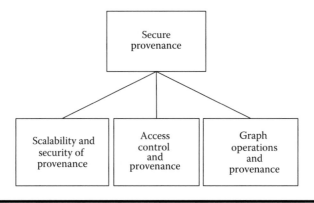

Figure 2.1   Concepts in secure provenance.

2.2 Scalability and Security of Provenance

There are some related works in the area of access control that deal with reasoning and scalability issues (Cirio et al. 2007; Finin et al. 2008; Kolovski et al. 2007; Liu et al. 2008; Masood et al. 2006; Zhao et al. 2005). In Cirio et al. (2007), an approach for supporting RBAC in a Semantic Web environment using DL is discussed. This work combines RBAC with other context-aware access control mechanisms (e.g., attribute-based access control [ABAC] to add flexibility to RBAC), which suffers from using static assignments. In Cirio et al. (2007), a high-level OWL ontology is used to express RBAC, which is combined with a domain specific ontology about the application domain.

Another approach is that of Zhao et al. (2005). They describe a formalism of RBAC using the DL language $\mathcal{ALCQ}$. In their work, they show how to use DL to model policy constraints. Finin et al. (2008) show different approaches to support RBAC in OWL by investigating the use of OWL in unifying parallel approaches to policy needs in real-world domains. Rules were also used in Finin et al. (2008) for enforcing policies written in N3, a language developed by Tim Berners Lee (Berners-Lee et al. 2008). There is also work on access control based on other policy languages such as eXtensible Access Control Markup Language (XACML), which is a standard from OASIS (Organization for the Advancement of Structured Information Standards). Furthermore, the work in Kolovski et al. (2007) addresses reasoning aspects of access control and the work in Liu et al. (2008) focuses on the scalability aspects.

There are also some existing works on partitioning knowledge bases and combining query answers over many knowledge bases. In Guo and Heflin (2006), an approach is discussed for partitioning a large OWL ABox with respect to a TBox so that specific kinds of reasoning can be performed separately on each partition and the results combined in order to achieve complete answers. Note that the terms ABox and TBox are used to describe two different types of statements in ontologies. TBox statements are sometimes associated with object-oriented classes and ABox statements are associated with instances of those classes (http://en.wikipedia.org/wiki/Abox). In Soma and Prasanna (2008), the authors examine the problem of speeding up and scaling the inferencing process for OWL knowledge bases that employ rule-based reasoners. They propose a data partitioning approach for the problem in which the input data are partitioned into smaller chunks that are then processed independently. In Dolby et al. (2008), the focus is on addressing aspects related to answering partial queries and then combining the results. Other works in this area include the discussions in Owens et al. (2009) and Sirin and Parsia (2006).

We also found ongoing works addressing distributed reasoning in a Semantic Web environment. These include the works in Kaoudi et al. (2010), Oren et al. (2009), Serafini and Tamilin (2005), and Tonti et al. (2003). In Kaoudi et al. (2010), the focus is on RDF reasoning and MapReduce, while in Oren et al. (2009) the focus is on using a divide-conquer-swap strategy for processing large amounts of RDF data. In Serafini and Tamilin (2005), a distributed reasoning approach is presented whereby the result is based on the combination of local reasoning chunks. This approach uses a tableau-based distributed reasoning procedure. The work in Tonti et al. (2003) is a comparison of different Semantic Web languages for policy representation and reasoning in multiagent and distributed systems. Levandoski and Mokbel (2009) store RDF data into relational databases and use clustering and partitioning to reduce the number of joins and improve querying time. Database approaches to reasoning, however, require all instances of the data in the entire knowledge base (KB). Furthermore, works along this line could be used for supporting provenance in a relational database.

Our goal is to add scalability to our framework. In particular, we would like to (1) build a scalable Semantic Web framework that is capable of performing inferencing over both traditional data and provenance data that are represented in an OWL knowledge base, (2) identify existing techniques for performing inferencing over large ABoxes, (3) identify ways to efficiently answer queries over large distributed provenance knowledge bases, and (4) explore ideas on how to apply access control mechanisms to a Semantic Web framework.

2.3 Access Control Languages and Provenance

There are some recent works related to access control in provenance. These include the work in Braun and Shinnar (2002), which emphasizes the need for a separate security model for provenance. This work also points out that existing access control models do not support the directed acyclic graph of provenance. The authors in Rosenthal et al. (2009) discuss the shortcomings of RBAC and instead propose ABAC, which supports a fine-grained access control based on attributes rather than roles. In Syalim et al. (2009), the authors present an access control method for provenance over a directed acyclic graph. They build their access control model over a relational database that controls access to nodes and edges. They apply a grouping strategy to the provenance graph to create resources that need to be protected. In Corcoran et al. (2007), the authors propose a grouping of provenance into blocks and then apply a labeling strategy over these blocks. They also provide a language, SELinks, to encode their security policies. In Ni et al. (2009), the issues with existing access control models in provenance are addressed by proposing a general language. This language supports fine-grained policies and personal preferences and obligations as well as decision aggregation from different applicable policies.

Research has also focused on general access control languages that are based on XML, logic, and algebra (Bray et al. 2000). XACML is an OASIS standard for an access control language that is based on XML (Lorch et al. 2003). This language is very flexible and expressive. The work in Ni et al. (2009) builds on XACML features to create a general access control language for provenance. Logic-based languages offer features such as decidability and a formal proof of security policies

(Abadi 2003). The work given in Bonatti et al. (2002) shows how policies possibly expressed in different languages can be formulated in algebra. The algebra offers a formal semantics such as in logic-based languages.

Our goals are manifold: (1) We want to extend our access control model to support RDF triple stores in addition to relational databases. We also want to support the idea of grouping by defining dynamic paths that are evaluated at query time based on incorporating regular expressions in our policies. (2) We would like to extend the language given in Ni et al. (2009) with support for regular expressions. Our language should also incorporate other features of a general access control language such as support for fine-grained access control over the indivisible parts of a provenance graph, and integration of existing access control policies. (3) Finally, we want our language to extend the XML-based policies in Ni et al. (2009) for several reasons, such as it is easy to write policies in XML and XML also provides a schema that can be used to verify the policies (Bray et al. 2000).

2.4 Graph Operations and Provenance

Previous works on using graph transformation approaches to model security aspects of a system include Corradini et al. (2006), Koch et al. (2005), and Koch and Parisi-Presicce (2006). In Corradini et al. (2006), an extension of the double-pushout (DPO) rewriting, called Sesqui pushout (SqPO), was used to represent the subjects and objects in an access control system as nodes, and the rights of a subject on an object as edges. In Koch et al. (2005), the authors used the formal properties of graph transformation to detect and resolve inconsistencies within the specification of access control policies. In Koch and Parisi-Presicce (2006), the authors proposed a methodology to integrate the specification of access control policies into Unified Modeling Language (UML). This provides a graph-based formal semantics for access control, which can allow software engineers to reason about the coherence of access control policies. The works in Braun et al. (2008), Ni et al. (2009), and Tan et al. (2006) focus on some unique features of provenance with respect to the security of provenance itself. For example, it is recognized that we need suitable access control for provenance, which has distinct characteristics from traditional data. While Ni et al. (2009) prescribe a generalized access control model for provenance, the flow of information between various sources and the causal relationships among entities are not immediately obvious in this work. We recognize that we can extend the work in Ni et al. (2009) to make obvious these causal relationships, which we have done in Cadenhead et al. (2011). In Tan et al. (2006), the authors try to address basic security issues related to a provenance system in the context of a service-oriented architecture (SOA) view as well as the security issues for scaling such a system. Some of these issues involve the aggregation and combination of processes in an SOA view to achieve the right granularity of access control. Our work is also motivated by the discussions in Braun et al. (2008), Moreau et al. (2011), and

Zhao (2010), where the focus is on representing provenance as a directed graph structure. In Braun et al. (2008), it is suggested that provenance needs its own security model, while in Moreau et al. (2011) and Zhao (2010), an abstract graph model is proposed and a corresponding vocabulary for describing the relationships between nodes in a provenance graph is also presented.

We also found previous works related to the efficiency of a graph rewriting system in Blostein et al. (1996), Dodds and Plump (2006), and Dorr (1995). In the general case, graph pattern matching, which finds a homomorphic (or isomorphic) image of a given graph in another graph a nondeterministic polynomial time (NP)-complete problem. However, various factors make it tractable in a graph rewriting system (Blostein et al. 1996). Our aim is to explore the relevant related works in order to gain better insights into performing graph operations over the directed graph structure of provenance. We will discuss our approach and contributions in Sections II and III of this book.

2.5 Summary and Directions

In this chapter we provided some background information on provenance relevant to our work. First we discussed scalability issues for a secure provenance framework. As mentioned earlier, building a scalable framework is our major goal. Then we discussed aspects of an access control language for provenance. We will discuss details of our language in Section II. Finally, we discussed graph operations on provenance. We have used graph structures to represent provenance. In particular, we have utilized Semantic Web technologies for representing provenance. Therefore, the graph operations are an essential part of manipulating provenance.

In Section II we will discuss our approach to securing provenance. In particular, we will describe our framework, access control on provenance, as well as graph operations on provenance. Inference control on provenance will be discussed in Section III. Provenance has become an integral part of data and information management. With the vast quantities of data and information on the Web, including social media, it is important to have a history of each piece of data so that malicious operations on the data can be detected. Furthermore, maintaining the history of the data will also enable one to determine the trustworthiness of the data. Many of these aspects will be discussed throughout this book.

References

Abadi, M., Logic in access control, Proceedings of the 18th Annual Symposium on Logic in Computer Science, 2003, pp. 228–233.

Berners-Lee, T., Connolly, D., Kagal, L., Scharf, Y. and Hendler, J., N3Logic: A logical framework for the World Wide Web, *Theory and Practice of Logic Programming*, Vol. 8, No. 3, 2008, pp. 249–269.

Blaustein, B., Seligman, L., Morse, M., Allen, M. D. and Rosenthal, A., PLUS: Synthesizing privacy, lineage, uncertainty and security, ICDEW 2008, IEEE 24th Data Engineering Workshop, 2008.

Blostein, D., Fahmy, H. and Grbavec, A., Issues in the practical use of graph rewriting, in *Graph Grammars and Their Application to Computer Science,* Kuny, J., Ehrig, H., Engels, G. and Rozenberg, G. (eds.), Springer-Verlag, Berlin, 1996, pp. 38–55.

Bonatti, P., De Capitani di Vimercati, S. and Samarati, P., An algebra for composing access control policies, *ACM Transactions on Information and System Security* (TISSEC), Vol. 5, No. 1, 2002, pp. 1–35.

Braun, U. and Shinnar, A., A security model for provenance, project thesis, Harvard University, 2002.

Braun, U., Shinnar, A. and Seltzer, M., Securing provenance, Proceedings of the 3rd Conference on Hot Topics in Security, 2008.

Bray, T., Paoli, J., Sperberg-McQueen, C. M., Maler, E. and Yergeau, F., Extensible markup language (XML) 1.0, W3C Recommendation, Vol. 6, 2000.

Cadenhead, T., Khadilkar, V., Kantarcioglu, M. and Thuraisingham, B., A language for provenance access control, Proceedings of the First ACM Conference on Data and Application Security and Privacy, 2011.

Cirio, L., Cruz, I. F. and Tamassia, R., A role and attribute based access control system using Semantic Web technologies, On the Move to Meaningful Internet Systems 2007: OTM 2007 Workshops, Springer, Berlin.

Corcoran, B. J., Swamy, N. and Hicks, M., Combining provenance and security policies in a web-based document management system, On-line Proceedings of the Workshop on Principles of Provenance (PrOPr), 2007.

Corradini, A., Heindel, T., Hermann, F. and Konig, B., Sesqui-pushout rewriting, *Graph Transformations,* Vol. 4178, 2006, pp. 30–45.

Davidson, S. B. and Freire, J., Provenance and scientific workflows: Challenges and opportunities, SIGMOD Conference, 2008.

Dodds, M. and Plump, D., Graph transformation in constant time, *Graph Transformations,* Corradini, A. et al, (eds.), Springer-Verlag, Berlin Heidelberg, 2006, LNCS 4178, pp. 367–382.

Dolby, J., Fokoue, A., Kalyanpur, A., Ma, L., Schonberg, E., Srinivas, K. and Sun, X., Scalable grounded conjunctive query evaluation over large and expressive knowledge bases, *The Semantic Web—ISWC 2008.*

Dorr, H., *Efficient Graph Rewriting and Its Implementation,* Springer-Verlag, Berlin, 1995.

Finin, T., Joshi, A., Kagal, L., Niu, J., Sandhu, R., Winsborough, W. and Thuraisingham, B., ROWLBAC: Representing role based access control in OWL, Proceedings of the 13th ACM Symposium on Access Control Models and Technologies, 2008.

Gil, Y., Deelman, E., Ellisman, M., Fahringer, T., Fox, G., Gannon, D., Goble, C., Livny, M., Moreau, L. and Myers, J., Examining the challenges of scientific workflows, *IEEE Computer,* Vol. 40, No. 12, 2007, pp. 24–32.

Golbeck, J. and Hendler, J., A Semantic Web approach to the provenance challenge, *Concurrency and Computation: Practice and Experience,* Vol. 20, No. 5, 2008, pp. 431–439.

Groth, P., Jiang, S., Miles, S., Munroe, S., Tan, V., Tsasakou, S. and Moreau, L., An architecture for provenance systems, ECS, University of Southampton, 2006.

Guo, Y. and Heflin, J., A scalable approach for partitioning OWL knowledge bases, Proceedings of the 2nd International Workshop on Scalable Semantic Web Knowledge Base Systems, Athens, GA, 2006.

Hasan, R., Sion, R. and Winslett, M., Introducing secure provenance: Problems and challenges, Proceedings of the 2007 ACM Workshop on Storage Security and Survivability, 2007.

http://en.wikipedia.org/wiki/Abox.

Kaoudi, Z., Miliaraki, I. and Koubarakis, M., RDFS reasoning and query answering on top of DHTs, *The Semantic Web–ISWC,* 2010.

Koch, M., Mancini, L. V. and Parisi-Presicce, F., Graph-based specification of access control policies, *Journal of Computer and System Sciences,* Vol. 71, No. 1, 2005, pp. 1–33.

Koch, M. and Parisi-Presicce, F., UML specification of access control policies and their formal verification, *Software and Systems Modeling,* Vol. 5, No. 4, 2006, pp. 429–447.

Kolovski, V., Hendler, J. and Parsia, B., Analyzing web access control policies, Proceedings of the 16th International Conference on World Wide Web, 2007.

Levandoski, J. J. and Mokbel, M. F., RDF Data-Centric Storage, 2009 IEEE International Conference on Web Services, 2009.

Liu, A. X., Chen, F., Hwang, J. H. and Xie, T., Xengine: A fast and scalable XACML policy evaluation engine, *ACM SIGMETRICS Performance Evaluation Review,* Vol. 36, No.1, 2008, pp. 265–276.

Lorch, M., Proctor, S., Lepro, R., Kafura, D. and Shah, S., First experiences using XACML for access control in distributed systems, Proceedings of the 2003 ACM Workshop on XML Security, 2003.

Masood, A., Ghafoor, A. and Mathur, A., Scalable and effective test generation for access control systems that employ RBAC policies, Purdue University, 2006, Technical Report.

Moreau, L., The foundations for provenance on the Web, *Foundations and Trends in Web Science,* Vols. 2–3, 2009, pp. 99–241.

Moreau, L., Clifford, B., Freire, J., Gil, Y., Groth, P., Futrelle, J., Kwasnikowska, N., Miles, S., Missier, P. and Myers, J., The open provenance model core specification, *Future Generation Computer Systems,* Vol. 27, No. 6, 2011, pp. 743–756.

Moreau, L., Ludscher, B., Altintas, I., Barga, R. S., Bowers, S., Callahan, S., Chin, J. R., Clifford, B., Cohen, S. and Cohen-Boulakia, S., Special issue: The first provenance challenge, *Concurrency and Computation: Practice and Experience,* Vol. 20, No. 5, 2008.

Ni, Q., Xu, S., Bertino, E., Sandhu, R. and Han, W., An access control language for a general provenance model, Proceedings Secure Data Management Workshop, Lyons, France, 2009.

Oren, E., Kotoulas, S., Anadiotis, G., Siebes, R., ten Teije, A. and van Harmelen, F., Marvin, distributed reasoning over large-scale Semantic Web data, *Web Semantics: Science, Services and Agents on the World Wide Web,* Vol. 7, No. 4, 2009, pp. 305–316.

Owens, A., Seaborne, A., Gibbins, N. and Schraefel, M., Clustered TDB: A clustered triple store for Jena, In 18th International World Wide Web Conference (WWW 2009), Madrid, Spain, April 20–24, 2009.

Rosenthal, A., Seligman, L., Chapman, A. and Blaustein, B., Scalable access controls for lineage, First Workshop on the Theory and Practice of Provenance, 2009.

Seltzer, M., Muniswamy-Reddy, K. K., Holland, D. A., Braun, U. and Ledlie, J., Provenance-aware storage systems, Harvard University Technical Report TR-18-05, 2005.

Serafini, L. and Tamilin, A., Drago: Distributed reasoning architecture for the Semantic Web, *The Semantic Web: Research and Applications,* Gómez-Pérez, A. and Euzenat, J. (eds.), Springer-Verlag, Berlin Heidelberg, 2005, LNCS 3532, pp. 361–376.

Simmhan, Y. L., Plale, B. and Gannon, D., A survey of data provenance in e-science, *ACM SIGMOD Record,* Vol. 34, No. 3, 2005, pp. 31–36.

Simmhan, Y. L., Plale, B. and Gannon, D., A survey of data provenance techniques, Computer Science Department, Indiana University, Bloomington, IN. Technical Report IUB-CS-TR618.

Sirin, E. and Parsia, B., Optimizations for answering conjunctive ABox queries: First results, 2006 International Workshop on Description Logics DL, 2006.

Soma, R. and Prasanna, V. K., A data partitioning approach for parallelizing rule based inferencing for materialized OWL knowledge bases, Proceedings of the 21st International Conference on Parallel and Distributed Computing and Communication Systems, 2008.

Syalim, A., Hori, Y. and Sakurai, K., Grouping provenance information to improve efficiency of access control, *Advances in Information Security and Assurance,* Park, J. H., Chen, H., Atiquzzaman, M., Lee, C., Kim, T. and Yeo, S. (eds.), Springer-Verlag, Berlin Heidelberg, 2009, LNCS 5576, pp. 51–59.

Tan, V., Groth, P., Miles, S., Jiang, S., Munroe, S., Tsasakou, S. and Moreau, L., Security issues in a SOA-based provenance system, In Proceedings of 2006 International Conference on Provenance and Annotation of Data, 2006.

Tonti, G., Bradshaw, J., Jeffers, R., Montanari, R., Suri, N. and Uszok, A., Semantic Web languages for policy representation and reasoning: A comparison of KAoS, Rei, and Ponder, *The Semantic Web–ISWC,* 2003.

Zhao, C., Heilili, N. M., Liu, S. and Lin, Z., Representation and reasoning on RBAC: A description logic approach, In Proceedings of the International Colloquium on Theoretical Aspects of Computing-ICTAC 2005, Hanoi, Vietnam, October 17–21, 2005.

Zhao, J., Open Provenance Model Vocabulary Specification, latest version, http://open-biomed.sourceforge.net/opmv/ns.html, 2010.

Chapter 3

Access Control and Semantic Web

3.1 Overview

While the current Web technologies facilitate the integration of information from a syntactic point of view, there is still a lot to be done to handle the different semantics of various systems and applications. That is, current Web technologies depend a lot on the "human-in-the-loop" for information management and integration. Tim Berners Lee, the father of the World Wide Web, realized the inadequacies of current Web technologies and subsequently strived to make the Web more intelligent. His goal was to have a web that would essentially alleviate humans from the burden of having to integrate disparate information sources as well as to carry out extensive searches. He then came to the conclusion that one needs machine-understandable Web pages and the use of ontologies for information integration. This resulted in the notion of the Semantic Web (Berners-Lee and Hendler 2001). The Web services that take advantage of Semantic Web technologies are Semantic Web services.

A Semantic Web can be thought of as a web that is highly intelligent and sophisticated so that one needs little or no human intervention to carry out tasks such as scheduling appointments, coordinating activities, and searching for complex documents, as well as integrating disparate databases and information systems. While much progress has been made toward developing such an intelligent web, there is still a lot to be done. For example, technologies such as ontology matching, intelligent agents, and markup languages are contributing a lot toward developing the Semantic Web. Nevertheless, one still needs a human to make decisions and take actions. Since the 2000s there have been many developments on the Semantic Web. The World

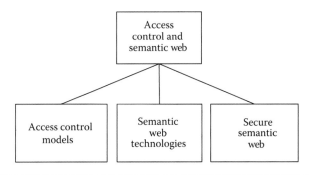

Figure 3.1   Access control and semantic web.

Wide Web Consortium (W3C) is specifying standards for the Semantic Web (World Wide Web Consortium, http://www.w3c.org). These standards include specifications for eXtensible Markup Language (XML), RDF, and interoperability.

As the demand for data and information management increases, there is also a critical need for maintaining the security of the databases, applications, and information systems. Data and information have to be protected from unauthorized access as well as from malicious corruption. To address this critical need, various access control models have been proposed since the 1980s. These include models such as RBAC, where access to the data is granted based on the roles of the users. With the advent of the Web, it is even more important to protect the data and information as numerous individuals now have access to these data and information. Therefore, we need effective mechanisms to secure the Semantic Web technologies. In particular, we need to secure XML and RDF documents as well as other components such as ontologies.

In this chapter, we present a brief background on access control and the Semantic Web. A large part of this book is devoted to providing a mechanism for extending the traditional definition of access control policies. As a result, Section 3.2 will cover access control models in general and RBAC in particular. This is a good starting point for explaining the components of an access control model. Section 3.3 will give an overview of key Semantic Web technologies used in this book. Securing the Semantic Web will be discussed in Section 3.4. The chapter is summarized in Section 3.5. Figure 3.1 illustrates the concepts discussed in this chapter.

3.2 Access Control

Access control models include RBAC, mandatory based access control (MAC), discretionary access control (DAC), lattice-based access control (LBAC), temporal access control, and ABAC, to name a few (Bertino et al. 2001; Cirio et al. 2007; Ferraiolo et al. 2003; Denning 1976; Lindqvist 2006; Moffett et al. 1990; Sandhu 1993). These can be grouped into three main classes, which differ by the constraints they place on the sets of *users*, *actions*, and *objects* (access control models often refer to resources as objects) (Samarati and de Capitani di Vimercati 2001; Sandhu and Samarati 1994). These classes are (1) RBAC, which restricts access based on roles, (2) DAC, which controls access based on the identity of the user, and (3) MAC, which controls access based on mandated regulations determined by a central authority.

MAC usually enforces access control by attaching security labels to users (subjects) and objects. DAC enforces access control on an object on the basis of permissions and denials configured by the object's owner. Mandatory policy is particularly applicable to military environments, whereas discretionary policy typically applies to commercial, industrial, and educational environments. These two access control models can be simulated by RBAC (Osborn et al. 2000); therefore we focus on RBAC in this book. Below we provide the definition of RBAC. More details can be found in (Ferraiolo et al. 2001, 2003).

RBAC. This model is generally comprised of loosely coupled components: (1) a user is usually a human or an autonomous agent, (2) a role is a collection of permissions needed to perform a certain job function, (3) a permission is an access mode that can be exercised on an object, and (4) a session relates a user to roles.

- *PA:Roles* → *Permissions*: the permission assignment function that assigns to roles the permissions needed to complete their jobs
- *UA:Users* → *Roles*: the user assignment function that assigns users to roles
- *user:Sessions* → *Users*: assigns each session to a single user
- *role:Session* → 2^{Roles}: assigns each session to a set of roles
- *RH* ⊆ *Roles* × *Roles*: a partially ordered role hierarchy (written)

3.3 Semantic Web

Figure 3.2 illustrates the layered technology stack for the Semantic Web. This is the stack that was developed by Tim Berners Lee. Essentially the Semantic Web

Trust
SWRL
OWL
RDF
XML
Foundations

Figure 3.2   Technology stack for the semantic web.

consists of layers where each layer takes advantage of the technologies of the previous layer. The lowest layer is the protocol layer and this is usually not included in the discussion of the semantic technologies. The next layer is the XML layer. XML is a document representation language. While XML is sufficient to specify syntax, semantics such as "the creator of document D is John" is hard to specify in XML. Therefore, the W3C developed RDF, which uses XML syntax. The Semantic Web community then went further and came up with a specification of ontologies in languages such as OWL. Note that OWL addresses the inadequacies of RDF. In order to reason about various policies, the Semantic Web community has come up with Web rules languages such as Semantic Web Rules Language (SWRL) and Rule Markup Language (RuleML). Next we will describe the various technologies that constitute the Semantic Web.

XML. XML is needed due to the limitations of Hypertext Markup Language (HTML) and complexities of Standard Generalized Markup Language (SGML). XML is an extensible markup language specified by the W3C and designed to make the interchange of structured documents over the Internet easier. An important aspect of XML used to be document type definitions (DTDs) that define the role of each element of text in a formal model. XML schemas have now become critical to specify the structure of data. XML schemas are also XML documents (Bray et al. 1997).

RDF. RDF is a standard for describing resources on the Semantic Web. It provides a common framework for expressing this information so it can be exchanged between applications without loss of meaning. RDF is based on the idea of identifying things using Web identifiers (called uniform resource identifiers [URIs]), and describing resources in terms of simple properties and property values (Klyne et al. 2004).

The RDF terminology T is the union of three pairwise disjoint infinite sets of terms: the set U of URI references, the set L of literals (itself partitioned into two sets, the set L_p of plain literals and the set L_t of typed literals), and the set B of blanks. The set U∪L of names is called the vocabulary.

Definition 3.1 RDF Triple

An RDF Triple (s, p, o) is an element of $(U \cup B) \times U \times T$
An RDF graph is a finite set of triples.   ■

An RDF triple can be viewed as an arc from s to o, where p is used to label the arc. This is represented as $s \xrightarrow{p} o$. We also refer to the ordered triple (s, p, o) as the subject, predicate, and object of a triple.

RDF has a formal semantics that provides a dependable basis for reasoning about the meaning of a RDF graph. This reasoning is usually called entailment.

Entailment rules state which implicit information can be inferred from explicit information. In general, it is not assumed that complete information about any resource is available in an RDF query. A query language should be aware of this and tolerate incomplete or contradicting information. The notion of class and operations on classes are specified in RDF through the concept of RDF Schema (Antoniou and Van Harmelen 2008).

Simple Protocol and RDF Query Language (SPARQL). SPARQL (Prud'hommeaux and Seaborne 2006) is a powerful query language. It is a key Semantic Web technology and was standardized by the RDF Data Access Working Group of the W3C. SPARQL syntax is similar to SQL, but it has the advantage whereby it enables queries to span multiple disparate data sources that consist of heterogeneous and semistructured data. SPARQL is based around graph pattern matching (Prud'hommeaux and Seaborne 2006).

Definition 3.2: Graph Pattern

A SPARQL graph pattern expression is defined recursively as follows:
    A triple pattern is a graph pattern.

If $P1$ and $P2$ are graph patterns, then expressions ($P1$ *AND* $P2$), ($P1$ *OPT* $P2$) and

($P1$ *UNION* $P2$) are graph patterns.

If P is a graph pattern, V a set of variables and $X \in U \cup V$ then (X *GRAPH* P)

is a graph pattern.

1. If P is a graph pattern and R is a built-in SPARQL condition, then the expression (P *FILTER* R) is a graph pattern. ■

OWL. OWL (McGuinness and van Harmelen 2004) is an ontology language that has more expressive power and reasoning capabilities than RDF and RDF Schema (RDF-S). It has additional vocabulary along with a formal semantics. OWL has three increasingly expressive sublanguages: OWL Lite, OWL DL, and OWL Full. These are designed for use by specific communities of implementers and users. The formal semantics in OWL is based on DL, which is a decidable fragment of first-order logics.

DL. DL is a family of knowledge representation (KR) formalisms that represent the knowledge of an application domain (Baader et al. 2003). It defines the concepts of the domain (i.e., its terminology) as sets of objects called classes, and it uses these concepts to specify properties of objects and individuals occurring in the domain. DL is characterized by a set of constructors that allow one to build complex concepts and roles from atomic ones.

$\mathcal{ALCQ}$. A DL language $\mathcal{ALCQ}$ consists of a countable set of individuals *Ind*, a countable set of atomic concepts *CS*, a countable set of roles *RS*, and the concepts built on *CS* and *RS* as follows:

$$C,D: = A|{-}A|C{\sqcap}D|C{\sqcup}D|\exists R.C|\forall R.C|({\leq}nR.C)|({\geq}nR.C)$$

where $A{\in}CS$, $R{\in}RS$, *C*, and *D* are concepts and *n* is a natural number. Also, individuals are denoted by *a,b,c, . . .* (e.g., lowercase letters of the alphabet).

This language includes only concepts in negation normal form. The complement of a concept $-(C)$ is inductively defined, as usual, by using the law of double negation, de Morgan laws, and the dualities for quantifiers. Moreover, the constants $\top$ and $\perp$ abbreviate $A \sqcup{-}A$ and $A{\sqcap}{-}A$, respectively, for some $A{\in}CS$.

An interpretation *I* consists of a nonempty domain, Δ^{I}, and a mapping, $.^{\mathrm{I}}$, that assigns

- To each individual $a{\in}Ind$ an element $a^{\mathrm{I}} \in \Delta^{\mathrm{I}}$
- To each atomic concept $A{\in}CS$ a set $A^{\mathrm{I}} \subseteq \Delta^{\mathrm{I}}$
- To each role $R{\in}RS$ a relation $R^{\mathrm{I}} \subseteq \Delta^{\mathrm{I}} \times \Delta^{\mathrm{I}}$

The interpretation extends then on concepts as follows:

$$-A^{\mathrm{I}} = \Delta^{\mathrm{I}}\backslash A^{\mathrm{I}}$$

$$(C \sqcup D)^{\mathrm{I}} = C^{\mathrm{I}} \cup D^{\mathrm{I}}$$

$$(C \sqcap D)^{\mathrm{I}} = C^{\mathrm{I}} \cap D^{\mathrm{I}}$$

$$(\exists R.C)^{\mathrm{I}} = \{x \in \Delta^{\mathrm{I}}|\exists y((x, y) \in R^{\mathrm{I}} \wedge y \in C^{\mathrm{I}})\}$$

$$(\forall R.C)^{\mathrm{I}} = \{x \in \Delta^{\mathrm{I}}|\forall y((x, y) \in R^{\mathrm{I}} \Rightarrow y \in C^{\mathrm{I}})\}$$

$$(\leq R.C)^{\mathrm{I}} = \{x \in \Delta^{\mathrm{I}}|\#\{y|((x, y) \in R^{\mathrm{I}} \wedge y \in C^{\mathrm{I}})\} \leq n\}$$

$$(\geq R.C)^{\mathrm{I}} = \{x \in \Delta^{\mathrm{I}}|\#\{y|((x, y) \in R^{\mathrm{I}} \wedge y \in C^{\mathrm{I}})\} \geq n\}$$

We can define the notion of a knowledge base and its models. An $\mathcal{ALCQ}$ knowledge base is the union of

1. A finite terminological set (TBox) of inclusion axioms that have the form $\top{\sqsubseteq}C$, where *C* is called inclusion concept.

2. A finite assertional set (ABox) of assertions of the form *a:C* (concept assertion) or (*a*, *b*) : *R* (role assertion) where *R* is called the assertional role and *C* is called the assertional concept.

We denote the set of individuals that appear in *KB* by *Ind(KB)*. An interpretation *I* is a model of

- An inclusion axiom $T \sqsubseteq C (I \vDash T \sqsubseteq C)$ if $C^I = \Delta^I$
- A concept assertion a:$C (I \vDash a:C)$ if $a^I \in C^I$
- A role assertion *a*, *b*: $R (I \vDash (a, b) : R)$ if $(a^I, b^I) \in R^I$

Let *K* be the $\mathcal{ALCQ}$-knowledge base of a TBox, *T* and an ABox A. An interpretation *I* is a model of *K* if $I \vDash \phi$, for every $\phi \in T \cup \mathcal{A}$. A knowledge base *K* is consistent if it has a model. Moreover, for φ, an inclusion axiom or an assertion, we say that $K \vDash \varphi$ (in other words, *K* entails φ) if for every model *I* of *K*, $I \vDash \varphi$ also holds.

The consistency problem for $\mathcal{ALCQ}$ is ExpTime-complete. The entailment problem is reducible to the consistency problem as follows:

Let *K* be an $\mathcal{ALCQ}$ knowledge base and *d* be an individual not belonging to *Ind(K)*. Then

- $K \vDash T \sqsubseteq C$ iff $K \cup \{d: -C\}$ is inconsistent
- $K \vDash a: C$ iff $K \cup \{a: -C\}$ is inconsistent

This shows that an entailment can be decided in ExpTime. Moreover, the inconsistency problem is reducible to the entailment problem and so deciding an entailment is an ExpTime-complete problem, too.

Inferencing. The basic inference problem for DL is checking a knowledge base consistency. A knowledge base *K* is consistent if it has a model. The additional inference problems are

- *Concept satisfiability.* A concept *C* is satisfiable relative to *K* if there is a model *I* of *K* such that $C^I \neq \emptyset$.
- *Concept subsumption.* A concept *C* is subsumed by concept *D* relative to *K* if, for every model *I* of *K*, $C^I \sqsubseteq D^I$.
- *Concept instantiation.* An individual *a* is an instance of concept *C* relative to *K* if, for every model *I* of *K*, $a^I \in C^I$.

All these reasoning problems can be reduced to KB consistency. For example, concept *C* is satisfiable with regard to the knowledge base *K* if $K \cup C(a)$ is consistent where *a* is an individual not occurring in *K*.

SWRL. SWRL extends the set of OWL axioms to include Horn-like rules, and it extends the Horn-like rules to be combined with an OWL knowledge base (Horrocks et al. 2004).

Definition 3.3: Horn Clause

A Horn clause C is an expression of the form $D_0 \leftarrow D_1 \cap \ldots \cap D_n$, where each D_i is an atom. The atom D_0 is called the head and the set $D_1 \cap \ldots \cap D_n$ is called the body. Variables that occur in the body at most once and do not occur in the head are called unbound variables; all other variables are called bound variables.

The proposed rules are of the form of an implication between an antecedent (body) and a consequent (head). The intended meaning can be read as follows: whenever the conditions specified in the antecedent hold, the conditions specified in the consequent must also hold. Both the antecedent (body) and consequent (head) consist of zero or more atoms. An empty antecedent is treated as trivially true (i.e., satisfied by every interpretation), so the consequent must also be satisfied by every interpretation. An empty consequent is treated as trivially false (i.e., not satisfied by any interpretation), so the antecedent must not be satisfied by any interpretation.

Multiple atoms are treated as a conjunction, and both the head and body can contain conjunction of such atoms. Note that rules with conjunctive consequents could easily be transformed (via Lloyd-Topor transformations) into multiple rules, each with an atomic consequent. Atoms in these rules can be of the form $C(x)$, $P(x,y)$, $SameAs(x,y)$ or $DifferentFrom(x,y)$ where C is an OWL description, P is an OWL property, and x,y are either variables, OWL individuals, or OWL data values.

3.4 Semantic Web and Security

We first provide an overview of security issues for the Semantic Web and then discuss some details on XML security, RDF security, and secure information integration that are components of the secure Semantic Web. As more progress is made on investigating these various issues, we hope that appropriate standards would be developed for securing the Semantic Web. Security cannot be considered in isolation. Security cuts across all layers.

For example, consider the lowest layer. One needs secure Transmission Control Protocol/Internet Protocol (TCP/IP), secure sockets, and secure Hypertext Transfer Protocol (HTTP). There are now security protocols for these various lower-layer protocols but end-to-end security is needed. That is, one cannot just have secure TCP/IP built on untrusted communication layers; network security is needed. The next layer is XML and XML schemas. Secure XML is needed. That is, access must be controlled to various portions of the document for reading, browsing, and modifications. There is research on securing XML and XML schemas. The next step is securing RDF. Now with RDF not only is secure XML needed, we also need security for the interpretations and semantics. For example, under certain contexts, portions of the document may be unclassified while under certain other contexts the document may be classified.

Once XML and RDF have been secured, the next step is to examine security for ontologies and interoperation. That is, ontologies may have security levels attached to them. Certain parts of the ontologies could be secret while certain other parts may be unclassified. The challenge is how does one use these ontologies for secure information integration? Researchers have done some work on the secure interoperability of databases. We need to revisit this research and then determine what else needs to be done so that the information on the Web can be managed, integrated, and exchanged securely. Logic, proof, and trust are at the highest layers of the Semantic Web. That is, how can we trust the information that the Web gives us? Next we discuss the various security issues for XML, RDF, ontologies, and rules.

XML security: Various research efforts have been reported on XML security (see for example [Bertino and Ferrari 2002]). We briefly discuss some of the key points. The main challenge is whether to give access to the entire XML documents or parts of the documents. Bertino et al. have developed authorization models for XML. They have focused on access control policies as well as on dissemination policies. They also considered push and pull architectures and specified the policies in XML. The policy specification contains information about which users can access which portions of the documents. In Bertino and Ferrari (2002), algorithms for access control as well as computing views of the results are presented. In addition, architectures for securing XML documents are also discussed. In Bertino et al. (2004) and Bhatti et al. (2004), the authors go further and describe how XML documents may be published on the Web. The idea is for owners to publish documents, subjects to request access to the documents, and untrusted publishers to give the subjects the views of the documents they are authorized to see. W3C is specifying standards for XML security. The XML security project is focusing on providing the implementation of security standards for XML. The focus is on XML-Signature Syntax and Processing, XML-Encryption Syntax and Processing, and XML Key Management. W3C also has a number of working groups including the nXML Signature Working Group and the nXML Encryption Working Group. While the standards are focusing on what can be implemented in the near-term, much research is needed on securing XML documents.

RDF security: RDF is the foundation of the Semantic Web. While XML is limited in providing machine-understandable documents, RDF handles this limitation. As a result, RDF provides better support for interoperability as well as searching and cataloging. It also describes contents of documents as well as relationships between various entities in the document. While XML provides syntax and notations, RDF supplements this by providing semantic information in a standardized way (Antoniou and Van Harmelen 2008).

The basic RDF model has three components: resources, properties, and statements. Resource is anything described by RDF expressions. It could be a Web page or a collection of pages. Property is a specific attribute used to describe a resource. RDF statements are resources together with a named property plus the value of the property. Statement components are subject, predicate, and object. So for example, if we have a sentence of the form "John is the creator of xxx," then xxx is the subject or resource, property or predicate is "creator," and object or literal is "John." There are RDF diagrams very much like, say, entity relationship (ER) diagrams or object diagrams to represent statements. It is important that the intended interpretation be used for RDF sentences. This is accomplished by RDF schemas. A schema is sort of a dictionary and has interpretations of various terms used in sentences.

More advanced concepts in RDF include the container model and statements about statements. The container model has three types of container objects and they are bag, sequence, and alternative. A bag is an unordered list of resources or literals. It is used to mean that a property has multiple values but the order is not important. A sequence is a list of ordered resources. Here the order is important. Alternative is a list of resources that represent alternatives for the value of a property. Various tutorials in RDF describe the syntax of containers in more detail. RDF also provides support for making statements about other statements. For example, with this facility one can make statements of the form "The statement A is false" where A is the statement "John is the creator of X." Again one can use object-like diagrams to represent containers and statements about statements. RDF also has a formal model associated with it. This formal model has a formal grammar. The query language to access RDF document is SPARQL. For further information on RDF, we refer to the excellent discussion in the book by Antoniou and van Harmelen (2008).

Now to make the Semantic Web secure, we need to ensure that RDF documents are secure. This would involve securing XML from a syntactic point of view. However, with RDF, we also need to ensure that security is preserved at the semantic level. The issues include the security implications of the concepts resource, properties, and statements. That is, how is access control ensured? How can statements and properties about statements be protected? How can one provide access control at a finer grain of granularity? What are the security properties of the container model? How can bags, lists, and alternatives be protected? Can we specify security policies in RDF? How can we resolve semantic inconsistencies for the policies? What are the security implications of statements about statements? How can we protect RDF schemas? These are difficult questions and we need to start research to provide answers. XML security is just the beginning. Securing RDF is much more challenging (see also Carminati et al. 2004).

Security and ontologies: Ontologies are essentially representations of various concepts in order to avoid ambiguity. Numerous ontologies have been developed. These ontologies have been used by agents to understand the Web pages and conduct operations such as the integration of databases. Furthermore, ontologies can be represented in languages such as RDF or special languages such as OWL. Now, ontologies have to be secure. That is, access to the ontologies has to be controlled. This means that different users may have access to different parts of the ontology. On the other hand, ontologies may be used to specify security policies just as XML and RDF have been used to specify the policies. That is, we will describe how ontologies may be secured as well as how ontologies may be used to specify the various policies.

Secure query and rules processing: The layer above the secure RDF layer is the secure query and rule processing layer. While RDF can be used to specify security policies (see for example Carminati et al. 2004), the Web rules language being developed by W3C is more powerful to specify complex policies. Furthermore, inference engines are being developed to process and reason about the rules (e.g., the Pellet engine developed at the University of Maryland). One could integrate ideas from the database inference controller that we have developed (see Thuraisingham et al. 1993) with Web rules processing to develop an inference or privacy controller for the Semantic Web. The query-processing module is responsible for accessing the heterogeneous data and information sources on the Semantic Web. Researchers are examining ways to integrate techniques from Web query processing with Semantic Web technologies to locate, query, and integrate the heterogeneous data and information sources. Much of the discussion in this book is related to secure query processing for Semantic Web technologies.

3.5 Summary and Directions

This chapter has provided the foundations needed to understand the contents of this book. They are access control and the Semantic Web. We first provided an overview of access control models and then discussed RBAC. This was followed by a discussion of the technologies for the Semantic Web including XML, RDF, ontologies, and OWL. Finally, we discussed security issues for the Semantic Web. More details on security for the Semantic Web can be found in Thuraisingham (2007).

In the remaining chapters of Section I, we describe inferencing and inference controllers. In Section II we describe techniques for securing data provenance and in Section III we describe the inference controller we have developed. We have chosen provenance data as an example to illustrate the concepts. However, our techniques are general enough to be applicable to any type of data.

References

Antoniou, G. and Van Harmelen, F., *A Semantic Web Primer,* MIT Press, Cambridge, MA, 2008.

Baader, F., Calvanese, D., McGuinness, D., Nardi, D. and Patel-Schneider, P., *The Description Logic Handbook: Theory, Implementation and Applications,* Cambridge University Press, Cambridge, UK, 2003.

Berners Lee, T. and Hendler, J., The Semantic Web, *Scientific American,* Vol. 284, No. 5, May 2001.

Bertino, E., Bonatti, P. A. and Ferrari, E., TRBAC: A temporal role-based access control model, *ACM Transactions on Information and System Security* (TISSEC), Vol. 4, No. 3, 2001.

Bertino, E. and Ferrari, E., Secure and selective dissemination of XML documents, *ACM Transactions on Information and System Security* (TISSEC), Vol. 5, No. 3, 2002.

Bertino, E., Guerrini, G. and Mesiti, M., A matching algorithm for measuring the structural similarity between an XML document and a DTD and its applications, *Information Systems,* Vol. 29, No. 1, 2004.

Bhatti, R., Bertino, E., Ghafoor, A. and Joshi, J., XML-based specification for Web services document security, *Computer,* Vol. 37, No. 4, 2004.

Bray, T., Paoli, J., Sperberg-McQueen, C. M., Maler, E. and Yergeau, F., Extensible markup language (XML), *World Wide Web Journal,* Vol. 2, No. 4, 1997.

Carminati, B., Ferrari, E. and Thuraisingham, B. M., Using RDF for policy specification and enforcement, DEXA Workshops, 2004.

Cirio, L., Cruz, I. and Tamassia, R., A role and attribute based access control system using Semantic Web technologies, *Proceedings OTM Confederated Conference* (On the Move to Meaningful Internet Systems, Volume II), pp. 1256–1266, Springer-Verlag, 2007.

Denning, D. E., A lattice model of secure information flow, *Communications of the ACM,* Vol. 19, 1976.

Ferraiolo, D., Kuhn, D. R. and Chandramouli, R., *Role-Based Access Control,* Artech House, Norwood, MA, 2003.

Ferraiolo, D. F., Sandhu, R., Gavrila, S., Kuhn, D. R. and Chandramouli, R., Proposed NIST standard for role-based access control, *ACM Transactions on Information and System Security* (TISSEC), Vol. 4, No. 3, 2001.

Horrocks, I., Patel-Schneider, P. F., Boley, H., Tabet, S., Grosof, B. and Dean, M., SWRL: A Semantic Web rule language combining OWL and RuleML, W3C Member Submission, 2004.

Klyne, G., Carroll, J. J. and McBride, B., Resource description framework (RDF): Concepts and abstract syntax, W3C Recommendation 10, 2004.

Lindqvist, H., Mandatory access control, Master's Thesis, Umea University, 2006.

McGuinness, D. L. and van Harmelen, F. OWL web ontology language overview, W3C Recommendation, 2004.

Moffett, J., Sloman, M. and Twidle, K., Specifying discretionary access control policy for distributed systems, *Computer Communications,* Vol. 13, No. 9, 1990.

Osborn, S., Sandhu, R. and Munawer, Q., Configuring role-based access control to enforce mandatory and discretionary access control policies, *ACM Transactions on Information and System Security* (TISSEC), Vol. 3, No. 2, 2000.

Prud'hommeaux, E. and Seaborne, A. SPARQL query language for RDF, W3C Working Draft, 2006.

Samarati, P. and de Capitani di Vimercati, S., Access control: Policies, models, and mechanisms, *Foundations of Security Analysis and Design,* LCNS 2171, Springer-Verlag, Berlin-Heidelberg, 2001, pp. 137–196.

Sandhu, R. S., Lattice-based access control models, *Computer,* Vol. 26, No. 11, 1993.

Sandhu, R. S. and Samarati, P., Access control: Principle and practice, *IEEE Communications Magazine,* Vol. 23, No. 9, 1994.

Thuraisingham, B., *Building and Securing the Semantic Web,* CRC Press, Boca Raton, FL, 2007.

Thuraisingham, B. M., Ford, W., Collins, M. and J. O'Keeffe, Design and implementation of a database inference controller, *Data & Knowledge Engineering,* Vol. 11, No. 3, 1993.

World Wide Web Consortium, http://www.w3c.org.

Chapter 4

The Inference Problem

4.1 Overview

As stated in Chapter 1, inference is the process of forming conclusions from premises. This process is harmful if the user draws unauthorized conclusions from the legitimate responses he or she receives. This problem has come to be known as the inference problem. An inference controller is the device that prevents a user from drawing unauthorized conclusions. We have studied the inference problem extensively in the past. Specifically, we have defined various types of inference strategies and developed inference controllers that handle certain types of inference strategies. However, our prior work focused on inference in relational databases. Our current work, described in this book, is about inference controllers that act on Semantic Web data. Specifically, we utilize the inference strategies built into the Semantic Web technologies.

This chapter describes the inference problem and the desired features of an inference controller. We first discuss the inference problem, and then we discuss some key criteria for an inference controller. Next, we introduce various inference strategies followed by a list of security constraints, also known as security policies, that must be enforced by any inference controller in order to protect a provenance database. We then discuss our approach to handling the inference process. Finally, we give a historical perspective. The organization of this chapter is as follows. Section 4.2 describes the inference problem including a discussion of inference strategies. Our approach is discussed in Section 4.3. A historical perspective is given in Section 4.4. A note on the privacy problem and its relationship to the inference problem is discussed in Section 4.5. The chapter is concluded in Section 4.6. Figure 4.1 illustrates the concepts discussed in this chapter.

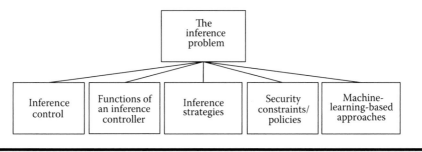

Figure 4.1   The inference problem.

4.2 The Inference Problem

The inference problem is typical of systems where the databases store both public and secured views of the underlying data. The intended use of these database systems is to allow users to interact with the system through an interface that directs the user query to subsets of the database. These subsets are governed by a set of policies that determine which subsets of the database are considered secure with respect to the user and which subsets are considered safe to release. Normally, in these systems, users pose multiple queries that may result in the release of unauthorized information via inferences. It is always possible to draw inferences from the responses returned to a query by a database system. The inferred knowledge could depend on data obtained from the database or it could depend on some prior knowledge possessed by the user in addition to the data obtained from the database. The situation where the inferred knowledge is something the user is not authorized to acquire has come to be known as the inference problem. Various approaches have been suggested previously to handle the inference problem. Such approaches have been used to build software systems that use strategies such as machine learning techniques (e.g., decision trees) and logic-based approaches (e.g., deductions and semantic associations).

4.2.1 Functions of an Inference Controller

In order for an inference controller to be functional, it must have the capabilities to carry out key operations. These operations include

- *Identifying threats:* The user can combine collections of data to infer new knowledge. Therefore, we need to protect against the association and correlation between the data that is confidential.
- *Handling different types of inferences:* The Semantic Web has reasoning capabilities. This could be used to implement the system to detect inference threats or enhance the inference capabilities of the system.

- *Specifying the granularity of protection:* Different granularity includes class level, instance level, and attribute level protection. At the finest level, we could iterate all the triples in a graph and process the subject, object, and property separately.
- *Protecting against security violations:* The inference controller has to ensure that the user does not acquire knowledge that he or she is not authorized to know.
- *Tracking previously released information:* A release knowledge base functions as a checkpoint where queries and responses are evaluated against previously released information.
- *Performing reasoning about the activities of a user:* A query log records all the previous queries in order to identify query trends and patterns. The log is a great database about the user profile.

4.2.2 Inference Strategies

A successful design of an inference controller is one that is capable of identifying the inference strategies that are available to an adversary. The possible inference strategies include

- *Inference by deductive reasoning:* In this strategy, new information is inferred using well-formed rules; for example, implication rules.
- *Inference by inductive reasoning:* In this strategy, well-formed rules are used to infer hypotheses from the example observed. For example, we could infer a function f from observing the values $f(0)$, $f(1)$, and $f(2)$.
- *Inference by analogical reasoning:* In this strategy, statements such as "X is like Y" are used to infer properties of X given the properties of Y.
- *Inference by heuristic reasoning:* Heuristics are criteria, methods, or principles for deciding which among several alternative courses of action promises to be the most effective in order to achieve some goal.
- *Inference by semantic association:* In this strategy, association between entities is inferred from the knowledge of the entities themselves. Examples of associations include content-based associations, aggregation-based associations, and dependency-based associations.
- *Inference by inferred existence:* In this strategy, one can infer the existence of an entity Y from certain information about Y. For example, from the information "Radiologist performs an x-ray on patient John," it is reasonable to infer that there is some entity who is a radiologist.
- *Statistical inference:* In this strategy, from the various statistics computed on a set of entities, information about an individual entity in the set is inferred.

The success of the inference controller depends on the software that is available and the reasoning strategies supported by the software.

4.2.3 Security Constraints

Security constraints are essentially security policies (Thuraisingham et al. 1993; Thuraisingham and Ford 1995). They determine the type of access that a user has to the data. We use the term constraints instead of policies to be consistent with the terminology we used in our prior work. We will, however, use the terms policies and constraints interchangeably. One approach for implementing an inference controller is to build a software device that is capable of enforcing security constraints. The security constraints include

- *Constraints that classify a knowledge base.* These are called simple constraints.
- *Constraints that classify any part of the knowledge base depending on the value of some data.* These are called content-based constraints.
- *Constraints that classify any part of a knowledge base depending on the occurrence of some real-world event.* These are called event-based constraints.
- *Constraints that classify associations between data.* These are called association-based constraints.
- *Constraints that classify the knowledge base or any part of the knowledge base depending on the information that has been previously released.* These constraints are called release-based constraints.
- *Constraints that classify collections of data.* These are called aggregate constraints.
- *Constraints that specify implication.* These are called logical constraints.

4.2.4 Machine Learning and Inference

Machine learning is a branch of artificial intelligence concerned with the design and development of algorithms that allow computers to evolve behaviors based on empirical examples. A learner can take advantage of examples to capture characteristics of interest of their unknown underlying probability distribution. A learner automatically learns to recognize complex patterns and to make intelligent decisions based on the examples. Usually the learner generalizes from the given examples to be able to produce a useful output in new cases.

4.3 Our Approach

We have developed an inference controller to act on provenance data. Our data and policies (i.e., the constraints) are represented using Semantic Web technologies

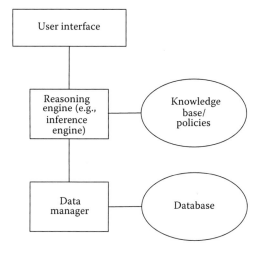

Figure 4.2   Inference controller.

(e.g., OWL and RDF). The inference controller augments a Semantic Web data management system. An example of a Semantic Web data management system is Jena. It can be augmented with a system such as Pellet for reasoning. The reasoner reasons about the policies and determines whether the data should be released to the user.

Figure 4.2 illustrates our approach to designing an inference controller. The Semantic Web data manager manages the database. The policy database stores the policies. The policies specify the type of access that a user has on the data. The inference controller reasons about the policies using Semantic Web-based reasoning strategies and determines whether the data should be released to the user. For example, if the user John has access to A and does not have access to B and if A implies B, then the inference controller will determine that John is not given access to A. Details of our approach are given in Section III.

4.4 Historical Perspective

The inference problem was studied extensively in statistical databases for several years before it became a very popular topic for multilevel secure database management systems. In such a system, the data are assigned sensitivity levels and the users are granted clearance levels. The goal is for users to query and update data to which they have authorized access. As stated earlier, inference is the process of posing queries and deducing information from the legitimate response received. It becomes a problem if the information deduced is something that a user is not authorized to know. For example, if one deduces, say, secret information from unclassified pieces of data, then the inference problem has occurred.

In the case of statistical databases, Dorothy Denning and others were the first to study the problem extensively (see Denning 1979). Here the idea is to give out, for example, averages and sums while protecting the individual pieces of data. The census bureau also studied the inference problem in collecting and maintaining census data. However, it was not until the late 1980s when there were many activities on multi-level secure database management systems (MLS/DBMSs) that the inference problem was investigated extensively. Morgenstern (1987) at SRI International, Thuraisingham (1987) at Honeywell, and Hinke (1988) at TRW developed the early solutions. Later, Thuraisingham at MITRE carried out extensive work on the problem together with Ford, Rubinovitz, and Collins (see Thuraisingham 1989; Thuraisingham et al. 1993; Thuraisingham and Ford 1995). Since then many efforts have been reported by Marks, Farkas, Wiederhold, and others (see Farkas et al. 2001; Marks 1996; Wiederhold 2000). The early approaches were divided into two categories: one that was an active approach where the security constraints are processed when the data are being queried or updated (Thuraisingham et al. 1993) and one that was a passive approach where the constraints are examined when designing the database (Thuraisingham 1992). In 1990, Thuraisingham (1990) proved that the general inference problem was unsolvable and in October 1990, at the National Computer Security Conference, Dr. John Campbell of the National Security Agency stated that this was a significant development in database security for that year (Campbell 1990).

Today the inference problem is resurfacing due to technologies such as data warehousing, data mining, and the Semantic Web. This is because data warehousing, data mining, and the Semantic Web have reasoning capabilities and therefore they exacerbate the inference problem and also contribute toward privacy violations via inference. For example, data mining tools may be applied to extract sensitive nuggets from unclassified data. Semantic Web technologies such as RDF have reasoning capabilities and could therefore lead to unauthorized inferences. Our work will focus on the inference problem in Semantic Web data. More details on the inference problem can be found in Thuraisingham (2005). More details of the

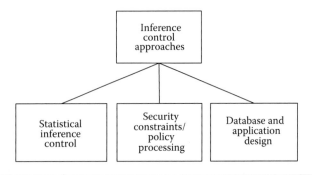

Figure 4.3   Historical perspective.

historical perspective will be given in Appendix C. Design and implementation of one of the earliest inference controllers is given in Appendix D.

Figure 4.3 illustrates the historical perspective of the inference problem.

4.5 A Note on the Privacy Problem

While the inference problem has focused on confidentiality, the privacy problem deals with protecting information about individuals. Furthermore, an individual can, for example, specify to a Web service provider the information that can be released about him or her. Privacy has always been a topic of great discussion, especially when it relates to protecting medical information about patients. Social scientists as well as technologists continue to work on privacy issues. However, privacy has received enormous attention in recent years. This is mainly because of the advent of the Web, the Semantic Web, counterterrorism, and national security. For example, data mining tools are being examined in order to extract information about various individuals and perhaps prevent and/or detect potential terrorist attacks. We have heard much about national security versus privacy in the media. This is mainly due to the fact that people are now realizing that to handle terrorism, the government may need to collect data about individuals and mine that data to extract useful information. Data may be in relational databases or it may be text, video, and images. This is causing major concerns with various civil liberties unions (Thuraisingham 2003).

The privacy problem has been studied within the context of data mining. That is, how can we effectively mine the data but at the same time ensure that the sensitive attribute values of individuals (e.g., medical records) are kept private (Agrawal

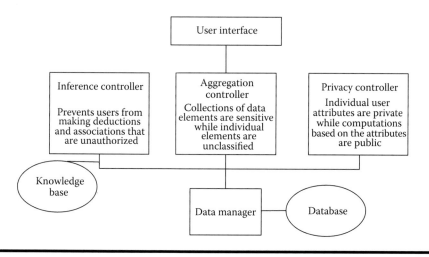

Figure 4.4   Inference, aggregation, and privacy problems.

and Srikant 2000)? On the other hand, some researchers have studied the privacy problem as a variation of the inference problem. That is, while the inference problem deals with deducing confidential information, the privacy problem deals with deducing sensitive information private to individuals. In the latter situation, the privacy controller could be developed to ensure that private information is protected. We will revisit privacy in Section IV of this book after we have presented the design and implementation of our inference controller.

Figure 4.4 illustrates the inference problem, aggregation problem, and privacy problem.

4.6 Summary and Directions

This chapter has provided details about the inference problem and inference controllers. First we discussed the inference problem. In particular, we defined the inference problem and discussed the inference strategies. We also defined various types of security constraints, also known as security policies. Then we discussed our approach to developing an inference controller. The next two chapters will continue to discuss inference control. Chapter 5 will discuss the various tools that we have examined to develop the inference controller. In Chapter 6 we give examples of inference strategies. The contents of these chapters will provide the foundations for our work on inference control, which will be discussed in Section III.

The inference problem has been studied extensively since the 1980s. However, at that time we did not have sophisticated reasoning tools. Therefore, the solutions that we developed were not efficient. With the development of Semantic Web technologies and machine-learning tools, we now have the capability to develop more powerful inference controllers. The work described in this book is the first step. We believe that with the developments in reasoning tools together with the development of security and privacy technologies, significant progress can be made on inference control.

References

Agrawal, R. and Srikant, R., Privacy-Preserving Data Mining, SIGMOD Conference, 2000, pp. 439–450.

Campbell, J., Database security, a year in progress, Proceedings of the National Computer Security Symposium, Washington, DC, October 1990.

Denning, D., The tracker: A threat to statistical database security, *ACM Transactions in Database Systems,* Vol. 4, No. 2, 1979.

Farkas, C. et al., The inference problem and updates in relational databases, Proceedings of the IFIP Database Security Conference, Lake Niagara, Canada, 2001.

Hinke, T., Inference aggregation detection in database management systems, Proceedings of the IEEE Symposium on Security and Privacy, Oakland, CA, April 1988.

Marks, D., Inference in MLS database systems, *IEEE Transactions on Knowledge and Data Engineering*, Vol. 8, No. 1, 1996.

Morgenstern, M., Security and inference in multilevel database and knowledge base systems, Proceedings of the ACM SIGM CD Conference, San Francisco, May 1987.

Thuraisingham, B., Security checking in relational database management systems augmented with inference engines, *Computers & Security*, Vol. 6, December 1987.

Thuraisingham, B., Secure query processing in intelligent database systems. In Proceedings of the Computer Security Applications Conference, Tucson, AZ, 1989.

Thuraisingham, B., Recursion theoretic properties of the inference problem, Computer Security Foundations Workshop, Franconia, NH, June 1990 (also available as MITRE Report MTP 291, June 1990).

Thuraisingham, B., The use of conceptual structures to handle the inference problem, Proceedings of the IFIP Database Security Conference, Shepherdstown, WV (proceedings published by North Holland, 1992).

Thuraisingham, B., Data mining, national security and privacy, *ACM SIGKDD*, Explorations Vol. 4, No. 2, pp. 1–5, January 2003.

Thuraisingham, B., *Database and Applications Security*, CRC Press, Boca Raton, FL, 2005.

Thuraisingham, B. M. and Ford, W., Security constraints in a multilevel secure distributed database management system, *IEEE Transactions on Knowledge and Data Engineering*, Vol. 7, 1995.

Thuraisingham, B. M., Ford, W., Collins, M. and O'Keeffe, J., Design and implementation of a database inference controller, *Data & Knowledge Engineering*, Vol. 11, No. 3, 1993.

Wiederhold, G., Release control in database systems, Proceedings IFIP Database Security Conference, Amsterdam, August 2000.

Chapter 5

Inference Engines

5.1 Overview

Now that we have provided an overview of the inference problem, we describe the concepts and systems that have been developed for reasoning. These concepts and systems are essentially based on Semantic Web technologies. For example, the concepts include the closed world assumption, negation by failure, and OWL. The systems include Jena, Euler, and Sesame, which essentially manage RDF data and reason about the data. We have utilized these concepts and systems in our design and development of the inference controller.

As mentioned in Chapter 4, we developed multiple inference controllers in the 1990s. These inference controllers operated on relational databases and used mainly logical inferencing. However, with the sophisticated reasoning tools based on Semantic Web technologies and machine-learning techniques that have been developed during the past decade, we can now build more powerful inference controllers. This book will lay the foundations for developing such powerful inference controllers. Some of the technologies and reasoning tools are discussed in this chapter. The organization of this chapter is as follows. Concepts such as the closed world assumption are discussed in Section 5.2. The various systems such as Jena and Sesame are discussed in Section 5.3. The chapter is summarized in Section 5.4. Figure 5.1 illustrates the concepts and systems.

5.2 Concepts for Inference Engines

Our inference controller uses a set of tools to build its inference engine. We therefore benefit from using the existing tools that support inferencing over RDF and

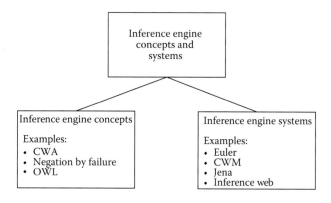

Figure 5.1 Concepts and systems for inference engines.

OWL. By leveraging the existing inference tools, we can make use of state-of-the-art reasoners, such as Pellet, and the Semantic Web framework, Jena. In addition, we make use of DL-based reasoners, RDF-S, forward and backward reasoners, and SWRL. The three major concepts on which we have designed inference controller are (1) the closed world assumption, (2) negation by failure, and (3) OWL. We describe them next.

Closed world assumption (CWA). In previous implementations of an inference controller, inferred knowledge that depends on data obtained from the database alone is used to disclose what is and what is not in the database. This is the case when a closed world is assumed. A positive answer to a query describes what is in a database and a negative answer could be interpreted as what is not present in the database. This interpretation of the responses to a query is a consequence of the fact that the information is complete in the database.

Negation by failure (NF). Negation by failure means that if a fact cannot be proved, then the fact is assumed not to be true. In CWA this negation by failure is equal to the logical negation. When using RDF on the Semantic Web, an open world assumption is the rule and NF is translated as "not found."

OWL. OWL is designed for use by applications that need to process the content of information instead of just presenting information to humans. OWL facilitates greater machine interpretability of Web content than that supported by XML, RDF, and RDF-S by providing additional vocabulary along with a formal semantics (McGuinness and van Harmelen 2004).

OWL can be used to explicitly represent the meaning of terms in vocabularies and the relationships between those terms. This representation of terms and their interrelationships is called an ontology. OWL has more facilities for expressing meaning and semantics than XML, RDF, and RDF-S, and thus OWL goes beyond these languages in its ability to represent machine interpretable content on the Web.

OWL has been designed to meet this need for a Web ontology language. OWL is part of the growing stack of W3C recommendations related to the Semantic Web.

- XML provides a surface syntax for structured documents, but imposes no semantic constraints on the meaning of these documents
- XML Schema is a language for restricting the structure of XML documents and also extends XML with datatypes
- RDF is a data model for objects ("resources") and relations between them, provides a simple semantics for this data model, and these data models can be represented in an XML syntax
- RDF-S is a vocabulary for describing properties and classes of RDF resources with a semantics for generalization-hierarchies of such properties and classes
- OWL adds more vocabulary for describing properties and classes: among others, relations between classes (e.g., disjointness), cardinality (e.g., "exactly one"), equality, richer typing of properties, characteristics of properties (e.g., symmetry), and enumerated classes

OWL provides three increasingly expressive sublanguages designed for use by specific communities of implementers and users:

1. OWL Lite supports those users primarily needing a classification hierarchy and simple constraints. For example, while it supports cardinality constraints, it only permits cardinality values of 0 or 1. It should be simpler to provide tool support for OWL Lite than its more expressive relatives, and OWL Lite provides a quick migration path for thesauri and other taxonomies. OWL Lite also has a lower formal complexity than OWL DL; see the section on OWL Lite in the OWL reference for further details.
2. OWL DL supports those users who want the maximum expressiveness while retaining computational completeness (all conclusions are guaranteed to be computable) and decidability (all computations will finish in finite time). OWL DL includes all OWL language constructs, but they can be used only under certain restrictions (for example, while a class may be a subclass of many classes, a class cannot be an instance of another class). OWL DL is so named due to its correspondence with description logics, a field of research that has studied the logics that form the formal foundation of OWL.
3. OWL Full is meant for users who want maximum expressiveness and the syntactic freedom of RDF with no computational guarantees. For example, in OWL Full a class can be treated simultaneously as a collection of individuals and as an individual in its own right. OWL Full allows an ontology to augment the meaning of the predefined (RDF or OWL) vocabulary. It is unlikely that any reasoning software will be able to support complete reasoning for every feature of OWL Full.

Each of these sublanguages is an extension of its simpler predecessor, both in what can be legally expressed and in what can be validly concluded. The following set of relations hold. Their inverses do not.

- Every legal OWL Lite ontology is a legal OWL DL ontology
- Every legal OWL DL ontology is a legal OWL Full ontology
- Every valid OWL Lite conclusion is a valid OWL DL conclusion
- Every valid OWL DL conclusion is a valid OWL Full conclusion

Ontology developers adopting OWL should consider which sublanguage best suits their needs. The choice between OWL Lite and OWL DL depends on the extent to which users require the more-expressive constructs provided by OWL DL. The choice between OWL DL and OWL Full mainly depends on the extent to which users require the metamodeling facilities of RDF-S (e.g., defining classes of classes, or attaching properties to classes). When using OWL Full as compared to OWL DL, reasoning support is less predictable since complete OWL Full implementations do not currently exist.

5.3 Software Systems

The foundational systems for supporting inferences over RDF and OWL include

- Euler, which takes as input a triple database and a query file then applies backward chaining reasoning. Euler is graph-oriented, which makes it suitable for applications that require reasoning over a graph representation of the domain (Euler Proof Mechanism, http://www.agfa.com/w3c/euler/).
- CWM, which applies forward chaining reasoning and has support for built-in properties such as math:sum (Berners-Lee 2000).
- Jena, which supports forward and backward reasoning (Carroll et al. 2004). It also has the capability to allow other reasoners to be plugged in (e.g., Pellet [Sirin et al. 2007]).
- Inference Web, which supports a variety of inference engines. Inference Web supports the compatibility of different inference engines and has a Web-based registry on details about the information sources and reasoners. It provides an explanation of a proof, where every inference step has a link to at least one inference engine (McGuinness and van Harmelen 2004).

This section elaborates on the above systems, describes some other systems for inferencing, and surveys some existing mechanisms for incorporating application domain and datatype knowledge into RDF inferences.

Euler. Euler is a program (Euler Proof Mechanism, http://www.agfa.com/w3c/euler/) that does inferencing and also implements a great deal of OWL. The program reads one or more triple databases that are merged together and it also reads a query file. The merged databases are transformed into a linked structure (Java objects that point to other Java objects). The philosophy of Euler is graph-oriented.

Euler is essentially a backward-chaining reasoner, using rules similar to those defined for CWM. Euler also supports a range of CWM's built-in properties. Euler treats built-in properties in a rule antecedent as terms to be unified, just like any others, except that the unification is handled by special code rather than by reference to the knowledge base. The terms in the antecedent of a rule are taken in the order they are given and unified one at a time, adding new variable bindings as they arise. Ordering of terms in the antecedent is important because unification of terms that appear later in the antecedent may depend on bindings created by unification of preceding terms. Individual terms (statements) in a rule antecedent are generally required to have at least their objects bound to specific values, and new bindings may be created as required for variables used in the subject position (see also http://www.agfa.com/w3c/euler/easterP. n3 for an example of Euler using CWM built-ins to calculate a date for Easter.)

CWM. CWM is a general-purpose data processor for the Semantic Web developed by Berners-Lee (Berners-Lee 2000). It is a forward-chaining reasoner that can be used for querying, checking, transforming, and filtering information. CWM is widely used for creating RDF applications with the ability to perform inferencing.

A rule could be expressed in CWM thus:

{?v :seatedCapacity ?c1.
?v :standingCapacity ?c2.
(?c1 ?c2) math:sum ?c3.}

=>

{?v :totalCapacity ?c3.}

Points to note are

- The term ?name indicates a name that is universally quantified within the scope of the rule. Standard RDF does not provide any way to express universal quantification. It is in the nature of a rule that it generalizes some assertion over many things arbitrarily rather than asserting information about a single thing.
- The property math:sum is a built-in property with special semantics known to CWM. It embodies knowledge of the relationship between numbers and their arithmetic sum. CWM defines a number of such built-in properties.
- The CWM built-in properties are not specifically linked to RDF datatypes, though many reasonably could be. In many cases, the CWM built-ins refer to RDF plain literal values.
- CWM requires that the built-in properties be used in the antecedent of a rule.

TRIPLE and RuleML. TRIPLE is an RDF query, inference, and transformation language for the Semantic Web. It is based on Horn logic and borrows many features from F-Logic (Angele et al. 2009; Kifer and Lausen 1989). TRIPLE is the successor to F-Logic. RuleML is an effort to define a specification of rules for use in the World Wide Web (Sintek and Decker 2002). The kernel of RuleML is datalog logic programs (Grosof et al. 2003). It is a declarative logic programming language with model-theoretic semantics.

The Inference Web. The Inference Web was introduced by a series of recent articles (Da Silva et al. 2006; McGuinness and van Harmelen 2004). When the Semantic Web evolves, it is to be expected that a variety of inference engines will be used on the Web. A software system is needed to ensure the compatibility between these engines. The Inference Web is a software system consisting of

- A Web-based registry containing details on information sources and reasoners called the Inference Web Registry.
- An interface for entering information in the registry called the Inference Web Registrar.
- A portable proof specification. In the Inference Web Registry, data about inference engines are stored. These data contain details about authoritative sources, ontologies, inference engines, and inference rules. In the explanation of a proof, every inference step should have a link to at least one inference engine.

(a) The Web Registrar is an interface for entering information into the Inference Web Registry.
(b) The portable proof specification is written in the language DAML+OIL. In the future it will be possible to use OWL.

There are four major components of a portable proof:

(1) Inference rules
(2) Inference steps
(3) Well-formed formulae
(4) Referenced ontologies

These are the components of the inference process and thus produce the proof of the conclusion reached by the inferencing.

- An explanation browser. The explanation browser shows a proof and permits to focus on details and asks additional information,

DARPA Agent Markup Language (DAML) Rules Language. DAML Rules is a layered rule language for supporting applications that need RDF reasoning and transformation. It extends the existing forms of OWL ontology axioms and facts with a form of rule axiom.

Jena Inference Engine. Jena is a general purpose RDF toolkit that includes an inference engine. The Jena inference engine incorporates a hybrid forward- and backward-chaining reasoner with provision for extension through the addition of additional inference code written in Java (Carroll et al. 2004). Jena also incorporates a general purpose rule engine that can be with simple rules, performing a combination of both forward- and backward-chaining.

Sesame. Sesame is an open source Java framework for storing, querying, and reasoning with RDF and RDF-S (Broekstra et al. 2002). It can be used as a database for RDF and RDF-S or as a Java library for applications that need to work with RDF internally. Sesame is an architecture for efficient storage and expressive querying of large quantities of RDF metadata.

Intellidimension RDF Gateway. Intellidimension's RDF Gateway is a platform for building RDF applications, which includes an inference rule processor (Intellidimension, RDF Gateway, http://www.intellidimension.com). The general style of inference supported is forward-chaining, similar to CWM, though the details are different. The package also supports function rules that can be used to create additional variable bindings for use in new statements deduced using a rule. These function rules serve a purpose comparable to CWM's built-in properties.

RDF Inference Language (RIL). The RDF Inference Language (RIL) is a language for defining inference rules (Olson 2001). It appears to be implemented in the 4suite platform (4Suite 2008). RIL describes a simple forward-chaining inference process similar to CWM and Intellidimension's RDF gateway described above. (Unlike those, it allows a rule antecedent to contain disjunctions and negations.) (See also http://www2.gca.org/knowledgetechnologies/2001/proceedings/ogbuji/index.html.)

Metalog. Metalog is a SW3C project. It appears that Metalog is an attempt to provide a pseudonatural-language expression to a Prolog-like rule language over RDF. This suggests a backward-chaining reasoner over Horn-clauses (Marchiori and Saarela 1998).

Pellet. Pellet is a reasoner based on OWL-DL that was developed at the University of Maryland (Sirin et al. 2007). It has been shown to be sound and complete. Jena has been augmented with Pellet to access RDF triples and reason about the data.

We have taken a plug and play approach to designing our inference controller. For example, while Jena manages RDF graphs, it may be augmented with Pellet to carry out reasoning. Such an inference controller is illustrated in Figure 5.2.

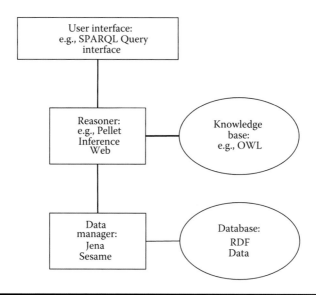

Figure 5.2 Plug-and-play approach to building an inference controller.

5.4 Summary and Directions

This chapter has provided an overview of the concepts and systems for the various inference engines that have been developed. These include concepts such as CWA, NF, and OWL as well as systems such as Jena, Sesame, and the Inference Web. These inference engines reason with Semantic Web data. We have taken a plug and play approach to developing inference controllers. For example, we have integrated Jena with Pellet for building an inference controller where Jena managed RDF graphs and Pellet carried out reasoning.

Chapters 4, 5, and 6 provide the necessary background information for inference control. For example, Chapter 4 discussed the inference problem and inference control while Chapter 5 discussed inference engines. Examples of inference strategies will be given in Chapter 6. The concepts and techniques discussed in these chapters will be utilized in Section III when we describe the design and implementation of an inference controller. Our inference controllers operate on provenance data. Therefore, in Section II we will describe the systems we have developed for securing provenance data.

References

Angele, J., Kifer, M. and Lausen, G., Ontologies in F-logic, in *Handbook on Ontologies,* Staab, S. and Studer, R. (eds.), Springer-Verlag, Berlin, 2009.

Berners-Lee, T., CWM—closed world machine, http://www. w3. org/2000/10/swap/doc/ cwm. html, 2000.

Broekstra, J., Kampman, A. and Van Harmelen, F., Sesame: A generic architecture for storing and querying RDF and RDF schema, *The Semantic Web*–ISWC, 2002.

Carroll, J. J., Dickinson, I., Dollin, C., Reynolds, D., Seaborne, A. and Wilkinson, K., Jena: Implementing the Semantic Web recommendations, Proceedings of the 13th International World Wide Web Conference, 2004.

Da Silva, P. P., McGuinness, D. L. and Fikes, R., A proof markup language for Semantic Web services, *Journal of Information Systems,* Vol. 31, No. 4–5, 2006.

Euler Proof Mechanism, http://www.agfa.com/w3c/euler/.

Grosof, B. N., Horrocks, I., Volz, R. and Decker, S., Description logic programs: Combining logic programs with description logic, Proceedings of the 12th International Conference on World Wide Web, 2003.

Intellidimension, RDF Gateway, http://www.intellidimension.com.

Kifer, M. and Lausen, G., F-logic: A higher-order language for reasoning about objects, inheritance, and scheme, *ACM SIGMOD Record,* Vol. 18, No. 2, 1989.

Marchiori, M. and Saarela, J., Query+ metadata+ logic = metalog, W3C Query Languages Workshop, 1998.

McGuinness, D. L. and van Harmelen, F., OWL web ontology language overview, W3C Recommendation 10, 2004.

Olson, M., RDF Inference Language (RIL), http://xml.coverpages.org/RIL-20010510.html, 2001.

Sintek, M. and Decker, S., TRIPLE—A query, inference, and transformation language for the Semantic Web, *The Semantic Web*–ISWC, Springer, 2002.

Sirin, E., Parsia, B., Grau, B. C., Kalyanpur, A. and Katz, Y., Pellet: A practical OWL-DL reasoner, *Web Semantics: Science, Services and Agents on the World Wide Web,* Vol. 5, No. 2, 2007.

4Suite. http://sourceforge.net/projects/foursuite/, March 2008.

Chapter 6

Inferencing Examples

6.1 Overview

At the heart of our approach is the notion of inference. That is, what are the strategies for carrying out inferencing and how can we build a system that implements the strategies? The basic concept of inferencing is the notion of an inference function. An inference function essentially takes data and generates new data from the original data using the inference strategies.

To best illustrate the notion of inference, we focus on the medical domain that generates provenance for a patient's medical record. The medical records usually consist of some sensitive provenance information. The provenance of a patient's record is used for purposes such as verification of medical procedures, or tracking the medication usage while under the care of a health care professional. We use the synthetic provenance generated from a toy hospital for our running examples. This provenance will be shown as an RDF graph in order to highlight the sensitive nodes, edges, and paths that our inference controller will protect. In order to understand our approach to secure data provenance and inference control, we will set the stage by describing various inference scenarios whereby we pinpoint possible inference attacks.

The organization of this chapter is as follows. We describe inference functions in Section 6.2. Aspects of classifying knowledge bases is discussed in Section 6.3. Inference strategies with examples are given in Section 6.4. Approaches to handling the inference problem are discussed in Section 6.5. Inference-related provenance data are discussed in Section 6.6. The chapter is summarized in Section 6.7. Figure 6.1 illustrates the concepts in this chapter. Some useful references include Johnson-Laird (1999), Lipton (2004), O'Rourke (1990), and Pearl (1984).

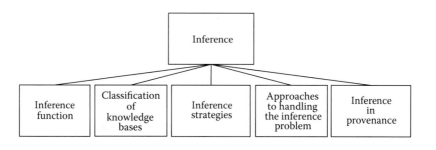

Figure 6.1   Aspects of inference.

6.2 Inference Function

An inference function takes a piece of data or a collection of data elements and derives new data elements using a particular inference strategy. We illustrate the notion of an inference function with an example. Assume we have a process defined by a function $\oplus$ with two inputs and one output. The various inferences are

$$1 \oplus 1 = 0$$

$$1 \oplus 0 = 1$$

$$0 \oplus 0 = 0$$

$$0 \oplus 1 = 1$$

It is possible to see that we can employ an inference strategy based on dependencies:

- Revealing the input and output would identify the function type
- Revealing the function and output would reveal the input and revealing the input and process would reveal the output

This inference strategy is more likely to apply in cases where multiple queries are posed to a system containing this XOR function. Another example could be where an artifact and a process in a provenance graph imply an agent. We could combine a medical record (artifact) and an x-ray process to infer that a radiologist performs some operation on the patient. The notion of an inference function will be clearer when we discuss examples in Section 6.4. In the next section, we will discuss various aspects of classifying a knowledge base that will illustrate our approach.

It should also be noted that an alternative definition of an inference function is given in Thuraisingham (1990) in order to prove that the inference problem was unsolvable. This definition uses deductive databases in its formulation (Gallaire and Minker 1978). A deductive database consists of a database and a set of rules, which enable new data to be deduced from the extensional data. The inference function essentially applies the rules to deduce the new data. It also utilizes concepts from recursive function theory (Rogers 1967). For more details we refer the reader to Thuraisingham (1990).

6.3 Classification of a Knowledge Base

There are many ways for classifying a knowledge base containing provenance data. Some of them are

- Using an ontology, which shows the subsumption of concepts in the form of a hierarchy.
- Considering a class D, a class X, and two individuals x and y. We form a new concept $\forall R.A$, which is given a meaning of $x \in D$ s.t. $\forall (x, y) \in R, y \to A$. This classifies a concept based on a value restriction.
- Using a released knowledge base. This classifies data based on what is released. For example, if a knowledge base contains six doctors in the radiology unit and if we already revealed that a patient had an x-ray procedure and that four of the doctors were on a shift not overlapping with the period in which the x-ray procedure was performed, then if we answer a new query about the shift of any of the two remaining doctors, we would have revealed the doctor who performed the procedure.

Semantic Web technologies can be used to express provenance information (e.g., we could store and represent provenance as RDF or OWL). We could query for provenance information by using SPARQL to retrieve answers to a query. We could perform inference over provenance, using the support of a DL reasoner. We could also benefit from rule-based supports on the Semantic Web to write our policies. These Semantic Web technologies are both flexible and expressive, although sometimes we trade off expressiveness with decidability. Nevertheless, these technologies are well-suited for modeling a domain, such as our medical domain.

Provenance helps make the systems in a domain transparent. It can be used to determine whether a piece of information is appropriate for a specific purpose under a set of health care procedures. It can also be used to provide accountability of the systems and information used to make critical decisions in a health care domain. Provenance is the origin or source of a data item. It offers a means to verify data products, to infer data quality, to analyze a process that leads to a data product, and to help decide whether to trust a data product.

The problem we are trying to solve is to determine whether an attacker can use his or her prior knowledge to successfully carry out an inference attack. An inference attack may occur when a low user is able to infer sensitive information from common knowledge and authorized query responses. We are trying to find practical tools for dealing with the inference problem and are trying to determine whether there is a controller for a specific instance of the inference problem. In general, this is a nonpolynomial (NP)-complete problem. Sometimes an attacker may carry out imprecise or partial inference. An imprecise or partial inference is a compromise that occurs when a low user is able to infer an exact value or a set of possible values—an information chunk—for a sensitive attribute with a certain probability. The granularity of the inferred chunk may be small enough and/or its probability high enough to constitute a security breach.

For a specific domain, we could build heuristics to determine the dependencies or associations among data items, but there is no general way of doing this. These heuristics could be used to build certain classes of rules; for example, if a doctor can be identified by the set of processes he or she performs or the notes he or she makes, we may need to hide the tasks performed by the doctor. A "where" provenance query could identify the immediate processes that are responsible for a particular version of a patient's record. The immediate context of a patient's record that is revealed by a where query could indicate the most current set of operations on that record. For example, assume that the current record reveals that the patient has a disease or illness, which we are trying to hide. Then, revealing the immediate context of the record could send an alarm to the querying user, who may question whether the patient is immunized or vaccinated. Also, it could lead an insurance company to drop the health coverage given to a patient or increase the premiums for the patient's health insurance policy in anticipation that the treatments administered to the patient may lead to higher claims costs.

There are many ways of identifying or describing a concept. We could ask a provenance knowledge base if the description of a context exists in the knowledge base. We may also ask a knowledge base if a pattern exists by formulating regular expression queries. When the description of the concept or the pattern exists explicitly, the inference controller may attempt to prevent an attack. This is often unsuccessful when the user has some prior knowledge not explicitly known to the inference controller. There may be cases when the patterns or descriptions are implicit in the knowledge base or the answers given to a user. We may be able to use a reasoner to compute the implicit information, but this may still be approximate at guessing what a user can learn.

Inference is a method to subvert access control in database systems. An inference occurs when a user is able to infer some data without directly accessing them. In multilevel database systems, early work on inference detection used a graph to represent the functional dependencies among the attributes in the database schema. An inference occurs when there are two or more paths among the attributes and the paths are labeled at different classification levels. The inference path is eliminated by upgrading some attributes along the path. Lunt points out that some inference problems can be avoided by redesigning the database schema and classifying the attributes properly (Lunt 1989). However, as stated by Lunt, redesigning the database schema results in data duplication, which leads to update anomalies. It also requires modifications to the existing application programs.

There is also work on incorporating external knowledge into the inference detection systems. More recently, researchers suggest using data of the database to generate a richer set of functional dependencies for inference detection. Hinke et al. use cardinality associations to discover potential inference paths (Hinke et al. 1997). Hale et al. incorporate imprecise and fuzzy database relations into their inference detection system. However, existing efforts still simply employ functional dependencies to detect inferences (Hale and Shenoi 1997).

As noted by SRI researchers (Qian et al. 1993), monitoring user activities may lead to detecting more inferences. A simple way to monitor user accesses is to examine each user query and reject any query that accesses sensitive data. However, as stated by Qian et al., it is possible for a user to use a series of unsuspicious queries to infer data in the database. Motro et al. (1994) address a similar problem, but their work focuses on detecting aggregation instead of inference attacks. In the statistical database security community, various techniques have been proposed to protect individual records; for example, query-set-size control, cell suppression, and data perturbation (Adam and Worthmann 1989). However, these techniques are not suitable for detecting inferences using general-purpose queries. A certain group of attribute values of a tuple may uniquely identify the tuple. The unique identification rule handles this situation. Another way to identify a return tuple is to compare it with other return tuples that have already been identified. Another possibility is that only some return tuples of a query correspond to some return tuples of another query. The overlapping inference rule identifies the corresponding return tuples that are common to both queries.

Modern database systems allow multiple users access to data. When users are not to be allowed access to every item of data in the database, an access control system is needed. An access control system has two components: the access control policy and the access control mechanism. The access control policy specifies the accesses that are allowed or disallowed for each user in the database system. The access control mechanism enforces the policy. A mechanism is sound with respect to a policy if it allows accesses that are allowed by the policy, and disallows accesses that are not allowed by the policy. The mechanism is complete with respect to a policy if it addresses all accesses as specified in the policy.

Each user accesses the database system using queries. For each query issued to the database system, the access control system determines if the query is allowed by the database system. The allowed queries are processed by the database system, and the results are returned to the user. The disallowed queries can be handled in various ways. For example, the user may simply be notified that the query violates the access control policy and is not processed by the database system, or the database system intentionally returns incorrect responses to the user in order to protect the data. The invalid accesses might also be recorded for further investigation.

6.4 Inference Strategies and Examples

A user may employ different inference strategies in order to arrive at new information from the available background information and answers to all previous queries. When the newly inferred information is private, we say the confidentiality of the system is compromised. To prevent the release of the confidential information, a first step is to identify the possible inference strategies available to the user (Thuraisingham and Ford 1991; Thuraisingham et al. 1993).

Inference by deductive reasoning. In this strategy, new information is inferred using well-formed rules. This strategy allows deriving β as a consequence of α. In other words, deductive reasoning is the process of deriving the consequences of what is assumed. Given the truth of the assumptions, a valid deduction guarantees the truth of the conclusion.

Example 6.1

If it is true (given) that the sum of the angles is 180 in all triangles, and if a certain triangle has angles of 90° and 30°, then it can be deduced that the third angle is 60°.

There are two types of deductions: classical logic-based deduction and nonclassical logic-based deduction. We discuss each type of deduction next.

■ *Classical logic-based deduction*: Rules in classical logic enable new information to be deduced (an example is the logical implication rule).
■ *Nonclassical logic-based deduction*: We call the deductions not made within classical logic nonclassical logic-based deductions. They include deductions based on probabilistic reasoning, fuzzy reasoning, nonmonotonic reasoning, default reasoning, temporal logic, dynamic logic, and modal logic. hInferences based on this strategy are also made according to well-formed rules.

Deductive reasoning is the process of deriving the consequences of what is assumed. Given the truth of the assumptions, a valid deduction guarantees the truth of the conclusion (Johnson-Laird 1999). In other words, deduction is the process of drawing inferences about a specific case on the basis of a general principle.

Example 6.2

Consider the use case in Figure 6.2.

If it is true that whenever med:HeartSurgery_n_1 is controlled by med:Surgeon_n_1, then the patient has a critical disease. If we know that John's record was used by a process med:HeartSurgery_n_1 that was controlled by med:Surgeon_n_1, we can conclude that John has a critical disease.

Let *r* be an encoding of the rule: If it is true that whenever med:HeartSurgery_n_1 is controlled by med:Surgeon_1 then the patient has a critical disease, where *r* is a prior knowledge. In order to prevent a user from learning that John has a critical disease, we would add *r* to our knowledge base.

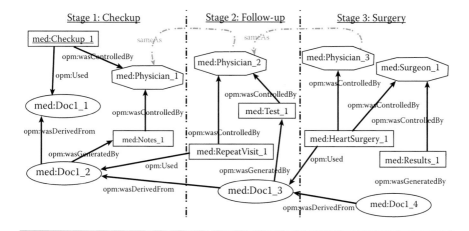

Figure 6.2 **Use case diagram.**

Assume *KB'* contains the following triples:

```
<med:HeartSurgery_n_1><opm:Used><med:Doc_{John}_3>
<med:HeartSurgery_n_1><opm:wasControlledBy><med:Surgeon_n_1>
```

Encode *r* as a DL constraint

$$HeartSurgery \sqcap \exists wasControlledBy.Surgeon \sqsubseteq Critical.$$

Encode r as a SWRL rule

$$(?\,pwasControlledBy\,?s) \wedge Surgeon(?s) \wedge HeartSurgery(?p) \rightarrow Critical(?p)$$

Forms of reasoning:

1. *If A then B; A; therefore B. (modus ponens)*
2. *If A then B; not B; therefore not A. (modus tollens)*
3. *If A then B; If B then C; therefore If A then C. (Hypothetical Syllogism)*
4. *Either A or B; Not A; therefore B. (Disjunctive Syllogism)*
5. *If A then B; B; therefore A. (affirming the consequent premise)*
6. *If A then B; not A; therefore not B. (denying the antecedent premise)*

Invalid Inferences:

■ *Affirming the Consequent*
   (1) $P \rightarrow Q$
   (2) Q
   (3) *Therefore*: P

■ *Denying the Antecedent*
   (1) $P \rightarrow Q$
   (2) $\neg P$
   (3) *Therefore*: $\neg Q$

Inference by inductive reasoning. Induction is the process of inferring probable conditional relevance as a result of observing multiple antecedents and consequents. An inductive statement requires empirical evidence for it to be true. In this strategy, well-formed rules are utilized to infer hypotheses from the examples observed. This allows inferring β entails α from multiple instantiations of α and β at the same time.

Example 6.3

The statement "it's snowing, so it must be cold" can be induced from the experience of the two being true together.

Example 6.4

Consider the following three observations:

> *Premise 1: Bob had a checkup at day 1 and a follow-up at day 4, Bob went into surgery.*
> *Premise 2: Jack had a checkup at day 1 and a follow-up at day 5, Jack went into surgery.*
> *Premise 3: Joe had a checkup at day 1 and a follow-up at day 4, Joe went into surgery.*

> *Conclusion: Patient with follow-up visit three days after a checkup will undergo surgery.*

Assume that a hospital has the following procedure: Patients diagnosed with critical heart complications are required to follow up with their physician within three days of being tested, after which time the physician should prepare the patient for heart surgery. Let *KB'* contain the following triples:

```
<med:CheckUp_{Bob}_1><opm:Used><med:Doc_{Bob}_1>
<med:CheckUp_{Bob}_1><med:TimeStamp><"1">
<med:RepeatVisit_{Bob}_1><opm:Used><med:Doc_{Bob}_1>
<med:RepeatVisit_{Bob}_1><med:TimeStamp><"4">
<med:CheckUp_{Jack}_1><opm:Used><med:Doc_{Jack}_1>
<med:CheckUp_{Jack}_1><med:TimeStamp><"1">
<med:RepeatVisit_{Jack}_1><opm:Used><med:Doc_{Jack}_1>
<med:RepeatVisit_{Jack}_1><med:TimeStamp><"4">
<med:CheckUp_{Joe}_1><opm:Used><med:Doc_{Joe}_1>
<med:CheckUp_{Joe}_1><med:TimeStamp><"1">
<med:RepeatVisit_{Joe}_1><opm:Used><med:Doc_{Joe}_1>
<med:RepeatVisit_{Joe}_1><med:TimeStamp><"4">
```

In order to prevent the user from learning this rule, we could limit the amount of cases the user can observe. For example, we could enforce the following constraint in the knowledge base:

$$(CheckUp \sqcap \geq 3Used) \sqcap (RepeatVisit \sqcap \geq 3Used) \sqsubseteq Critical$$

Abduction. Abduction allows inferring a as an explanation of b. Because of this, abduction allows the precondition a to be inferred from the consequence b.

Deduction and abduction thus differ in the direction in which a rule like "a entails b" is used for inference. As such, abduction is formally equivalent to the logical fallacy affirming the consequent or *post hoc ergo propter hoc,* because there are multiple possible explanations for b. Abduction is typically defined as inference to the best explanation (e.g., Levandoski and Mokbel 2009; O'Rourke 1990). Given α,β and the rule R1:$\alpha \vdash \beta$, then deduction is using the rule and its preconditions to make a conclusion ($\alpha \wedge R_1 \Rightarrow \beta$), induction is learning R_1 after seeing numerous examples of α and β, and abduction is using the postcondition and the rule to assume that the precondition could explain the postcondition ($\beta \wedge R_1 \Rightarrow \alpha$). More formally, abduction is the search for assumptions A which, when combined with some theory T, achieves some set of goals G without causing some contradiction (Burkleaux et al. 2005). That is

$$EQ_1: V \cup A \vdash G$$

$$EQ_2: T \cup A \vdash \perp$$

$$EQ_1: V \cup A \vdash G$$

$$EQ_2: T \cup A \nvdash \perp$$

Consider the use case in Figure 9.4 and the following rule:

Whenever med:HeartSurgery_1 is controlled by med:Surgeon_1 then the patient has a critical disease. If we know that a patient Bob has a critical disease, we try to infer that med:Surgeon_1 performed the process med:HeartSurgery_1 as the explanation for Bob's disease. In other words, the explanation is that a surgeon who is identified as med:Surgeon_1 performed the surgery on Bob.

It could be that Bob's disease is not related to heart surgery. The set of conditions leading to critical conditions varies and is not limited to one rule, or there may not be any one (best) explanation for an observation. Abductive reasoning starts when an inquirer considers a set of seemingly unrelated facts armed with an intuition that they are somehow connected:

D is a collection of data
Hypothesis H explains D
No other hypothesis explains D as well as H does
Therefore, H is probably correct

This allows inferring *a* as an explanation of *b*. Because of this, abduction allows the precondition *a* to be inferred from the consequence *b*. Deduction and abduction thus differ in the direction in which a rule like "*a* entails *b*" is used for inference. As such, abduction is formally equivalent to the logical fallacy affirming the consequent or *post hoc ergo propter hoc,* because there are multiple possible explanations for *b*.

Induction allows inferring *b* from *a*, where *b* does not follow necessarily from *a*. *a* might give us very good reason to accept *b*, but it does not ensure *b*.

Example 6.5

If all of the swans that we have observed so far are white, we may induce that all swans are white. We have good reason to believe the conclusion from the premise, but the truth of the conclusion is not guaranteed. (Indeed, it turns out that some swans are black.)

Abductive reasoning starts when an inquirer considers a set of seemingly unrelated facts armed with an intuition that they are somehow connected.

D is a collection of data
Hypothesis H explains D
No other hypothesis explains D as well as H does
Therefore, H is probably correct

Inference by analogical reasoning. In reasoning by analogy, statements such as "X is like Y" are used to infer properties of X when given the properties of Y. This type of reasoning is common to frame-based systems (Fikes and Kehler 1985).

Example 6.6

The properties of an entity A are a secret and the properties of an entity B are prior knowledge of a user. Further, if the statement "A is like B" is also prior knowledge, then a user could infer the properties of A.

Example 6.7

Patient 2 had a checkup and went into surgery immediately after the follow-up visit. Patient 1 also had a checkup and a follow-up visit. The user also knows that Patient 1 and Patient 2 are the same age, the same height, and the same ethnicity. The user may reason that Patient 1 also had the same disease as Patient 2 and therefore underwent the same surgery procedure.

An analogy can be seen as reasoning or explaining from parallel cases. In other words, an analogy is a comparison between two different things in order to highlight some point of similarity. An argument from analogy could be an argument that has the form:

All P are like Q
Q has such-and-such characteristic
Thus P has such-and-such characteristic

Inference by heuristic reasoning. Heuristics are criteria, methods, or principles for deciding which among several alternative courses of action promises to be the most effective in order to achieve some goal (Oinn et al. 2004; Pearl 1984). In general, a heuristic is not well-defined and may be a rule of thumb that is used to guide one's actions. Experts often use heuristics in order to solve a problem. Inference by heuristic reasoning is the process of deducing new information using various heuristics.

Example 6.8

Given some information α, heuristic rules and past experience are used to infer some information β.

The Web contains many sources of information about patients, hospital procedures, and physicians. There may be many formal procedures, tests, and treatments for a disease. Given some information α, which describes Bob, the user may wish to determine Bob's disease. However, the user may not be able to acquire all relevant information to derive the correct disease for Bob: It may not be possible to use our question-answering interface to get all the information about Bob and it may not be possible to research all possible explanations for Bob's condition given the sheer size of the Web (and prior knowledge). In this situation, the user may use shortcuts (or heuristic rules) and past experiences to infer Bob's disease.

Inference by semantic association. In this strategy, association between entities is inferred from the knowledge of the entities themselves (Thuraisingham and Ford 1991). Various types of semantic associations have been identified. They include context-based associations, aggregation-based associations, and dependency-based associations.

Example 6.9

Consider the use case in Figure 6.2.

Assume there is a semantic relation between med:Surgeon_1 and the process med:HeartSurgery_1. Then, revealing either the surgeon identified as med:Surgeon_1 or the the process identified as med:HeartSurgery_1 would reveal the identities of the surgeon or the process. Further, these two entities, med:Surgeon_1 and med:HeartSurgery_1, taken together would reveal a critical condition about Patient 1.

Inferred existence. Using the strategy of inferred existence, one can infer the existence of an entity Y from certain information on Y (Thuraisingham et al. 1993).

Example 6.10

From the triple

```
med:HeartSurgery_1 opm:wasControlledBy med:Surgeon_1
```

we can infer that there is a surgeon.

Example 6.11

From the information "Champion sails to Japan," it is reasonable to infer that there is some entity called "Champion."

Statistical inference. In this strategy, a user could infer information about an individual entity in the set from the various statistics computed on a set of entities.

Invoking inference rules. Any rule can be invoked in forward-chaining, backward-chaining, or proof-checking modes:

■ Forward-chaining: given some set of statements, uses the rule to deduce new statements. In principle, repeated application of forward-chaining will find all facts that can be deduced by the inference rule from some initial knowledge base.

■ Backward-chaining: given some expression, determine all of the antecedents that must be satisfied in order for the given consequent expression to be true.

■ Inference checking: given some antecedent expressions and a consequent expression, determine whether the inference rule can deduce the consequent from the antecedents.

6.5 Approaches to the Inference Problem

Different approaches can be employed for building an inference controller. For example, we can use state-of-the-art machine-learning techniques to build a learner that automatically learns to recognize complex patterns and make intelligent decisions based on some explicit data. We can also build an inference that uses Semantic Web technologies equipped with reasoners that perform inferences over the data in the knowledge base. In this book, we will build an inference controller that is based on the use of Semantic Web technologies.

Aggregation problem is a special case of the inference problem: collections of data elements are secret but the individual elements are unclassified.

$$A \sqcup B \sqcup C \sqsubseteq Secret$$

We could enforce this rule by checking if there are any sensitive concepts in the provenance KB or the released KB.

$$A \sqcap B \sqcap C \sqsubseteq Secret$$

$$\geq 10 \ R.(A \sqcap B \sqcap C)$$

If we know that at least 10 people have a property, then classify KB.

Association problem is when attributes A and B taken together are secret, but individually they are unclassified.

Example 6.12

A and B and C → Secret

We could encode this as a SWRL rule, then check the provenance KB or the released KB if there is anything secret.

Example 6.13

Something that is all three classes is private:

$$A \sqcap B \sqcap C \sqsubseteq Secret$$

Example 6.14

If at most one individual is in all three classes, then classify KB:

$$\leq 1R.(A \sqcap B \sqcap C)$$

Domain Restriction

Range restriction: a qualified value for a role is secret (e.g., "something with nine digits"). Restriction on Social Security Number (SSN) is nine digits; if something with nine digits is released, then classify KB.

Similarly, we could specify that something with 16 digits is a credit card number. The approaches covered by Thuraisingham and Ford (1995) included the following.

- *Handling inference during database design.* This approach is considered rather static. It depends mainly on schema design and integrity constraints. It was also pointed out that it is not very convenient to keep changing the database schema in response to each user's query.
- *Handling inference during query processing.* The bulk of the research mainly focuses on query modification because queries are dynamic.

Inference by deduction reasoning have been applied in Thuraisingham et al. (1993). These involve using a set of sound and complete deduction systems to derive other pieces of information.

Inference by semantic association have been discussed in Thuraisingham et al. (1993). They have been powerful in addressing some of the issues in this domain.

Similar strategies to heuristic reasoning are discussed in Thuraisingham et al. (1993), which includes abductive reasoning.

Statistical reasoning has been applied to handle the inference problem in statistical databases. Given the summary data, the object is to learn macro properties about a population. However, the objective is to ensure that the individual attribute values be kept sensitive. This is an aspect of the privacy problem discussed in Chapter 4. As well, machine-learning techiques also perform reasoning (Mitchell 1997). These techniques are based on having a machine learn from a set of test cases to construct a model, then applying the model to real-world situations. Building software systems to support machine-learning techniques and association-based reasoning have seen some success. However, other techniques require artificial intelligence techniques to capture a human cognitive process.

In Thuraisingham et al. (1993), the main functions of the inference controller were on classical logic-based inference by deductive reasoning and on semantic-based associations. With the use of semantic technologies, the inference controller has new ways of performing inferences. Thus, we can better detect some inferences that were not addressed by previous implementations of an inference controller in Thuraisingham et al. (1993). The Semantic Web provides a family of knowledge representation formalisms, which are well-suited for reasoning, for example, about (1) terminological knowledge, (2) ontologies, and (3) database schemata, including schema design, evaluation and query optimization, and source integration in heterogeneous databases.

Machine-learning techniques. In Chang and Moskowitz (1998), the authors approach the inference problem with a parsimonious downgrading framework using decision trees. The assumption is that when Low needs information for purposes such as performance and functionality, High must decide whether to give (i.e., downgrade) information to Low. In other words, when High wishes to downgrade a set of data to Low, it may be necessary, because of inference channels, to trim the set. Basically, decision trees are used to form rules from the downgraded data High makes available to Low. Remember that we can use the nonsensitive attributes of an individual to arrive at (i.e., predict) the sensitive attribute using rules that are trained on similar individuals (occurring in previously released data). In parsimonious downgrading, a cost measure is assigned to the potential downgraded information that is not sent to Low. The idea is to determine if the loss of functionality (to Low) associated with (High) not downgrading these data is worth the extra confidentiality. Decision trees assist in analyzing the potential inference channels in the data that one wishes to downgrade. The authors assign penalty functions to this parsimonious downgrading in order to minimize the amount of information that is not downgraded, and compare the penalty costs to the extra confidentiality that is obtained.

6.6 Inferences in Provenance

Implicit information in provenance. Provenance can be recorded in any knowledge representation language (e.g., RDF, RDFS, and OWL). Using these languages allows us to later perform inference over the provenance graph, and therefore we could determine the implicit information over the provenance graph.

Use cases of provenance. A case study can serve as guidance with regard to what we want to achieve with the Semantic Web. Whenever standards are approved, they should be such that important case studies remain possible to implement. Discussing all possible application fields here would be out of scope. However, one case study will help to clarify the goals of the research.

Provenance has many use cases, as outlined in (xg-prov 2010). In this book we discuss some of these using a toy hospital.

See http://arxiv.org/PS_cache/arxiv/pdf/1002/1002.0433v1.pdf for a quick summary of provenance for scientific data.

Identifying private information in query logs. There are pieces of information that can also be identifying. Queries for phone numbers, addresses, and names of individuals are all useful in narrowing down the population, and thus increases the chance of a successful attack.

From the query logs, we can know the distribution of queries for a user, query timing, and also the content of many queries. Furthermore, it should still be possible to cluster users and to some extent augment search engine responses with user behavior. More significantly, if only the first of our techniques is used (that of masking unique queries) we can also correlate queries (e.g., those who query for X also query for Y).

$$a \ r{:}b \ c$$

$$c \ r{:}v \ f$$

Processing rules. There is a difference between a query engine that just does querying on an RDF graph but does not handle rules and an inference engine that also handles rules. In the literature this difference is not always so clear. The complexity of an inference engine is a lot higher than a query engine. The reason is that rules permit making sequential deductions. In the execution of a query these deductions are to be constructed. This is not necessary in the case of a query engine. We do not discuss query engines. Some examples are DQL, RQL, and XQUERY.

Rules also suppose a logic base that is inherently more complex than the logic in the situation without rules. For an RDF query engine, only the simple principles of entailment on graphs are necessary. RuleML is an important effort to define rules that are usable for the World Wide Web. The Inference Web (McGuinness and da Silva 2003, 2004) is a recent realization that defines a system for handling different inferencing engines on the Semantic Web.

6.7 Summary and Directions

This chapter has elaborated on the notion of inference. We first defined inference functions. Next we discussed aspects of classifying knowledge bases. This was followed by a detailed discussion of inference strategies and examples for each strategy. For examples, strategies such as inference by deduction, inference by induction, and inference by analogical reasoning were discussed. Finally, aspects of inference and provenance were discussed.

The discussion in this chapter has provided background information on the notion of inference. We will use some of the strategies discussed in this chapter when we describe the inference controller we have developed. Our inference controller works on provenance data. Therefore, first we discuss details of securing provenance data in Section II of this book. This is followed by a discussion of inference control in Section III.

References

Adam, N. R. and Worthmann, J. C., Security-control methods for statistical databases: A comparative study, *ACM Computing Surveys*, Vol. 21, No. 4, 1989.

Burkleaux, T., Menzies, T. and Owen, D., Lean = (LURCH+ TAR3) = reusable modeling tools, Proceedings of the WITSE, 2005.

Chang, L. W. and Moskowitz, I. S., Parsimonious downgrading and decision trees applied to the inference problem, Proceedings of the 1998 Workshop on New Security Paradigms, 1998.

Fikes, R. and Kehler, T., The role of frame-based representation in reasoning, *Communications of the ACM*, Vol. 28, No. 9, 1985.

Gallaire, H. and Minker, I., *Logic and Databases*, Plenum Press, New York, 1978.

Hale, J. and Shenoi, S., Catalytic inference analysis: Detecting inference threats due to knowledge discovery, Proceedings, IEEE Security and Privacy Symposium, 1997.

Hinke, T. H., Delugach, H. S. and Wolf, R. P., Protecting databases from inference attacks, *Computers & Security*, Vol. 16, 1997.

Johnson-Laird, P. N., Deductive reasoning, Annual review of psychology, Annual Reviews, Vol. 50, No. 1, 1999.

Levandoski, J. and Mokbel, M. REF data-centric storage, Proceedings of 2009 IEEE International Conference on Web Services, 2009, pp. 911–918.

Lipton, P., *Inference to the Best Explanation*, Second Edition, Routledge, London, 2004.

Lunt, T., Aggregation and inference: Facts and fallacies, Proceedings IEEE Security and Privacy Symposium, 1989.

McGuinness, D. L. and da Silva, P. P., Infrastructure for web explanations, *The Semantic Web*–ISWC 2003, pp. 113–129.

McGuinness, D. L. and da Silva, P. P., Explaining answers from the Semantic Web: The Inference Web approach, *Web Semantics: Science, Services and Agents on the World Wide Web*, Vol. 1, 2004.

Mitchell, T. M., *Machine Learning*, McGraw Hill Series in Computer Science, McGraw-Hill, Boston, 1997.

Motro, A., Marks, D. G. and Jajodia, S., Aggregation in relational databases: Controlled disclosure of sensitive information, *ESORICS 94,* 1994, pp. 431–445.

Oinn, T., Addis, M., Ferris, J., Marvin, D., Greenwood, M., Carver, T., Pocock, M., Wipat, A. and Taverna, P., A tool for the composition and enactment of bioinformatics workflows, *Bioinformatics*, Vol. 20, No. 17, 2004, pp. 3045–3054.

O'Rourke, P., Working Notes of the 1990 Spring Symposium on Automated Abduction, University of California, Irvine, CA, 1990.

Pearl, J., *Heuristics: Intelligent Search Strategies for Computer Problem Solving*, Addison-Wesley, Reading, MA, 1984.

Qian, X., Stickel, M. E., Karp, P., Lunt, T. F. and Garvey, T. D., Detection and elimination of inference channels in multilevel relational database systems, Proceedings of the IEEE Computer Society Symposium on Research in Security and Privacy, 1993.

Rogers, H., Jr., *Theory of Recursive Functions and Effective Computability*, McGraw-Hill, New York, 1967.

Thuraisingham, B., Recursion theoretic complexity of the inference problem in Proceedings, Computer Security Foundations Workshop, 1990 (also MITRE Technical Report, MPT-291).

Thuraisingham, B. and Ford, W., Issues on the design and implementation of an intelligent database inference controller, Proceedings of the IEEE Conference on Systems, Man, and Cybernetics, 1991.

Thuraisaingham, B. and Ford, W., Security constraints in a multilevel secure distributed database management system, *IEEE Transactions on Knowledge and Data Engineering*, Vol. 7, No. 2, pp. 214–293, 1995.

Thuraisingham, B., Ford, W., Collins, M. and O'Keeffe, J., Design and implementation of a database inference controller, *Data & Knowledge Engineering*, Vol. 11, No. 3, 1993.

xg-prov, W3C Provenance Incubator Group Wiki, http://www.w3.org/2005/Incubator/prov/, 2010.

Chapter 7

Cloud Computing Tools and Frameworks

7.1 Overview

Provenance captures the history of a data item. A particular data item may have many previous versions, each associated with its own chain, where each chain corresponds to a workflow. It is normally assumed that the provenance can grow much faster than the data item it is associated with, and so we need the ability to capture large provenance data graphs. In addition, we often need fine-grained recording of the provenance to ensure the quality, the trustworthiness, and the correctness of any shared information. For example, a repeat of an execution for a data item should reveal similar provenance and should not differ due to omissions because we failed to capture important steps in the execution. The granularity is the degree of detail for which provenance metadata are collected. In order to develop systems that allow fine-grained-level recording of provenance, we need massive scalable storage mechanisms.

We protect provenance with policies. These policies determine who can access a document and under what conditions access is to be granted, and when access is allowed or disallowed. We need to develop policies that scale with the large provenance graphs and also take into account any implicit relationships among various components in the provenance graph. In other words, we need to build large data stores for provenance. Some major challenges are how to successfully manage the huge datasets involved and how to effectively query large provenance graphs efficiently while still maintaining system responsiveness and enforcing security constraints. We believe that cloud computing offers a viable solution to this problem.

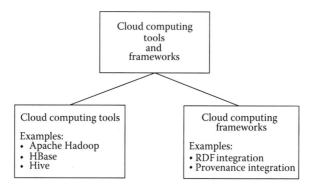

Figure 7.1   Cloud computing tools and frameworks.

The Cloud Computing paradigm emerged after the seminal work carried out on the implementation of the Google File System as well as the MapReduce framework (Dean and Ghemawat 2008; Ghemawat et al. 2003). The development of Hadoop and a subsequent list of open-source tools opened up the cloud computing ecosystem to a host of new users at virtually no cost (Shvachko et al. 2010; White 2010). In this chapter we first discuss a cloud computing framework for capturing and storing provenance recorded as RDF graphs and then give a brief survey of the uses of cloud computing tools being adapted for the Semantic Web of data.

In this chapter we discuss the cloud computing tools and frameworks on which we have built our solutions. The organization of this chapter is as follows. In Section 7.2 we discuss cloud computing tools and in Section 7.3 we discuss cloud computing frameworks. Our prior work on building an XACML-based policy manager using a cloud computing framework is discussed in Section 7.4. In Section IV we will describe assured information sharing as well as inference control in a cloud computing environment that is based on the framework discussed in Section 7.4. The chapter is summarized in Section 7.5. Figure 7.1 illustrates the concepts discussed in this chapter.

7.2 Cloud Computing Tools

Processing large volumes of provenance data requires sophisticated methods and tools. In recent years, cloud computing tools, such as cloud-enabled NoSQL systems, MongoDB, and CouchDB, as well as frameworks such as Hadoop, offer appealing alternatives and great promises for systems with high availability, scalability, and elasticity (Anderson et al. 2010; Cattell 2011; Chodorow and Dirolf 2010; White 2010). In this section, we briefly survey these systems and their applicability and usefulness for processing large-scale datasets.

Apache Hadoop. Apache Hadoop is an open-source software framework that allows batch processing tasks to be performed on vast quantities of data (White 2010). Hadoop uses the Hadoop Distributed File System (HDFS), a Java-based open-source distributed file system that employs the Google File System as its underlying storage mechanism. HDFS provides several advantages such as data replication and fault tolerance (Ghemawat et al. 2003). HDFS uses a master/slave architecture that consists of a single namenode process (running on the master node) and several datanode processes (usually one per slave node). A MapReduce job consists of three phases: (1) a "map" phase in which each slave node performs some computation on the data blocks of the input that it has stored. The output of this phase is a key-value pair based on the computation that is performed. (2) An intermediate "sort" phase in which the output of the map phase is sorted based on keys. (3) A "reduce" phase in which a reducer aggregates various values for a shared key and then further processes them before producing the desired result.

CouchDB. Apache CouchDB is a distributed, document-oriented database that can be queried and indexed in a MapReduce fashion (Anderson et al. 2010). Data are managed as a collection of JavaScript Object Notation (JSON) documents (Crockford 2006). Users can access the documents with a Web browser via HTTP as well as querying, combining, and transforming documents with JavaScript.

HBase. Apache HBase is a distributed, versioned, column-oriented store modeled after Google' Bigtable, written in Java. Organizations such as Mendeley, Facebook, and Adobe use HBase (George 2011).

MongoDB. MongoDB is an open-source, schema-free, (JSON) document-oriented database written in C++ (Chodorow and Dirolf 2010). It is developed and supported by 10gen and is part of the NoSQL family of database systems. MongoDB stores structured data as JSON-like documents with dynamic schemas (MongoDB calls the format BSON), making the integration of data in certain types of applications easier and faster.

Hive. Apache Hive is a data warehousing framework that provides the ability to manage, query, and analyze large datasets stored in HDFS or HBase (Thusoo et al. 2010). Hive provides basic tools to perform extract-transfer-load (ETL) operations over data, project structure onto the extracted data, and query the structured data using an SQL-like language called HiveQL. HiveQL performs query execution using the MapReduce paradigm while allowing advanced Hadoop programmers to plug in their custom-built MapReduce programs to perform advanced analytics not supported by the language. Some of the design goals of Hive include dynamic scale-out, user defined analytics, fault-tolerance, and loose coupling with input formats.

Apache Cassandra. Apache Cassandra is an open-source distributed database management system (Hewitt 2010). Apache Cassandra is a fault-tolerant, distributed data store that offers linear scalability, allowing it to be a storage platform for large high-volume websites. Cassandra is designed to handle big data workloads across multiple nodes with no single point of failure. Its architecture is based on the understanding that system and hardware failures can and do occur.

7.3 Cloud Computing Framework

In this section, we introduce a cloud computing framework that we have utilized in the implementation of our systems (e.g., the Policy Manager to be discussed in Chapter 22). In particular, we discuss our framework for RDF integration and provenance data integration.

7.3.1 RDF Integration

The reasons for using RDF as our data model are as follows: (1) RDF allows us to achieve data interoperability between the seemingly disparate sources of information that are cataloged by each agency or organization separately. (2) The use of RDF allows participating agencies to create data-centric applications that make use of the integrated data that are now available to them. (3) Since RDF does not require the use of an explicit schema for data generation, it can be easily adapted to ever-changing user requirements. The policy engine's flexibility is based on its accepting high-level policies and executing them as rules or constraints over a directed RDF graph representation of the provenance and its associated data. The strength of our policy engine is that it can handle any type of policy that could be represented using RDF technologies, Horn logic rules (e.g., SWRL), and OWL constraints. The power of these Semantic Web technologies can be successfully harnessed in cloud computing environment to provide the user with the capability to efficiently store and retrieve data for data-intensive applications. Storing RDF data in the cloud brings a number of new features, such as scalability and on-demand services, resources and services for users on demand, ability to pay for services and capacity as needed, location independence, guarantee quality of service for users in terms of hardware and central processing unit (CPU) performance, bandwidth, and memory capacity. We examined the following efforts in developing our framework for RDF integration.

In Sun and Jin (2010), the authors adopted the idea of Hexastore and considered both the RDF data model and HBase capability. They stored RDF triples into six HBase tables (S_PO, P_SO, O_SP, PS_O, SO_P, and PO_S), which covered all combinations of RDF triple patterns. They indexed the triples with HBase-provided index structure on row key. They also proposed a MapReduce strategy for SPARQL Basic Graph Pattern (BGP) processing, which is suitable for their storage schema. This strategy uses multiple MapReduce jobs to process a typical BGP. In each job, it uses a greedy method to select a join key and eliminates multiple triple patterns. Their evaluation result indicated that their approach worked well against large RDF datasets. In Husain et al. (2009), the authors described a framework that uses Hadoop to store and retrieve large numbers of RDF triples. They described a schema to store RDF data in HDFS. They also presented algorithms to answer SPARQL queries. This made use of Hadoop's MapReduce framework to actually answer the queries. In Huang et al. (2011), the authors introduced a scalable RDF data management system. They introduced techniques for (1) leveraging state-of-the-art, single-node RDF-store technology and (2) partitioning the data across nodes in a manner that helps accelerate query processing through locality optimizations. In Papailiou et al. (2012), the authors presented H2RDF, which is a fully distributed RDF store that combines the MapReduce processing framework with a NoSQL distributed data store. Their system features unique characteristics that enable efficient processing of both simple and multijoin SPARQL queries on virtually unlimited numbers of triples. These include join algorithms that execute joins according to query selectivity to reduce processing and include adaptive choice among centralized and distributed (MapReduce-based) join execution for fast query responses. They claim that their system can efficiently answer both simple joins and complex multivariate queries as well as scale up to 3 billion triples using a small cluster consisting of nine worker nodes. In Khadilkar et al. (2012), the authors designed a Jena-HBase framework. Their HBase backed triple store can be used with the Jena framework. Jena-HBase provides end users with a scalable storage and querying solution that supports all features from the RDF specification.

7.3.2 Provenance Integration

While our approach is general enough for any type of data, we have utilized provenance data as an example. We discuss the various approaches that we have examined in our work on provenance data integration.

In Ikeda et al. (2011), the authors considered a class of workflows that they call generalized map and reduce workflows (GMRWs). The input datasets are processed by an acyclic graph of map and reduce functions to produce output results. They also showed how data provenance (lineage) can be captured for map and reduce functions transparently. In Chebotko et al. (2013), the authors explored and addressed the challenge of efficient and scalable storage and querying of large collections of provenance graphs serialized as RDF graphs in an Apache HBase database. In Park et al. (2011), the authors proposed Reduce And Map Provenance (RAMP) as an extension to Hadoop that supports provenance capture and tracing for workflows of MapReduce jobs. The work discussed in Abraham et al. (2010) proposed a system to show how HBase Bigtable-like capabilities can be leveraged for distributed storage and querying of provenance data represented in RDF. In particular, their ProvBase system incorporates an HBase/Hadoop backend, a storage schema to hold provenance triples, and a querying algorithm to evaluate SPARQL queries in their system. In Akoush et al. (2013), the authors' research introduced HadoopProv, a modified version of Hadoop that implements provenance capture and analysis in MapReduce jobs. Their system is designed to minimize provenance capture overheads by (1) treating provenance tracking in map and reduce phases separately, and (2) deferring construction of the provenance graph to the query stage. The provenance graphs are later joined on matching intermediate keys of the map and reduce provenance files.

7.4 Secure Query Processing in a Cloud Environment

To illustrate how the various cloud computing tools can be utilized, we describe a prototype system that we have developed. Our prototype is a Web-based secure cloud query processing system. It enforces XACML-based policies for access control during query processing. We have combined HDFS with Hive to provide a common storage area for participating organizations. Users of our system are divided into groups based on the kinds of queries that they can run, such as SELECT and INSERT. Our system provides a secure login feature to users based on a salted hash technique. When a user logs into our system, he or she is provided with different options based on the group to which they belong. We allow collaborating organizations to load data to the shared storage space in the form of relational tables and views. Users can also define fine-grained XACML access control policies on tables and views for groups of users. Users can then query the entire database based on the credentials that they have. We have provided some basic query rewriting rules in our system that abstract users from the query language of Hive (HiveQL). This allows them to enter regular SQL queries in the Web application that are translated into HiveQL using basic rewriting rules. Our system also allows new users to register, but only a designated special user "admin" can assign these users to the appropriate groups.

Figure 7.2 shows the architecture of our system. Each rectangle in the figure represents a different component of our framework. The various line styles for arrows indicate the flow of control for a specific task that can be accomplished with this system. Next, we present each of the component layers in the architecture. More details of our prototype, including the experimental results, can be found in Khaled et al. (2010) and Thuraisingham (2013). In Chapter 20 we will describe a more robust implementation of our cloud query processing system that carries out both assured information sharing and inference control on provenance data.

7.4.1 The Web Application Layer

The Web application layer is the only interface provided by our system to the user to access the cloud infrastructure. We provide different functions based on the permissions assigned to a user. The Web application provides a log-in page that can be used by any user to log into the system. We use the Java simplified encryption (JASYPT) library's salted hash technique to store user names and passwords in a file. Further, that file is stored in a secure location that is not accessible to any user (JASYPT—Java simplified encryption, http://www.jasypt.org/index.html). The system currently supports three types of users:

1. Users who can only query the existing tables/views
2. Users who can create tables and views and define XACML policies on them in addition to querying all tables and views

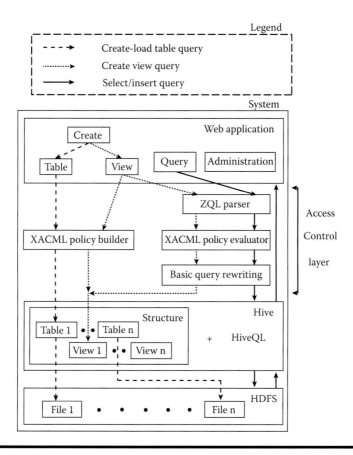

Figure 7.2 System architecture.

3. A special "admin" user who in addition to the functions described above can also assign new users to either of the above categories

7.4.2 The ZQL Parser Layer

The ZQL parser layer takes as input any query submitted by a user and either proceeds to the XACML policy evaluator if the query is successfully parsed or returns an error message to the user (Zql: A Java SQL parser, http://zql.sourceforge.net/). The ZQL parser is an SQL parser written in Java that takes a SQL query as input and fills different Java vectors with different parts of the query. For example, consider the following query:

```
SELECT a.id, a.name FROM a WHERE a.id > 5;
```

The ZQL parser parses the query and constructs different Java vectors for every part of the query (SELECT, FROM, and WHERE). In our system, the vector of attribute names in the SELECT clause for the query above is returned to the Web application layer to be used in displaying the results returned by the query. The vector of table/view names in the FROM clause is passed to the XACML policy evaluator to ensure that the current user has permissions to access all tables/views specified in the query. If the evaluator determines that the current user has the required permissions, the query is processed further; otherwise, an error message is returned to the Web application layer. The ZQL parser currently supports the SQL DELETE, INSERT, SELECT, and UPDATE statements. Our future work involves adding support for other keywords such as CREATE and DROP.

7.4.3 The XACML Policy Layer

XACML is an XML-based language that is used to define access control policies on resources. The same language is also used to determine whether access is allowed for a particular resource based on the policy defined for that resource (Zql: A Java SQL parser, http://zql.sourceforge.net/). Next we explain how we have defined and used XACML policies in our framework.

XACML policy builder. In our framework, the tables and views defined by users are treated as resources for building XACML policies. Further, we have defined RBAC policies on these resources based on the kinds of queries that are provided by our system (Ferraiolo and Kuhn 1992). For every type of query supported by our framework, we define a mapping between this type and all users that are allowed to run that kind of query. A sample listing of such a mapping is given below:

```
INSERT admin user1 user2
SELECT admin user1 user3
```

In our system, for every table/view that a user wants to create, they are given the option of uploading their own predefined XACML policy or having the framework build a policy for them. If a user selects the latter option, they must also specify the kinds of queries (e.g., INSERT, SELECT) that will be allowed on the table or view. We then use Sun's XACML implementation (Sun XACML Implementation, http://sunxacml.sourceforge.net/) to build a policy for that table or view with the groups specified by that particular user.

XACML policy evaluator. Our system uses Sun's XACML implementation to evaluate if the current user has access to all tables or views that are defined in any user query. If permission is granted for all tables or views, then the query is processed further; otherwise, an error message is returned to the user. The policy evaluator is used both during regular user query execution as well as during view creation, since the only way to create a view in Hive is by specifying a SELECT query on the existing tables or views. The current user must have access to all tables or views specified in this SELECT query before the view can be created.

The basic query rewriting layer. This layer enables us to add another layer of abstraction between the user and HiveQL by allowing users to enter SQL queries that are rewritten according to HiveQL's syntax. In our current system, we provide two basic rewriting rules for user-specified SQL queries.

HiveQL does not allow multiple tables in the FROM clause of a query, but rather expects this kind of query to be given as a sequence of JOIN statements. The user is abstracted from this fact by being allowed to enter a regular SQL query with multiple tables in the FROM clause that we transform to a sequence of JOIN statements in conformance with HiveQL's syntax. The following is an example:

```
SELECT a.id, b.age FROM a, b; → SELECT a.id, b.age FROM a JOIN
b;
```

HiveQL uses a modified version of SQL's INSERT-SELECT statement, INSERT OVERWRITE TABLE <tablename> SELECT, rather than INSERT INTO <tablename> SELECT. Again we abstract this from the user by allowing him or her to enter the traditional INSERT INTO <tablename> SELECT that we then rewrite into HiveQL's INSERT OVERWRITE TABLE <tablename> SELECT. The following is an example:

```
INSERT INTO a SELECT * FROM b; → INSERT OVERWRITE TABLE a
SELECT * FROM b;
```

As part of our future work, we plan to extend these basic rewriting rules with more complicated rules in a complete query rewriting engine.

7.4.4 The Hive Layer

Hive is a data warehouse infrastructure built on top of Hadoop (Apache Hive, https://cwiki.apache.org/confluence/display/Hive/Home%3bjsessionid=8946C5F 66E7FBD0CE2466BAA5C699289). Hive provides the ability to structure the data in the underlying HDFS as well as to query these data. The arrows in Figure 7.2 between the tables in this layer and the files in the HDFS layer indicate that each table in Hive is stored as a file in the HDFS. These files contain the data that this table represents. There are no arrows between the views in this layer and the files in the HDFS layer since a view is only a logical concept in Hive that is created with a SELECT query. In our framework, Hive is used to structure the data that will be shared by collaborating organizations. Further, we use Hive's SQL-like query language, HiveQL, to enable access to these data. The advantage of using Hive in our system is that users can query the data using a familiar SQL-like syntax.

7.4.5 HDFS

HDFS is a distributed file system that is designed to run on basic hardware (Borthakur 2010). The HDFS layer in our framework stores the data files corresponding to tables that are created in Hive [Thusoo et al. 2009]. Our security assumption is that these files cannot be accessed using Hadoop's Web interface or Hadoop's command line interface but only by using our system.

Our system provides the following features (Khaled et al. 2010):

- A mechanism to load and query shared data securely that are stored in HDFS using Hive
- An additional layer of security above HDFS and Hive using a XACML policy-based mechanism
- Basic query rewriting rules that abstract a user from HiveQL and allows him or her to enter SQL queries
- Incorporation of the above mechanisms into a Web-based system

7.5 Summary and Directions

Provenance data represent the history of the data. It is collected to answer questions such as, Where did the data originate from? Who accessed the data? Who owns the data? When was the data created? When was the data updated? We have represented provenance data as a graph structure. Over time the graph structures could become massive. We need scalable solutions to manage large amounts of provenance data. Cloud computing offers a solution to the problem.

As stated by the National Institute of Standards and Technology (http://csrc.nist.gov/publications/nistpubs/800-145/SP800-145.pdf), "Cloud computing is an example of computing in which dynamically scalable and often virtualized resources are provided as a service over the Internet. Users need not have knowledge of, expertise in, or control over the technology infrastructure in the 'cloud' that supports them." Various technologies have been developed to support cloud computing. More details on cloud computing and security issues for cloud computing can be found in Thuraisingham (2013).

This chapter has described cloud computing tools and frameworks and our use of these technologies in a prototype secure cloud query processing system implementation. In Chapter 20 we will describe a more robust system that operates in the cloud and carries out assured information sharing and inference control on provenance data.

References

Abraham, J., Brazier, P., Chebotko, A., Navarro, J. and Piazza, A., Distributed storage and querying techniques for a Semantic Web of scientific workflow provenance, Proceedings Services Computing (SCC), 2010 IEEE International Conference on Services Computing, 2010.

Akoush, S., Sohan, R. and Hopper, A., HadoopProv: Towards provenance as a first class citizen in MapReduce, Proceedings of the 5th USENIX Workshop on the Theory and Practice of Provenance, 2013.

Anderson, C., Lehnardt, J. and Slater, N., *CouchDB: The Definitive Guide,* O'Reilly Media, Sebastopol, CA, 2010.

Apache Hive, https://cwiki.apache.org/confluence/display/Hive/Home%3bjsessionid=8946 C5F66E7FBD0CE2466BAA5C69928.

Borthakur, D., HDFS Architecture, http://hadoop.apache.org/common/docs/r0.19.2/hdfs_ design.pdf, 2010.

Cattell, R., Scalable SQL and NoSQL data stores, *ACM SIGMOD Record,* Vol. 39, No. 4, 2011, pp. 12–27.

Chebotko, A., Abraham, J., Brazier, P., Piazza, A., Kashlev, A. and Lu, S., Storing, indexing and querying large provenance data sets as RDF graphs in Apache HBase, IEEE International Workshop on Scientific Workflows, Santa Clara, CA, 2013.

Chodorow, K. and Dirolf, M., *MongoDB: The Definitive Guide,* O'Reilly Media, Sebastopol, CA, 2010.

Crockford, D., The application/json media type for JavaScript Object Notation (JSON), 2006.

Dean, J. and Ghemawat, S., MapReduce: Simplified data processing on large clusters, *Communications of the ACM,* Vol. 51, No. 1, 2008, pp. 107–113.

Ferraiolo, D. F. and Kuhn, D. R., Role-based access controls, National Computer Security Conference, 1992, pp. 554–563.

George, L., *HBase: The Definitive Guide,* O'Reilly Media, Sebastopol, CA, 2011.

Ghemawat, S., Gobioff, H. and Leung, S.-T., The Google file system, *ACM SIGOPS Operating Systems Review,* Vol. 37, No. 5, 2003, pp. 29–43.

Hewitt, E., *Cassandra: The Definitive Guide,* O'Reilly Media, Sebastopol, CA, 2010.

http://csrc.nist.gov/publications/nistpubs/800-145/SP800-145.pdf.

Huang, J., Abadi, D. J. and Ren, K., Scalable SPARQL querying of large RDF graphs, *Proceedings of the VLDB Endowment,* Vol. 4, No. 11, 2011.

Husain, M. F., Doshi, P., Khan, L. and Thuraisingham, B., Storage and retrieval of large RDF graph using Hadoop and MapReduce, *Cloud Computing,* 2009.

Ikeda, R., Park, H. and Widom, J., Provenance for generalized map and reduce workflows, Stanford InfoLab, 2011.

JASYPT—Java simplified encryption, http://www.jasypt.org/index.html.

Khadilkar, V., Kantarcioglu, M., Castagna, P. and Thuraisingham, B., Jena-HBase: A distributed, scalable and efficient RDF triple store, technical report, http://www.utdallas. edu/~vvk072000/Research/Jena-HBase-Ext/tech-report.Pdf, 2012.

Khaled, A., Husain, M. F., Khan, L., Hamlen, K. W. and Thuraisingham, B. M., A token-based access control system for RDF data in the clouds, CloudCom, 2010.

Papailiou, N., Konstantinou, I., Tsoumakos, D. and Koziris, N., H2RDF: Adaptive query processing on RDF data in the cloud, Proceedings of the 21st International Conference Companion on World Wide Web, 2012.

Park, H., Ikeda, R. and Widom, J., Ramp: A system for capturing and tracing provenance in MapReduce workflows, Stanford InfoLab, 2011.

Shvachko, K., Kuang, H., Radia, S. and Chansler, R., The Hadoop distributed file system, mass storage systems and technologies (MSST), 2010 IEEE 26th Symposium on Mass Storage Systems and Technologies (MSST), 2010.

Sun, J. and Jin, Q., Scalable RDF store based on HBase and MapReduce, Proceedings *Advanced Computer Theory and Engineering (ICACTE), 2010 3rd International Conference on,* Vol. 1, 2010, pp. V1–633.

Sun XACML Implementation, http://sunxacml.sourceforge.net/.

Thuraisingham, B., *Developing and Securing the Cloud,* CRC Press, Boca Raton, FL, 2013.

Thusoo, A., Sarma, J. S., Zheng, S., Jain, N., Chakka, P., Anthony, S., Liu, H., Wycoff, P., and Murthy, R., Hive–A Warehousing solution over a map-Reduce framework. *VLDB,* Vol. 2, No. 2, 2009, pp. 1626–1629.

Thusoo, A., Sarma, J. S., Jain, N., Shao, Z., Chakka, P., Zhang, N., Antony, S., Liu, H. and Murthy, R., Hive–A petabyte scale data warehouse using Hadoop, Proceedings Data Engineering, 2010 IEEE 26th International Conference on Data Engineering (ICDE), 2010.

White, T., *Hadoop: The Definitive Guide,* O'Reilly Media, Sebastopol, CA, 2010.

Zql: A Java SQL parser, http://zql.sourceforge.net/.

CONLUSION

Section I, which described supporting technologies, consisted of six chapters: 2, 3, 4, 5, 6, and 7. Chapter 2 provided some background information on provenance relevant to our work. First, we discussed scalability issues for a secure provenance framework and then we discussed aspects of an access control language for provenance. Finally, we discussed graph operations on provenance. Chapter 3 provided the foundations needed to understand the contents of this book, which is access control and the Semantic Web. We first provided an overview of access control models and then discussed role-based access control. This was followed by a discussion of the technologies for the Semantic Web including XML, RDF, ontologies, and OWL. Finally, we discussed security issues for the Semantic Web.

Chapter 4 provided details about the inference problem and inference controllers. First, we discussed the inference problem. In particular, we defined the inference problem and discussed the inference strategies. We also defined various types of security constraints, also known as security policies. Then we discussed our approach to developing an inference controller. Chapter 5 provided an overview of the various inference engines that have been developed. These included Jena, Sesame, and the Inference Web. These inference engines reason with Semantic Web data. We have utilized some of these systems in our work and they form the foundations of the next generation inference controllers. Chapter 6 elaborated on the notion of inference. We first defined inference functions and then we discussed aspects of classifying knowledge bases. This was followed by a detailed discussion of inference strategies and examples for each strategy. For example, strategies such as inference by deduction, inference by induction, and inference by analogical reasoning were discussed. Finally, aspects of inference and provenance were discussed.

Chapter 7 discussed cloud computing. Provenance data represents the history of the data. It is collected to answer questions such as, Where did the data originate from? Who accessed the data? Who owns the data? When was the data created? When was the data updated? We have represented provenance data as a graph structure. Over time the graph structures could become massive. We need scalable solutions to manage large amounts of provenance data. Cloud computing offers a solution to the problem.

Now that we have described the supporting technologies, we are now ready to embark on the first major objective of this book, which is secure data provenance. The chapters in Section II will describe in detail our approach to achieving this major objective.

SECURE DATA PROVENANCE

INTRODUCTION II

As stated in the book's introduction, provenance means the origin of a source; the history of ownership of a valued object or a work of art or literature. It allows us to share and verify data, to repeat experiments, and to discover dependencies. Organizations rely on information sharing as a way of conducting their day-to-day activities, but with this ease of information sharing comes a risk of information misuse. For example, an EPR is a log of all activities including patient visits to a hospital, diagnoses and treatments for diseases, and processes performed by health care professionals on a patient. This EPR is often shared among several stakeholders (for example researchers and insurance and pharmaceutical companies). Before this information can be made available to these third parties, the sensitive information in an EPR must be circumvented or hidden from the released information. In Section I we described approaches to secure such provenance data.

Section II consists of Chapters 8, 9, and 10. Chapter 8 discusses how we create flexible and scalable access control policies by extending RBAC using key Semantic Web technologies. We also describe a prototype which shows that we can scale and reason over a set of access control policies efficiently. Chapter 9 provides a definition of an access control policy language for provenance. This language retains the properties of traditional access control to gain access to data. Furthermore, the language provides an additional advantage whereby we can write one policy that is a pattern for several policies, thus contracting the policy set. We also describe our prototype that utilizes Semantic Web technologies, which allows a user to query for data and provenance based on access control policies defined using our policy language. Chapter 10 discusses the application of a graph grammar technique that can be used to perform redaction over provenance. In addition, we provide an architectural design that allows a high-level specification of policies, thus separating the business layer from a specific software implementation. We also describe a prototype of the architecture based on open-source Semantic Web technologies.

Chapter 8

Scalable and Efficient RBAC for Provenance

8.1 Overview

In Section I we discussed the supporting technologies needed for the concepts in this book. In particular, we looked at access control models and Semantic Web technologies as well as data provenance, RBAC, and a discussion of the inference problem. In this section we discuss one of the major objectives of this book, which is secure data provenance. In particular, the design and implementation of our system based on Semantic Web technologies that enforces RBAC on provenance data will be described.

In this chapter, we first discuss the drawbacks of using the current access control policies in a heterogeneous environment. These heterogeneous environments can contain either relational data or semistructured data in the form of a tree (e.g., XML) or a graph (e.g., the World Wide Web, RDF). We focus mainly on RBAC systems, but the discussion applies equally well to the other access control models. We identify the key drawbacks of access control over provenance by concentrating on a simple case; single data items within a provenance graph. We discuss the reasons why we need flexible policies, which are both dynamic and interoperable, and then present a Semantic Web approach for overcoming these challenges.

The organization of this chapter is as follows. In Section 8.2 we discuss the motivation of our work as well as our contributions. In Section 8.3 we describe flexible policies. Supporting inferences in RBAC are discussed in Section 8.4. Our approach is discussed in Section 8.5. Extending RBAC to support provenance is discussed in Section 8.6. Query processing is discussed in Section 8.7. Experiments

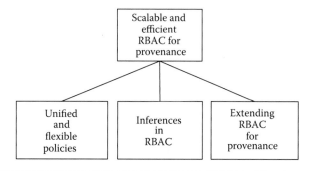

Figure 8.1   Scalable and efficient RBAC for provenance.

are discussed in Section 8.8. The chapter is summarized in Section 8.9. Figure 8.1 illustrates the concepts discussed in this chapter. More details of our work in secure data provenance can be found in Cadenhead et al. (2010).

8.2 Motivation and Contributions

There is a need for a scalable access control model that simplifies the management of security policies and handles the heterogeneity inherent in an information system with both traditional data and provenance. We now support this claim with a motivating example taken from the medical domain, where provenance is recorded (Kifor et al. 2006) and heterogeneity is present (Kataria et al. 2008; Winter et al. 2001).

1. Bob's history shows that he only visits his primary physician Sam to receive health care. Therefore, only Sam is preassigned a role to access Bob's record when Bob is under his care. One day Bob requires emergency care, but Sam is off duty. Kelly is on duty in the emergency room, but Kelly is not preassigned to view or update Bob's record. Therefore, Bob cannot get immediate treatment.
2. Kelly is eventually assigned to a role that allows access to Bob's record. However, Kelly needs to collaborate with other specialists who are in different wards. To expedite the care given to Bob, the information given to Kelly must be coherent and unambiguous.

The main points of this chapter are

1. A flexible RBAC using existing semantic technologies
2. Scalable support for large instances
3. Efficient and accurate reasoning about access rights

8.3 Unified and Flexible Policies

One of our overall goals is to provide a general access control model that can support multiple domains. To achieve this, we need an access control policy that can unify existing and disparate access control policies. RBAC models have enjoyed popularity by simplifying the management of security policies using roles and also simulating existing access control policies (Ferraiolo et al. 2003). Therefore, RBAC is a good choice for unifying the different policies in a heterogeneous environment.

In Figure 8.2, we show that we need a stronger notion of simplification of policies than that provided by RBAC. Large organizations are often distributed across different geographical locations. Each department may also have its own jargon and set of terms that are common to that department. We can extend RBAC (Ferraiolo et al. 2003) with ontologies with the use of Semantic Web technologies that will enable RBAC to support these departments (Berners-Lee et al. 2001). Furthermore, we can integrate different ontologies by importing them into one ontology or we could use a framework for combining them.

Semantic Web technologies have been increasingly used to build rules that enforce access control (Finin et al. 2008; Kolovski et al. 2007; Qin and Atluri 2003; Zhang et al. 2009; Zhao et al. 2005). Though many of the previous works were about enforcing access control over traditional relational databases, the migration

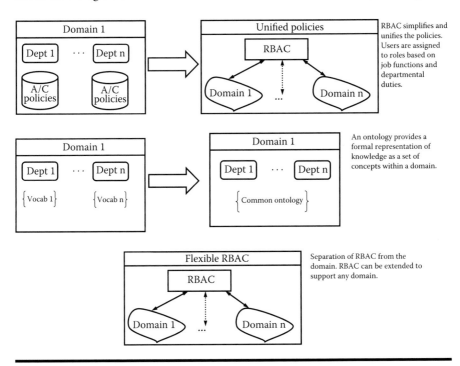

Figure 8.2 A unified and flexible RBAC.

of relational databases to the Semantic Web environment is also on the way (Bizer 2003; Chen et al. 2006; Cullot et al. 2007). As well, with the increasing use of the Semantic Web for e-commerce and Web services, we need access control models and mechanisms for this new environment (Agarwal and Sprick 2004; Agarwal et al. 2004; Kagal et al. 2003; Priebe et al. 2006; Tonti et al. 2003; Yague et al. 2003). Therefore, we hope that the work in this chapter plays a part in this shift to a new environment that supports and enforces access control.

Flexible RBAC. In the case of Bob in the emergency room, an RBAC model that has a temporal dimension could have given Kelly temporary access to Bob's record. These models are well covered in the literature (Bertino et al. 2001; Joshi et al. 2005). A temporal access control model (TRBAC) can be summarized as one that supports periodic role enabling and disabling. TRBAC is generally expressed by means of role triggers, which are active rules that are automatically executed when a specified action occurs. The triggers are basically used to constrain the set of roles that a particular user can activate at a given time instant.

Other models that extend RBAC are also given in Ardagna et al. (2006), El Kalam and Benferhat (2003), Freudenthal et al. (2002), Kulkarni and Tripathi (2008), and Yuan and Tong (2005). These models are an attempt to overcome the static nature of traditional access control models. They cater to environments where access to resources is required based on some context, like attributes, location, organization structure, and coalition.

Interoperability. In the case of information being shared across different wards (sometimes departments), a framework that allows a global naming scheme and a standard syntax for describing things would resolve the ambiguities. Within a Semantic Web framework, an access control mechanism could respond to a changing vocabulary and therefore adapt to different environments. We can achieve interoperability by representing the information about RBAC and the domain using RDF or OWL, both knowledge representation languages (Klyne et al. 2004; McGuinness and Van Harmelen 2004). RDF is a standard for describing resources on the Semantic Web. It provides a common framework for expressing information so it can be exchanged between applications without loss of meaning. RDF uses Web identifiers (URIs) for identifying and describing resources in terms of simple properties and property values. OWL facilitates greater machine interpretability of Web content than that supported by XML, RDF, and RDF-S by providing additional vocabulary along with a formal semantics.

8.4 Supporting Inferences in RBAC

We also support inferencing with respect to RBAC in a Semantic Web environment. We represent RBAC and the domain ontology in OWL ontologies; in particular we are concerned with the DL $\mathcal{ALCQ}$ REF BIB_baader2003description * MERGEFORMAT for our knowledge bases (Baader et al. 2003; McGuinness and Van Harmelen 2004). These knowledge bases consist of a TBox and an ABox. A TBox is a terminology box, which stores the ontology. The TBox organizes a domain by a concept hierarchy and relationships between the concepts. An ABox is the assertional box, which contains instances based on the TBox. Reasoning can be performed by different DL tools, such as Pellet or FaCT++ (Sirin et al. 2007; Tsarkov and Horrocks 2006).

The RBAC policies can be specified in terms of rules in a Semantic Web environment. There are different mechanisms for encoding these policies; we consider two of them here but will choose one for addressing some scalability aspects of RBAC. A rule can be encoded using DL, as shown in Kolovski et al. (2007), Zhao et al. (2005), and Zhang et al. (2009). These rules can be used to encode the constraints in the binary relationships of RBAC. Another approach for enforcing the RBAC constraints and policy rules is with SWRL (Horrocks et al. 2004). This is more expressive than using DL alone, but with this expressivity, there is a complexity trade-off. SWRL rules are normally written as DL-safe rules in order to be decidable; therefore, each variable of a rule is required to occur in a non-DL-atom in the rule body (Motik et al. 2005).

Our solution is based on the more expressive rule language, SWRL, which is normally preferred for its ability to support complex relationships between properties as well as expressing access control with semantic information (Li et al. 2005; Shields et al. 2006). The expressiveness of SWRL would allow the formulation of policies such as

StudentOf(Mary, ?x) ∧ colleagueOf(?x, ?z) ∧ isProhibittedReadWith(?x, ?note1) → *isProhibittedReadWith(?z, ?note1)*

This policy states that a student Mary uploaded a note and specifies that if her teachers are prohibited from reading this note, then so too are their colleagues.

We came across one major challenge in using SWRL in our knowledge base, which was due to the availability of memory on the machine utilized. Our observation was that as we increase the number of rules in the knowledge base, the longer it takes to perform reasoning tasks (i.e., determining the consistency of the knowledge base). Table 8.1 shows the performance of when we add all the individual assertions and rules into one knowledge base, which resulted in a memory exception.

Table 8.1   Memory Exception after Adding 1000 Individuals + 16 (Rules)

Inference Statistics					
Individuals	112	336	560	784	1008
Time(ms)	152	211	276	448	552

Distributed reasoning. A solution that we implemented for handling the memory constraint problem was to partition the knowledge base (Cadenhead et al. 2010). At first this appeared as a very naive solution; arbitrary partitioning would not return the same answers to an access control query as that obtained by querying one knowledge base in memory. An access control query is formulated to answer questions like: Does Kelly currently have access to Bob's record? What is the duration of such access? Is there a conflict between two roles? After examining the current model for RBAC, we apply the basic tenet of RBAC; this states that a subject (therefore a user or autonomous agent) must assume a role before any access is allowed to a resource. Further, a role is associated with a permission, which is a combination of actions and objects (see Figure 8.3).

Next, we consider the impact of an access control query for Bob's record in relation to another patient's records. For example, if Bob is under 18 years old, would

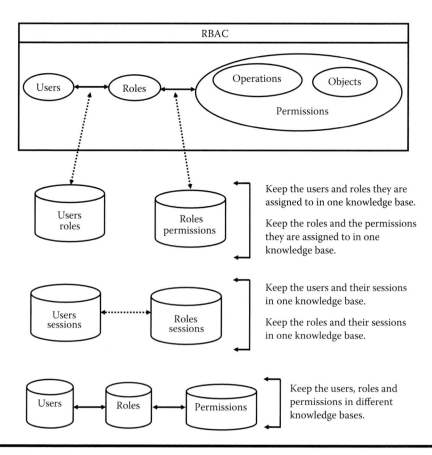

Figure 8.3 Distributed knowledge bases.

an access query for Bob's record depend on another query for Michelle's record if Michelle is Bob's guardian? Here we are concerned with a written consent for a minor. Another situation would be where we need to access Michelle's record if Michelle is related to Bob by blood (therefore a biological parent).

For the first situation, a policy would have to be in place to ensure that Michelle gives consent to share the contents of Bob's record with Kelly (or other hospital personnel or third party). This policy would have to be evaluated before another policy could determine that Kelly (or any other hospital personnel) has access to Bob's record. The second situation is similar; Michelle would give consent to release her information to Kelly, who is in the emergency room. The sequential execution of these policies would indicate that we could create a control environment where one policy is evaluated and a note is made of the decision, and then the second policy is evaluated based on the effect of the first policy. A third situation would be when Bob and Michelle are unrelated to each other. In this case, there are no causal dependencies between the execution of policies to consider.

These situations led us to consider a distributed approach to the memory problem. We now describe this approach. We partition the KB in memory, which we call KB_{global} into n smaller knowledge bases.

$KB_{global} = (\mathcal{T}, \mathcal{A}_{global})$ and we distribute the ABox, $\mathcal{A}_{global}$, over each KB_i such that $\mathcal{A}_{global} = \mathcal{A}_1 \cup \mathcal{A}_2 \cup \ldots \cup \mathcal{A}_n$. $KB_i = (\mathcal{T}, \mathcal{A}_i)$.

The TBox remains the same in each knowledge base, but the ABox is distributed. The rationale is that in the general case, the number of instances in a knowledge base grows much faster than the TBox. This is normally observed in relational databases, where the schema is usually fixed, but the instances (or data) increase with the number of daily transactions. This situation is also observed in DL knowledge bases (Guo and Heflin 2006).

8.5 Overview of Our Approach

We now present an overview of our approach, which we use to address the memory constraint problem. We take both the size of the ABox and the number of rules into consideration in order to devise a suitable approach for handling both the scalability issues and efficiency issues we observe in Table 8.1. This approach involves three stages as depicted in Figure 8.4. Note that Figure 8.4 describes an instance related to the medical domain, but it can be applied to different domains as well.

We now define these three stages:

1. We partition the global KB, KB_{global} into n smaller KBs. This reduces the size of a partition in memory. We then store each partition onto disk. In order to ensure acceptable query performances, we index each assertion in a partition. This is done by indexing an RDF triple by its subject, predicate, and object. This stage is normally performed before we answer the access queries and

$$Disk \xrightarrow{load} KB_i \xrightarrow{query} KB_{inf} \xrightarrow{add} New\ Facts$$

(a)

$$KB_{inf} \xrightarrow{addrules} KB_{inf}$$

(b)

$$KB_{global} \xrightarrow{partition} KB_i ...KB_{inf} \xrightarrow{store} Disk$$

(c)

Figure 8.4   Architecture. (a) Stage 1, (b) stage 2, (c) stage 3.

often leads to significantly low overhead at query time. There is one important restriction when performing this stage—each partition must be small
enough to fit into the memory on the machine at query time.

2. Instead of loading the SWRL rules into a knowledge base with all the
   instances of KB_{global}, we load them into a new KB, KB_{inf}. Adding these rules
   to KB_{inf} reduces the impact of performing inferencing at query time. This is
   due to the fact that we are only retrieving a small subset of the entire triple
   set into memory. Also, a reasoner will only have to deal with a smaller set of
   symbols in the ABox even in the presence of a large rule set.

3. Finally, at query time we only perform an access query for one patient. This
   is mainly due to the fact that an access decision for Bob is either independent
   of Michelle's or we can perform the access queries in sequence (therefore, at
   different temporal intervals). We retrieve the relevant assertions from disk,
   one step at a time, and update our inference KB, KB_{inf}. Observe that once
   this loading is performed, the rules in KB_{inf} should cause new facts to be
   added to KB_{inf}. A major assumption we make is that the cascading effect of
   firing the rules will eventually halt, indicating that all the access control policy rules are satisfied. Our goal will be to show that a controlled sequence for
   applying the rules produces acceptable performance times. Another observation is that some rules will function only to add special facts (or metadata
   about the activities in KB_{inf}). Querying for these metadata provides feedback
   about conflicts, such as a role is both enabled and disabled within the same
   session.

Discussion. When there is an access request for a specific patient, stages 2 and
3 are executed in sequence. This sequence ensures that KB_{inf} will only contain the

relevant facts for one patient. The main advantages of the architecture in Figure 8.4 can be summarized as follows:

■ We can instantiate many iterations over stages 2 and 3. At each iteration i we start with a new knowledge base KB_{inf_i}. This would handle cases where we need to make decisions about patients concurrently.

■ There are performance improvements. We now discuss two of them.

1. The partitions, $KB_1, \ldots, KB_n$, are materialized. We perform consistency tests over KB_n before putting it on disk. This is done to avoid doing these inferencing tests at querying time. The inference tests are usually expensive (Calvanese 1996; Donini 2003) and OWL reasoning is exponential in time and memory in the worst case (Baader et al. 2003).

2. KB_{inf} stores SWRL rules. The effect of this is that the rules are applied to a small number of individuals in the knowledge base.

Scalable RBAC. A global knowledge base normally resides in memory and offers real-time reasoning and querying but is not scalable as we stream more data to it. The main reason is that the instances in the ABox grow as we scale our implementation, while the size of the TBox remains relatively the same. We would like to handle a large number of instances without sacrificing efficiency. To achieve this we partition a knowledge base into a set of smaller knowledge bases. Each smaller knowledge base has the same TBox as the original knowledge base but only a subset of the ABox. What we would like is to be able to do arbitrary partitioning whenever any of the partitions become too large. We can achieve this by using the same argument we use to partition KB_{global}. Therefore, $KB_{patient}$ could be further partitioned into $KB_{patient_1}$, $KB_{patient_2}, \ldots, KB_{patient_n}$.

8.6 Extending RBAC to Support Provenance

Our system consists of the standard RBAC modules, *Users*, *Roles*, *Sessions*, *Permissions*, and *Objects*, plus some domain-specific modules. The RBAC module could be described in terms of an access control vocabulary or ontology while the domain modules would reflect the descriptions and vocabulary of the domain. This separation of RBAC from the domain would make our approach more flexible; therefore, we could support any domain by leveraging from the benefits of the Semantic Web.

In this section, we first define the modules in one domain, but this definition is not limited to the health care domain. Next, we define the binary constraints in our example domain. These binary relations extend those that are already in place for RBAC. We would also like to point out that our example domain could extend to any other access control model or variant of the access control model we use for this chapter.

Definition 8.1: Domain Modules

The set $\mathfrak{D}$ consists of disjoint modules, where

- RBAC defines *Users, Roles, Sessions, Permissions,* and *Objects*
- The hospital extends *Users* to employees, *Roles* to the organizational structure, *Objects* to *Records* (plus other resources, such as equipment)
- The hospital defines *Patients* (plus other stakeholders, such as suppliers)

Definition 8.2: Mapping Function

The set $\mathcal{M}$ consists of unique atomic properties (binary relations) connecting two domain modules in $\mathfrak{D}$ so that we have:

- RBAC assignments: the mappings *user-role, role-user, role-permission, permission-role, user-session, role-role,* and *role-session*
- Hospital extensions: the mappings *patient-user, user-patient,* and *patient-session*
- *Patient-Record* constraint: the one-to-one mappings *patient-record* and *record-patient*

where *user* $\in$ *Users*, *role* $\in$ *Roles*, *permission* $\in$ *Permissions*, *session* $\in$ *Sessions*, *patient* $\in$ *Patients*, and *record* $\in$ *Records*.

Connecting RBAC partitions. In order to ensure that we get the desired behavior using our partition approach as that of using one knowledge base, we need to ensure that we can hop from one module to the next. This flow will enable us to gather the pieces we need in order to make an access decision.

In this section, we first present the notion of a home partition. The purpose of defining a home partition is so that we have a unique partition to locate an RDF triple. In the global approach, all the triples are in KB_{global}. However, without a home partition in the distributed approach, we have no predetermined method for retrieving a triple effectively. We take advantage of the fact that a subject in an RDF triple is a URIref that identifies a unique resource. Therefore, we use this unique name to get to a home partition. Next, we define the notion of a link. The idea of this link is to enable us to navigate the partitions. We can think of a link as a way of linking two RDF graphs; therefore, a link connects two home partitions, where the subject of triple t_i is in KB_i and its object is the subject of another triple t_{i+1} in KB_{i+1}.

Definition 8.3: Home Partition

We define a home partition KB_i, for all the triples, where $i = 1, 2, \ldots, n$ such that

- The TBox, T, is in KB_i
- For all assertions of form $C(x)$ and $R(x, Y)$, both have the same home, KB_i, and C is a concept, R is an atomic property, x is restricted to individuals in $\mathfrak{D}$, and Y is either an individual or a literal (for object or datatype property, respectively). In particular, the home is determined by x, the domain of R.

Definition 8.4: P-Link

A P-link is a directed arc that allows navigation from one materialized KB to the next. An atomic property $\rho \in RS$, the set of properties in $\mathcal{ALCQ}$, is a *P-link* if $\rho \in \mathcal{M}$. Also, a *P-link* has a home partition.

8.7 A Query-Retrieval Process

We now present an example in which we show how we carry out steps two and three in Figure 8.4. This example illustrates the controlled sequence of applying the rules in order to ensure good performance. We first present a notion of a policy query, which is encoded with the controlled sequence.

Policy query. Let KS be a set of partitions, a policy (or access) query q against KS is a tuple (s, α, K, Ψ, o), where s is of the form $[t_1, t_2]$, α is an individual, K is an ordered set of partitions, Ψ is a set of access policy rules, and o is the output of a positive query.

- K represents a flow and is of the form $(KB_1 \prec \ldots \prec KB_m)$ such that $KB_i \prec KB_{i+1}$ means that KB_i precedes KB_{i+1} and the query process starts from KB_1 and ends in KB_m. Note that $i < m$.
- KB_i and KB_{i+1} are connected by a special P-link.
- Ψ is a set of SWRL rules of the form $H_1 \wedge \ldots \wedge H_{m'} \leftarrow B_1 \wedge \ldots \wedge B_{n'}$ where B_i, H_j, $1 < i < n'$, $1 < j < m'$ are atoms of the following form $C(i)$ or $P(i,j)$.

8.7.1 Example of a Policy Query

A policy query for a patient *Bob* in session $[t_1, t_2]$ would be

$$([t_1, t_2], Bob, \prec KB_{patient} \prec KB_{user} \prec KB_{role} \succ, \Psi, o)$$

8.7.2 Example of a SWRL Rule

A rule in Ψ would be

> *Patient*(?x1) ∧ *patUser*(?x1, ?x2) ∧ *patSess*(?x1, ?x4) ∧ *patRec*(?x1, ?x3) ∧
> *userRole*(?x2, ?x5) ∧ *userSess*(?x2, ?x4) ∧ *roleSess*(?x5, ?x4) ∧
> *rolePerm*(?x5, ?x6) → *canAccess*(?x2, ?x3) ∧ *grantPerm*(?x2, ?x6)

which means that a *user* on duty, who plays the appropriate *role* (e.g., patient's physician) will be granted access to the patient's *record* within the specified *session* (e.g., the patient's session).

8.7.3 Example of a Trace

A policy query is decomposed into several queries so that g_i is evaluated over KB_i. Figure 8.5 outlines a trace of a policy query for a patient *Bob* entering the hospital at interval $[t_1, t_2]$. At each stage of the query, we are retrieving a set of results (on the right) for the individual (possibly many) and session on the left. In the diagram, we assume *Sam* is *Bob*'s physician.

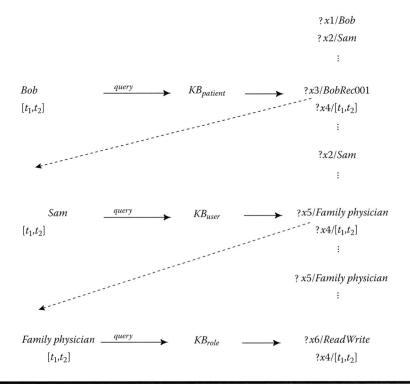

Figure 8.5   A trace (for a patient *Bob*).

8.7.4 Output of the Trace

The output of a trace is $o = o_1 \cup \ldots \cup o_3$

1. The first output, o_1, is determined by issuing q_1 against $KB_{patient}$. We add o_1 to KB_{inf}.
2. The second output, o_2, is determined by issuing q_2 against KB_{doctor}. We add o_2 to KB_{inf}.
3. The third output, o_3, is determined by issuing q_3 against KB_{role}. We add o_3 to KB_{inf}.

8.7.5 Comment

Queries are also used to retrieve facts from the knowledge base KB_{inf}; these include facts inferred by the SWRL rules in KB_{inf}. Under the open world assumption (OWA) of OWL and SWRL, a negative response to a query is not treated as failure to prove the query. This is because a knowledge base is assumed to be incomplete; that is, OWL assumes monotonic reasoning. However, under CWA, what is not known to be true is believed to be false. This is the common reasoning over a relational database, which uses default reasoning.

Under OWA the Semantic Web approach does not quite give the output we desire; instead, we would like the output returned under CWA. Many access control mechanisms make use of policy resolution techniques that handle situations where the effect of a policy is neither true (i.e., a permit) nor false (i.e., a deny). In these situations a default effect is assumed, which could be a denial-takes-precedence effect. Therefore, in the partitioned approach we presented for RBAC, a policy query is positive if $o_i \neq \emptyset \forall i$ and false otherwise. This ensures that a user does not have the ability to perform unnecessary and potentially harmful actions merely as a side effect of granting access using incomplete knowledge from a set of KBs.

Optimization and Heuristics. In the case where everything fits into memory, inferencing is fast but not scalable. In our distributed approach, we address the scalability aspects by using a combination of disk and memory. The distributed approach incurs overhead in creating the partitions and combining the relevant facts to answer an access query.

We identify two places where we need to apply indexing. The first place is in a partition on disk and the second place is in a table that stores the home partitions.

1. We index each triple $t = (s,p,o)$ in order to have faster retrieval at query time. We employ the services of LARQ (http://jena.sourceforge.net/ARQ/lucene-arq.html), which is an extension of the SPARQL implementation of Jena using Apache Lucene. Using this indexing application programming interface (API) allows us to find a triple by its subject (s), its predicate (p), or its object (o) without the cost of a linear search over all the triples in a partition.

2. We keep a lookup table that is an index of the location of a partition on disk. This time we employ the services of Lucene (Gospodnetic and Hatcher 2004). When we are ready to process an access request, we use this index to locate the home partition for an RDF triple. Using this lookup table, we are able to locate a triple in at most linear time with respect to the number of partitions.

We apply two heuristics in order to have greater performances.

1. A concept C could be of the form $\geq nR.C \geq nR.C$ or $\leq nR.C$. These concepts are used in RBAC to enforce minimum and maximum cardinality on roles. We limit n for concepts $C \sqsubseteq \geq nR.C$ and $C \sqsubseteq \leq nR.C$.
2. For n_u users and n_r roles, the combination of users and roles is at most $n_u \times n_r$. A user, a, could theoretically have n_r assertions of form $R(a, r_i)$, $i = 1 \dots n_r$. In these situations, arbitrary partitioning may seem too naive. In practice, however, this is less likely to be the case, since there are different competences among users and roles are based on the user's ability to perform a job.

Correctness. For a $\mathcal{ALCQ}$ knowledge base *KB*, complex concepts are built from atomic concepts in *CS*, and properties in *RS*. Table 8.2 displays the predicate logic translation of these concepts (Baader et al. 2003).

Let F infer assertions from KB_i such that $F(T, A_i) = Inf_i$, Q be a query over a set of triples, and S be a subset of $\mathcal{ALCQ}$ KBs. For an RBAC system discussed in this

Table 8.2 $\mathcal{ALCQ}$ Rule Engine

Group 1	
$D(x) \leftarrow C(x)$	$C \sqsubseteq D$
$C(x) \leftarrow R(x,y), D(x)$	$\exists R.D \sqsubseteq C$
$D(y) \leftarrow R(x,y), C(x)$	$C \sqsubseteq \forall R.D$
$\neg A(x)$	$\neg A$
Group 2	
$C(x) \leftarrow \exists y_1 \dots y_n.R(x,y_1) \wedge \cdots \wedge R(x,y_n) \wedge \bigwedge_{i<j} y_i \neq y_j$	$C \sqsubseteq \geq nR.D$
$\bigwedge_{i<j} y_i = y_j \leftarrow \forall y_1 \dots y_{n+1}.R(x,y_1) \wedge \cdots$	$C \sqsubseteq \leq nR.D$
$\wedge R(x,y_{n+1}), C(x)$	
Group 3	
$C(x) \leftarrow D_1(x) \wedge \cdots \wedge D_n(x)$	$D_1 \sqcap \cdots \sqcap D_n \sqsubseteq C$
$C(x) \leftarrow D_1(x) \vee \cdots \vee D_n(x)$	$D_1 \sqcup \cdots \sqcup D_n \sqsubseteq C$

chapter, our partitioning based reasoning scheme correctly infers all the necessary triples needed for enforcing security policy.

Theorem 8.1

$$Q\left(F(KB_{global})\right) \equiv F\left(\bigcap_{i \in s} Q_{S_i}\left(F(KB_i)\right)\right)$$

Our goal is to prove that our partitioning scheme correctly infers all the relevant triples associated with a given session, user, role, and permission. Basically, we argue that in order to correctly infer all the triples associated with the KB_{global}, we can just do reasoning using each partition and combine the selected results of the local reasoners. (Note that all the local reasoners share the same TBox.)

To prove this claim, we will use the rule engine given in Table 8.2. First, we argue that the information needed to use the rules given in Table 8.2 is already captured by the TBox and the local ABox instances. To prove this we will examine all the rules given above and argue that correct application of those rules could be done without combining instances in different partitions.

Note that the first rule in group 1 could be correctly applied by just using the TBox. The second and third rules in group 1 could be correctly applied by using the triple (xRy) given in some local partition and TBox since the definition of R in TBox precisely specifies the domain and the range of the relation. The fourth rule in group 1 is just the negation of an atomic concept.

For rules in group 2, for correct reasoning we need to find out triples of the form (xRy_i), $\forall i$. Since our partitioning puts all the triples with subject xo in the same partition, all needed triples for correct inference will be in the same partition.

For the rules in group 3, we need to have all concepts D_i to be present at the time of reasoning. Clearly some of the concepts could be in different partitions. The way our system works is we query all the materialized results for each partition (i.e., $F[KB_i]$) related to the RBAC query and get the D_i concepts needed. Using these D_i concepts and a TBox, we infer all $C(x)$ and associated triples in memory (i.e., in KB_{inf}).

In our partition approach, we evaluate each policy query (s, α, K, Ψ, o) against the ordered set K of materialized KBs.

Therefore, $Q(K) \equiv Q(\langle KB_i \prec \ldots \prec KB_m \rangle) \equiv Q(\langle KB_{global} \rangle)$.

8.8 Experimental Evaluation

Our experiments were conducted on a Dell Inspiron 2.4 GHz with 8GB RAM. We used various open sources to build a prototype. For keeping track of the partitions, we used a Lucene index (Gospodnetic and Hatcher 2004) and to query a partition, we used LARQ and SPARQL (Prud'hommeaux and Seaborne 2006). We used

Java 1.5 as the main programming language for writing the logic in our code and Pellet as the main reasoner (Sirin et al. 2007). We used synthetic data to build in-memory models using the Jena API (http://jena.sourceforge.net/ARQ/lucene-arq. html; Carroll et al. 2004). The individuals and their properties in our knowledge bases were created randomly. We used Protégé to build our TBox and Jena to build our ABoxes and programmatically extend the TBox (Knublauch et al. 2004). Each user and patient had on average 30 object and datatype properties. We used various information sources, such as WebMD, pubmed, and related literature to investigate and gain insight into the health care domain (http://www.webmd.com/; http://www.ncbi.nlm.nih.gov/pubmed/).

For our base line, we compared our performances to those in Kolovski et al. (2007), which evaluates reasoning for a similar policy language, XACML. We used a naive approach to generate assertions for an in-memory KB (see Table 8.1). We perform various runs, each time with different combinations of individuals from our toy hospital domain. The time to build a set of materialized KBs ranged from 1 to 3 hours. We scaled one variable in the set {(D)octors, (N)urses, (P)atients (R)ules, TBox} at a time while keeping the other variables constant. We recorded the time for performing inferencing over KB_{inf}. The time to retrieve the assertions and validate the policies in KB_{inf} are presented in Figures 8.6 and 8.7.

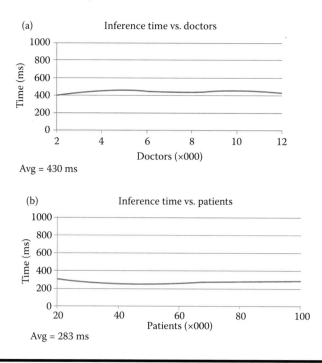

Figure 8.6 Scaling individuals. (a) Scaling doctors using constants: 4200(N), 2100(P), 16(R), (b) scaling patients using constants: 3862(D), 3940(N), 16(R).

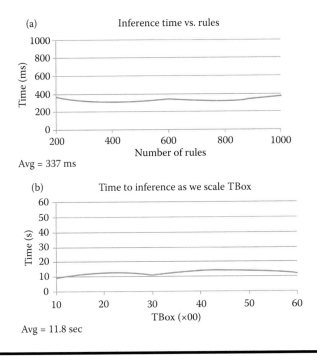

Figure 8.7 **Scaling TBox and rules. (a) Scaling rules using constants: 320(D), 640(N), 1280(P), (b) scaling TBox using constants: 320(D), 640(N), 1280(P), 16(R).**

The performance of our inference knowledge base, KB_{inf}, displays fluctuations as we simulate various activities. This is due to the fact that the index of any of the most accessed KBs will cache previous results, and this has unpredictable behavior. The results in Figure 8.6 a and b show that we can achieve almost constant time for determining a policy decision even in the presence of large instances. The results in Figure 8.7a show that we can support large number rules. The constant run-time in Figure 8.6 is due to our approach of only supporting one instance of a patient per access query. The results in Figure 8.7b show that scaling our TBox does have some performance limitations. This could be because the DL reasoner must perform more expensive tests each time the TBox size increases.

Our implementation is quite scalable with respect to the ABox size and number of SWRL rules. However, it does not scale as well with the TBox. We expect the TBox size to be fairly constant in practice. Our implementation performs fairly well in comparison to our chosen baseline.

8.9 Summary and Directions

In this chapter, we discussed the drawbacks of using the current access control policies in a heterogeneous environment. These heterogeneous environments can contain either relational data or semistructured data. We focused mainly on RBAC systems, but the discussion can apply equally well to the other access control models. We first identified the key drawbacks of access control over provenance by concentrating on a simple case with single data items within a provenance graph. Then we discussed the reasons why we need flexible policies that are both dynamic and interoperable. We then presented a Semantic Web approach for overcoming these challenges.

Essentially, in this chapter, we tell a part of the story where traditional access control does not extend over RDF graph data. We proposed an approach to handle policies on the Semantic Web. In the rest of this book, we will continue to address concerns about traditional policies. In particular, we will turn our attention to the case where provenance takes the form of a directed graph. Moreover, we will continue to use RDF graphs to represent and store provenance, since an RDF graph data model can be restricted to capture the unique features of provenance such as a directed acyclic structure and causality among entities. Next we describe our detailed design and implementation of our system for secure data provenance.

References

Agarwal, S. and Sprick, B., Access control for semantic web services, In Proceedings of Intl Conference on Web Services, 2004.

Agarwal, S., Sprick, B. and Wortmann, S., Credential based access control for Semantic Web services, AAAI Spring Symposium–Semantic Web Services, 2004.

Ardagna, C. A., Cremonini, M., Damiani, E., di Vimercati, S. D. C. and Samarati, P., Supporting location-based conditions in access control policies, Proceedings of the 2006 ACM Symposium on Information, Computer and Communications Security, 2006.

Baader, F., Calvanese, D., McGuinness, D. L. and Nardi, D. (eds.), *The Description Logic Handbook: Theory, Implementation, and Applications*, Cambridge University Press, Cambridge, UK, 2003.

Berners-Lee, T., Hendler, J. and Lassila, O., The Semantic Web, *Scientific American,* Vol. 284, No. 5, 2001.

Bertino, E., Bonatti, P. A. and Ferrari, E., TRBAC: A temporal role-based access control model, *ACM Transactions on Information and System Security* (TISSEC), Vol. 4, No. 3, 2001.

Bizer, C., D2R MAP—A database to RDF mapping language, Proceedings WWW, 2003.

Cadenhead, T., Kantarcioglu, M. and Thuraisingham, B., Scalable and efficient reasoning for enforcing role-based access control, Proceedings Data and Applications Security and Privacy Conference, 2010.

Calvanese, D., Reasoning with inclusion axioms in description logics: Algorithms and complexity, ECAI, 1996.

Carroll, J. J., Dickinson, I., Dollin, C., Reynolds, D., Seaborne, A. and Wilkinson, K., Jena: Implementing the Semantic Web recommendations, Proceedings of the 13th International World Wide Web Conference, 2004.

Chen, H., Wu, Z., Wang, H. and Mao, Y., RDF/RDFS-based relational database integration, In Proceedings of the Intl. Conf. on Data Engineering, 2006.

Cullot, N., Ghawi, R. and Yetongnon, K., DB2OWL: A tool for automatic database-to-ontology mapping, Proceedings of the 15th Italian Symposium on Advanced Database Systems (SEBD 2007), Torre Canne di Fasano (BR), Italy, 2007.

Donini, F. M., Complexity of reasoning, in *The Description Logic Handbook: Theory, Implementation, and Applications,* Baader, F., Calvanese, D., McGuinness, D. L., and Nardi, D. (eds.), Cambridge University Press, Cambridge, UK, 2003.

El Kalam, A. A. and Benferhat, S., Organization based access control, In Proceedings of Policies for Distributed Systems and Networks (POLICY 2003), 2003.

Ferraiolo, D. F., Chandramouli, R., Ahn, G.-J. and Gavrila, S. I., The role control center: Features and case studies, SACMAT, pp. 12–20, 2003.

Finin, T., Joshi, A., Kagal, L., Niu, J., Sandhu, R., Winsborough, W. and Thuraisingham, B., ROWLBAC: Representing role based access control in OWL, Proceedings of the 13th ACM Symposium on Access Control Models and Technologies, 2008.

Freudenthal, E., Pesin, T., Port, L., Keenan, E. and Karamcheti, V., dRBAC: Distributed role-based access control for dynamic coalition environments, In Proceedings of the Intl Conference on Distributed Computing Systems, 2002.

Gospodnetic, O. and Hatcher, E., Lucene in action, Manning Publications, Stanford, CT, 2004.

Guo, Y. and Heflin, J., A scalable approach for partitioning OWL knowledge bases, Proceedings of the 2nd International Workshop on Scalable Semantic Web Knowledge Base Systems, Athens, GA, 2006.

Horrocks, I., Patel-Schneider, P. F., Boley, H., Tabet, S., Grosof, B. and Dean, M., SWRL: A Semantic Web rule language combining OWL and RuleML, W3C Member Submission, Vol. 21, 2004.

http://jena.sourceforge.net/ARQ/lucene-arq.html.

http://www.ncbi.nlm.nih.gov/pubmed/.

http://www.webmd.com/.

Joshi, J. B. D., Bertino, E., Latif, U. and Ghafoor, A., A generalized temporal role-based access control model, *IEEE Transactions on Knowledge and Data Engineering,* Vol. 17, No. 1, 2005.

Kagal, L., Finin, T. and Joshi, A., A policy based approach to security for the Semantic Web, *The Semantic Web* (ISWC), 2003.

Kataria, P., Juric, R., Paurobally, S. and Madani, K., Implementation of ontology for intelligent hospital wards, Proceedings HICCS, 2008.

Kifor, T., Varga, L. Z. and Vazquez-Salceda, J. Provenance in agent-mediated healthcare systems, *IEEE Intelligent Systems,* Vol. 21, No. 6, 2006.

Klyne, G., Carroll, J. J. and McBride, B., Resource description framework (RDF): Concepts and abstract syntax, http://www.w3.org/TR/rdf.concepts/, 2004.

Knublauch, H., Fergerson, R. W., Noy, N. F. and Musen, M. A., The Protege OWL plugin: An open development environment for Semantic Web applications, *The Semantic Web*–ISWC, 2004.

Kolovski, V., Hendler, J. and Parsia, B., Analyzing web access control policies, Proceedings of the 16th International Conference on World Wide Web, 2007.

Kulkarni, D. and Tripathi, A., Context-aware role-based access control in pervasive computing systems, Proceedings of the 13th ACM Symposium on Access Control Models and Technologies, 2008.

Li, H., Zhang, X., Wu, H. and Qu, Y., Design and application of rule based access control policies, Proceedings of the Semantic Web and Policy Workshop, Galway, Ireland, 2005.

McGuinness, D. L. and Van Harmelen, F., OWL web ontology language overview, W3C Recommendation 10, 2004.

Motik, B., Sattler, U. and Studer, R., Query answering for OWL-DL with rules, *Web Semantics: Science, Services and Agents on the World Wide Web,* Vol. 3, No. 1, 2005.

Priebe, T., Dobmeier, W. and Kamprath, N., Supporting attribute-based access control with ontologies, In Proceedings of the Intl Conference on Availability, Reliability and Security (ARES), 2006.

Prud'hommeaux, E. and Seaborne, A., SPARQL query language for RDF, W3C Working Draft, Volume 20, 2006.

Qin, L. and Atluri, V., Concept-level access control for the Semantic Web, Proceedings of the ACM Workshop on XML Security, 2003.

Shields, B., Molloy, O., Lyons, G. and Duggan, J., Using semantic rules to determine access control for web services, Proceedings of the 15th International Conference on World Wide Web, 2006.

Sirin, E., Parsia, B., Grau, B. C., Kalyanpur, A. and Katz, Y., Pellet: A practical OWL-DL reasoner, *Web Semantics: Science, Services and Agents on the World Wide Web,* Vol. 5, No. 2, 2007.

Tonti, G., Bradshaw, J., Jeffers, R., Montanari, R., Suri, N. and Uszok, A., Semantic Web languages for policy representation and reasoning: A comparison of KAoS, Rei, and Ponder, *The Semantic Web* (ISWC), 2003.

Tsarkov, D. and Horrocks, I., FaCT++ description logic reasoner: System description, Proceedings of the Third International Joint Conference on Automated Reasoning (IJCAR'06), 2006.

Winter, A., Brigl, B. and Wendt, T., A UML-based ontology for describing hospital information system architectures, *Studies in Health Technology and Informatics,* pp. 778–782, 105 Press, Amsterdam, 2001.

Yague, M. I., Mana, A., Lopez, J. and Troya, J. M., Applying the Semantic Web layers to access control, Proceedings 14th International Workshop on Database and Expert Systems Applications, 2003.

Yuan, E. and Tong, J., Attributed based access control (ABAC) for Web services, In Proceedings of Intl. Conf. on Web Services (ICWS), 2005.

Zhang, R., Artale, A., Giunchiglia, F. and Crispo, B., Using description logics in relation based access control, International Workshop on Description Logics (CEUR Workshop Proceedings), 2009, Grau et al. (eds.).

Zhao, C., Heilili, N. M., Liu, S. and Lin, Z., Representation and reasoning on RBAC: A description logic approach, *Theoretical Aspects of Computing—ICTAC,* Hung, D. V. and Wirsing, M. (Eds.), pp. 381–393, LNCS 3722, Springer-Verlag, Berlin, Heidelberg, 2005.

A Language for Provenance Access Control

9.1 Overview

In Chapter 8, we discussed the design of a scalable and efficient access control model for securing both data and its provenance. We assumed that both the traditional data and provenance were represented in a RDF format and therefore we could take advantage of an integrated Semantic Web environment to represent and reason over RBAC policies. Besides the scalability and efficiency of an access control mechanism for managing a provenance system, there are other concerns we need to address before we arrive at a unified framework for provenance.

Traditional access control models focus on individual data items, whereas in provenance we are concerned with protecting both the data items and their relationships (Braun et al. 2008). The various paths in a provenance graph from a resource to all its sources are important in proving the validity of that resource. Furthermore, these paths contain the pertinent information needed to verify the integrity of the data and establish trust between a user and the data. However, we do not want to divulge any exclusive information in the path that could be used by an adversary to gain advantages (for example, in military intelligence).

Our main focus in this chapter is on the definition of an access control policy language for provenance. With this language, we can treat provenance not only as being comprised of single data items but also as paths in a connected directed graph. This language also retains the properties of traditional access control to

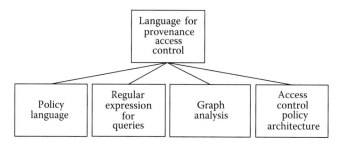

Figure 9.1   Language for provenance access control.

gain access to data. Furthermore, the language provides an additional advantage whereby provenance not only acts as an access control mechanism, but also as an integrity mechanism for giving access to the data. We also describe a prototype that uses Semantic Web technologies and allows a user to query for data and provenance based on access control policies defined using our policy language.

The organization of this chapter is as follows. In Section 9.2 we discuss the challenges involved and the drawbacks of the current approaches. In Section 9.3 we describe our policy language. Our approach based on regular expressions queries is discussed in Section 9.4. Graph analysis is discussed in Section 9.5. We describe our architecture in Section 9.6. Our use case with a medical example is discussed in Section 9.7. Our prototype and experiments are discussed in Section 9.8. The chapter is summarized in Section 9.9. Figure 9.1 illustrates the concept discussed in this chapter.

9.2   Challenges and Drawbacks

The major challenges we face in implementing an access control policy for provenance are related to the definition of a provenance resource. This identification is one of the major distinguishing factors between a provenance access control model and existing access control models. In order to define an access control policy for provenance, it is imperative that we identify the parts of the provenance graph that we want to protect. Therefore, we must have a clear definition of the users, their actions, and the resources to be protected. Provenance takes the form of a directed acyclic graph (DAG) that establishes causal relationships between data items (Moreau et al. 2009). The provenance graph structure not only poses challenges to access control models but also to querying languages (Holland et al. 2008).

9.2.1   Drawbacks of Current Access Control Mechanisms

An access control policy authorizes a set of *users* to perform a set of *actions* on a set of *resources* within an *environment*. Unless authorized through one or more access control policies, users have no access to any resource of the system. There are many access control policies defined in the literature. These can be grouped into three main classes that differ by the constraints they place on the sets of *users, actions,* and *objects* (access control models often refer to resources as objects) (Samarati and de Vimercati 2001). These classes are (1) RBAC, which restricts access based on roles, (2) DAC, which controls access based on the identity of the user, and (3) MAC, which controls access based on mandated regulations determined by a central authority. There are two major concerns with these policies. The first is the number of user to object assignments and the second is that these policies are defined over a single resource.

RBAC models have enjoyed popularity by simplifying the management of security policies. These models depend on the definition of roles as an intermediary between users and permissions (which is a combination of actions and objects). The core model defines two assignments: a user-assignment that associates users with roles and a permission-assignment that associates roles with permissions. In Ferraiolo et al. (2003), the authors argue that there is a direct relationship between the cost of administration and the number of mappings that must be managed. The drawbacks with using RBAC include (1) a new role is needed each time a user does not have access to an object through an existing role, and (2) as the policies become more fine-grained, a role is needed for each combination of the different resources in the provenance (Rosenthal et al. 2009).

Clearly, applying these traditional access control policies for fine-grained access control in provenance would result in prohibitive management costs. Moreover, their usage in provenance would be an arduous task for the administrator. In Section 9.4, we provide an analysis that shows that the number of resources in a provenance graph is exponential in the number of nodes in the graph. We address these drawbacks in this chapter and provide an implementation of a prototype mechanism, which shows that we can greatly reduce these mappings.

We need appropriate access control mechanisms for provenance that prevent the improper disclosure of any sensitive information along a path in the provenance graph. We need to extend the traditional access control definition that protects a single data item to one where we now want to protect any resources along a path of arbitrary length. In summary, the general expectations of an access control language for provenance are (1) to be able to define policies over a directed acyclic graph, (2) to support a fine-grained access control on any component of the graph, and (3) to seamlessly integrate existing organizational policies.

9.3 Policy Language

We propose a policy language that extends the definition of traditional access control languages to allow specification of policies over data items and their relationships in a provenance graph. This language will allow a policy author to write policies that specify who accesses these resources. The language provides natural support for traditional access control policies over data items.

We provide an adaptation of the access control language for provenance given in Ni et al. (2009). We extend the syntax of this XML policy language in order to incorporate regular expressions in the policy. This existing provenance language in Ni et al. (2009) was developed as a generalized model of access control for provenance but did not address resources with arbitrary path lengths within the provenance graph. Therefore, it now suffers from the fact that a resource must be identified beforehand rather than be given as a string that is matched against the graph at execution time.

An example of our adaptation of the language in Ni et al. (2009) is shown in Figure 9.2, which now allows the policy to be written using the regular expression syntax. We place an emphasis on the target, effect, and condition elements given in Ni et al. (2009), but make slight modifications to their meanings to incorporate regular expressions on a provenance graph. Since our focus in this chapter is on specifying a policy for access control in provenance, we provide only the relevant XML elements in this chapter. The interested reader can find other interesting elements of the language, such as obligation and originator preference, in Ni et al. (2009).

The description of each element in Figure 9.2 is as follows:

- The *subject* element can be the name of a user or any collection of users (e.g., physician or surgeon) or a special user collection *anyuser* that represents all users.
- The *record* element is the name of a resource.
- The *restriction* element is an (optional) element that refines the applicability established by the subject or record.
- The *scope* element is an (optional) element that is used to indicate whether the target applies only to the record or its entire ancestry.

```
<policy ID="1">
<target>
<subject>anyuser</subject>
<record>Doc1_2</record>
<restriction>
    Doc1_2 [WasGeneratedBy] process AND
    process [WasControlledBy]
physician|surgeon
</restriction>
<scope>non-transferable</scope>
</target>
<condition>purpose == research</condition>
<effect>Permit</effect>
</policy>
```

Figure 9.2 Policy language.

- The *condition* element is an (optional) element that describes under what conditions access is to be given or denied to a user.
- The *effect* element indicates the policy author's intended consequence for a true evaluation of a policy.

The scope element is useful, in particular, when we want to protect the record only if it is along a specified path in the provenance graph. This is achieved by using the predefined value "nontransferable." This element can also be used when we need to protect a path in the provenance graph if a particular record is along that path. This is achieved by the predefined value "transferable." The condition element is necessary when we want to specify system or context parameters for giving access, such as permitting access to the provenance when it is being used for research. It is important that we keep the number of policies to a minimum by combining them using regular expressions. This will improve the effectiveness of an access control system that protects sensitive information from unauthorized users. It was also pointed out in Ni et al. (2009) that when the policy size is not small, detecting abnormal policies is essentially an SAT problem (Boolean Satisfiability). The reason is that the effects of different semantics for the predicates used in the condition and restriction elements may cause incorrect policy specifications, which may generate conflicting or redundant policies.

We achieve fine-grained access control by allowing a record value to be any (indivisible) part of a provenance graph. The regular expressions in the "restriction" element allow us to define policies over paths of arbitrary length in a provenance graph that apply to a subject or record. Also, since XML is an open and extensible language, our policy language is both customizable and readily supports integration of other policies.

The grammar. We define a grammar for each of the tags in the language we propose.

```
<exp>  :: = <char>+ ("." <char>+)?
<char> :: = [a-z] | [A-Z] | "_" | "-" |
<reg>  :: = "*" | "+" | "?"
<bool> :: = " AND " | " OR " | "|"
<op>   :: = " = = " | " < = " | " > = " | " < " | " > "
<num>  :: = ([0-9])+
<sp>   :: = "[" <exp> "]"
```

We now define the set of strings accepted by each element in our language.

```
subject = <char>+ | <num>

record = <exp>

restriction = (<exp><num>?)+ (<op> | <sp><reg>?)
        (<exp><num>?)+
        (<bool> (<exp><num>?)+
        (<op> | <sp><reg>?)? (<exp><num>?)+)*
```

```
scope = <char>+

condition = (<exp><num>?)+ (<op> | <sp><reg>?)
        (<exp><num>?)+
        (<bool> (<exp><num>?)+
        (<op> | <sp><reg>?)? (<exp><num>?)+)*

effect = <char>+ | <num>
```

The grammar defined above allows us to evaluate the policy for correctness and also allows a parser to unambiguously translate the policy into a form that can be used by the appropriate layer in our architecture.

9.4 Solution Based on Regular Expression Queries

The traditional definition of access control policies is extended in our policy language to include relationships over data items in the provenance graph by making use of regular expressions. The use of an existing access control language to build policies over the provenance graph would require enumerating all the possible paths that we want to protect in the graph as separate policies. The use of regular expressions in our language not only solves this problem, since many paths can be specified using the same regular expression, but also allows the same policy to be applied to multiple provenance graphs.

Consider a medical example where we may want to give access to everything in a patient's record that was updated by processes controlled only by the patient's physician and surgeon. For this example, the system would evaluate two policies. The first policy would check if the user has access to the medical record. This policy would be applied over all the medical records in the system with the traditional access control policies in place. The second policy would check if the patient's medical record has indeed only been modified by the patient's physician and surgeon. This second policy would be applied over the provenance graph associated with the given medical record. This example not only shows how existing access control policies can be integrated in our language, but also how traditional access control can be used to allow access to provenance.

In contrast to the previous example, these regular expressions can be used to first verify the quality of the data items and second, act as a "pseudo" access control mechanism for giving data access to the user. Consider a military example where access to an intelligence report can only be given to a user if the report was created by a particular field agent belonging to a specific agency in a particular country. In this example, the system would evaluate the regular expression in the policy over the provenance graph for the given intelligence report to check if that report was indeed created by the specified field agent belonging to the given agency in the specified country. If such a path exists in the provenance graph, only then is access granted to the querying user for the report. This example emphasizes how provenance can be used to first determine the integrity of the data in order to guarantee high-quality information before access to the actual data items is given.

9.4.1 Data Representation

We require a suitable data representation for storing provenance. Such a data representation must naturally support the directed graph structure of provenance and also allow path queries of arbitrary length. OPM does not specify protocols for storing or querying provenance information but it does specify properties that any data model should have (Moreau et al. 2009). One such property includes allowing provenance information to be shared among systems. Provenance data can be stored in the relational database model, the XML data model, or the RDF data model (Klyne et al. 2004). Each of these in their current form has drawbacks with respect to provenance (Holland et al. 2008). A relational model suffers from the fact that it needs expensive joins on relations (tables) for storing edges or paths. Also, current SQL languages that support transitive queries are complex and awkward to write. XML supports path queries, but the current query languages XQuery and XPath only support a tree structure. RDF naturally supports a graph structure, but the current W3C Recommendation for SPARQL (the standard query language for RDF) lacks many features needed for path queries. There are recent works on extending SPARQL with path expressions and variables. These include SPARQL Query 1.1, which is now a W3C recommendation. The SPARQL 1.1 query language includes new features such as aggregates, subqueries, property paths, negation, and regular expressions, but this is still a W3C Working Draft as of this writing (Harris and Seaborne 2010).

In the case of access control in provenance, we may have two different sets of access control policies: one for traditional access control and one for provenance access control. This may result in the management of two different sets of policies if both the traditional data items and provenance are placed in the same data store. If we allow this scenario, all requests from a user would be evaluated against both the policies for the traditional access control and the policies for provenance. This would be the case even when the user is only working with the traditional data and is not requesting the provenance information. In general, the lineage or ancestry of a data item may involve many sources and processes that influence a resource. Recording all these sources and paths may result in very large databases. Therefore, provenance may grow much faster than the actual data items and may be better served by a separate database. To this end, we will use a separate data store for provenance in our design of an architecture and prototype for provenance.

9.4.2 Graph Data Model

Of the many data models in the literature, we model our prototype based on an RDF data representation for provenance. This data model meets the specification of the OPM recommendation. RDF allows the integration of multiple databases describing the different pieces of the lineage of a resource and naturally supports the directed structure of provenance. This data model has been successfully applied for provenance capture and representation (Ding et al. 2005; Zhao et al. 2008).

The RDF terminology T is the union of three pairwise disjoint infinite sets of terms: the set U of URI references, the set L of literals (itself partitioned into two sets, the set L_p of plain literals and the set L_t of typed literals), and the set B of blanks. The set $U \cup L$ of names is called the vocabulary.

We can view each RDF triple (s,p,o) as an arc from s to o, where p is used to label the arc. This is represented as $s \xrightarrow{p} o$. Our provenance graph is constructed from a set of these RDF triples. RDF is intended to make assertions about a resource. This includes making multiple assertions about the same two resources; for example, a heart surgery h was controlled by a surgeon s, and the inverse relation: s performed a heart surgery h. This would be modeled as a directed loop in an RDF graph. In order to preserve the properties of a provenance graph, we need to place restrictions on the assertions made in a RDF graph. That is, we require a directed acyclic RDF graph to retain the causal dependencies among the nodes as needed in provenance.

Definition 9.1: Provenance Graph

Our provenance graph is a restricted RDF graph with the following properties:

1. Causality. For any RDF triple (s,p,o) (represented graphically as $s \xrightarrow{p} o$), s is causally dependent on o. We refer to s as the effect and o as the cause of s.
2. Acyclic. For any cause o and effect s there exists no path from o to s.

■

Let $H = (V,E)$ be a RDF graph where V is a set of nodes with $|V| = n$, and $E \subseteq (V \times V)$ is a set of ordered pairs called edges. A provenance graph $G = (V_G, E_G)$ with n entities is defined as $G \subseteq H$, $V_G = V$ and $E_G \subseteq E$ such that G is a directed graph with no directed cycles.

We define a resource in a provenance graph recursively as follows:

- The sets V_G and E_G are resources.
- ε is a resource.

- The set of provenance graphs are closed under intersection, union, and set difference. Let H_1 and H_2 be two provenance graphs, then $H_1 \cup H_2$, $H_1 \cap H_2$ and $H_1 - H_2$ are resources, such that if $t \in H_1 \cup H_2$ then $t \in H_1$ or $t \in H_2$; if $t \in H_1 \cap H_2$ then $t \in H_1$ and $t \in H_2$; or if $t \in H_1 - H_2$ then $t \in H_1$ and $t \notin H_2$.

9.4.3 Provenance Vocabulary

We define the nodes in the provenance graph using the nomenclature in Moreau et al. (2009). This nomenclature defines three entities: artifacts, processes, and agents. These entities form the nodes in V_G in our provenance graph G. An artifact is an immutable piece of state that may have a physical embodiment in a physical object or a digital representation in a computer system (Moreau 2009). A process is an action or series of actions performed on or caused by artifacts and resulting in new artifacts (Moreau 2009). An agent is a contextual entity acting as a catalyst of a process, enabling, facilitating, controlling, and affecting its execution (Moreau 2009). In RDF representation, an artifact, a process, and an agent could be represented as

```
<opm:Agent><rdf:type><opm:Entity>
<opm:Artifact><rdf:type><opm:Entity>
<opm:Process><rdf:type><opm:Entity>
```

The property rdf:type is used to indicate the class of a resource and the prefix opm: is reserved for the entities and relationships in the OPM nomenclature in Moreau et al. (2009).

Let V_G be the set of names appearing in a provenance graph G and $V_G^P \subseteq V_G$ be a set of names on the arcs in G. The label on each $e \in V_G^P$ defines a relationship between the entities in G and also allows us to navigate across the different nodes by a single hop. A list of predicate names in V_G^P describing the causal relationships among the nodes in G are as follows:

```
<opm:Process><opm:WasControlledBy><opm:Agent>
<opm:Process><opm:Used><opm:Artifact>
<opm:Artifact><opm:WasDerivedFrom><opm:Artifact>
<opm:Artifact><opm:WasGeneratedBy><opm:Process>
<opm:Process><opm:WasTriggeredBy><opm:Process>
```

These predicates are the ones defined in Moreau (2009) and they form the edges in our edge set, E_G, in our provenance graph G.

Definition 9.2: Path

A path in an RDF graph is a sequence of RDF triples, where the object of each triple in the sequence coincides with the subject of its successor triple in the sequence. ■

Definition 9.3: Provenance Path

In G, a provenance path (s,p,o) is a path $s(\xrightarrow{\;p\;})o$ that is defined over the provenance vocabulary $\mathcal{V}_G^P$ using regular expressions. ■

Definition 9.4: Regular Expressions

Let Σ be an alphabet of terms in $\mathcal{U} \cap \mathcal{V}_G^P$, then the set $RE\,(\Sigma)$ of regular expressions is inductively defined by

- $\forall\, x \in \Sigma,\, x \in RE(\Sigma)$
- $\Sigma \in RE(\Sigma)$
- $\varepsilon \in RE(\Sigma)$
- If $A \in RE(\Sigma)$ and $B \in RE(\Sigma)$ then

$$A|B,\; A/B,\; A^*,\; A^+,\; A? \in RE(\Sigma).$$

■

The symbols $|$ and $/$ are interpreted as logical OR and composition, respectively.

Our intention is to define paths between two nodes by edges equipped with * for paths of arbitrary length, including length 0 or + for paths that have at least length 1. Therefore, for two nodes x,y and predicate name $p, x(\xrightarrow{\;p\;})^*\, y$ and $x(\xrightarrow{\;p\;})^+\, y$ are paths in G.

9.4.4 Path Queries

SPARQL is based around graph pattern matching (Prud'hommeaux and Seaborne 2006).

Definition 9.5: Graph Pattern

A SPARQL graph pattern expression is defined recursively as follows:

1. A triple pattern is a graph pattern
2. If P1 and P2 are graph patterns, then expressions (P1 AND P2), (P1 OPT P2), and (P1 UNION P2) are graph patterns

3. If P is a graph pattern and R is a built-in SPARQL condition, then the expression (P FILTER R) is a graph pattern
4. If P is a graph pattern, V is a set of variables and $X \in \mathcal{U} \cup V$, then (X GRAPH P) is a graph pattern

The current W3C recommendation for SPARQL does not support paths of arbitrary length; therefore, extensions are needed to answer the queries over the provenance graph (Detwiler et al. 2008). Many approaches to supporting paths of arbitrary length have been proposed in the literature, which include Alkhateeb et al. (2009), Detwiler et al. (2008), and Koch et al. (2005). A W3C recommendation extending SPARQL to support property paths can be found in Harris and Seaborne (2010). We use the following basic SELECT query structure to map a regular expression that is part of a policy or part of a user provenance query into a query over the provenance graph.

$$\text{SELECT } \vec{B} \text{ WHERE P}$$

where P is a graph pattern and $\vec{B}$ is a tuple of variables appearing in P.

9.5 Graph Analysis

In this section, we evaluate the impact of querying over a provenance graph with many subgraphs as resources. We will first address the complexity of protecting the resources in a provenance-directed acyclic graph (digraph) and then examine the case where two digraphs overlap, which may conflict with each other.

9.5.1 Analysis of Digraphs

We now provide a simple analysis addressing the concerns with traditional access control policies. We use the convention that a permission is a unique pair of (*action*, *resource*). Given n resources, m users, and a set of only two actions (read, write), we have a maximum of $2 \times n$ possible permissions. This gives $m \times (2 \times n) = c_1 n$ mappings. To analyze RBAC, we assume the case where there is at least one role with two or more users assigned to it from a possible set of r roles. Therefore, we have $r \times (2 \times n) = c_2 n$ mappings and we also assume that $c_2 n \leq c_1$.

We continue our analysis by considering the varying number of relationships among the resources in a provenance graph. We assume that we have n nodes in our graph G. The first case is when the provenance paths are of length 0. This is similar to the case of access control policies over single resources. Next we consider the case where the provenance paths are of length 1. This is equivalent to counting the number of edges in E_G. We use the notion that a resource is a set of triples in G and therefore a resource is a directed acyclic graph (or digraph) from among all the allowed digraphs that can be formed from *G*. In general, the total number of ways of constructing a digraph from *n* nodes in Robinson (1971, 1977) is given recursively as

$$a_n = \sum_{k=1}^{n} (-1)^{k-1} \binom{n}{k} 2^{k(n-k)} a_{n-k} \tag{9.1}$$

Given *n* nodes in a provenance graph *G*, a_n would represent the upper limit of resources to be protected in *G*. The work done in Robinson (1977) shows that the number of ways of constructing a directed acyclic graph is exponential in the size of *n* single resources.

In general, a node in a digraph can have both an in-degree and an out-degree. OPM restricts the relationships we can have among the nodes in a provenance graph (see Moreau 2009 for a formal definition of a provenance graph). This restriction is on the dependency relationships involving agents; in simple terms the only relation involving an agent is a directed edge from a process to an agent. That is, agents in a provenance graph can only have an in-degree, and although this restriction limits the maximum number of resources to be protected (as given in Equation 9.1) by a factor, the upper bound for the maximum number of digraphs is still exponential. The OPM specification for a provenance graph describes how to trace an artifact or process back to its direct source (or cause), which could be a process, an artifact, or an agent, using the edges in the graph. It does not, however, provide a standard arc name that explains the causes or sources for an agent in the graph. Therefore, a more useful definition of provenance according to OPM in the context of our analysis would describe how an artifact or process came to be in its current form. This definition is still consistent with the ones in the literature. Hence, even in the cases where we only consider *n'* artifacts and processes in our provenance graph, where $2 \leq n' \leq n$, the number of digraphs is still exponential in *n'*.

A traditional access control policy would first require identifying a provenance path and then expressing a policy for each of the resources on this path. The regular expressions presented in Section 9.4 allow us to specify a pattern for resources that need to be protected with an access control policy. Since a regular expression pattern can match many paths (each of arbitrary length), we can replace all policies that protect a resource on any of these paths with one policy.

9.5.2 Composition of Digraphs

Access control systems normally contain policies that are used to handle situations where two policies have opposite values for the *effect* element of a policy. This happens when one policy has a permit (or positive authorization) effect whenever it evaluates to true, while another policy has a deny (or negative authorization) whenever it evaluates to true, and both of these policies protect the same digraph. The conflict could be a result of two policies overlapping with each other to form a common digraph or when a digraph associated with a negative authorization overlaps with a digraph that results from the execution of a user's query. Different conflict resolution policies have been proposed to resolve conflicts that result from opposite access authorizations on a resource (Samarati and de Vimercati 2001). These policies include Denials-take-precedence, Most-specific-takes-precedence, and Most-specific-along-a-path-takes-precedence.

There are three possibilities that could occur when two digraphs overlap with each other. We discuss these possibilities when the Denials-take-precedence conflict resolution policy is applied.

1. $G1 \subseteq G2$. The digraph $G1$ is associated with a policy that denies viewing its contents and the digraph $G2$ is associated with a policy that permits viewing of its contents. In this situation, the system would have the effect of permitting viewing of the digraph $G2-G1$.
2. $G1 \supseteq G2$. The digraph $G1$ is associated with a policy that denies viewing its contents and the digraph $G2$ is associated with a policy that permits viewing of its contents. In this situation, the user would be denied from viewing the contents of both $G1$ and $G2$.
3. $G1 \cap G2$. The digraph $G1$ is associated with a policy that denies viewing its contents and the digraph $G2$ is associated with a policy that permits viewing its contents. In this situation, the system would have the effect of denying access to digraphs $G1$ and $G1 \cap G2$.

These three cases also apply when a user's query execution returns the digraph $G2$, and the effect of the policy for $G1$ is "deny."

9.6 Access Control Policy Architecture

Our system architecture assumes that the available information is divided into two parts: the actual data and provenance. Both the data and provenance are represented as RDF graphs. The reader should note that we do not make any assumptions about how the actual information is stored. A user may have stored data and provenance in two different triple stores or in the same store. Access control policies are defined in our XML-based language for both the data and the provenance. These policies define access for users on resources in the data graph and on agents, artifacts, processes, and paths in the provenance. A user application can submit a query for access to the data and its associated provenance or vice versa. In this discussion we first present the various modules in our prototype implementation. We then give an example of a scenario where the user already has access to the data item and is requesting additional information from the provenance. The same logic applies when we want to give high-quality information to a user where we would first verify the information against the provenance store before allowing access to the data item.

9.6.1 Modules in Access Control Policy Architecture

We now present a detailed description of the different layers in Figure 9.3 followed by an example.

User Interface Layer. The User Interface Layer is an abstraction layer that allows a user to interact with the system. A user can pose either a data query or provenance query to this layer. This layer determines whether the query should be evaluated against the data or provenance. Our interface hides the use of regular expression queries (i.e., the actual internal representation of a provenance query) from a user by providing a simple question-answer mechanism. This mechanism allows the user to pose standard provenance queries such as why a data item was created, where in the provenance graph it was generated, how the data item was generated, and when and in what location it was created. We show an example of a provenance query in Figure 9.5a that a user would pose to the system. This layer also returns results after they have been examined against the access control policies.

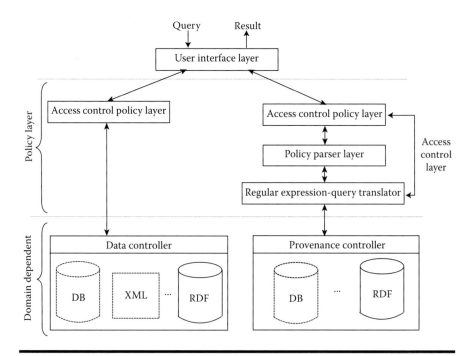

Figure 9.3   Access control policy layer.

Access Control Policy Layer. The Access Control Policy Layer is responsible for ensuring that the querying user is authorized to use the system. It also enforces the access control policies against the user query and results to make sure that no sensitive information is released to unauthorized users. This layer also resolves any conflicts that resulted from executing the policies over the data stores. An example of a provenance policy that can be used in this layer is given in Figure 9.3.

Policy Parser Layer. The Policy Parser Layer is a program that takes as input a policy set and parses each policy to extract the information in each element. The parser verifies that the structure of the policy conforms to a predefined XML schema. Further, the parser also validates the value of each element in a policy using the grammar specified in Section 9.3.

Regular Expression-Query Translator. The regular expression-query translator takes a valid regular expression string and builds a corresponding graph pattern from these strings. It associates a provenance query from a user to a corresponding template query by invoking the necessary parameters associated with the user's provenance query. For example, Figure 9.5a shows a user query and the corresponding translation in Figure 9.5b.

Data Controller. The data controller is a suite of software programs that stores and manages access to data. The data could be stored in any format such as in a relational database, in XML files, or in an RDF store. The controller accepts requests for information from the access control policy layer if a policy allows the requesting user access to a data item. This layer then executes the request over the stored data and returns results back to the access control policy layer where it is reevaluated based on the access control policies.

Provenance Controller. The provenance controller is used to store and manage provenance information that is associated with data items that are present in the data controller. The provenance controller stores information in the form of logical graph structures in any appropriate data representation format. This controller also records the on-going activities associated with the data items stored in the data controller. This controller takes as input a regular expression query and evaluates it over the provenance information. This query evaluation returns a subgraph back to the access control layer where it is reexamined using the access control policies.

9.7 Use Case: Medical Example

In this section we provide examples of provenance queries. These queries can be used to identify resources for a policy or identify the answer for a user query. The examples in this section are based on the provenance graph in Figure 9.4. This provenance graph shows a workflow that updates a fictitious record for a patient who went through three medical stages at a hospital. In the first phase, the physician performed a checkup on the patient. At checkup, the physician consulted the history in the patient's record, med:Doc1_1 and performed the task of recording

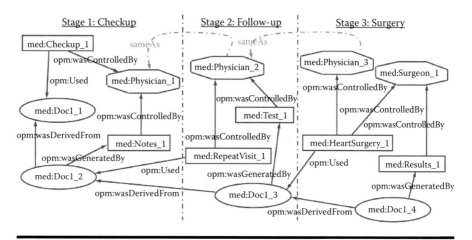

Figure 9.4 Provenance graph.

notes about the patient. At the end of the checkup, the physician then updated the patient's record, which resulted in a newer version, med:Docl_2. In the second phase, the patient returned for a follow-up visit at the physician's request. During this visit, the physician consulted with the patient's record for a review of the patient's history and then performed a series of tests on the patient. At the end of this visit, the physician then updated the patient's record, which results in a newer version, med:Docl_3. In the third phase, the patient returned to undergo heart surgery. This was ordered by the patient's physician and carried out by a resident surgeon. Before the surgeon started the surgery operation, a careful review of the patient's record was performed by both the patient's physician and surgeon. During the surgery process, the surgeon performed the task of recording the results at each stage of the heart surgery process. At the end of the surgery, the patient's record was updated by the surgeon, which resulted in a newer version, med:Docl_4.

We assume that a hospital has a standard set of procedures that govern every health care service that the hospital provides. Therefore, each patient that needs to use a health care service will need to go through this set of procedures. We use a fixed set of notations in Figure 9.4 to represent an entity in the provenance graph; for example

```
<med:Checkup_n_1>.
```

The "n" denotes a particular patient who is undergoing a procedure at the hospital. Therefore, n = 1 identifies a patient with id = 1, n = 2 identifies a patient with id = 2, and so on. A larger number in the suffix of each process, agent, and artifact signifies that the particular provenance entity is used at a later stage in a medical procedure. In practice, "n" would be instantiated with an actual patient id; this leads to the following set of RDF triples for a patient with id = 1 at stage 1:

Table 9.1   RDF Annotations

Entity	RDF annotation
Process	Performed on
Agent	Name, sex, age, and zip code
Artifact	Updated on

```
<med:Checkup_1_1><opm:WasControlledBy><med:Physician_1_1>
<med:Checkup_1_1><opm:Used><med:Doc_1_1>
<med:Doc_1_2><opm:WasDerivedFrom><med:Doc_1_1>
<med:Doc_1_2><opm:WasGeneratedBy><med:Notes_1_1>
<med:Notes_1_1><opm:WasControlledBy><med:Physician_1_1>
```

The sameAs annotations on the light shaded arrows illustrate that the reference to physician is meant to be the same person in all the three phases. We use Figure 9.4 as a running example through the rest of this thesis.

This is not a complete picture of the provenance graph; it would be further annotated with RDF triples to indicate for example, location, time, and other contextual information. Each entity in the graph would have a unique set of RDF annotations based on its type. Table 9.1 shows a set of compatible annotations for each type of provenance entity. A usage of these annotations in RDF representation for a physician associated with a patient with id = 1 would be

```
<med:Physician_1_1><med:Name> "John Smith"
<med:Physician_1_1><med:Sex> "M"
<med:Physician_1_1><med:Age> "35"
<med:Physician_1_1><med:Zip> "76543"
```

9.7.1 Query Templates

We can use the set of names in $\mathcal{V}_G$ to answer common queries about provenance such as why-provenance, where-provenance, and how-provenance (Moreau 2009). To anticipate the varying number of queries a user could ask, we create templates that are parameterized for a specific type of user query. This simplifies the construction of queries by allowing us to map a user query to a suitable template. This in turn allows us to build an interface through which a user could interact with the system as well as create an abstraction layer that hides the details of the graph from the user.

Why Query:

```
med:Doc1_3 gleen:OnPath("([opm:WasDerivedFrom] |
[opm:WasGeneratedBy] | [opm:WasTriggeredBy] |
[opm:WasControlledBy] | [Used])*" ?x).
```

This allows us to specify all the resources reachable from med:Doc1_3 by issuing a query against the provenance graph. This query explains why med:Doc1_3 came to be in its current form. Figure 9.5 shows a part of the graph in Figure 9.4 that would result from executing a why-provenance query.

Where Query:

```
med:Doc1_4 gleen:OnPath("([opm:WasDerivedFrom] |
[opm:WasGeneratedBy])" ?x).
```

This query would return the following triples:

```
(med:Doc1_4, opm:WasDerivedFrom, med:Doc1_3)
(med:Doc1_4, opm:WasGeneratedBy, med:Results_1)
```

A where query would be useful if we need to pinpoint where in the process a possible risk could occur as a result of performing a surgery on the patient. For example, a where-provenance could be used to identify at which phase in the flow any medication administered to the patient had a negative interaction with the ones the patient is already taking. By using this query, we could compare the information in med:Doc1_3 with those in med:Doc1_4 (which incorporates the recording of events during the surgery operation).

9.7.2 Additional Templates

The OPM in general allows us to extend $\mathcal{V}_G$ to support annotations on the nodes and edges in our provenance graph (Moreau et al. 2009). These annotations allow us to capture additional information relevant to provenance such as time and location

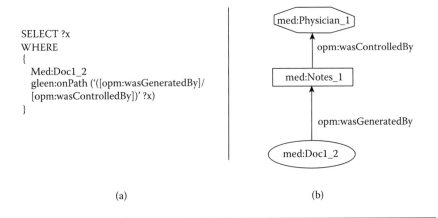

```
SELECT ?x
WHERE
{
  Med:Doc1_2
  gleen:onPath ('([opm:wasGeneratedBy]/
  [opm:wasControlledBy])' ?x)
}
```

(a)

(b)

Figure 9.5 Why query.

that pertain to execution. The annotations are not part of the vocabulary provided by OPM. The idea of not providing annotations as part of the predicate vocabulary is to allow a user the flexibility of creating his or her own vocabulary for the nodes and edges. The annotations themselves can be added as RDF triples since RDF allows us to make assertions about any node in a RDF graph. This allows us to capture more contextual information about resources, which in turn would allow us to model the provenance information to capture the semantics of the domain. While a particular causal relation, such as process P_2 was triggered by process P_1, may imply that P_1 occurs before P_2 on a single logical clock, it does not tell us the exact physical time both processes occur. Such additional information plays a critical role in the intelligence domain. These additional annotations allow us to build more templates, which give our prototype the ability to respond to queries like when was a resource generated, what was a resource based on, and at which location was a resource created or modified. We show a simple example of a when query below:

When Query

```
Select ?x
{
med:Doc1_4 med:modifiedOn ?x.
}
```

This query would return the timestamp value as a binding for the variable ?x if the graph pattern in the where clause successfully matches a triple in the extended annotated provenance graph.

9.7.3 Access Control Example

We show an example of how a user query and a policy query are executed in our prototype system. The user query given in Figure 9.6a is submitted to the User Interface Layer. This query asks for a complete explanation of why Doc1_2 came to be in existence. Doc1_2 is an internal node in the example provenance graph. This means that the user would have had access for the actual patient record in the traditional database before submitting a query about its provenance. Our Regular Expression-Query Translator in the Access Control Layer would transform this query into the query shown in Figure 9.6b. The result of executing this query against the provenance graph shown in Figure 9.4 returns the results shown in Figure 9.6c. This result is passed back to the Access Control Policy Layer. This layer also passes the policy given in Figure 9.2 to the Policy Parser Layer that parses the policy against an XML schema and the grammar given in Section 9.3. If the policy is well constructed, it is passed to the Regular Expression-Query Translator Layer that constructs the query given in Figure 9.6a. This query is also evaluated against the provenance graph in Figure 9.4. The result of this query execution would return the digraph shown in Figure 9.6d. This digraph represents the resource that the

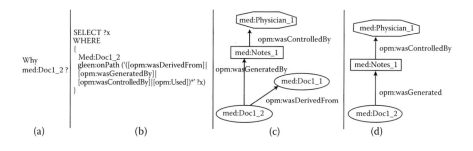

Figure 9.6 A resource protected by a policy.

policy is protecting and is returned back to the Access Control Layer. The Access Control Layer would then compare the resource from Figure 9.6c with the digraph in Figure 9.6d. Since the digraph in Figure 9.6c contains the digraph in Figure 9.6d, the Access Control Policy Layer would need to execute the effect that is given in the policy. Since in this case, the effect is Permit, the results in Figure 9.6c are passed to the User Interface Layer that in turn will return the results to the user. For the second case where we want to verify the integrity of the data, the process will be the same as described above, except that the user query would be about a leaf node stored in the traditional database and this leaf node is the last node of an ancestral chain in provenance.

9.8 Prototype

To implement the layers in our architecture we use various open-source tools. To implement the Access Control Layer, we use the policy files written in XML 1.0 and Java 1.6 to write the logic that enforces the policies. To implement the Policy Parser Layer, we use Java 1.6 and the XML schema specification. The XML schema allows us to verify the structure of our policy file. This layer was also programmed to apply the grammar in Section 9.3 against the values in the elements in the policies stored in the policy file. To implement the Regular Expression-Query Translator, we use the Gleen regular expression library. This library extends SPARQL to support querying over a RDF graph using regular expressions (Detwiler et al. 2008). To create the provenance store, we use the OPM toolbox (http://openprovenance. org/). This toolbox allows us to programmatically build workflows that use the OPM vocabulary and also allows us to generate RDF graphs corresponding to the workflow (with some tweaking to generate the RDF graphs for this prototype). There are other tools that support automatic provenance generation such as Taverna (Oinn et al. 2004), but they are not as easy to use as the OPM toolbox. We use the OPM vocabulary, which is based on RDF rather than existing vocabularies that have support for a more expressive representation of provenance, for example the vocabulary specification in (Zhao 2010). Our aim in this chapter is to demonstrate a general way of navigating a provenance graph rather than capturing the semantics of the domain associated with the provenance paths.

We use synthetic data to build in-memory models using the Jena API (Carroll et al. 2004, http://jena.sourceforge.net/). This tool allows us to add annotations to the existing RDF triples generated from executing the provenance workflows. We then issue different provenance queries such as why, where, how, when, and who against each of the provenance graphs in the Jena model. The graphs vary in size, as shown in Figures 9.7 and 9.8. The execution times vary for each query template as well. A why-provenance query retrieves the transitive closure of the edges that justifies the existence of the resource, and so its execution time varies as the number of triples in its transitive closure grows. The main impact on the how-provenance execution time is the length of each ancestry chain starting from the resource. A how-provenance query returns a polynomial representation of the structure of the proof explaining how the resource was derived. This normally involves counting the number of times a provenance entity occurs at the beginning of an ancestry-chain for the resource. The other queries show almost constant execution times ranging from 1 to 2 ms. This is not surprising since these queries usually retrieve provenance information in the locality of the resource; for example, the when query just returns the RDF triple whose subject is the resource and whose predicate associates a time value with the resource and the where-provenance query finds the entities whose contents create the resource (i.e., where the resource was copied from).

Our experiments were conducted on a Dell Inspiron 2.4 GHz with 8-GB RAM. For each pair of query and Jena model, we use the average execution time

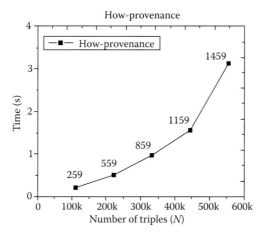

Figure 9.7   Why-provenance queries.

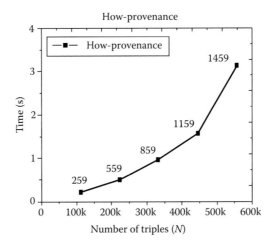

Figure 9.8 How-provenance queries.

for the longest diameter in the graph. Each point of the graphs in Figures 9.7 and 9.8 is labeled with the longest diameter, which is the path with the most edges starting from the resource. This approximates the maximum number of hops needed to create a new digraph from the original provenance graph involving the starting resource. Our prototype is efficient for both finding the provenance resources (which involve single resources and their relationships) that an access control system is protecting and for finding the provenance resources a querying user is requesting.

9.9 Summary and Directions

Our main contribution in this chapter is the definition of an access control policy language for provenance. With this language, we can treat provenance not only as being comprised of single data items, but also as paths in a connected directed graph. This language also retains the properties of traditional access control to gain access to data. Furthermore, the language provides an additional advantage whereby provenance not only acts as an access control mechanism, but also as an integrity mechanism for giving access to the data. We also described a prototype that utilizes Semantic Web technologies and allows a user to query for data and provenance based on access control policies defined using our policy language.

In this chapter, we have told another part of the story where traditional access control policies do not extend over provenance data. We proposed a language that can be used to express access control over provenance that takes the form of a directed graph. In the rest of this book, we will continue to address concerns about security and provenance. Next, we will focus on another kind of policy that governs the release of provenance. We refer to this release policy as redaction, which is used to specify the sensitive information that must be removed before the provenance is shared.

References

Alkhateeb, F., Baget, J. and Euzenat, J., Extending SPARQL with regular expression patterns (for querying RDF), *Web Semantics: Science, Services and Agents on the World Wide Web,* Vol. 7, No. 2, 2009.

Braun, U., Shinnar, A. and Seltzer, M., Securing provenance, Proceedings of the 3rd Conference on Hot Topics in Security, USENIX Association, 2008, p. 4.

Carroll, J., Dickinson, I., Dollin, C., Reynolds, D., Seaborne, A. and Wilkinson, K., Jena: Implementing the Semantic Web recommendations, Proceedings of the 13th International World Wide Web Conference, Alternate Track Papers and Posters, 2004.

Detwiler, L., Suciu, D. and Brinkley, J., Regular paths in SparQL: Querying the NCI thesaurus, *AMIA Annual Symposium Proceedings,* Vol. 2008, American Medical Informatics Association, 2008, p. 161.

Ding, L., Finin, T., Peng, Y., da Silva, P. and McGuinness, D., Tracking RDF graph provenance using RDF molecules, Proceedings of the 4th International Semantic Web Conference (poster), 2005.

Ferraiolo, D., Kuhn, D. and Chandramouli, R., *Role-Based Access Control,* Artech House, Norwood, MA, 2003.

Harris, S. and Seaborne, A., SPARQL 1.1 Query Language, W3C Working Draft, 2010.

Holland, D., Braun, U., Maclean, D., Muniswamy-Reddy, K. and Seltzer, M., Choosing a data model and query language for provenance, International Provenance and Annotation Workshop, Citeseer, 2008.

http://jena.sourceforge.net/.

http://openprovenance.org/.

Klyne, G., Carroll, J. and McBride, B., Resource description framework (RDF): Concepts and abstract syntax, http://www.w3.org/TR/rdf.concepts/, 2004.

Koch, M., Mancini, L. and Parisi-Presicce, F., Graph-based specification of access control policies, *Journal of Computer and System Sciences,* Vol. 71, No. 1, 2005.

Moreau, L., The Foundations for Provenance on the Web, *Foundations and Trends in Web Science,* 2009.

Moreau, L., Clifford, B., Freire, J., Gil, Y., Groth, P., Futrelle, J., Kwasnikowska, N., Miles, S., Missier, P., Myers, J. et al., The Open Provenance Model—Core Specification, *Future Generation Computer Systems,* 2009.

Ni, Q., Xu, S., Bertino, E., Sandhu, R. and Han, W., An access control language for a general provenance model, in: *Secure Data Management*, Jonker, W. and Petković, M. (Eds.), pp. 68–88, Springer Verlag, Berlin, 2009.

Oinn, T., Addis, M., Ferris, J., Marvin, D., Greenwood, M., Carver, T., Pocock, M., Wipat, A. and Li, P., Taverna: A tool for the composition and enactment of bioinformatics workflows, *Bioinformatics,* Vol. 20, No. 17, 2004.

Prud'hommeaux, E. and Seaborne, A., SPARQL query language for RDF, W3C Working Draft, Volume 20, 2006.

Robinson, R., Counting labeled acyclic digraphs, Proceedings of the Third Ann Arbor Conference on Graph Theory, University of Michigan, 1971.

Robinson, R., Counting unlabeled acyclic digraphs, in: *Combinatorial Mathematics V*, Little, C. (Ed.), pp. 28–43, Springer-Verlag, Berlin, 1977.

Rosenthal, A., Seligman, L., Chapman, A. and Blaustein, B., Scalable access controls for lineage, First Workshop on On Theory and Practice of Provenance, USENIX Association, 2009.

Samarati, P. and de Vimercati, S., Access control: Policies, models, and mechanisms, in: *Foundations of Security Analysis and Design (FOSAD)*, Focardi, R. and Gorrieri, R. (Eds.), pp. 137–196, LCNS 2171, Springer-Verlag, Berlin, 2001.

Zhao, J., Open Provenance Model Vocabulary Specification, latest version, http://open-biomed.sourceforge.net/opmv/ns.html, 2010.

Zhao, J., Goble, C., Stevens, R. and Turi, D., Mining Taverna's Semantic Web of provenance, *Concurrency and Computation: Practice and Experience,* Vol. 20, No. 5, 2008.

Chapter 10

Transforming Provenance Using Redaction

10.1 Overview

So far we have mainly focused on access control policies that are mostly used to control access to a document. In this chapter we explore other policies (namely redaction) that enable the sharing of provenance. Our idea of executing an access control policy over a provenance graph is to identify those resources of the graph that a user is permitted or denied to view. An access control policy is used to determine whether a user is allowed access to a subset (a single node, a path, or a subgraph) of the provenance graph. Such a subset is found by queries that operate over graph patterns. A generalized XML-based access control language for protecting provenance was proposed in Ni et al. (2009). This language was further extended to show how to effectively apply access control over provenance graphs by extending SPARQL queries with regular expressions in Chapter 9. However, these policies do not specify any formal graph models for applying policies over a provenance graph or focus on the need for sharing provenance. We now address these shortcomings by writing the redaction policies as graph operations over a provenance graph (Cadenhead et al. 2011). A provenance graph has a formal foundation based on a graph grammar (Rozenberg 1997).

We address the shortcomings by applying redaction policies that completely or partially remove sensitive attributes of the information being shared. Such policies have been traditionally applied to text, portable document formats (PDFs), and images using tools such as Redact-It (http://www.redact-it.com/). Redaction is often required by regulations that are mandated by a company or by laws such as HIPAA. The risks of unintentional disclosure of sensitive contents of an EPR document can be severe and costly (Heath 1997). Such risks may include litigation proceedings related to noncompliance of HIPAA regulations (Heath 1997).

Commercially available redaction tools have been so far applied over single resources but not to provenance graphs. Therefore, we now explore new mechanisms for supporting redaction policies over a provenance graph. The current commercially available redaction tools block out (or delete) the sensitive parts of documents that are available as text and images. These tools are not applicable to provenance since provenance is a DAG that contains information in the form of nodes and relationships between nodes. Therefore, new approaches are needed for redacting provenance graphs. In this chapter, we apply a graph transformation technique (generally called graph grammar) that is flexible enough to perform fine-grained redaction over data items and their associated provenance graphs (Rozenberg 1997). A graph is best described in a graphical data model such as RDF (Klyne et al. 2004), which is equipped with features for handling both representation and storage of data items and provenance. Our approach utilizes this graph data model for applying a set of redaction policies, which involves a series of graph transformation steps until all the policies are applied. At each step, a policy specifies how to replace a sensitive subset of the graph (such as a data item or a relationship between data items such as edge, path, or subgraph) with another graph in order to redact the sensitive content. The final graph is then shared among the various stakeholders.

Our main focus in this chapter is the application of a graph grammar technique to perform redaction over provenance. In addition, we provide an architectural design that allows a high-level specification of policies, thus separating the business layer from a specific software implementation. We also implement a prototype of the architecture based on open source Semantic Web technologies. The organization of this chapter is as follows. In Section 10.2 we discuss graph grammar that we have utilized in our work for redaction policies. In Section 10.3 we describe our architecture for redaction policies. Our experiments are discussed in Section 10.4. The chapter is summarized in Section 10.5. Figure 10.1 illustrates the concepts discussed in this chapter.

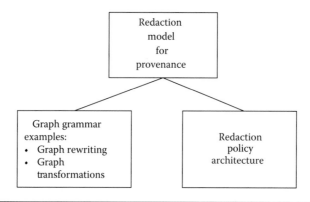

Figure 10.1   Redaction model for provenance.

10.2 Graph Grammar

There are two steps to apply redaction policies over general directed labeled graphs: (1) Identify a resource in the graph that we want to protect. This can be done with a graph query (i.e., a query equipped with regular expressions). (2) Apply a redaction policy to this identified resource in the form of a graph transformation rule. For the rest of this section, we will focus on a graph grammar (or a graph rewriting system) that transforms an original graph to one that meets the requirements of a set of redaction policies. We first describe two graph data models that are used to store provenance. Next, we present the graph rewriting procedure, which is at the heart of transforming a graph, by describing the underlying graph operations. We support the general descriptions of our graph rewriting system with use cases taken from a medical domain.

Graph data models. Graphs are a very natural representation of data in many application domains, such as precedence networks, path hierarchy, family tree, and concept hierarchy. In particular, we emphasize applying graph theory to redaction by using two existing data models, namely RDF and OPM (Klyne et al. 2004; Moreau et al. 2009). In addition, directed graphs are a natural representation of provenance (Braun et al. 2008; Moreau et al. 2009; Zhao 2010). We begin by giving a general definition of a labeled graph suitable for any graph grammar system, and then we introduce a specific labeled graph representation for our prototype. This specific representation is referred to as RDF, which we use to support the redaction procedure over a provenance graph.

Definition 10.1: Labeled Graph

A labeled graph is a 5-tuple, $G_\ell = (V, E, \mu, \nu, \ell)$ where V is a set of nodes, $E = V \times V$ is a set of edges, $\ell = \langle \ell_V, \ell_E \rangle$ is a set of labels, $\mu: V \to \ell_V$ is a function assigning labels to nodes, and $\nu: E \to \ell_E$ is a function assigning labels to edges. In addition, the sets ℓ_V and ℓ_E are disjoint.

Definition 10.2: RDF Graph

Recall that an RDF graph is a finite collection of RDF triples. A RDF graph used in this chapter restricts Definition 10.1 as follows:

1. $\ell_V \subset (\mathcal{V} \cup \mathcal{B} \cup \mathcal{L})$
2. $\ell_E \subset \mathcal{V}$
3. An RDF triple (s,p,o) is a directed labeled edge p in G_ℓ with endpoints s and o.

Definition 10.3: Provenance Graph

Let $H = (V, E)$ be an RDF graph where V is a set of nodes with $|V| = n$ and $E \subseteq (V \times V)$ is a set of ordered pairs called edges. A provenance graph $G = (V_G, E_G)$ with *n* entities is defined as $G \subseteq H$, $V_G = V$, and $E_G \subseteq E$ such that G is a directed graph with no directed cycles.

Graph rewriting. A graph rewriting system is well suited for performing transformations over a graph. Further, provenance is well represented in a graphical format. Thus, a graph rewriting system is well suited for specifying policy transformations over provenance. Graph rewriting is a transformation technique that takes as input an original graph and replaces a part of that graph with another graph. This technique, also called graph transformation, creates a new graph from the original graph by using a set of production rules. Popular graph rewriting approaches include the single-pushout approach and the double-pushout approach (Corradini et al. 1997; Rozenberg 1997). For the purpose of this thesis, we define graph rewriting as follows:

Definition 10.4: Graph Rewriting System

A graph rewriting system is a three tuple, (G_ℓ, q, P) where

> G_ℓ is a labeled directed graph as given by Definition 10.1;
> q is a request on G_ℓ that returns a subgraph G_q
> P is a policy set. For every policy $p = (r, e)$ in P, $r = (se, re)$ is a production rule, where *se* is a starting entity, *re* is a regular expression string, and *e* is an embedding instruction
>
> - Production rule, *r*. A production rule, $r: L \rightarrow R$, where L is a subgraph of G_q and R is a graph. We also refer to L as the left-hand side (LHS) of the rule and R as the right-hand side (RHS) of the rule. During a rule manipulation, L is replaced by R and we embed R into $G_q - L$.
> - Embedding information, *e*. This specifies how to connect R to $G_q - L$ and also gives special postprocessing instructions for graph nodes and edges on the RHS of a graph production rule. This embedding information can be textual or graphical.

This general graph rewriting system can be used to perform redaction over a directed labeled graph, in particular a provenance graph. A graph query is used to determine the resources in the provenance graph that are to be shared with other parties. These resources take the form of a single node, a relationship between two nodes, or a sequence of nodes along a path in the provenance graph. A set of redaction policies is used to protect any sensitive information that is contained within these resources. Such policies are a formal specification of the information that must not be shared. We formulate these policies in our graph grammar system as production rules in order to identify and remove any sensitive (e.g., proprietary, legal, competitive) content in these resources. These production rules are applied on the provenance graph as one of the following graph operations: a vertex contraction, an edge contraction, a path contraction, or a node relabeling operation.

In order for our graph rewriting system to manipulate the provenance graph, we use a graph manipulation language over RDF called SPARQL (Prud'hommeaux and Seaborne 2008). In addition, we use one of the features in SPARQL (Harris and Seaborne 2010), namely regular expressions, to identify paths of arbitrary length in a provenance graph. We formulate our SPARQL queries around regular expression patterns in order to identify both the resources being shared and the LHS and RHS of the production rules of a policy set. The regular expressions are used to qualify the edges of a triple pattern so that a triple pattern is matched as an edge or a path in the provenance graph.

Graph operations. We now define the graph operations that manipulate a provenance graph in order to effectively apply a set of redaction policies. These graph operations remove or circumvent parts of the graph identified by a query. In addition, a graph rewriting system can be constructed so that the rules and embedding instructions ensure that specific relationships are preserved (Blostein and Schürr 1997). Therefore, we specify embedding information that will ensure that our graph rewriting system returns a modified but valid provenance graph. These graph operations are implemented as an edge contraction, a vertex contraction, a path contraction, or a node relabeling.

Edge contraction. Let $G = (V, E)$ be a directed graph containing an edge $e = (u, v)$ with $v \neq u$. Let f be a function that maps every vertex in $V\backslash\{u, v\}$ to itself, and otherwise maps it to a new vertex w. The contraction of e results in a new graph $G' = (V', E')$, where $V' = V\backslash\{u, v\} \cup \{w\}$, $E' = (E\backslash\{e\})$, and for every $x \in V$, $x' = f(x) \in V$ is incident to an edge $e' \in E'$ if and only if the corresponding edge, $e \in E$, is incident to x in G. Edge contraction may be performed on a set of edges in any order. Contractions may result in a graph with loops or multiple edges. In order to maintain the definition of a provenance graph given in Definition 10.3, we delete these edges.

Figure 10.2 is an example of an edge contraction for our use case (see Figure 9.4). In this example, our objective is to prevent a third party from determining a specific procedure (i.e., a heart surgery) as well as the agent who performed that procedure (i.e., a surgeon). The triangle refers to a merge of the heart surgery process and the surgeon who performed the said process. The cloud represents predecessors, which could be the remaining provenance graph or a redacted graph.

We would like to make clear that an edge contraction will serve as the basis for defining both vertex contraction and path contraction: A vertex contraction can be implemented as an edge contraction by replacing two arbitrary vertices u, v, and an edge drawn between them with a new vertex w. Similarly, a path contraction can be implemented as a series of edge contractions where each edge is processed in turn until we reach the last edge on the path. We will therefore exploit these two implementation details to make clear that both our vertex and path contractions are in fact edge contractions and therefore they are both consistent with our graph rewriting system.

Vertex contraction. This removes the restriction that contraction must occur over vertices sharing an incident edge. This operation may occur on any pair (or subset) of vertices in a graph. Edges between two contracting vertices are sometimes removed in order to maintain the definition of the provenance graph given in Definition 10.3.

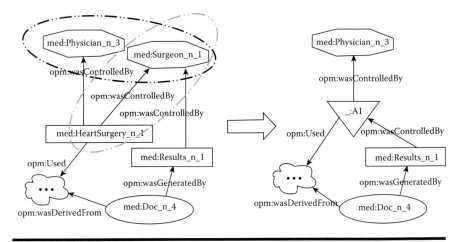

Figure 10.2   Edge contraction.

A vertex contraction of the LHS of Figure 10.3 would therefore replace Physician1_1 and Surgeon1_1 with a triangle that denotes a merge of these two nodes.

This vertex contraction could show for example how a third party is prevented from knowing the identities of agents (i.e., both a patient's primary physician and surgeon) who controlled the processes (i.e., a heart surgery and a logging of results of a surgery into a patient's record).

Path contraction. This occurs on a set of edges in a path that contract to form a single edge between the end points of the path. Edges incident to vertices along the path are either eliminated or arbitrarily connected to one of the end points. A path contraction over the provenance graph given in Figure 9.4 for a patient with id = 1 would involve circumventing the entire ancestry chain of Doc_1_4 as well as the entities affected by Doc_1_4. Figure 10.4 shows an example of a path contraction.

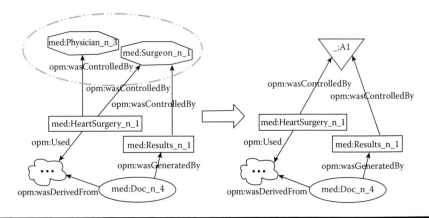

Figure 10.3   Vertex contraction.

A path contraction is necessary when we want to prevent the release of the history of patient 1 prior to surgery as well as the details of the surgery procedure. We show the resulting triples after conducting path contraction on Figure 10.4.

```
<med:Doc_1_4><opm:WasDerivedFrom><_:A1>
<med:Doc_1_4><opm:WasGeneratedBy><_:A2>
```

Node relabeling. A node relabeling operation replaces a label in a node with another label. This is generally a production rule whose LHS is a node in G_q and whose RHS is also a node normally with a new label. The entities shown in Figure 10.4 have generic labels but in practice each entity would be annotated with contextual information. This information serves as identifiers for the respective entity. Before sharing information about these entities it is imperative that we remove sensitive identifiers from them. For example, a physician's cell phone number and social security number are considered unique identifiers and these should be redacted whenever this physician's identity is sensitive. Other attributes such as date of birth, sex, and zip code, when taken together, may also uniquely identify a physician (see further details in the work by Sweeney [2002]). Figure 10.5 shows an example of node relabeling.

We motivate this idea of node relabeling with the following RDF triples taken from our use case:

```
<med:Physician_1_1><med:Sex> "M"
<med:Physician_1_1><med:Age> "35"
<med:Physician_1_1><med:Zip> "76543"
```

After performing a node relabeling on the above set of RDF triples we would then share the following triples:

```
<med:Physician_1_1><med:Sex> "X"
<med:Physician_1_1><med:Age> "30-40"
<med:Physician_1_1><med:Zip> "765XX"
```

Figure 10.4   Path contraction.

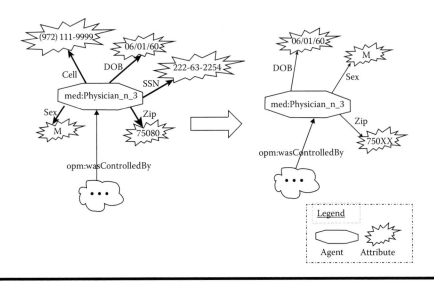

Figure 10.5   Node relabeling.

10.2.1 An Example Graph Transformation Step

We show the general steps of the medical procedure only for one patient in Figure 9.4 for clarity. However, in reality Figure 9.4 would be a subgraph of a much larger graph that describes provenance for *n* patients. We next support the transformation step over Figure 9.4 with an example.

Example 10.1

After *Bob* underwent a heart surgery operation, the hospital must submit a claim to *Bob*'s insurance company. In order to completely process the claim, the insurance company requests more information about the heart surgery procedure.

In this example, the entity representing patient 1 in the provenance graph would be annotated with an attribute *name* and a value *Bob*. The hospital may wish to share this information in order to receive payment from *Bob*'s insurance company. However, based on guidelines related to this sharing of medical records with third parties, the hospital may not wish to share *Bob*'s entire medical history, as doing so could adversely affect *Bob*'s continued coverage from his insurance company. So, in this case, the hospital shares the relevant information related to the surgery operation but not *Bob*'s entire medical history. From Figure 9.4, the provenance of Doc1_4 involves all the entities that can be reached from Doc1_4 by following the paths that start at Doc1_4. The hospital's first step is to identify the resources in the provenance graph related to patient 1. For this we would evaluate a regular expression SPARQL query over the provenance graph

G by using the following graph patterns with Doc1_4 as the starting entity for the first graph pattern and HeartSurgery1_1 as the starting entity of the second graph pattern.

```
{{med:Doc1_4 gleen:OnPath("([opm:WasDerivedFrom]+/
  ([opm:WasGeneratedBy]/[opm:WasControlledBy]))")}
 UNION {med:HeartSurgery1_1 gleen:OnPath("([opm:Used]|
 [opm:WasControlledBy])*")}}
```

This would return G_q as the following RDF triples:

```
<med:Doc_1_4><opm:WasDerivedFrom><med:Doc_1_3>
<med:Doc_1_3><opm:WasDerivedFrom><med:Doc_1_2>
<med:Doc_1_2><opm:WasDerivedFrom><med:Doc_1_1>
<med:Doc_1_3><opm:WasGeneratedBy><med:Test_1_1>
<med:Test_1_1><opm:WasControlledBy><med:Physician_1_2>
<med:Doc_1_2><opm:WasGeneratedBy><med:Notes_1_1>
<med:Notes_1_1><opm:WasControlledBy><med:Physician_1_1>
<med:Doc_1_4><opm:WasGeneratedBy><med:Results_1_1>
<med:Results_1_1><opm:WasControlledBy><med:Surgeon_1_1>
<med:HeartSurgery1_1><opm:WasControlledBy><med:Physician_1_3>
<med:HeartSurgery1_1><opm:WasControlledBy><med:Surgeon_1_1>
<med:HeartSurgery1_1><opm:Used><med:Doc_1_3>
```

We would then evaluate a set of production rules against these RDF triples, where each production rule has a starting entity in G_q. This set of rules governs the particulars relating to how information is shared based on the hospital procedures or an even bigger set of regulatory guidelines (e.g., HIPAA). Figure 10.6a is the first production rule applied to G_q and Figure 10.6b and c, respectively, show the transformation before and after applying the rule. This rule reveals some information about the heart surgery procedure that was done for patient 1, but not the entire history of the record, which may contain sensitive information. The graph pattern for the regular expression SPARQL query used to generate the LHS of the rule in Figure 10.6a is

```
{{med:Doc1_4 gleen:OnPath("([opm:WasDerivedFrom]+/
  ([opm:WasGeneratedBy]/[opm:WasControlledBy])")}
 UNION {med:RepeatVisit1_1 gleen:OnPath("([opm:Used]|
 [opm:WasControlledBy])")}
 UNION {med:Checkup1_1 gleen:OnPath("([opm:Used]|
 [opm:WasControlledBy])")}}
```

The graph representing the RHS would be given by **_:A1** and the embedding instruction for gluing the RHS to G_q – *LHS* given by

```
<med:HeartSurgery_1_1><opm:Used><:_A1>
```

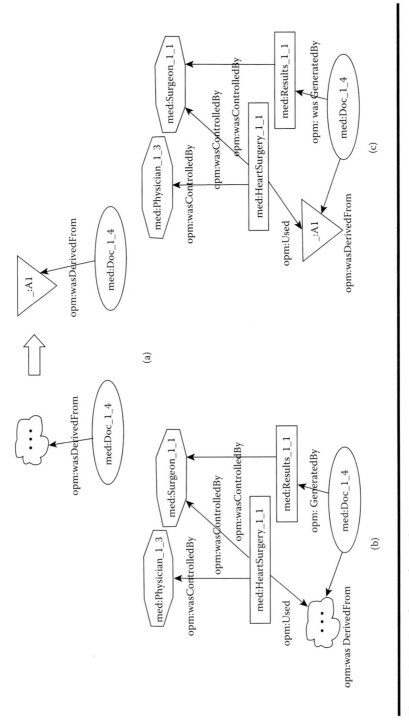

Figure 10.6   Graph transformation step.

The transformed G_q would now be

```
<med:Doc_1_4><opm:WasDerivedFrom><_:A1>
<med:Doc_1_4><opm:WasGeneratedBy><med:Results_1_1>
<med:Results_1_1><opm:WasControlledBy><med:Surgeon_1_1>
<med:HeartSurgery1_1><opm:WasControlledBy><med:Physician_1_3>
<med:HeartSurgery1_1><opm:WasControlledBy><med:Surgeon_1_1>
<med:HeartSurgery1_1><opm:Used><_:A1>
```

10.2.2 Valid Provenance Graph

A graph rewriting system should be capable of specifying under what conditions a graph manipulation operation is valid. The embedding instructions normally contain a fair amount of information and are usually very flexible. Therefore, allowing the policy designer to specify the embeddings may become error-prone. The OPM nomenclature places restrictions on the set of admissible RDF graphs, which we call valid OPM graphs. These restrictions serve to control a graph transformation process (also a graph rewriting process) by ruling out transformations leading to nonadmissible graphs.

Let there be a rule in Figure 10.7a that replaces a subgraph of phase 1 in Figure 9.4 with a null (or empty) graph. Figure 10.7b–d shows the effects of carrying out a graph transformation step using an embedding instruction. Figure 10.7b is the result of performing a transformation using the rule in Figure 10.7a and the following embedding instruction:

```
<med:Doc_n_3><opm:wasDerivedFrom><med:Doc_n_1>
<med:RepeatVisit_n_1><opm:Used><med:Doc_n_1>
```

Figure 10.7c is the result of performing a transformation using the rule in Figure 10.7a but with an empty embedding instruction.

Figure 10.7d is the result of performing a transformation using the rule in Figure 10.7a and the following embedding instruction:

```
<med:Doc_n_3><opm:wasDerivedFrom><med:Doc_n_1>
<med:RepeatVisit_n_1><opm:wasControlledBy><med:Checkup_n_1>
```

The only provenance graph of interest to us is the one in Figure 10.7b. This is a valid OPM graph under the transformation of the rule in Figure 10.7a. Figure 10.7b conforms to the OPM nomenclature convention, and each causal dependency in Figure 10.7b existed in Figure 9.4. Figure 10.7c is a valid OPM graph, but the causal relationships are not preserved; for example, there is a causal relationship between med:Doc_n_3 and med:Doc_n_1 in Figure 9.4 that is absent in Figure 10.7c. Figure 10.7d is not a valid OPM graph since the RDF triple

```
<med:RepeatVisit_n_1><opm:wasControlledBy><med:Checkup_n_1>
```

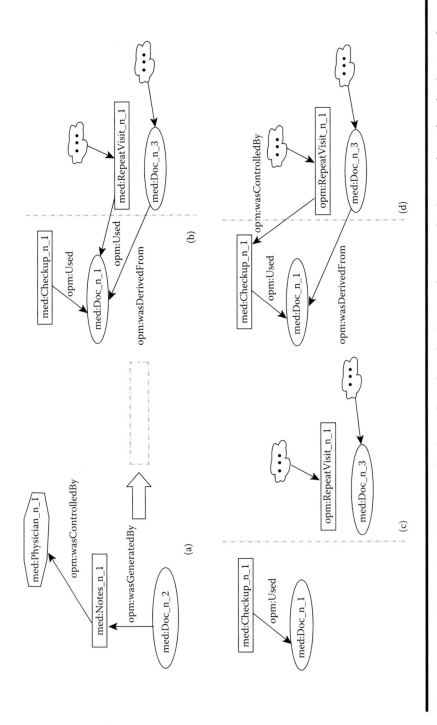

Figure 10.7 Graph transformations. (a) Redaction policy, (b) redaction graph 1, (c) redaction graph 2, (d) redaction graph 3.

does not conform to the OPM nomenclature convention. In addition, there is no causal relationship between med:RepeatVisit_n_1 and med:Checkup_n_1 in Figure 9.4.

10.2.3 Discussion

We acknowledge the impact of an adversarial model when doing an analysis of our approach. Determining which adversary is violating privacy safeguards, in what ways they would do it, and what their capabilities are, is an art in itself and may not be something a community is capable of doing correctly. Also, with so many regulations restricting an institution's sharing ability and with a high demand for quality and trustworthy information, there is a need for very flexible redaction policies. However, redaction policies alone may not anticipate various potential threats that may occur after the information is released from our prototype system.

We identify a unit of provenance that is to be protected as a resource. We could describe this resource as a concept, where modifying the resource produces a description of a possibly new concept that may no longer be sensitive. This modification could be performed by an operation, such as deletion, insertion, or relabeling. We could also describe a resource as a unit of proof; this means that the evidence for the starting entity (or some entity) exists in the rest of the resource. Tampering with this evidence would then reduce the utility of the resource. We attempt to strike the right balance between these two descriptions.

We note that for the standard procedures in our use case, a set of similar procedures give provenance graphs with similar topologies. This allows us to define the resources in the provenance graph by regular expressions, which match a specific pattern. These patterns are our concepts. An advantage of regular expressions in queries is that we do not need the contents of the provenance graph to determine the resource we are protecting; we only need the structure of the graph since all graphs generated in accordance with the same procedure have similar topologies.

One drawback with our prototype is that if we change (or sanitize) only the content of a single resource node before releasing it to a third party, other identifying characteristics still remain in the released resource. For example, if we hide the physician in stage 2 of Figure 9.4, the contextual information associated with that physician (such as age, zip code, and sex) could reidentify the physician. Another drawback in releasing information is that the querying user, in the real world, usually has knowledge of the application domain. Let us assume a resource having the following regular expression pattern: opm:WasGeneratedBy/opm:WasControlledBy was released. Then, a user could infer the sequence of entities along the path identified by this regular expression pattern. In addition, if we apply this regular expression pattern to stage 2 of Figure 9.4, we could determine that only a physician could have performed or ordered the particular test.

In order to minimize the above drawbacks, we apply our graph grammar approach, which transforms a provenance graph to a new graph and at each stage of the transformation determines if a policy is violated before performing further transformations. When this transformation process is completed, we hope to successfully redact the piece of provenance information we share as well as maximize its utility.

10.3 Redaction Policy Architecture

Figure 10.8 shows an overview of our redaction policy architecture. We will now discuss the modules in this redaction policy architecture.

The *User Interface Layer* hides the actual internal representation of a query and a redaction policy from a user. This allows a user to submit a high-level specification of a policy without any knowledge of grammar rules and SPARQL regular expression queries. This layer also allows a user to retrieve any information irrespective of the underlying data representation.

The *High-Level Specification Language Layer* allows the user to write the redaction policies in a language suitable for their application needs. This layer is not tied to any particular policy specification language. Any high-level policy language can be used to write the redaction policies as long as there is a compatible parser that translates these policies to the graph grammar specification. We provide a simple default policy language for writing redaction policies. The syntax uses XML, which is an open and extensible language and is both customizable and readily supports integration of other domain descriptions (Bray et al. 2000). The following is a

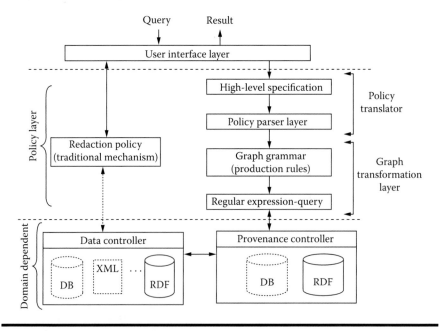

Figure 10.8   Redaction policy layer.

high-level specification of the rule in Figure 10.6a using our default policy language for patient 1.

```
<policy ID = "1" >
<lhs>
        start = Doc1_4
        chain = [WasDerivedFrom]+ artifact AND
        artifact [WasGeneratedBy] process AND
        process [WasControlledBy] physician|surgeon.
        start = RepeatVisit1_1
        chain = [Used] [WasControlledBy].
        start = Checkup1_1
        chain = [Used] [WasControlledBy].
</lhs>
<rhs>_:A1</rhs>
<condition>
<application>null</application>
<attribute>null</attribute>
</condition>
<embedding>
<pre>null</pre>
<post>(HeartSurgery_1_1,Used, _:A1)</post>
</embedding>
</policy>
```

The description of each element is as follows: The *lhs* element describes the left-hand side of a rule. The *rhs* element describes the right-hand side of a rule. Each path in the *lhs* and *rhs* begins at a starting entity. The *condition* element has two optional subelements, the *application* defines the conditions that must hold for rule application to proceed, and the *attribute* element describes the annotations in *lhs*. Similarly, the *embedding* element has two optional subelements, *pre* describes how *lhs* is connected to the provenance graph, and the *post* describes how *rhs* is connected to the provenance graph.

The Policy Parser Layer, Redaction Policy Layer, Regular Expression-Query Translator, Data Controller and Provenance Controller all have the same default behavior like the modules in Chapter 9, except that the Access Control Policy Layer is replaced with the Redaction Policy Layer. The Redaction Policy Layer enforces the redaction policies against the information retrieved to make sure that no sensitive or proprietary information is released for unauthorized uses.

There is a similarity between the access control policy architecture in Figure 9.3 and the redaction policy architecture in Figure 10.8. This redundancy allows us to use the Redaction Policy Layer without installing the Access Control Policy Layer. Sometimes we may want to hide information using only access control policies and other times hide information using redaction policies. Our design architecture provides a high-level policy user with this option. Another advantage of this redundancy is that we can extend the modules in one policy layer without changing the functionality of the other policy layer.

10.4 Experiments

Our experiments were conducted on an IBM workstation with 8 × 2.5-GHz processors and 32 GB RAM. Our prototype is efficient for both finding the shared resource over an original provenance graph and evaluating the production rules over the shared resource. We choose three conventions for preordering the production rules: (1) the original ordering (O,O), (2) lowest to highest utility (*LHO*), and (3) highest to lowest utility (*HLO*). We believe that provenance is more useful when it is least altered. Therefore, we define utility as $\left(1 - \dfrac{\text{altered triples}}{\text{original triples in } G_q}\right) \times 100$, which captures this notion. For implementing the second and third conventions we use a sorting mechanism based on our definition of utility. This sorting mechanism is used in Algorithm 10.1, which is an overview of the redaction procedure discussed in Section 10.2.

Algorithm 10.1: *REDACT* (G_q, *RS*)

1. $LI \leftarrow SORT(G_q, RS)$;   {Initial sort of rule set (*RS*)}
2. **while** *diff* > 0 **do**
3. $G_q'' = G_q$
4. $p = LI.top$
5. $G_q \leftarrow p.e\left(p.r\left(G_q'\right)\right)$ {$T_{Redact} += T_{Rule} + T_{Emb}$}
6. $LI = SORT(G_q, RS - p)$ {$T_{Redact} += T_{Sort}$}
7. $diff = difference\left(G_q, G_q'\right)$ {$T_{Redact} += T_{Diff}$}
8. **end while**
9. **return** G_q'

Algorithm 10.2: *SORT*(G_q, *RS*)

1. $SL = $ new List()
2. **for all** $r \in RS$ **do**
3. **if** $r.se \in G_q$ **then**
4. **if** $G_q \models r$ **then**
5. $SL.add(r)$
6. **end if**
7. **end if**
8. **end for**
9. **return** SL

Table 10.1 shows a comparison of the average redaction time for two graphs given to Algorithm 10.1 with the same rule patterns. Both graphs are constructed from the original provenance graph such that each starts at the beginning of the longest path in the provenance graph. Further, the first graph retrieves all the ancestry chains for that starting entity while the second graph determines the agents that are two hops away from every artifact at least one hop away from the said starting entity. Algorithm 10.1 updates the redaction time at each graph transformation step. Our first observation from Table 10.1 is that the major component of the redaction time is the time spent in sorting the rule set when using our notion of utility. We further explore the performance of Algorithm 10.1 using different graph sizes and rule patterns.

Figure 10.9 shows a comparison of the redaction time and utility versus graph size while keeping the rule set size constant (RS = 200 rules). The labels on every point in Figure 10.9 show the actual provenance graph size. Figure 10.9a compares the redaction time for our three utility conventions as the input graph to Algorithm 10.1 increases in size. The inset to Figure 10.9a shows that OO takes the least redaction time because this strategy does not execute lines 1, 4, and 6 of Algorithm 10.1 for each rule in the rule set. The difference in times between the different strategies is compensated by the higher utility gained from applying the *HLO* as shown in Figure 10.9b.

Figure 10.10 shows a comparison of the redaction time and utility as the size of the rule set increases while keeping the size of G_q constant (G_q = 87 triples). At each

Table 10.1 Query Comparison in Milliseconds

G_q	Order	T_{Redact}	T_{Rule}	T_{Emb}	T_{Sort}	T_{Diff}
1	HLO	17,304	19	3	17,241	41
	LHO	41,012	1853	7	39,137	15
2	HLO	35,270	28	2	35,187	53
	LHO	9044	2904	7	6106	27

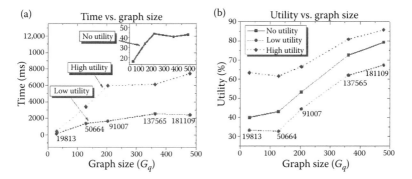

Figure 10.9 Comparison of redaction time and utility versus graph size.

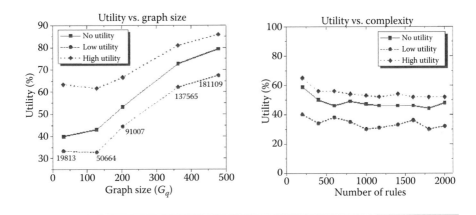

Figure 10.10 Experimental comparison of complexity.

transformation step, Algorithm 10.1 picks a rule that alters the least triples in G_q for *HLO* while it picks a rule that alters the most triples in G_q for *LHO*. Algorithm 10.1 picks any rule for OO.

At each transformation step, Algorithm 10.1 transforms G_q by using rule p at line 5. Rule p is determined by applying either *LHO* or *HLO* to a sorted rule set returned by Algorithm 10.2. Line 4 of Algorithm 10.2 performs graph matching to determine if $G_q \vDash p.r$. This operation tests if $G_q \vDash s \xrightarrow{p} o$ where $\rho \in RE(\Sigma)$. This further evaluates whether $G_q \vDash t$ for each triple t along $s \xrightarrow{p} o$. In conclusion, the time and utility of the entire redaction process is dependent on (1) the current G_q, (2) the current rule set, *RS*, (3) a given rule $r \in RS$ that transforms G_q, and (4) the given *RHS* of r and the embedding instruction, *p.e.*

10.5 Summary and Directions

Our main focus in this chapter was the application of a graph grammar technique to perform redaction over provenance. In addition, we provided an architectural design that allows a high-level specification of policies, thus separating the business layer from a specific software implementation. We also implemented a prototype of the architecture based on open-source Semantic Web technologies. Essentially, in this chapter, we tell yet a third part of the story of our work. We proposed a graph rewriting approach for redacting a provenance graph. We used a simple utility-based strategy to preserve as much of the provenance information as possible. This ensures a high quality in the information shared. We also implement a prototype based on our redaction policy architecture and on Semantic Web technologies (RDF, SPARQL) in order to evaluate the effectiveness of our graph rewriting system.

There are several areas for further work. We utilized one type of a redaction model. Are there other redaction models that could be utilized together with

Semantic Web? How can we build a unified system that includes both access control and redaction? There are lot of opportunities for research in this area. Finally, now that we have described the first major objective of this book, next we will discuss the systems for our second major objective, which is inference control with provenance data. In particular, we will discuss the various aspects related to the inference problem and describe the inference controller we have developed.

References

Blostein, D. and Schürr, A., Computing with graphs and graph rewriting, *FACHGRUPPE INFORMATIK, RWTH*, 1997.

Braun, U., Shinnar, A. and Seltzer, M., Securing provenance, Proceedings of the 3rd Conference on Hot Topics in Security, USENIX Association, 2008, pp. 1–5.

Bray, T., Paoli, J., Sperberg-McQueen, C., Maler, E. and Yergeau, F., Extensible Markup Language (XML) 1.0, W3C Recommendation, Vol. 6, 2000.

Cadenhead, T., Khadilkar, V., Kantarcioglu, M. and Thuraisingham, B., A language for provenance access control, Proceedings of the ACM Conference on Data Application and Security and Privacy, 2011.

Corradini, A., Montanari, U., Rossi, F., Ehrig, H., Heckel, R. and Löwe, M., Algebraic approaches to graph transformation. Part I: Basic concepts and double pushout approach, in *Handbook of Graph Grammars and Computing by Graph Transformation*, Volume 1, Rozenberg, G. (ed.), World Scientific Publishing, Singapore, 1997.

Harris, S. and Seaborne, A., SPARQL 1.1 Query Language, W3C Working Draft, 2010.

Heath, G., Redaction defined: Meeting information disclosure requests with secure content delivery, Informative Graphics white paper, 1997.

http://www.redact-it.com/.

Klyne, G., Carroll, J. and McBride, B., Resource description framework (RDF): Concepts and abstract syntax, W3C Recommendation, http://www.w3.org/TR/rdf-concepts/, 2004.

Moreau, L., Clifford, B., Freire, J., Gil, Y., Groth, P., Futrelle, J., Kwasnikowska, N., Miles, S., Missier, P., Myers, J. et al., The Open Provenance Model core specification (v1. 1), *Future Generation Computer Systems*, 2009.

Ni, Q., Xu, S., Bertino, E., Sandhu, R. and Han, W., An access control language for a general provenance model, *Secure Data Management*, 2009.

Prud'hommeaux, E. and Seaborne, A., SPARQL query language for RDF, W3C Recommendation, 2008.

Rozenberg, G. (ed.), *Handbook of Graph Grammars and Computing by Graph Transformation*, Volume 1, World Scientific Publishing, Singapore, 1997.

Sweeney, L., K-anonymity: A model for protecting privacy, *International Journal on Uncertainty, Fuzziness, and Knowledge-Based Systems*, Vol. 10, No. 5, 2002.

Zhao, J., Open Provenance Model Vocabulary Specification, latest version, http://purl.org/net/opmv/ns-20100827, 2010.

CONCLUSION

II

Section II, which described secure data provenance, consisted of Chapters 8, 9, and 10. In Chapter 8, we discussed the drawbacks of using the current access control policies in a heterogeneous environment. These heterogeneous environments can contain either relational data or semistructured data. We began this chapter by discussing RBAC systems. We identified the key drawbacks of access control over provenance. Then we discussed the reasons why we need flexible policies that are both dynamic and interoperable. We then presented a Semantic Web approach for overcoming these challenges. Essentially, we argued that traditional access control does not extend over RDF graph data. We proposed an approach to handle policies on the Semantic Web.

In Chapter 9, we defined an access control policy language for provenance. We also described a prototype using Semantic Web technologies that allows a user to query for data and provenance based on access control policies defined using our policy language. Essentially, we argued that traditional access control policies do not extend over provenance data. We proposed a language that can be used to express access control over provenance, which takes the form of a directed graph. In Chapter 10 we applied a graph grammar technique to perform redaction over provenance. In addition, we provided an architectural design that allows a high-level specification of policies, thus separating the business layer from a specific software implementation. We also described a prototype of the architecture based on open-source Semantic Web technologies.

Since we have described our approaches to secure data provenance, we are now ready to embark on the second major objective of this book which is inference control. The chapters in Section III will describe in detail our approach to achieving this second major objective.

INFERENCE
CONTROL

INTRODUCTION

As stated in the introduction, inference is the process of forming conclusions from premises. The inferred knowledge is harmful when the user is not authorized to acquire such information from legitimate responses that he or she receives. Providing a solution to the inference problem where users issue multiple requests and consequently infer unauthorized knowledge is an open problem. An inference controller is a device that is used to detect or prevent the occurrence of the inference problem. We have provided solutions to certain aspects of the inference problem that occur in provenance data.

Section III consists of seven chapters: 11, 12, 13, 14, 15, 16, and 17. It addresses the very important notion of inference control within the context of provenance and Semantic Web. Chapter 11 gives an overview of the architecture of our controller. Chapter 12 describes inference control with two users. Chapter 13 describes the provenance layer for inference control. Chapter 14 describes a query processing approach for inference control. Query modification for inference control is discussed in Chapter 15. Inference control with provenance data is discussed in Chapter 16. Implementation of the system is discussed in Chapter 17.

Chapter 11

Architecture for an Inference Controller

11.1 Overview

In this part we describe the second major objective of this book, which is inference control. As stated in Chapter 4, an inference controller is a device that is used to detect or prevent the occurrence of the inference problem. We describe the design and implementation of a prototype inference controller that operates over a provenance graph and protects important provenance information from unauthorized users. Previous work to build an inference controller to protect data confidentiality was described in the late 1980s and early 1990s; however, this work was mainly in the area of multilevel secure databases and supported limited reasoning capabilities. Our current work is a substantial improvement over prior efforts with more sophisticated reasoning and policy representation techniques through the use of Semantic Web technologies. We use as our data model RDF, which supports the interoperability of multiple databases having disparate data schemas. In addition, we express policies and rules in terms of Semantic Web rules and constraints, and we classify data items and relationships between them using Semantic Web software tools such as Pellet, Jena, and Protégé (Carroll et al. 2004; Knublauch et al. 2004; Sirin et al. 2007).

Our main focus is on classifying and protecting provenance data, which are a kind of metadata that capture the origins of single data items of interest, as well as other relevant information such as data manipulation operations and temporal information. Though it is acceptable to represent provenance in any data format, it is sometimes easier to visualize its structure using a directed graph layout.

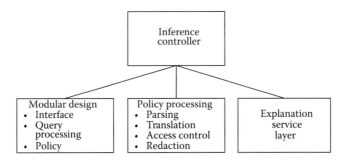

Figure 11.1 Architecture for an inference controller.

Therefore, we will refer to the provenance data as a directed graph, since a directed graph structure, besides being popular, has many advantages with respect to data modeling in a Semantic Web environment. The Semantic Web extends the RDF graph data model to have reasoning capabilities through the use of formal semantics. In our work, we use the reasoning capabilities of the Semantic Web to support the inference strategies of the inference controller. Furthermore, we present several new query modification (i.e., rewriting) techniques that can be used to enforce security policies over a provenance graph.

In this chapter, we present our architecture of an inference controller that employs inference strategies and techniques built around Semantic Web technologies. The organization of this chapter is as follows. Our design is discussed in Section 11.2. Modular approach to the design is provided in Section 11.3. Policy processing is the subject of Section 11.4. Some desirable features (e.g., providing explanations) are discussed in Section 11.5. The chapter is summarized in Section 11.6. Figure 11.1 illustrates the concepts in this chapter. Note that we provide a perspective of the inference problem in Appendix C. Design and implementation of one of the earliest inference controllers is discussed in Appendix D.

11.2 ■ Design of an Inference Controller

The unsolvability of the inference problem was proved in Thuraisingham (1990). Its complexity is an open problem. While there is a need to analyze the complexity classes of the inference problem, still a lot of research has been pivoted around the implementations based on traditional databases. However, since provenance has a logical graph structure, it can also be represented and stored in a graph data model; therefore, it is not limited to any particular data format. Although our focus in this design is on building an inference controller over the graph representation of provenance, our inference controller could be used to protect the case with the traditional database as well. Also, the use of an RDF data model does not overburden our implementation with restrictions, since other data formats are well served by an RDF data model. Furthermore, tools such as the one discussed in Bizer (2003) convert relational data to RDF data.

Our architecture takes a user's input query and returns a response that has been pruned using a set of user-defined policy constraints. We assume that a user could interact with our system to obtain both traditional and provenance data. However, since our focus will be on protecting provenance, we will focus more on the design of the inference controller and the provenance data layers.

In our design we will assume that the available information is divided into two parts: the actual data and provenance. Both the data and provenance are represented as RDF graphs. The reader should note that we do not make any assumptions about how the actual information is stored. A user may have stored data and provenance in two different triple stores or in the same store. A user application can submit a query for access to the data and its associated provenance or vice versa. Figure 11.2 shows our design and some modules in our prototype implementation of an inference controller over provenance data. We present a description of the modules in Figure 11.2.

User interface manager. The user interface manager is responsible for processing the user's requests, authenticating the user, and providing suitable responses back to the user. The interface manager also provides an abstraction layer that allows a user to interact with the system. A user can therefore pose either a data query or a provenance query to this layer. The user interface manager also determines whether the query should be evaluated against the traditional data or provenance.

Policy manager. The policy manager is responsible for ensuring that the querying user is authorized to use the system. It evaluates the policies against a user's query and

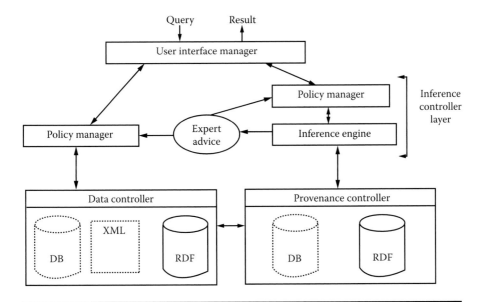

Figure 11.2   Architecture.

associated query results to ensure that no confidential information is released to unauthorized users. The policy manager may enforce the policies against the traditional data or against the provenance data. Each data type may have its own policy manager; for example, the traditional data may be stored in a different format from the provenance data. Hence, we may require different implementations of each policy manager.

Inference engine. The inference engine is the heart of the inference controller. The engine is equipped to use a variety of inference strategies that are supported by a particular reasoner. Since there are many implementations of reasoners available, our inference controller offers an added feature of flexibility whereby we can select from among any reasoning tool for each reasoning task. We can improve the efficiency of the inference controller since each inference strategy (or a combination of strategies) could be executed on a separate processor. An inference engine typically uses software programs that have the capability of reasoning over some data representation; for example, a relational data model or an RDF graph model representation.

Data controller. The data controller is a suite of software programs that stores and manages access to data. The data could be stored in any format such as in a relational database, in XML files, or in an RDF store. The controller accepts requests for information from the policy manager (or the inference engine layer) if a policy allows the requesting user access to the data item. This layer then executes the request over the stored data and returns results back to the policy layer (or inference engine layer) where it is reevaluated based on a set of policies.

Provenance controller. The provenance controller is used to store and manage provenance information that is associated with data items that are present in the data controller. In the case when we select a graph representation of provenance, the provenance controller stores information in the form of logical graph structures in any appropriate data representation format. This controller also records the ongoing activities associated with the data items stored in the data controller. This controller takes as input a graph query and evaluates it over the provenance information. This query evaluation returns a subgraph back to the inference controller layer where it is reexamined using a set of policies.

11.3 Modular Design

The inference controller is built using a modular approach; therefore, it is very flexible in that most of the modules can be extended or replaced by another application module. For example, an application user may substitute the policy parser module that handles the parsing of the high-level policies to a low-level policy object. This substitution would allow the application user to continue using his or her business policies independent of our software implementation of the provenance inference controller.

Inference tools. Newly published data, when combined with existing public knowledge, allow for complex and sometimes unintended inferences. Therefore, we need semiautomated tools for detecting these inferences prior to releasing provenance information. These tools should give data owners a fuller understanding of the implications of releasing the provenance information as well as helping them adjust the amount of information they release in order to avoid unwanted inferences.

The inference controller is a tool that implements some of the inference strategies that a user may utilize to infer confidential information that is encoded into a provenance graph. Our inference controller leverages from existing software tools that perform inferencing, such as Pellet, Fact++, Racer, HermiT, and CWM (Berners-Lee 2000; Haarslev and Moller 2001; Shearer et al. 2008; Sirin et al. 2007; Tsarkov and Horrocks 2006). Therefore, we can add more expressive power by replacing the default base engine of our inference controller with a more powerful reasoner. Furthermore, since there is a trade-off of expressivity and decidability, an application user has more flexibility in selecting the most appropriate reasoner for his or her application domain.

The *user-interface module* provides a layer of abstraction that allows a user to interact with the system. The user interacts with the provenance inference controller via an interface layer. This layer accepts a user's credentials and authenticates the user. Our interface module hides the actual internal representation of an inference controller from a user by providing a simple question-answer mechanism. This mechanism allows the user to pose standard provenance queries such as why a data item was created, where in the provenance graph it was generated, how the data item was generated, and when and in what location it was created. This layer also returns results after they have been examined against a set of policies. Figure 11.3 is a representation of our interface module that allows a user to interact with the underlying provenance store.

The *query-processing module* is responsible for accepting a user's query, parsing it, and submitting it to the provenance knowledge base. When the results are evaluated against the set of policies and rules, it is returned to the user via the interface layer. The query processing module can accept any standard provenance queries as well as any query written in the SPARQL format. The querying user is allowed to view the errors that are due to the syntax of a query as well as the responses constructed by the underlying processes of the inference controller.

The *policy module* is responsible for enforcing any high-level policy defined by a high-level application user or administrator. The policies are not restricted to any particular security policy definition, model, or mechanism. In fact, we can support different access control policies such as RBAC and access control based on context such as time (temporal role-based access control [TRBAC]) and location (LBAC). Besides the traditional and well-established security models built on top of access control mechanisms, we also support redaction policies that are based on sharing data for the ongoing mutual relationships among businesses and stakeholders. Finally, the policy layer interacts with the various reasoners in the inference engine, which offers further protection against inference attacks. The inference layer enforces policies that are in the form of DL constraints, OWL restrictions, or SWRL rules. We also observe that some of the access control policies can be expressed as inference rules or queries via query rewrite or views. Our policy module therefore has many layers equipped with security features, thus ensuring that we are enforcing the maximal protection over the underlying provenance store.

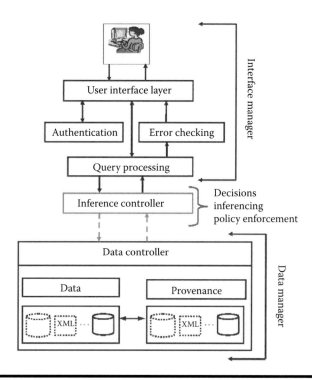

Figure 11.3   Interface module.

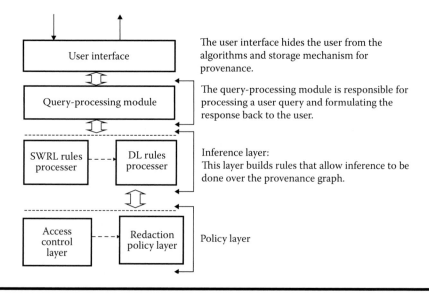

Figure 11.4   Policy module.

Figure 11.4 is the design of a policy module. The policy module interacts with the user via the query processing module. Each query passed to the policy manager from the query processing module is evaluated against a set of policies. These policies can be encoded as access control rules via any access control mechanism or suitable policy language. They can be expressed as rules that operate directly over a directed graph or they can be encoded as DL constraints or SWRL rules.

11.4 Policy Processing

11.4.1 Parsing Process

A high-level policy has to be translated to a suitable format and representation in order to be processed by a provenance inference controller. This often involves the parsing of a high-level policy to a low-level representation. Our design makes use of an extensible language for expressing policies. This language has been used successfully to write access control policies (Ni et al. 2009). Our policies are written as XML documents that reside on disk until they are requested. XML is also equipped with features for writing rules (e.g., RuleML; see also [Governatori 2005]) and representing OWL restrictions. Our choice of the XML language allows us to take as input any high-level policy specification and an associated parser that maps it to a low-level policy format. The high-level application user also benefits from our use of the XML language, since XML is an open standard that is widely used and many data exchange formats are based on XML. For the rest of the chapter we will refer to the policies as though they are in their XML standard form.

Figure 11.5 provides an overview of a policy parsing process. When a XML policy file is loaded, each policy in the policy file is parsed using a compatible parser. The parser is responsible for ensuring that the policies are well formed. The default policies (i.e., access control, redaction, inference rules) are written in an XML file

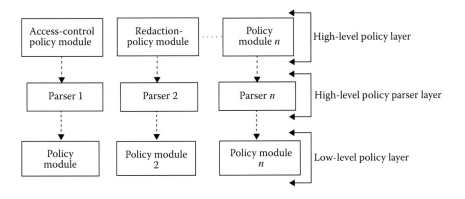

Figure 11.5 Parsing process.

and the parser evaluates the XML file against a XML schema file. The policies in a successfully parsed XML file are then translated to a low-level representation.

11.4.2 High-Level Policy Translation

We discuss how a correctly parsed high-level policy is translated to an internal low-level policy. We will first discuss two inference assemblers, the SWRL rule assembler and the DL rule assembler. Then we will discuss two policy assemblers that translate the access control and redaction high-level policies, respectively.

SWRL rule assembler. This module maps a high-level XML file onto a set of SWRL rules. A SWRL rule has a head and a body. The body is used to encode a condition that must be satisfied before the information encoded in the head is applied to the provenance knowledge base.

SWRL policy translation. The following is a policy which states that if a doctor has a patient then that doctor can also read the patient's record:

```
<policies>
<policy ID="1" >
<description>...some description....</description>
<body>
<atom>?x rdf:type provac:Doctor</atom>
<atom>?y rdf:type provac:Patient</atom>
<atom>?y provac:patientHasDoctor ?x</atom>
<atom>?y provac:hasRecord ?r</atom>
</body>
<head>
<atom>?x provac:canReadRecord ?r</atom>
</head>
</policy>
</policies>
```

This policy could be represented internally as

$$Doctor(?x) \land Patient(?y) \land patientHasDoctor(?y,?x) \land hasRecord(?y,?r) \rightarrow canReadRecord(?x,?r)$$

11.4.3 DL Rule Assembler

This module maps a high-level XML file onto a set of OWL restrictions.

Quantifier restrictions consist of three parts:

1. A quantifier, which is either the existential quantifier ($\exists$) or the universal quantifier ($\forall$)
2. A property, along which the restriction acts
3. A filler that is a class description

For a given individual, the quantifier effectively puts constraints on the relationships that the individual participates in. It does this by either specifying that at least one kind of relationship must exist or by specifying the only kinds of relationships that can exist (if they exist).

We currently support the following OWL restrictions:

1. **SomeValuesFromRestriction**. SomeValuesFromRestriction are existential restrictions that describe the set of individuals that have at least one specific kind of relationship to individuals that are members of a specific class.
2. **AllValuesFromRestriction**. AllValuesFromRestriction are universal restrictions that constrain the filler for a given property to a specific class.
3. **MinCardinalityRestriction**. MinCardinalityRestriction are cardinality restrictions that specify the minimum number of relationships that an individual must participate in for a given property. The symbol for a minimum cardinality restriction is the greater than or equal to symbol (≥).
4. **MaxCardinalityRestriction**. MaxCardinalityRestriction are cardinality restrictions that specify the maximum number of relationships that an individual can participate in for a given property. The symbol for a maximum cardinality restriction is the less than or equal to symbol (≤).
5. **DataRange**. DataRange is a built-in property that links a property (or some instance of the class rdf:Property) to either a class description or a data range. An rdfs:range axiom asserts that the values of this property must belong to the class extension of the class description or to data values in the specified data range.
6. **Domain**. Domain is a built-in property that links a property (or some instance of the class rdf:Property) to a class description. An rdfs:domain axiom asserts that the subjects of such property statements must belong to the class extension of the indicated class description.

11.4.4 DL Policy Translation

The following is a policy which states that any process that is controlled by a surgeon is a sensitive process.

```
<policies>
<policy ID="1" >
<description>...some description....</description>
<rule>
<restriction>AllValuesFromRestriction</restriction>
<property>opm:WasControlledBy</property>
<class>provac:Surgeon</class>
<label>provac:SensitiveProcess</label>
</rule>
</policy>
</policies>
```

This policy is converted internally as

$$\forall Wascontrolled By.Surgeon \sqsubseteq SensitiveProcess$$

11.4.5 Access Control Policy Assembler

The access control policy assembler module maps a high-level access control XML policy file to a low-level access control policy.

Access control policy translation. The following is a policy which states that any user has permission to access Doc_2 if it was generated by a process that was controlled by a surgeon.

```
<policies>
<policy ID="1" >
<description>description</description>
<target>
<subject>anyuser</subject>
<record>provac:Doc_2</record>
<restriction>Doc.WasGeneratedBy == opm:Process</restriction>
<restriction>process.WasControlledBy == provac:Surgeon
  </restriction>
</target>
<effect>NecessaryPermit</effect>
</policy>
</policies>
```

This policy could be translated to a query that retrieves the part of a provenance graph that this policy is allowing a user to view. A corresponding SPARQL query would then be

```
Select ?x
{
med:Doc1_2 gleen:OnPath("([opm:WasGeneratedBy]/
  [opm:WasControlledBy])" ?x
  ?x rdf:type provac:Surgeon).
}
```

11.4.6 Redaction Policy Assembler

This module maps a high-level XML redaction policy file to a low-level redaction policy.

Redaction policy translation. The following is a policy which states that if there is a path that starts at Doc_4 and Doc_4 was derived from an artifact that was generated by a process that was controlled by a physician, then we should redact this path from the provenance subgraph containing the path.

```
<policies>
<policy ID="1">
<description>description</description>
<lhs>
<chain>
<start> provac:Doc_4</start>
<path>
[opm:WasDerivedFrom]+ artifact AND artifact
   [opm:WasGeneratedBy] process AND process
   [opm:WasControlledBy] physician
</path>
</lhs>
<rhs>_:A1</rhs>
<condition>
<application>null</application>
<attribute>null</attribute>
</condition>
<embedding>
<pre>null</pre>
<post>(provac:HeartSurgery_1,opm:Used, _:A1)</post>
</embedding>
</policy>
</policies>
```

This policy would evaluate over a provenance graph, replacing any path that starts with a node labeled Doc_4 and connected to a process via a WasGeneratedBy link followed by a WasControlledBy link that has an end node labeled as physician (or is of type physician). Each such path would be replaced by a blank label _:A1 and :_A1 would be joined to the original provenance graph to some node labeled provac:HeartSurgery_1 using a link with the label opm:Used.

11.5 Explanation Service Layer

A novel feature to have is one where the reasoner derives new knowledge and then explains how it derived that new knowledge. For this we could rely on a reasoner that provides some explanation service. The default base reasoner, Pellet, has a service that can explain its inferences by providing the minimal set of facts or other knowledge necessary to justify the inference. For any inference that Pellet computes, we exploit Pellet inference service that will explain why a particular inference holds. The explanation itself is a set of OWL axioms which, taken together, justify or support the inference in question. There may be many (even infinitely many) explanations for an inference; Pellet heuristically attempts to provide a good explanation.

Our provenance inference controller can then provide information about the classification of the knowledge base. For example, we may be interested in why a set of RDF triples were classified as sensitive, or why a concept is considered sensitive. The answers to these questions are left to the Explanation Service Layer. This layer is built on top of Pellet explanation service and displays the set of axioms used to derive the concepts that are subsumed by another class. The Explanation Service Layer uses the services of a reasoner to provide justifications (also warrants) for each piece of the provenance that is classified as sensitive. The Explanation Service Layer is also useful for providing feedback to the application designer or policy administrator.

The explanations displayed back to a policy administrator may be in terms of the low-level descriptions. Furthermore, the explanations may reveal low-level details of the particular software implementation. This feature exists as an additional feature that can be turned on for policy designers familiar with DL or OWL. This service provides a desired feature whereby the application designer can view how his or her policies are interpreted by the low-level inference services. For example, since a high-level DL rule may be applied differently from what the author intended, the policy designer now has an opportunity to tweak the high-level policies for those who want it modified.

Populating the provenance knowledge base. The knowledge base is populated and added to a provenance store through a set of generators we have built. That is, there is a set of background generators that are responsible for extracting background information that is normally available online. We also build a workflow generator that produces the actual provenance. The workflow generator produces synthetic provenance data that are not available online. It is these provenance data that have subsets that we must hide.

We will revisit the discussion in this section when we describe the implementation of the inference controller in Chapter 17.

11.6 Summary and Directions

In this chapter we described the design of an inference controller that operates over a provenance graph and protects important provenance information from unauthorized users. Previous work to build an inference controller to protect data confidentiality was described in the late 1980s and early 1990s; however, this work was mainly in the area of multilevel secure databases and supported limited reasoning capabilities. Our current work is a substantial improvement over prior efforts with more sophisticated reasoning and policy representation techniques through the use of Semantic Web technologies. We used RDF as our data model as it supports the interoperability of multiple databases having disparate data schemas. In addition, we expressed policies and rules in terms of Semantic Web rules and constraints, and we classify data items and relationships between them using Semantic Web software tools.

In the next four chapters we give more details of our design. In Chapter 12 we discuss the philosophy of our design. In Chapter 13 we discuss provenance data representation. In Chapter 14 we discuss queries with regular expressions. In Chapter 15 we discuss query modification. Finally, in Chapter 16 we discuss inferencing with provenance data. The implementation of the inference controller is discussed in Chapter 17. This work is the first of its kind for secure data provenance and inference control with Semantic Web data.

References

Berners-Lee, T., CWM—closed world machine, http://www. w3.org/2000/10/swap/doc/cwm.html, 2000.

Bizer, C., D2R MAP—A database to RDF mapping language, The Twelfth International World Wide Web Conference (posters), 2003.

Carroll, J., Dickinson, I., Dollin, C., Reynolds, D., Seaborne, A. and Wilkinson, K., Jena: Implementing the Semantic Web recommendations, Proceedings of the 13th International World Wide Web Conference, Alternate Track Papers and Posters, 2004.

Governatori, G., Representing business contracts in RuleML, *International Journal of Cooperative Information Systems*, Vol. 14, No. 2–3, 2005.

Haarslev, V. and Moller, R., Description of the RACER system and its applications, *Description Logics*, 2001.

Knublauch, H., Fergerson, R., Noy, N. and Musen, M., The Protege OWL plugin: An open development environment for Semantic Web applications, ISWC 2004.

Ni, Q., Xu, S., Bertino, E., Sandhu, R. and Han, W., An access control language for a general provenance model, *Secure Data Management*, 2009.

Shearer, R., Motik, B. and Horrocks, I., HermiT: A highly-efficient OWL Reasoner, Proceedings of the 5th International Workshop on OWL: Experiences and Directions (OWLED 2008), 2008.

Sirin, E., Parsia, B., Grau, B., Kalyanpur, A. and Katz, Y., Pellet: A practical OWL-DL reasoner, *Web Semantics: Science, Services and Agents on the World Wide Web*, Vol. 5, No. 2, 2007.

Thuraisingham, B., Recursion theoretic properties of the inference problem, presented at the Computer Security Foundations Workshop, Franconia, NH, June 1990 (also MITRE Report, June 1990).

Tsarkov, D. and Horrocks, I., FaCT++ description logic reasoner: System description, *Automated Reasoning*, 2006.

Chapter 12

Inference Controller Design

12.1 Overview

Inference controller is a mechanism that (1) protects confidential information, (2) mimics a user's strategy used for inferring confidential information, and (3) performs inference over the provenance data. Data provenance in general contain both sensitive and public information. We need to disclose provenance information in order to ensure that the user has high-quality information. Provenance data have a unique characteristic that make them different from traditional data. This characteristic is DAG structure of provenance, which captures single data items and the causal relationships between them. Additionally, the DAG structure complicates any efforts to successfully build an inference controller over provenance data; surprisingly, this area has been unexplored by the research community. Although the research community has applied inference over provenance data—in particular the inference web, which has used provenance to provide proofs as justifications for data items—it has not considered inferencing from the point of view of provenance security.

The early inference controllers were developed in the 1990s (Thuraisingham et al. 1993). These inference controllers processed security policies, which were called security constraints at that time, during query, update, and database design operations. However, the early work in the area of MLS reasoning was rather limited due to inadequacies of policy representation and reasoning techniques. Ideally, an inference controller should be able to detect inference strategies that users utilize to draw unauthorized inferences and consequently protect the knowledge base from such security violations. Different approaches can be employed for building an inference controller. For example, it is desirable to use state-of-the-art machine-learning techniques to build a learner that automatically learns to recognize complex patterns and make intelligent decisions based on some input. One could also build an inference controller that uses Semantic Web technologies that are equipped with reasoners that perform inferences over the facts in a knowledge base. Semantic Web technologies have overcome the significant limitations that were present in the 1990s. In particular, our research has focused on designing and developing an inference controller with sophisticated reasoning and policy representation techniques using Semantic Web technologies. This chapter will describe the detailed design and implementation of an inference controller that draws inferences from a provenance graph store.

The inference controller that we have designed and developed protects the sensitive information in a provenance graph store from unauthorized users. The provenance is represented as a DAG. This graph-based structure of provenance can be represented and stored as an RDF graph. RDF, in conjunction with OWL (Klyne et al. 2004; McGuinness et al. 2004), allows us to associate semantics with the provenance information, thereby allowing us to further exploit various Semantic Web technologies. In our work, we have built a prototype to evaluate the effectiveness of the proposed inference controller. We store the provenance information as an OWL knowledge base and use OWL-compliant reasoners to draw inferences from the explicit information in the provenance knowledge base. We enforce policy constraints at the design phase as well as at runtime.

Provenance is metadata that capture the origin of a data source, the history or ownership of a valued object, or a work of art or literature. It allows us to verify the quality of information in a data store, to repeat manipulation steps, and to discover dependencies among data items in a data store. In addition, provenance can be used to determine the usefulness and trustworthiness of shared information. The

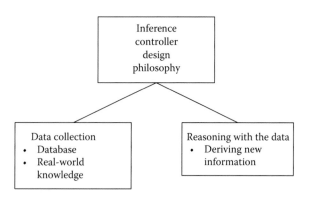

Figure 12.1   Inference controller.

utility of shared information relies on (1) the quality of the source of information and (2) the reliability and accuracy of the mechanisms (i.e., procedures and algorithms) used at each step of the modification (or transformation) of the underlying data items. Furthermore, provenance is a key component for the verification and correctness of a data item that is usually stored and then shared with information users.

This chapter describes the design of our provenance inference controller. Section 12.2 describes our design philosophy. The inference controller design is presented in Section 12.3. The chapter is summarized in Section 12.4. Figure 12.1 illustrates our approach.

12.2 Design Philosophy

Domains for provenance. Provenance and RDF define different domain spaces from traditional database problems. The provenance is mainly used for justification and proofs, verification and detection, trustworthiness of data items, auditing and history of a workflow process, establishing high integrity and quality data, and the reliability of information sources. RDF is mainly used for knowledge representation of a domain, to formulate a problem with a graph presentation, support the interoperability among data sources, and add semantics to data and support reasoning. Traditional databases are best suited for problems with fixed schema. RDF technologies have been used to build inference engines that support inferences and also to represent and store provenance information. In addition, OWL has been used to model different domains with private information and DL has been applied to the privacy problem. Our effort is to combine some of these efforts in order to build an inference controller over provenance. The provenance is represented as RDF graphs, and DL is used to support the inference tasks of our inference controller.

Traditionally, we protect data using various policies. These include access control policies that specify what can be accessed, sanitization and anonymization policies that specify how to share released information, and randomization and encryption techniques that can be used to scramble the data in transmission. These techniques alone do not prevent the inference problem. Therefore, we will build our inference controller to support existing rules and policies when protecting the provenance data.

Different approaches have been used to apply access control policies to provenance. For example, an approach was used to annotate the OPM entities with access control attributes. Another approach was to define policies for the artifacts, processes, and path dependencies. Our approach takes into consideration the structure of provenance and instead represents it as RDF data in order to leverage from the existing Semantic Web rule language, which has been shown to encode even the most complicated access control policies. Furthermore, our approach encodes some of the simpler access control policies as DL rules, thus allowing our inference controller to trade some of its expressive power for decidability.

Protecting the provenance by applying access control policies alone ignores the utility of the provenance given to the querying user. Therefore, an important feature of our inference controller is to build some mechanisms for associating a high utility to the query responses while ensuring the policies are not compromised. We rely on a formal graph transformation approach for visualizing the provenance after a policy is enforced. At each transformation step, the policy that preserves the highest utility is applied. We continue to apply the policies at different transformation steps until all the policies are enforced. Throughout this report, we refer to the policies that utilize the graph transformation approach as redaction policies. Our inference controller will therefore use a combination of policies when appropriate. We will protect data by using access control policies to limit access to the provenance data and we will use redaction policies to store the provenance information.

Inferences may be in two stages:

1. Data collection. This includes data in the database that is accessible to users, and real-world knowledge (which is not represented in the database) on the application domains.
2. Reasoning with the collected data. This is the act of deriving new information from the collected data.

The data collection and the reasoning stages are performed repeatedly by the adversary (i.e., by a human or autonomous agent) until the intended inference is achieved or the adversary gives up. The data that adversaries want to infer may include the existence of certain entity in the database or the associations among data. We provide the following examples to illustrate the kinds of inferences that are possible:

1. A user may want to find out *the specialty of a physician*. The user could ask if there exists such a physician who performed an operation and who used an equipment for that operation. The operation and equipment may be part of the provenance of some patient's record. The equipment may identify a set of possible specialties of surgeons (e.g., heart surgeon uses heart monitors, pacing wires, mediastinal tubes, intravenous [IV] lines). Revealing such provenance would allow an adversary to identify the specialty of the physician.
2. A user may want to find out *who performed a surgery on a patient*. Here, the user may ask if a surgeon exists in the provenance graph for the patient's record and then for the equipment on the provenance path. Assume the hospital zip code is known and a directory of all physicians and corresponding specialties/departments is also available that is sometimes published online (e.g., the North Shore Long Island Jewish [LIJ] Health System website, http://www.northshorelij.com/, allows one to identify physicians by name,

by specialty, and by affiliation). From these pieces of information, the user could identify the surgeon. Therefore, revealing the provenance could identify the surgeon.

3. A user may want to infer *the disease of a patient.* The user might try to find out if a physician exists whose specialty is heart surgery, if this physician updated the patient's record, and if this physician had used any special equipment while attending to the patient. Using the provenance to reveal the answers would identify the disease of the patient.

In some cases, instead of inferring the exact data values in the database (precise inference), users may be content with a set of possible data values (imprecise inference or approximate inference). For example, a user could infer that if a patient has a record in the provenance graph and that if according to the record's history, a heart surgeon performed an operation on the patient, then the user could practically infer that the patient has *some disease related to a heart problem.* Note that these examples could be a set of queries issued by a user in the above order.

Loading constraints in response to a query. It may be expensive to load all the policies in response to a user query. Not all queries compromise the system. We may be more interested in a particular strategy that effectively blocks a potentially benign query. Is there a way to select the smallest set of policies in response to a query? Does a query have a signature that describes it? Can our controller learn the patterns of query? Can we examine the projection BGP of a query? Can we build a model that determines the class of query that a user selects in order to exploit weaknesses of our inference controller?

Can our controller learn the patterns of query? This is a very interesting area to pursue. There have been several works on how to use data mining techniques to learn the implicit knowledge about the data and then build models that protect the data.

Can we examine the projection, BGP of a query? This strategy was applied in Thuraisingham et al. (1993), where a query modification engine was implemented to prevent inference attacks. Recently, there has been a lot of work in this area.

Can we build a model that determines the class of query that a user selects in order to exploit weaknesses of our inference controller? To build an effective inference controller, we make use of a game theoretic model to estimate the best strategy when responding to a user's query. A game theoretic model allows us to study the behavior of a user and estimate the basic characteristics of the next query that will be a best response by the user. Our assumption is that the next query is the one that will maximally exploit the weaknesses of our inference controller. By this we mean that a user who wants to maximize his or her opportunity to learn some protected data/information will pose the query that will best suit their objectives. In fact this is the query that is of interest to us.

Policy translation. Our inference controller should be able to determine how best to enforce a constraint. For example, we may have a high-level policy such as: give access to ?*d* if ?*d* is located in department *X*.

We would translate this internally to either a SWRL or DL rule:

$$(?d\ hasDept\ X) \wedge (?record\ locatedIn\ X) \rightarrow (?d\ hasAccess\ ?Record)$$

which could mean if a doctor is located in the patient's ward then allow the doctor to access the patients record.

$$\exists Dept.X \sqsubseteq \exists hasAccess.Record$$

which means that someone who is a doctor and is in dept X is someone who has access to a patient's record.

12.3 Inference Controller Process

To tackle the inference problem, we should explicitly represent all information available to users and mimic the reasoning strategies of users. A query log could identify the activities of the user and a database could record all information released to the user. These two activities could help identify some background profile of the user and what we know the user already knows. These are major challenges to the inference problem.

We could implement an inference controller that comprises a knowledge base for storing knowledge about the provenance entities. Each such entity is described by a set of RDF triples that makes various assertions about the entities. The inference processing unit receives a search pattern in the form of a query. The pattern is first examined to determine if it is a valid query before allowing access to the knowledge base on the basis of the search pattern. The query is then executed against the knowledge base in accordance with a specified set of policies specified by a constraint set in order to obtain the results from the inference controller.

We assume the user builds a machine M' that contains the history of all the answers, the modified background with relevant domain information, and a prior set of rules about the system. Further, the user can infer a subset of the private information using M'. Likewise, we build a machine M'' that simulates the inferencing mechanism of the user but with certain modifications to compensate for any differences. This machine M'' combines the history of all previous answers, the current query and associated provenance, and the rules that enforce the confidential policies. We use M'' to determine certain inferences occurring in M'. The major difference between M' and M'' is the user's background information. M' and M'' contain different sets of rules and M' keeps a repository of a user's input queries. This repository (or query log) is a rich source of information about the context of the user.

The inferencing capabilities of M'' are best realized by a language with formal semantics. RDF, RDFS, and OWL are knowledge representation languages that fit this criterion; these languages all use the RDF data model. The RDF data model is also a natural fit for a directed graph such as provenance.

We use SPARQL as a language to write the queries that are given to M''. These queries are extended with regular expressions in order to select graph patterns for both the user's query and the protected resources. In order to write the policy constraints (as rules), we use a mixture of queries, DL rules, and SWRL. These constraints (rules) specify the concepts that are to be protected. The concepts are the definitions (or descriptions) of resources in a provenance graph; these are normally written formally to avoid ambiguity in policy specification languages such as DL. Each DL concept can also be successfully defined by a SPARQL query or a SWRL rule. In some cases, the constraints may require more expressive languages for defining the concept and so we sometimes choose SWRL rules over DL rules.

12.4 Overview of a Query Process

Figure 12.2 shows a query as input and a response as output. Two machines take part in a query-answer process: The user system uses M' to formulate a query. The internal system uses M'' to formulate a response to the user's query. The user system handles a set of tasks on behalf of the user. The user system uses M' to perform the following operations:

1. Select a background $B_i i = \{1, 2, 3,..., n\}$, a set of most likely backgrounds. B is the set of prior knowledge available to the user.
2. Combine $B_i \in B$ with H_Q, a query history set. This improves the user's prior knowledge of the system.

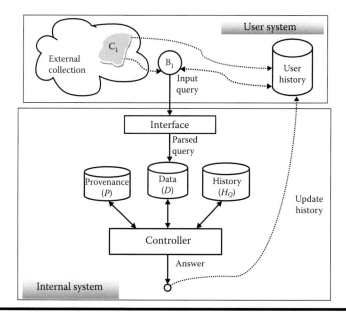

Figure 12.2   Query process.

3. Formulate a query Q_j. This query is the best the user can do given a background B and query history H_Q.

The internal system handles the processing of a user query in order to formulate the responses that preserve the confidentiality of the databases with respect to a set of constraints. The internal system has two parts: the interface module, which interacts with the user system, and a controller, which is built around Semantic Web technologies in order to protect the confidential contents of the knowledge base.

The Interface module uses M'' to perform the following:

1. Assign the user a label ℓ_u. This could be based on the context, attributes, authentication, credentials, and so forth, of the user.
2. Parse the current query Q_j. This could be used to modify the graph patterns of the query in order to ensure that the user is not given any answer that relies on the confidential information in the knowledge base.

The controller module has the task of using all the knowledge learned about the user so far and all the information already released as answers in response to the user's past queries in order to mimic the inference strategies of M'. Here, M'' must assume M' is using both the background knowledge and the information already released as answers to formulate the current query Q_j. The controller module performs the following:

1. $KB' = Ans(Q_j) \cup Prov(Ans(Q_j))$
   which adds the preliminary response to a knowledge base.
2. $KB' = KB' \cup H_Q$
   The query history is derived from all the queries answered so far (e.g., $(Q_1,\ldots,$ $Q_{j-1}) \rightarrow H_Q$. KB' is updated from the history.).
3. $R(KB') \rightarrow KB' + Inf(KB')$
   with R being an RDF-compatible reasoner
4. $J:Inf(KB') \rightarrow \ell$

$$A = \{x | x \in Inf(KB'), J(x) = \ell_1, \ell_2 > \ell_u\}$$

which determines all the triples to be protected in order to deny access to the user.
5. $Ans(Q_j) = Ans(Q_j) \cup Prov(Ans(Q_j)) - A$

$$H_Q = H_Q \cup Ans(Q_j).$$

The answer is then adjusted and the history reflects the new changes.

The controller employs a Semantic Web reasoner (i.e., one that is compatible with RDF, RDFS, or OWL). The main function of the reasoner is to use the current answers, provenance associated with the answers, and the history of past responses to the past queries in order to infer new information. The reasoner also may apply the rules corresponding to the constraints (written as SWRL rules) to infer new information. The inference controller must determine whether this new information should be made known to the querying user. By removing some triples from the answer set, we hope to limit what the user learns.

Step 4 above only prevents the release of confidential information from being a part of the answer returned to the querying user. We observe that M'' does not take into account the power of M'. If M' has at least the same power as M'', then M' would also derive the set A given in step 4. A better implementation would pinpoint the triples in KB' that took part in deriving each triple in $Inf(KB')$.

$$A = \{x \in Inf(KB') \mid B \subseteq KB' \wedge R(B) \rightarrow x\}$$

B is a minimal set such that $\forall B_i \subseteq KB' \wedge R(B_i) \rightarrow x$ and $B \subseteq KB' \wedge R(B_i) \rightarrow x$, $B \subseteq B_i$, and $\nexists B_j \subset B_i \wedge R(B_j) \rightarrow x$.

Now we can maximize the usefulness of the answers given to the user and at the same time prevent M' from inferring those triples that M'' can infer.

The controller. In order to mimic the inference strategies of M', we must program the controller to perform various inference strategies. Each inference strategy has a cost associated with implementing it and a factor that determines its effectiveness. We like to assume that the more effective the inference strategy implemented, the higher the cost. Also, we would like to think that the nature of the relationship between the cost of building an inference strategy and its effectiveness is nonlinear. That is, it costs more to improve the effectiveness by one more unit of utility. We could make use of utility theory to define the usefulness of each inference strategy we implement for M'', but this is outside the scope of this document.

In order to give the notion of the best controller for a set of test cases, we make an assumption that if two machines M_1'' and M_2'' are equally effective but the cost of M_1'' is less than M_2'', then we would select M_1'' as our controller. This qualitative measure of cost effectiveness would serve to determine the capabilities of the controller given current resources, an assumed background B, and a set of test cases. Note that in general it is also prohibitive to determine an exact cost effectiveness of the controller since the background knowledge of the user is not given to M''.

We could improve the effectiveness of the controller with the use of Semantic Web technologies. These technologies allow us to add new capabilities such as (1) associating the information in the knowledge base with semantics, (2) integrating different information formats and schemas, (3) using formal semantics for performing inferencing, and (4) increasing the expressiveness (or power) of the reasoner employed by M''.

We are interested in these new features given to us by incorporating Semantic Web technologies into *M″*. Previous implementations of an inference controller (Thuraisingham et al. 1993) suffer from the fact that when various parts of the system are provided in different formats and schemas, the integration process limits the ability of the controller to reason over all parts of the system. Also, without formal semantics the correct interpretation of all the schemas is not guaranteed. RDF is one step toward adding semantics and ease of schema integration to the various parts of the system. When information is represented as RDF, we can leverage on the state-of-the-art reasoners available on the Semantic Web. DF is usually associated with a formal vocabulary such as RDFS (Allemang and Hendler 2011) and OWL (McGuinness et al. 2004), which allow us to reason over RDFS or OWL data. OWL is usually more expressive than RDFS, but depending on the use case we may decide to use one over the other. For simple inferencing, we could use RDFS, which allows us to use a forward- or backward-chaining strategy. RDFS reasoners are available for free through open-source software such as Jena (Carroll et al. 2004). More expressive inference services are also available by open-source software such as Pellet (Sirin et al. 2007).

12.5 Summary and Directions

In this chapter we discussed our philosophy of designing an inference controller for provenance with Semantic Web data. Provenance and RDF define different domain spaces from traditional database problems. The provenance is used to study the history of the data, its quality as well as determine whether the data has been misused, among others. RDF is mainly used for knowledge representation of the data in a domain and reasoning about the data using DL. In our approach we design an inference controller where we use RDF for data resonation and reasoning of the data including provenance data and determine whether unauthorized inference could occur.

While we have made a significant improvement in migrating to Semantic Web data from relational data for inference control, we are still limited by the reasoning power inherent with the Semantic Web data. That is, the reasoning power of the Semantic Web is limited by the reasoning power of RDF, OWL, and SWRL. To handle more realistic inference strategies we need to include a variety of strategies such as reasoning by induction and probabilistic reasoning. Therefore, future work will include examining powerful machine-learning approaches for inference control.

References

Allemang, D. and Hendler, J., *Semantic Web for the Working Ontologist: Effective Modeling in RDFS and OWL,* Morgan Kaufmann, Waltham, MA, 2011.

Carroll, J., Dickinson, I., Dollin, C., Reynolds, D., Seaborne, A. and Wilkinson, K., Jena: Implementing the Semantic Web recommendations, Proceedings of the 13th International World Wide Web Conference, Alternate Track Papers and Posters, 2004.

Klyne, G., Carroll, J. and McBride, B., Resource description framework (RDF): Concepts and abstract syntax, http://www.w3.org/TR/rdf.concepts/, 2004.

McGuinness, D., van Harmelen, F. et al., OWL web ontology language overview, W3C Recommendation, Vol. 10, 2004.

Sirin, E., Parsia, B., Grau, B., Kalyanpur, A. and Katz, Y., Pellet: A practical OWL-DL reasoner, *Web Semantics: Science, Services and Agents on the World Wide Web,* Vol. 5, No. 2, 2007.

Thuraisingham, B., Ford, W., Collins, M. and O'Keeffe, J., Design and implementation of a database inference controller, *Data & Knowledge Engineering,* Vol. 11, No. 3, 1993.

Chapter 13

Provenance Data Representation for Inference Control

13.1 Overview

As stated earlier, provenance can be recorded in any knowledge representation language, for example, RDF, RDFS, and OWL (Antoniou and van Harmelen 2008; Klyne et al. 2004; McGuinness et al. 2004). Using these languages allows us to later perform inference over the provenance graph. Therefore, we could determine the implicit information in the provenance graph. Provenance data can be stored in the relational data model, the XML data model, or the RDF data model. Each of these in their current form has drawbacks with respect to provenance (Holland et al. 2008).

The directed nature of a provenance graph presents major challenges. A relational model suffers from the fact that it needs expensive joins on relations (tables) for storing edges or paths. In addition, current SQL languages that support transitive queries are complex and awkward to write. XML supports path queries, but the current query languages, XQuery and XPath, only support a tree structure. RDF naturally supports a graph structure, but the current W3C Recommendation for SPARQL (the standard query language for RDF) lacks many features needed for path queries. There are recent works on extending SPARQL with path expressions and variables. These include SPARQL Query 1.1, which is now a W3C recommendation (Harris and Seaborne 2010). Of these three data models, we represent provenance using an RDF data model. This data model meets the specification

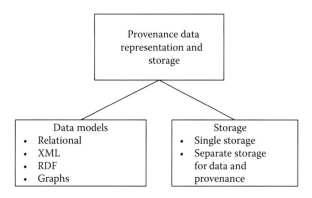

Figure 13.1   Provenance data representation and storage.

of the OPM recommendation (Moreau et al. 2011). In addition, RDF allows the integration of multiple databases describing the different pieces of the lineage of a resource (or data item), and naturally supports the directed structure of provenance. This data model has also been successfully applied for provenance capture and representation (Ding et al. 2005; Zhao et al. 2008).

In this chapter we describe different data formats for representing and storing provenance. We prefer a format representation that naturally supports the directed graph structure of provenance and naturally allows path queries of arbitrary lengths. We argue for a separate store for provenance in order to allow existing systems to continue supporting traditional data. This serves the purpose of decoupling the traditional data layer from the provenance data layer that operates on the provenance. The organization of this chapter is as follows: Data models for the inference controller are discussed in Section 13.2. Storage strategies for the data are discussed in Section 13.3. The chapter is summarized in Section 13.4, Figure 13.1 illustrates the concepts of this chapter.

13.2 ■ Data Models for the Inference Controller

The inference controller we implement can operate over different data models such as the relational database model, the XML model, and the RDF model. Each of these in their current form has drawbacks with respect to provenance.

Relational data. The inference controller described in Thuraisingham et al. (1993) was over relational databases. This data format has been used to represent provenance in tables, but it requires expensive joins on relations (tables) storing edges or paths. Also, the current SQL languages that support transitive queries are complex and awkward to write.

XML data. XML supports path queries, but the current query languages XQuery and XPath only support a tree structure.

RDF. RDF naturally supports graph structure, but the current W3C Recommendation for SPARQL lacks many features needed for path queries. However, recent works on extending SPARQL with path expressions and variables are promising and thus will make it easier to answer the kind of queries normally posed over a provenance graph. In addition, SPARQL Query 1.1 is part of a proposal put forward by W3C recently. SPARQL 1.1 query language includes new features such as aggregates, subqueries, negation, and regular expressions in the SELECT clause, but this is still a W3C Working Draft as of this writing.

Graph data. Graphs are a very natural representation of data in many application domains; for example, precedence networks, path hierarchy, family tree, and concept hierarchy. In addition, directed graphs are a natural representation of provenance (Braun et al. 2008; Moreau et al. 2011; Zhao 2010). We begin by giving a general definition of a labeled graph, and then we introduce a specific labeled graph representation for provenance. This specific representation is referred to as RDF, which will serve to represent and store a provenance graph. Note that an RDF graph is a set of triples that may have one or more machine-processable formats, such as RDF/XML, TURTLE, and N-TRIPLE.

Because of the structure of the provenance data, it requires a graph data model. This model should be suitable for storing provenance data as well as supporting inference tasks over the provenance chains and graph patterns. Two of the operations performed on the graph relevant to our work are graph matching and graph isomorphsim.

- *Graph matching* is used to determine if a condition is met in a provenance graph. A pattern in a provenance graph can be used for deciding what information is to be released.
- *Graph isomorphism* is a mechanism used to determine RDF graph entailment. This is also used as a supporting mechanism for the implementation of our release policies.

13.3 Separate Stores for Data and Provenance

In general, provenance records the origin of the data and how the data came about. The exact path taken to derive the data may involve many sources and processes that influence the data. Recording all these sources and paths may result in very large databases. This implies that the provenance data may grow much faster than the actual data and as such may be better served by a separate set of data management tools and databases. The approach we use in this chapter conforms to this paradigm and is illustrated in Figure 13.2.

Traditional data are normally expressed in a format that models an application domain and is suitable for the user's purposes and needs. Popular formats include relational databases that are suitable for well-structured data with a fixed schema format; XML and RDF are suitable for unstructured and changing data. We do not

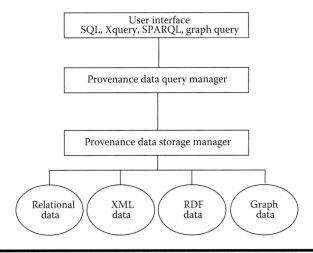

Figure 13.2   Provenance data storage.

put a constraint on how these data are modeled in our architecture. Provenance on the other hand may be derived from many sources, each with different schema, and so may be best represented in an open format that integrates with all these sources. We chose RDF as our preferred format because it captures the unique features of provenance such as the data flow, which is a causal relationship among data items and the directed graph nature of these patterns.

Even though the provenance is logically related to the actual data, it could be very large. A chain in a provenance graph may not be used in normal everyday transactions by all users, and so storing both the provenance and the data in the same database may impact the design and performances of the database. The needs of the provenance users and the normal users could still be served in a partitioned or distributed approach. Since the topic on provenance management is beyond the scope of this chapter. we do not discuss these concerns here. Normal data are already served with traditional models, which have their own security mechanisms to prevent the release of confidential data. These models do not naturally apply to the provenance. Keeping both the data and their provenance in the same database means we would have to manage two different sets of constraint policies on the same database. A request from a user for the traditional data must first be evaluated against all the policies, even though the user is not requesting the provenance data. In addition, in the case where both sets of policies are very large, their management could become intractable.

13.4 Summary and Directions

In this chapter we described different data formats for representing and storing provenance. We prefer a format representation that naturally supports the directed graph structure of provenance and naturally allows path queries of arbitrary lengths. We argued for a separate store for provenance in order to allow existing systems to continue supporting traditional data. This serves the purpose of decoupling the traditional data layer from the provenance data layer that operates on the provenance.

Appropriate data representation is one of the first steps to reasoning with the data. We have represented the provenance data using graph structures and Semantic Web technologies. We need to explore other forms of data representation including the logical languages to determine whether powerful machine-learning techniques may be applied to handle more sophisticated inference strategies. However, we need scalable techniques as provenance data may grow rapidly. Therefore, we need big data management and analytics techniques for inference control on provenance data.

References

Antoniou, G. and van Harmelen, F., *A Semantic Web Primer*, The MIT Press, Cambridge, MA, 2008.

Braun, U., Shinnar, A. and Seltzer, M., Securing provenance, Proceedings of the 3rd Conference on Hot Topics in Security, USENIX Association, 2008, pp. 1–5.

Ding, L., Finin, T., Peng, Y., da Silva, P. P. and McGuinness, D. L., Tracking RDF graph provenance using RDF molecules, Proceedings of the 4th International Semantic Web Conference (poster), 2005.

Harris, S. and Seaborne, A., SPARQL 1.1 Query Language, W3C Working Draft, 2010.

Holland, D., Braun, U., Maclean, D., Muniswamy-Reddy, K. and Seltzer, M., Choosing a data model and query language for provenance, International Provenance and Annotation Workshop, 2008.

Klyne, G., Carroll, J. and McBride, B., Resource description framework (RDF): Concepts and abstract syntax, http://www.w3.org/TR/rdf.concepts/, 2004.

McGuinness, D., Van Harmelen, F. et al., OWL web ontology language overview, W3C Recommendation 10, 2004–03, 2004.

Moreau, L., Clifford, B., Freire, J. et al., The open provenance model core specification, *Future Generation Computer Systems*, 2011.

Thuraisingham, B., Ford, W., Collins, M. and O'Keeffe, J., Design and implementation of a database inference controller, *Data & Knowledge Engineering*, Vol. 11, No. 3, 1993.

Zhao, J., Goble, C., Stevens, R. and Turi, D., Mining Taverna's Semantic Web of provenance, *Concurrency and Computation: Practice and Experience*, Vol. 20, No. 5, 2008.

Zhao, J., Open Provenance Model Vocabulary Specification, http://open-biomed.sourceforge. net/opmv/ns.html, 2010.

Chapter 14

Queries with Regular Path Expressions

14.1 Overview

In order for our graph rewriting system to manipulate the provenance graph, we use a graph manipulation language over RDF called SPARQL (Prud'hommeaux et al. 2006). In addition, we use one of the features of SPARQL, namely regular expressions, to identify paths of arbitrary length in a provenance graph (Harris and Seaborne 2010). We formulate our SPARQL queries around regular expression patterns in order to identify both the resources being shared and the LHS and RHS of the production rules of a policy set. The regular expressions are used to qualify the edges of a triple pattern so that a triple pattern is matched as an edge or a path in the provenance graph. Generally, any alteration to a provenance graph could alter the provenance (for example, changing the causal relationships among the entities in the provenance graph). This could change the history of some data items or alter the sequence of activities that caused a data item to exist in its current form (Cadenhead et al. 2011). This would therefore reduce the trustworthiness and value of provenance.

A graph rewriting system should be capable of specifying under what conditions a graph manipulation operation is valid. The embedding instructions normally contain a fair amount of information and are usually very flexible; however, allowing the policy designer to specify the embeddings may become error-prone. The OPM nomenclature places a restriction on the set of admissible RDF graphs, which we call valid OPM graphs. These restrictions serve to control a graph transformation process (also a graph rewriting process) by ruling out transformations

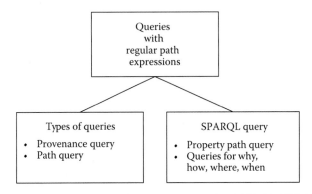

Figure 14.1 Queries with regular path expressions.

that lead to nonadmissible graphs. Our graph matching is based on regular expressions. We identify the patterns in the provenance graph by composing regular path queries in SPARQL. Therefore, this chapter is devoted to processing queries with regular expressions.

Query modification is at the cornerstone of our approach to inference control (Stonebraker 1975). Since we are dealing with SPARQL queries operating on RDF graphs, graph rewriting is the essence of our approach. Before we describe graph rewriting, we need to describe the types of queries we will consider. These queries are those with regular path expressions. The organization of this chapter is as follows. Background on regular expressions are given in Section 14.1. Processing SPARQL expressions are discussed in Section 14.2. The chapter is summarized in Section 14.3. Figure 14.1 illustrates the concepts discussed in this chapter.

14.2 Background

14.2.1 Regular Expressions

A subset of $\mathcal{U}$, the labels of RDF predicates, describes the terms of an alphabet Σ. A language over Σ defines the subgraphs accepted by a SPARQL query.

Definition 14.1: Regular Expressions

Let Σ be an alphabet of labels on RDF predicates, then the set $RE(\Sigma)$ of regular expressions is inductively defined by

- $\forall\, x \in \Sigma,\, x \in RE(\Sigma)$
- $\Sigma \in RE(\Sigma)$

- $\varepsilon \in RE(\Sigma)$
- If $A \in RE(\Sigma)$ and $B \in RE(\Sigma)$, then

$$A|B, A/B, A^*, A+, A? \in RE(\Sigma).$$

The symbols | and / are interpreted as logical OR and composition, respectively.

Our intention is to define paths between two nodes by edges equipped with * for paths of arbitrary length, including length 0 or + for paths that have at least length 1. Therefore, for two nodes x, y and predicate name p, $x(\overset{p}{\rightarrow})y$ and $x(\overset{p}{\rightarrow})^+ y$ are paths in G.

Provenance query. A provenance query usually answers questions of the form, Why X? How X, Where X, and When was X modified? The response to a provenance query could be a node, an edge, or a path in the original provenance graph. The responses to a provenance query is also referred to as a subgraph of the original provenance graph.

Path queries. The path queries we consider are navigational and are evaluated relative to some designated source vertex. Given a symbol x in Σ, the answer to a path query r is the set of all nodes x' reachable from x by some path whose labels spell a word in r. SPARQL is a RDF query language that is based around graph pattern matching (Prud'hommeaux et al. 2006).

Definition 14.2: Graph Pattern

A SPARQL graph pattern expression is defined recursively as follows:

1. A triple pattern is a graph pattern
2. If P1 and P2 are graph patterns, then expressions (P1 AND P2), (P1 OPT P2), and (P1 UNION P2) are graph patterns
3. If P is a graph pattern and R is a built-in SPARQL condition, then the expression (P FILTER R) is a graph pattern
4. If P is a graph pattern, V a set of variables, and $X \in \mathcal{U} \cup V$, then (X GRAPH P) is a graph pattern

The current W3C recommendation for SPARQL does not support paths of arbitrary length (Detwiler et al. 2008); therefore, extensions are needed to answer the queries over the provenance graph. Many approaches to supporting paths of arbitrary length have been proposed in the literature, which include Alkhateeb et al. (2009), Detwiler et al. (2008), and Kochut and Janik (2007). A W3C working draft for extending SPARQL to support property paths can be found in Harris and Seaborne (2010).

We use the following basic SELECT query structure to map a regular expression that is part of a policy or part of a user provenance query into a query over the provenance graph.

$$\text{SELECT } \vec{B} \text{ WHERE P,}$$

where P is a graph pattern and $\vec{B}$ is a tuple of variables appearing in P.

Query templates. We can use the set of names in Σ to answer common queries about provenance such as why-provenance, where-provenance, and how-provenance (Moreau 2009). To anticipate the varying number of queries a user could ask, we create templates that are parameterized for a specific type of user query. This simplifies the construction of queries by allowing us to map a user query to a suitable template. This in turn allows us to build an interface through which a user could interact with the system as well as create an abstraction layer that hides the details of the graph from the user.

14.3 SPARQL Queries

In this section, we provide examples of provenance queries. These queries can be used to identify resources for a policy or identify the answer for a user's query. The examples in this section are based on the provenance graph in Figure 9.4. The user interacts with the system by posing graph queries that support regular expressions.

Property path queries. These queries allow us to modify the property of a triple pattern. One important application is supporting regular expressions. These queries allow us to build constraints over the paths in a provenance graph in order to reduce leakages known as the inference problem. We write that can execute in accordance with the content of a user query. The code can examine various aspects of a user query, such as text or triple patterns, and take immediate actions to ensure that the appropriate constraints are intact. An example of a regular expression SELECT query that gives access to everything in a patient's record that was updated by processes controlled only by the patient's physician or surgeon, when the patient id = 1, is given as

```
{
        med:Doc_1_7 gleen:Subgraph("([opm:WasDerivedFrom]*/
        [opm:WasGeneratedBy]/
        [opm:WasControlledBy])" ?x).
}
```

The Gleen library function (Detwiler et al. 2008) is used to determine the set of nodes on the provenance path between med:Doc_1_7 and ?x. We can think of

s, ρ, and o for the provenance path, $s(\xrightarrow{\rho})o$, as placeholders for med:Doc_1_7, the expression given to the gleen:Subgraph function and the variable ?x, respectively. We can use the set of names in $\mathcal{V}_G^P$ of a provenance graph G to answer common queries about provenance such as why-provenance, where-provenance, and how-provenance (Moreau 2009). To anticipate the varying number of queries a user could ask, we create templates that are parameterized for a specific type of user query. This simplifies the construction of queries by allowing us to map a user query to a suitable template. This in turn allows us to build an interface through which a user could interact with the system as well as create an abstraction layer that hides the details of the graph from the user.

```
med:Doc_1_2 gleen:Subgraph("([opm:WasGeneratedBy]/
        [opm:WasControlledBy] | [Used])*" ?x).
```

This query pattern allows us to specify all the resources reachable from med:Doc_1_2 by issuing a query against the provenance graph in Figure 9.4. This query explains why med:Doc_1_2 came to be in its current form. Figure 14.2 shows the part of the graph from Figure 9.4 that would result from executing this why-provenance query for a patient with id = 1.

Example 14.1: How Query

```
compute leaf-set for med:Doc_1_3
for each XXX in leaf-set
computeFreq(XXX)
```

The Gleen API allows us to compute the leaf-set given the starting resource med:Doc_1_3. Each leaf in the leaf-set {med:Physician_1_1, med:Doc_1_1} is

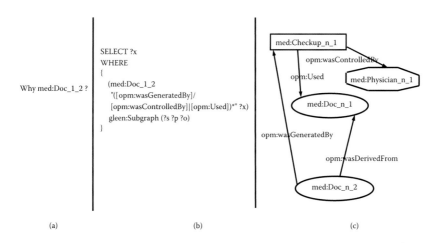

(a)   (b)   (c)

Figure 14.2   Why query.

the end of a unique path from med:Doc_1_3 to that leaf. We then compute the frequency of each leaf in the leaf-set. This query would return the following polynomials for a patient with id = 1:

```
med: med:Physician_1_1^3, med:Doc_1_1^4
```

A how-provenance query returns a polynomial representation of the structure of the proof explaining how the resource was derived. This normally involves counting the number of ways a provenance entity influences a resource.

Example 14.2: Where Query

```
med:Doc_1_7 gleen:Subgraph("([opm:WasDerivedFrom] |
[opm:WasGeneratedBy])" ?x).
med:Doc_1_5 gleen:Subgraph("([opm:WasDerivedFrom] |
[opm:WasGeneratedBy])" ?x).
```

This query would return the following triples:

```
(med:Doc_1_7, opm:WasGeneratedBy, med: Results_1_3)
(med:Doc_1_5, opm:WasGeneratedBy, med:Test_1_1)
```

A where query for a patient with id = 1 would be useful if we need to pinpoint where in the process a possible risk could occur as a result of performing a surgery on the patient. For example, a where-provenance query could be used to identify at which phase in the flow any medication administered to the patient had a negative interaction with the ones the patient is already taking. By using this query, we could compare the information in med:Doc_1_5 (which is generated prior to surgery) with that in med:Doc_1_7 (which incorporates the recording of events during the surgery). We show a simple example of a when query below for a patient with id = 1.

Example 14.3: When Query

```
Select ?x
{
med:Doc_1_5med:modifiedOn ?x.
}
```

This query would return the timestamp value as a binding for the variable $?x$, if the graph pattern in the where clause successfully matches a triple in the extended annotated provenance graph.

14.4 Summary and Directions

This chapter has described the processing of queries with regular path expressions. A graph rewriting system should be capable of specifying under what conditions a graph manipulation operation is valid. The embedding instructions normally contain a fair amount of information and are usually very flexible; however, allowing the policy designer to specify the embeddings may become error-prone. The OPM nomenclature places a restriction on the set of admissible RDF graphs, which we call valid OPM graphs. These restrictions serve to control a graph transformation process (also a graph rewriting process) by ruling out transformations that lead to nonadmissible graphs. Our graph matching was based on regular expressions. We identified the patterns in the provenance graph by composing regular path queries in SPARQL.

Now that we have described the design of our inference controller and the types of queries we will handle, in Chapter 15 we will discuss query modification in detail. It should be noted that our inference controller essentially implements query modification. Several examples will be provided in Chapter 16. Implementation details will be discussed in Chapter 17.

References

Alkhateeb, F., Baget, J. and Euzenat, J., Extending SPARQL with regular expression patterns (for querying RDF), *Web Semantics: Science, Services and Agents on the World Wide Web,* Vol. 7, No. 2, 2009.

Cadenhead, T., Kantarcioglu, M. and Thuraisingham, B. A., Framework for policies over provenance, Proceedings of the 3rd USENIX Workshop on the Theory and Practice of Provenance (TaPP '11), Heraklion, Crete, Greece, 2011.

Detwiler, L. T., Suciu, D. and Brinkley, J. F., Regular paths in SparQL: Querying the NCI thesaurus, AMIA Annual Symposium Proceedings, 2008.

Harris, S. and Seaborne, A. SPARQL 1.1 query language, W3C Working Draft, Vol. 14, 2010.

Kochut, K. and Janik, M., SPARQLeR: Extended SPARQL for semantic association discovery, The Semantic Web: Research and Applications, LNCS 4519, pp. 145–159 Springer-Verlag, Berlin Heidelberg, 2007.

Moreau, L., The foundations for provenance on the Web, *Foundations and Trends in Web Science,* Vol. 2, Nos. 2–3, 2009.

Prud'hommeaux, E., Seaborne, A. et al., SPARQL query language for RDF, W3C Working Draft, Vol. 20, 2006.

Stonebraker, M., Implementation of integrity constraints and views by query modification, SIGMOD Conference, 1975.

Chapter 15

Inference Control through Query Modification

15.1 Overview

The query modification technique has been used in the past to handle discretionary security and views (Stonebraker 1975). This technique has been extended to include mandatory security in Dwyer et al. (1987). In our design of the query processor, this technique is used by the inference engine to modify the query depending on the security constraints, the previous responses released, and real-world information. When the modified query is posed, the response generated will not violate security.

Consider the architecture for the inference controller discussed in Chapter 11. The inference engine has access to the knowledge base that includes security constraints, previously released responses, and real-world information. Conceptually, one can think of the database as part of the knowledge base. We illustrate the query modification technique with examples. The actual implementation of this technique could adapt any of the proposals given in Gallaire and Minker (1978) for deductive query processing.

We have conducted an extensive investigation on applying query modification for processing security policies (also known as constraints) to determine whether any unauthorized inferences can be deduced by the user (Thuraisingham et al. 1993). Our inference controller will then sanitize the data and give the results to the user. Much of our prior work has built inference controllers on top of relational databases. In our current work we have developed inference controllers for Semantic Web data. Our query modification technique for Semantic Web data will be the main focus of this chapter.

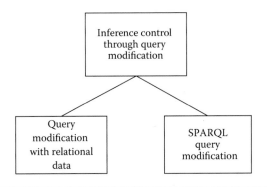

Figure 15.1   Inference control through query modification.

This chapter essentially describes the various methods that we use to enforce the constraints in the inference controller. The organization of this chapter is as follows. Background in query modification with relational data is discussed in Section 15.2. Query modification for SPARQL queries is discussed in Section 15.3. The chapter is concluded in Section 15.4. Figure 15.1 illustrates the content addressed in this chapter.

15.2 Query Modification with Relational Data

Security policies are rules (or constraints) that assign confidential values (or scores) to data items. In implementing these rules in a Semantic Web environment, we have several options available to help us implement these rules. A policy can be handled by TBox at design time by a query modification module at runtime and by a release knowledge base, which tracks the release of provenance.

In this section we discuss query modification with relational data. We have obtained this information from our prior work. More details can be found in Appendix C.

Query modification. We could modify the query according to the access control rules; for example, Retrieve all employee information where salary < 30K and Dept is not Security.

Query modification algorithm:

- **Inputs:** Query, Access Control Rules
- **Output:** Modified Query
- **Algorithm:**
  - Given a query Q, examine all the access control rules relevant to the query
  - Introduce a WHERE clause to the query that negates access to the relevant attributes in the access control rules

Example 15.1

> **Rules:** *John does not have access to Salary in EMP and Budget in DEPT*
> **Query:** *Join the EMP and DEPT relations on Dept #*
> **Modify Query:** *Join EMP and DEPT on Dept # and project on all attributes except Salary and Budget*
> **Output** *is the resulting query*

Security constraints/access control rules/security policies:

- *Simple constraint:* John cannot access the attribute Salary of relation EMP
- *Content-based constraint:* If relation MISS contains information about missions in the Middle East, then John cannot access MISS
- *Association-based constraint:* Ship's location and mission taken together cannot be accessed by John; individually each attribute can be accessed by John
- *Release constraint:* After X is released, Y cannot be accessed by John
- *Aggregate constraint:* Ten or more tuples taken together cannot be accessed by John
- *Dynamic constraint:* After the mission, information about the mission can be accessed by John

Security constraints for health care:

- *Simple constraint:* Only doctors can access medical records
- *Content-based constraint:* If the patient has AIDS, then this information is private
- *Association-based constraint:* Names and medical records taken together are private
- *Release constraint:* After medical records are released, names cannot be released
- *Aggregate constraint:* The collection of patients is private, individually public
- *Dynamic constraint:* After the patient dies, information about him or her becomes public

15.3 SPARQL Query Modification

RDF is increasingly used to store information as assertions about a domain. This includes both confidential and public information. SPARQL has been selected as a query language that extracts data from RDF graphs. Since confidential data are accessed during the querying process, we need to filter SPARQL queries so that only authorized information is released with respect to some confidentiality policy. Our aim is to rewrite the SPARQL queries so that the results returned are compliant with the confidential policies.

A considerable amount of work has been carried out in the area of databases that apply query modification techniques over the SQL querying language. These traditional approaches use rewrite procedures to modify the WHERE clause so that additional restrictions are added according to some constraints in the set of policies. More recently, the work in Oulmakhzoune et al. (2012) describes a query modification technique based on RDF/SPARQL. However, their techniques deal with privacy and do not take inference control into consideration. Our focus will be on applying similar query modification techniques to SPARQL queries.

We design security mechanisms that control the evaluation of SPARQL queries in order to prevent the disclosure of confidential provenance information. Our approach is to modify the graph patterns in the SPARQL query by adding filters and/or property functions that evaluate over a triple pattern. These approaches may return answers that are different from the user's initial query intent. It may be necessary to decide on appropriate actions in these cases. We propose two approaches that may be followed. The first approach checks the query validity against that of the initial query and notifies the user that the query validity is not guaranteed. The second approach takes into consideration that feedback about the validity of a query result may lead the user to draw undesirable inferences.

In some cases it may be possible to return only the answers that we know comply with the policy constraints. In other cases, it may be necessary to replace a restricted subgraph satisfying a query according to some transformation rules that leaves the released knowledge base consistent with the policy constraints. Yet another approach may be to lie; this is similar to polyinstantiation in multilevel secure databases where users at different clearance levels see different versions of reality.

15.3.1 Query Modification for Enforcing Constraints

Approaches for modifying the graph patterns in a SPARQL query make use of different techniques; for example SPARQL filters and property functions, graph transformations, and match/apply pattern. In order to determine the type of triple with respect to a security classification, the inference engine would use a domain ontology to determine the concept each data item belongs to (recall Example 15.2 above that shows a classification of an Abox based on the terminology in the TBox) as well as a query modification based on a SPARQL BGP transformation.

SPARQL query filter. The SPARQL specification provides another technique for modifying a graph pattern (Prud'hommeaux and Seaborne 2006). SPARQL filters restrict solutions to those for which the filter expression evaluates to TRUE. We briefly discuss how to rewrite a SPARQL query by applying SPARQL filters. The following is a SPARQL query requesting the age of a patient:

```
PREFIX med: http://cs.utdallas.edu/semanticweb/Prov-AC/
medical#
SELECT ?patient
WHERE {?patient med:age ?age}
```

After query modification, we restrict the query to only patients with ages greater than 18.

```
PREFIX med: http://cs.utdallas.edu/semanticweb/Prov-AC/
medical#
SELECT ?patient
WHERE {?patient med:age ?age
   FILTER (?age> 18)
}
```

Property paths. A property path is a possible route through a graph between two graph nodes. A trivial case is a property path of length exactly 1, which is a triple pattern. A property path expression (or just "path") is similar to a regular expression string but over properties, not characters. Table 15.1 describes regular path expressions as well as their descriptions.

Property path queries. These queries allow us to modify the property of a triple pattern (note that the property can be a directed label edge or a directed path between a subject and object). One important application is supporting regular

Table 15.1   Regular Path Expressions

Uri	A URI or a prefixed name; a path of length one
^*elt*	Reverse path (object to subject)
(*elt*)	A group path *elt*, brackets control precedence
*elt*1/*elt*2	A sequence path of *elt*1, followed by *elt*2
*elt*1^*elt*2	Shorthand for *elt*1^*elt*2, that is, *elt*1 followed by reverse *elt*2
*elt*1|*elt*2	An alternative path of *elt*1, or *elt*2 (all possibilities are tried)
*elt**	A path of zero or more occurrences of *elt*
elt+	A path of one or more occurrences of *elt*
elt?	A path of zero or one *elt*
elt{n,m}	A path between *n* and *m* occurrences of *elt*
elt{n}	Exactly *n* occurrences of *elt*; a fixed length path
elt{n,}	*n* or more occurrences of *elt*
elt{,n}	Between 0 and *n* occurrences of *elt*
!*uri*	A path matching a property that is not *uri* (negated property set)
!(*uri*₁|...|*uri*ₙ)	A path matching a property that is not any of (*uri*₁|...|*uri*ₙ) (negated property set)

expressions. We intend to build constraints over the paths in a graph pattern as a way of reducing leakages that cause the inference problem. We write code that can execute in accordance to the content of a user query. The code can examine various aspects of a user query, such as the literal text of a triple or triple patterns, and take immediate actions to ensure the appropriate policy constraints are intact. The following is an example of using regular expressions as part of the BGP of a SELECT query over a provenance graph, which uses the OPM vocabulary.

```
{
med:Doc_n_4 gleen:Subgraph("([opm:WasDerivedFrom]*/
   [opm:WasGeneratedBy]/
   [opm:WasControlledBy])" ?x).
}
```

This query pattern would give access to the artifacts, processes, and agents on the path to John's record. This query is written using the Gleen regular expression library (Detwiler et al. 2008). The Gleen library (Detwiler et al. 2008) provides two useful functions, OnPath and Subgraph. The OnPath function can be used to locate all of the resources in a graph that stand in a particular relationship pattern to a query resource by returning the set of reachable resources. The Subgraph function returns the set of resources and properties traversed on paths to these results.

15.3.2 Overview of Query Modification

An overview of a query modification for SPARQL could be as follows:

1. Iterate over the graph patterns
2. Identify the *sub(t)*, *obj(t)*, or *pred(t)* for each triple *t* in a graph pattern
3. If a *sub(t)*, *obj(t)*, or *pred(t)* is confidential then isolate *t* or transform it
4. Create a new query with modified graph patterns

15.3.3 Graph Transformation of a SPARQL Query BGP

SPARQL is based around graph pattern matching and a SPARQL query BGP is a graph pattern (i.e., a set of triples) (Prud'hommeaux and Seaborne 2006).

Definition 15.1: Graph Pattern

A SPARQL graph pattern expression is defined recursively as follows:

1. A triple pattern is a graph pattern
2. If P1 and P2 are graph patterns, then expressions (P1 AND P2), (P1 OPT P2), and (P1 UNION P2) are graph patterns

3. If P is a graph pattern and R is a built-in SPARQL condition, then the expression (P FILTER R) is a graph pattern
4. If P is a graph pattern, V is a set of variables and X ∈ U ∪ V then (X GRAPH P) is a graph pattern.

In a SPARQL query rewriting process, a BGP is replaced with an updated graph pattern. A graph transformation rule takes the original BGP as its LHS and specifies another pattern as the RHS.

Example 15.2: Hide the Surgery of a Patient

```
{
med:Doc_n_4 gleen:OnPath("([opm:WasDerivedFrom]*/
  [opm:WasGeneratedBy])" ?x).
}
```

This pattern matches a path where an entry in the patient's record, which is optionally derived from other versions of the patient's record, is created as a result of some process. That process is the surgery. This pattern, when it is the LHS of a graph transformation rule, could be replaced by another pattern, the RHS of the rule, so that the surgery is not disclosed. A possible RHS pattern would be the following:

```
{
med:Doc_n_4 gleen:OnPath("([opm:WasDerivedFrom])" ?x).
}
```

This pattern would only return the previous version of the patient's record without any entry that some version of the record had a path to the surgery.

15.3.4 Match Pattern/Apply Pattern

In Fine-Grained Access Control for RDF Data (http://docs.oracle.com/cd/E11882_01/appdev.112/e25609.pdf, 2012), a data access constraint is described using two graph patterns: a match pattern and an apply pattern. A match pattern determines the type of access restriction to enforce and binds one or more variables to the corresponding data instances accessed in the user query.

Example 15.3: A Data Access Constraint Using Match and Apply Patterns

```
Match: {?contract pred:hasContractValue ?cvalue}
Apply: {?contract pred:hasManageremp:Andy}
```

This example ensures that the *hasContractValue* of a contract can be accessed only if *Andy* is the manager of the contract being accessed. The important feature in Example 15.3 is that a variable defined in the match pattern is used in the corresponding apply pattern to enforce the access restrictions on the identified resources.

Processing rules. There is a difference between a query engine that simply queries an RDF graph but does not handle rules, and an inference engine that also handles rules. In the literature, this difference is not always clear. The complexity of an inference engine is a lot higher than a query engine. The reason is that rules permit us to make sequential deductions. In the execution of a query, these deductions are to be constructed. This is not necessary in the case of a query engine. Note that there are other examples of query engines that rely on a formal model for directed labeled graphs such as DQL and RQL (Fikes et al. 2002; Karvounarakis et al. 2002).

Rules also support a logic base that is inherently more complex than the logic in the situation without rules. For an RDF query engine, only the simple principles of entailment on graphs are necessary. RuleML is an important effort to define rules that are usable for the World Wide Web. The Inference Web is a recent realization that defines a system for handling different inference engines on the Semantic Web (McGuinness and da Silva 2004).

Enforcing constraints by graph rewriting. Graph rewriting, also called graph transformation, is a technique for creating a new graph out of an original graph by using some automatic machine. This is usually a compilation abstraction, where the basic idea is that the state of a computation can be represented as a graph, and further steps in the computation are then represented as transformation rules on the graph (Ehrig 2006; Rozenberg 1997).

Graph rewriting came out of logic and database theory, where graphs are treated as database instances, and rewriting operations as a mechanism for defining queries and views. Popular graph rewriting approaches include the double-pushout approach, the single-pushout approach, and the algebraic approach (Ehrig et al. 1991). The approach we describe is similar to the single-pushout approach.

A graph rewriting system consists of a set of rewrite rules of the form $p:L{\rightarrow}R$, with L being a graph pattern (or LHS) and R being the replacement graph (or RHS) of the rule. A graph rewrite rule is applied to the original graph by searching for an occurrence of the pattern graph and replacing the found occurrence by the existence of the replacement graph.

15.4 Summary and Directions

In this chapter we have discussed inference control through query modification. Query modification has also been referred to as query rewriting. In this approach the inference controller takes a user query and modifies the query according to the policies and gives a sanitized result to the query. We provided background information on query modification for relational data as well as aspects of modifying SPARQL queries. The implementation of our algorithms will be discussed in Chapter 17.

While moving to SPARQL queries from relational queries is the first step toward handling inferences for next generation inference controllers, our ultimate goal is to process queries with sophisticated logic-based reasoners that use machine-learning approaches. This way we can handle many more inference strategies than we have discussed in this book. As stated earlier, as the inference strategies become more complex, we need to keep scalability of the query processing techniques in mind. That is, while the data management system should release only authorized responses, users will require performance requirements to be met. Therefore, developing scalable inference controllers is one of our major goals.

References

Detwiler, L., Suciu, D. and Brinkley, J., Regular paths in SPARQL: Querying the NCI thesaurus, AMIA Annual Symposium Proceedings, American Medical Informatics Association, 2008.

Dwyer, P., Jelatis, G. D. and Thuraisingham, B. M., Multilevel security in database management systems, *Computers & Security,* Vol. 6, No. 3, 1987, pp. 252–260.

Ehrig, H., *Fundamentals of Algebraic Graph Transformation,* Springer-Verlag, New York, 2006.

Ehrig, H., Korff, M. and Lowe, M., Tutorial introduction to the algebraic approach of graph grammars based on double and single pushouts, in *Graph Grammars and Their Application to Computer Science,* Ehrig, H., Kreowski, H.-J. and Rozenberg, G. (eds.), Springer-Verlag, Belin, 1991.

Fikes, R., Hayes, P. and Horrocks, I., DQL—A query language for the Semantic Web, Knowledge Systems Laboratory, Report DR-05, Stanford University, 2002.

Fine-grained access control for RDF data, http://docs.oracle.com/cd/E11882_01/appdev. 112/e25609.pdf, 2012.

Gallaire, H. and Minker, J. (eds.), *Logic and Data Bases,* Plemum Press, New York, 1978.

Karvounarakis, G., Alexaki, S., Christophides, V., Plexousakis, D. and Scholl, M., RQL: A declarative query language for RDF, WWW2002, 2002, pp. 592–603.

McGuinness, D. L. and da Silva, P. P., Explaining answers from the Semantic Web: The Inference Web approach, *Web Semantics: Science, Services and Agents on the World Wide Web,* Vol. 1, No. 4, 2004.

Oulmakhzoune, S., Cuppens-Boulahia, N., Cuppens, F. and Morucci, S., Privacy policy preferences enforced by SPARQL query rewriting, ARES 2012, pp. 335–342.

Prud'hommeaux, E. and Seaborne, A., SPARQL query language for RDF, W3C Working Draft 20, 2006.

Rozenberg, G. (ed.), *Handbook of Graph Grammars and Computing by Graph Transformation,* Vol. 1, World Scientific Publishing, Singapore, 1997.

Stonebraker, M., Implementation of integrity constraints and views by query modification, SIGMOD Conference, 1975.

Thuraisingham, B., Ford, W., Collins, M. and O'Keeffe, J., Design and implementation of a database inference controller, *Data & Knowledge Engineering,* Vol. 11, No. 3, 1993.

Chapter 16

Inference and Provenance

16.1 Overview

Traditionally, we protect documents using policies such as access control policies and sanitization-based policies. However, current mechanisms for enforcing these policies do not operate over provenance that takes the form of a directed graph (Braun et al. 2008). Additionally, users can infer sensitive information from the results returned by performing frequent queries over a provenance graph. Such conclusions may include data that the user is not authorized to acquire. We refer to the process of forming these conclusions from the premises as inference. When the information inferred is something unauthorized for the user to see, we say we have an instance of the inference problem. This problem is always present in systems that contain both public and private information. The inferred knowledge could depend on data obtained from a knowledge base or on some prior knowledge possessed by the user in addition to the information obtained from the knowledge base (Thuraisingham et al. 1993).

The inferred knowledge obtained from a knowledge base alone could be used to reveal what is and what is not in a knowledge base. For example, if a user asks for information relating to a patient's x-ray procedure, any response could indicate whether the patient had an x-ray or not. In general, a positive answer to a query discloses what is in a knowledge base, while a negative answer could have more than one interpretation. For example, a user could interpret a negative answer to mean that the answer is not in the knowledge base, or the user could interpret that it is in the knowledge base, but the knowledge base chooses not to reveal the correct answer to the query. These two interpretations could also depend on whether the knowledge base uses a CWA or OWA (Reiter 1977). Normally, an OWA indicates that data are incomplete or they could be somewhere else in the system and are not restricted to a particular file or location. In a CWA, data are complete and a negative answer to a query usually indicates that the data are not present in the knowledge base. We assume an OWA; in particular, a user should not be able to distinguish, with accuracy, between the presence of facts hidden by the inference controller and the absence of facts that are available elsewhere.

Our main focus is on classifying and protecting provenance data, which are a kind of metadata that capture the origins of single data items of interest, as well as other relevant information such as data manipulation operations and temporal information. Though it is acceptable to represent provenance in any data format of choice, it is sometimes easier to visualize its structure using a directed graph layout. Therefore, we will refer to the provenance data as a directed graph, since a directed graph structure, besides being popular, has many advantages with respect to modeling data in a Semantic Web environment. The Semantic Web extends the RDF graph model to have inferencing capabilities by using formal semantics. It is this inferencing service that we use to support the inference strategies of the inference controller. Furthermore, we have shown how to perform new query modification techniques to enforce the security policies over a provenance graph.

A semantic reasoner enables us to infer logical consequences from a set of axioms. It provides a richer set of mechanisms that enables us to draw inferences from a provenance graph encoded using OWL vocabulary. We can specify the inference rules by means of an ontology language. Reasoners often use first-order predicate logic to perform reasoning. The inference proceeds by forward chaining and backward chaining.

In Chapters 11–15, we described our design of the inference controller including a discussion of data representation and query modification. In this chapter, we discuss the inference problem that can occur with provenance data and provide some examples. First, we discuss inference rules and then describe some of the approaches to handle the inference problem in provenance. Next, we discuss inferences and the implicit information in a provenance graph, and finally we briefly discuss how a user query log can be used to reveal a user's intent. The organization of this chapter is as follows. In Section 16.2 we discuss the invoking of inference rules. In Section 16.3 we discuss the approaches to the inference problem. In Section 16.4

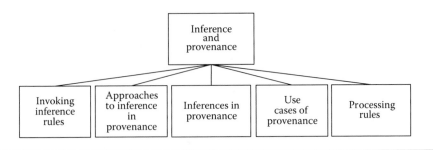

Figure 16.1   Inference and provenance.

we discuss inferences for provenance data. Use cases are discussed in Section 16.5. The approach to processing rules is discussed in Section 16.6. The chapter is summarized in Section 16.7. Figure 16.1 illustrates the contents of this chapter.

16.2 Invoking Inference Rules

Rules of inference can be used to infer a conclusion from a premise to create an argument. It is important to point out that a set of rules can be used to infer any valid conclusion if it is complete. A set of rules is sound if no invalid conclusion is drawn. Some rules may be redundant and thus a sound and complete set of rules need not include every rule when arriving at a conclusion. As stated earlier, when the conclusion is not something authorized to be seen by a user, we have a security leak and a case of the inference problem.

A rule can be invoked in forward chaining or backward chaining:

- If a forward-chaining mode, we are given some set of statements and we use the rules to deduce new statements. In principle, repeated application of forward chaining will find all facts that can be deduced by the inference rule from some initial set of facts from a knowledge base.

  Example 16.1

  Consider the following two rules:

  1. (med: HeartSurgery opm:wasControlledBy ?X) →(X rdf:type med:Surgeon)
  2. (med:Results_n_1 opm:Used med:Doc_n_6) ∧ (med:Results_n_1 opm:wasControlledBy ?X) → (X rdf:type med:Surgeon)

  If our knowledge base contains the following triples:

  ```
  <med:HeartSurgery_n_1><opm:Used><med:Doc_n_5>
  <med:Doc_n_6><opm:WasGeneratedBy><med:HeartSurgery_n_1>
  <med:Doc_n_6><opm:wasDerivedFrom><med:Doc_n_5>
  <med:Results_n_1><opm:Used><med:Doc_n_6>
  <med:Results_n_1><opm:WasControlledBy><med:Surgeon_n_1>
  <med:HeartSurgery_n_1><opm:WasControlledBy><med:Surgeon_n_1>
  ```

  we can conclude that ?X is a surgeon by using the last triple in the above knowledge base. The triple (med:Surgeon_n_1 rdf:type med:Surgeon) would then be added to the knowledge base. Note that the execution of rule 2 would also add this triple to the knowledge base.

- In backward chaining, we are given some expression and we determine all of the antecedents that must be satisfied in order for the given consequent expression to be true.

Example 16.2

Consider the following rules:

    1. (med: HeartSurgery opm:wasControlledBy ?X) → (X rdf:type med:Surgeon)
    2. (med:Results_n_1 opm:Used med:Doc_n_6) ∧ (med:Results_n_1 opm: wasControlledBy ?X) → (X rdf:type med:Surgeon)

If we want to satisfy rule 1, the reasoner would conclude that med: HeartSurgery opm:wasControlledBy ?X. Given the statement:

```
<med:HeartSurgery_n_1><opm:WasControlledBy><med:Surgeon_n_1>
```

this derivation will cause the reasoner to produce med:Surgeon_n_1 as the answer to the question

```
(X rdf:type med:Surgeon)
```

16.3 Approaches to the Inference Problem

Different approaches can be employed for building an inference controller. For example, we can use state-of-the-art machine-learning techniques to build a learner that automatically learns to recognize complex patterns and make intelligent decisions based on some explicit data. We can also build an inference controller that uses Semantic Web technologies equipped with reasoners that perform inferences over the data in the knowledge base. In this section, we illustrate some approaches of our inference controller that are based on the use of Semantic Web technologies.

The *aggregation problem* is a special case of the inference problem, where collections of data elements are secret but the individual elements are unclassified:

$$A \sqcup B \sqcup C \sqsubseteq Secret$$

We could enforce this rule by checking if there are any sensitive concepts in the provenance KB or the released KB:

$$A \sqcap B \sqcap C \sqsubseteq Secret$$

$$\geq 10R.(A \sqcap B \sqcap C)$$

If we know that at least 10 people have a property, then classify KB.

The *association problem* is where attributes A and B taken together are secret, but individually they are unclassified.

Example 16.3: AandBandC→Secret

We could encode this as an SWRL rule and then check the priovenance KB or the released KB if there is anything secret:

```
(med:Doc_n_6 opm:wasDerivedFrom med:Doc_n_5) ∧ (med:Doc_n_6 opm:
WasGeneratedBy med:HeartSurgery_n_1) ∧ (med:HeartSurgery_n_1
opm:WasControlledBy med:Surgeon_n_1) →
(med:HeartSurgery_n_1 med:Classification Secret)
```

If we consider the surgery operation to be sensitive, we can classify it as secret. Similary, the resulting version of the patient's record that was generated by the operation should be considered secret as well:

```
(med:Doc_n_6 opm:wasDerivedFrom med:Doc_n_5) ∧ (med:Doc_n_6 opm:
WasGeneratedBy med:HeartSurgery_n_1) ∧ (med:HeartSurgery_n_1
opm:WasControlledBy med:Surgeon_n_1) →
(med:Doc_n_6 med:Classification Secret)
```

Example 16.4

Something that is all three classes is private:

$$A \sqcap B \sqcap C \sqsubseteq Secret$$

Example 16.5

If at most one individual in all three classes, then classify KB:

$$\leq 1 R.(A \sqcap B \sqcap C)$$

Domain restriction. We can put a range restriction on a qualified value for a property as secret. For example, a property whose value is something with nine digits is sensitive. Note that a Social Security Number (SSN) contains nine digits; therefore if something with nine digits is released, then we need to classify the KB. Similarly, we could specify that something with 16 digits is a credit card number.

Statistical reasoning. In statistical reasoning we are given the summary data; the object is to learn macro properties about a population.

Example 16.6

If at most one heart surgeon on duty during a patient's visit and we reveal the following triple to a user:

```
<med:HeartSurgery_n_1><opm:WasControlledBy><_:b>
```

then the user can conclude that the surgeon on duty performed the surgery operation on the patient.

Machine-learning techniques. In (Chang and Moskowitz 1998), the authors approach the inference problem with a parsimonious downgrading framework using decision trees. The assumption is that when Low needs information for purposes such as performance and functionality, High must decide whether to give (i.e., downgrade) information to Low. In other words, when High wishes to downgrade a set of data to Low, it may be necessary, because of inference channels, to trim the set. Basically decision trees are used to form rules from the downgraded data High makes available to Low. Remember that we can use the nonsensitive attributes of an individual to arrive at (i.e., predict) the sensitive attribute using rules that are trained on similar individuals (occurring in previous released data). In parsimonious downgrading, a cost measure is assigned to the potential downgraded information that is not sent to Low. The idea is to determine if the loss of functionality (to Low) associated with (High) not downgrading these data is worth the extra confidentiality. Decision trees assist in analyzing the potential inference channels in the data that one wishes to downgrade. The authors assign penalty functions to this parsimonious downgrading in order to minimize the amount of information that is not downgraded and compare the penalty costs to the extra confidentiality that is obtained.

Other approaches covered by our inference engine include the following:

- *Handling inference during database design.* This approach is considered rather static. It depends mainly on schema design and integrity constraints. It was also pointed out that it is not very convenient to keep changing the database schema in response to each user's query.
- *Handling inference during query processing.* The bulk of the research mostly focuses on query modification mainly because queries are dynamic.

16.4 Inferences in Provenance

A user can infer sensitive information from the results returned from performing frequent queries over a provenance graph. Such conclusions may include data that the user is not authorized to acquire. Furthermore, our goal is to examine the inference problem that occurs with provenance data. We need automated software tools to discover and evaluate the interesting patterns and semantic associations in a provenance store. The amount of information generated by recording fine-grained provenance is an important but time-consuming work for security analysts. We can record the provenance using a Semantic Web language so that intelligent agents and reasoners can automate the inference without compromising the semantics of the underlying provenance.

16.4.1 Implicit Information in Provenance

A provenance document contains both data items and their relationships formulated as a directed graph. An intermediate node on a path in this graph may contain sensitive information such as the identity of an agent who filed an intelligence report, and so we need efficient tools for querying and inference as well. Also, we need to support large provenance graphs and the ability to query this graph so that we can build user views that filter user queries.

Security policies (i.e., security constraints) are used to determine who can access a document and under what conditions access is to be granted. In intelligence, it may be necessary to guard one's methods and sources; hence, an access control policy could limit access to the source of a report to sister agencies. However, these policies are limited to creating views and do not take into account implicit information in the provenance and so we need to develop policies that scale with the provenance data. We need to build large data stores for provenance. Provenance can be recorded in any knowledge representation language; for example, RDF, RDFS, and OWL. Using these languages allows us to later perform inference over the provenance graph. Therefore, we could determine the implicit information over the provenance graph.

16.5 Use Cases of Provenance

The use cases for provenance can be found at UseCases For Provenance Workshop (http://wiki.esi.ac.uk/UseCasesForProvenanceWorkshop).

Another useful source for use cases can be found at http://www.w3.org/2005/ Incubator/prov/wiki/Use_Cases. This gives the initial use cases gathered by the W3C incubator group.

For a list of security issues in provenance by the W3C group, see http://www. w3.org/2005/Incubator/prov/wiki/Security_issues_in_provenance_use_cases.

Use cases are also available at http://lists.w3.org/Archives/Public/public-xg-prov/ 2010Jan/0014.html and http://arxiv.org/PS_cache/arxiv/pdf/1002/1002.0433v1.pdf.

We construct use cases involving who/why/when/where queries. We may not know the answers to these queries for a particular domain, so revealing the provenance could be our best source for these answers. On the other hand, we may need to protect the who/when/where/why of a particular resource or node in a provenance graph. We present case studies in this section in order to illustrate what we want to achieve when we apply Semantic Web technologies to provenance information. In particular, we will discuss some of the use cases using a toy hospital example. While we will try to keep these use cases as close to our medical domain as possible, we also discuss use cases in other domains.

Data discovery. Data discovery encompasses the provenance of observing and capturing a patient's activities at all stages in a visit and operations.

A physician must rely on the historical information of a patient's record, such as who or what causes a record to be in its current state. Also the contents of the record can change with time, which can result in a temporal fine-grained capture of the provenance information for decision processes.

Dataset documentation. This allows physicians to retrieve the current and most up-to-date snapshot of a patient's record as well as its origin. This documentation supports further processing of the record by emergency personnel and drug dispensory units.

Pinpointing errors in a process. A where query for a patient would be useful if we need to pinpoint where in the process a possible risk could occur as a result of performing a surgery on the patient. For example, a where-provenance query could be used to identify at which phase in the flow any medication administered to the patient had a negative interaction with the ones the patient is already taking. By using where queries, we could compare the information in an earlier version of the record (which is generated prior to surgery) with that in a later version of the record (which incorporates the recording of events during the surgery).

Identifying private information in query logs. There are pieces of information that can also be used in identifying private information. Queries for phone numbers, addresses, and names of individuals are all useful in narrowing down the population and thus increase the chance of a successful attack. From the query logs, it is possible to generate the distribution of queries for a user, the query timing, and also the content of the queries. Furthermore, it is possible to cluster users and to some extent augment the query responses with the user behavior. Finally, we can also correlate queries (e.g., those who query for X also query for Y).

16.5.1 Use Case: Who Said That?

The scenario is based on a financial architecture being done for a government agency. This is a large architecture involving information, services and processes. Most of the stakeholders are nontechnical, and many are accountants. As with any such architecture, it is based on a successive set of inputs and meetings with stakeholders, not all at the same time. While this architecture was not being done with Semantic Web tools (it was Unified Modeling Language [UML]), the same situation arises despite the formalism used. Near the end of the project, one of the stakeholders was reviewing an information model for orders. This was not the first time this stakeholder had seen this part of the model, but they had not reviewed it in some time. The stakeholder pointed to a property on part of the model dealing with orders and asked, "Where did that come from? Who told you to put it in?" Certainly a reasonable question, but one we could not answer without a long dig through manual notes. There was nothing in the model to say where that property came from, when it was added, or under what authority. In addition, the stakeholder noted that something they thought was in the model had been removed and wanted to know where it had gone. Again, the tooling could not help. Conclusion: The source (both the person entering the data and who told them to put it there), the situation (such as a meeting), and the time of each assertion in the model needs to be tracked. This should be part of the core knowledge management infrastructure and leads directly to the trustworthiness of the knowledge base as it evolves over time.

16.5.2 Use Case: Cheating Dictator

It seems that certain intelligence activities look at things like the college transcripts of interesting people and use these to draw conclusions about their capability and character. The story (and it may just be a story) is that "Saddam Hussein" attended a college in Australia decades ago. The transcripts for that college were obtained and made part of his personal profile. This profile impacted important political and military activities. It became apparent that for propaganda purposes these transcripts had been modified. Analysts wanted to know what inferences had been made by human and automated means, what information was inferred, and how that could change Saddam's profile and potential actions. There was no way to trace this information path, making many of the opinions questionable. This is, of course, only one small example in the world where information may be intentionally falsified or obscured and where the resulting conclusions are critically important. The source and downstream impact of information is critical, particularly when sources and information quality are reevaluated. Conclusion: The track of inferences may span decades and this track may be of critical strategic value. In addition, inference is a combination of human and automated activities that affect downstream conclusions.

In this use case, we show that by annotating the entities in our generated workflow with actual attributes taken from the Web, we can verify qualifications of physicians and also point the querying user to appropriate URLs. These URLs could be part of the annotations about entities in our provenance graph, but they mainly serve to point to actual sources that verify the credentials of physicians.

Other uses cases include the following:

■ Aerospace engineering: maintain a historical record of design processes up to 99 years
■ Organ transplant management: tracking of previous decisions, crucial to maximize the efficiency in matching and recovery rate of patients

Below are some examples that illustrate policies relevant to the healthcare domain.

Example 16.7: Protecting the Name of the Physician

In this case any query that is issued should generate a response that does not divulge the name of the physician.

Example 16.8

For each patient, we generate workflows that capture the steps of various procedures generally performed in a hospital. In particular, we describe surgery, general check-ups, postcare operations, and so forth.

Details on generating workflows for inference control will be discussed in Chapter 17.

16.6 Processing Rules

The inference rules can be encoded and processed in more than one format. These include encoding the rules using SPARQL queries, encoding the rules using DL, and finally, the most expressive rules can be encoded as SWRL rules. There are differences in these approaches. A particular choice depends on the size of the knowledge base, the expressiveness of the rules, and decidability. A query processing engine does not handle inference rules, but is still powerful. For example, we can query for entailments in an RDF graph encoding of provenance. These queries can also be used to discover paths in a provenance graph (i.e., using regular expression path queries). The results of these queries can be combined to provide answers to complex inference problems. As well, where scalability is a factor, the best option is to query for the pieces of information and combine the relevant parts in a smaller knowledge base. On the other hand, there are cases where it may not be feasible to enumerate all the possible queries that will answer a particular inference problem. Therefore, we may need automated reasoners enriched with enough expressive power to do the inference for us. These reasoners may also produce new deductions that were previously unseen by a query engine alone. However, with this power comes a price: decidability.

Rules are normally inherently more complex than the logic in the situation without rules. For example, in an RDF query engine, only the simple principles of entailment on graphs are necessary. RuleML is an important effort to define rules that are usable for the World Wide Web. The Inference Web is a recent realization that defines a system for handling different inferencing engines on the Semantic Web (McGuinness and da Silva 2003).

16.7 Summary and Directions

Provenance is metadata that capture the origin of a data source, the history or ownership of a valued object, or a work of art or literature. It allows us to verify the quality of information in a data store, to repeat manipulation steps, and to discover dependencies among data items in a data store. In addition, provenance can be used to determine the usefulness and trustworthiness of shared information. The utility of shared information relies on (1) the quality of the source of information and (2) the reliability and accuracy of the mechanisms (i.e., procedures and algorithms) used at each step of the modification (or transformation) of the underlying data items. Furthermore, provenance is a key component for the verification and correctness of a data item, which is usually stored and then shared with information users. In this chapter, we discussed inference rules and then gave examples from some of the approaches to the inference problem in provenance. Next, we discussed inferences and the implicit information in a provenance graph, and finally we discussed how a user query log can be used to reveal a user's intent.

The last six chapters discussed the detailed design of the inference controller including the architecture, design philosophy, representing provenance data, the types of queries handled, the query modification process, and inferencing with provenance data. Our implementation will be discussed in Chapter 17. In particular, our implementation architecture as well as the development of the generators will be discussed. In Section IV we will discuss some advanced approaches for handling inference, including risk-based inference as well as playing games with the adversary to handle the inference problem.

References

Braun, U., Shinnar, A. and Seltzer, M., Securing provenance. In Proceedings of the 3rd conference on Hot topics in security, USENIX Association, 2008.

Chang, L. W. and Moskowitz, I. S., Parsimonious downgrading and decision trees applied to the inference problem, Proceedings of the 1998 Workshop on New Security Paradigms, 1998.

McGuinness, D. L. and da Silva, P. P., Inference Web: Portable and shareable explanations for question answering, Proceedings of the American Association for Artificial Intelligence Spring Symposium Workshop on New Directions for Question Answering, Stanford University, Stanford, CA, 2003.

Reiter, R., On closed world data bases, in *Logic and Databases,* Gallaire, H. and Minker, J. (eds.), Plenum Press, New York, 1977.

Thuraisingham, B., Ford, W., Collins, M. and O'Keeffe, J., Design and implementation of a database inference controller, *Data & Knowledge Engineering,* Vol. 11, No. 3, 1993.

Chapter 17

Implementing the Inference Controller

17.1 Overview

Chapters 11–16 discussed various aspects of the design of the inference controller. Chapter 11 described the architecture. Chapter 12 described details of the design of the inference controller. Chapter 13 discussed aspects of representing the provenance data. Queries based on regular expressions were the subject of Chapter 14. Inference through query modification was discussed in Chapter 15. Finally, in Chapter 16 we gave examples of inferencing with provenance data. In this chapter we present the implementation of an inference controller for provenance data. We have essentially used the design philosophy of building inference controllers that is discussed in Appendix D. Specifically, we augment a data management system with an inference engine. When a query is posed, this inference engine will reason about the policies and the data and determine whether the response should be released to the user.

The organization of this chapter is as follows. Implementation architecture is discussed in Section 17.2. Provenance in a health care domain is discussed in Section 17.3. Policy management including parsing the policies is discussed in Section 17.4. The explanation service layer is discussion in Section 17.5. Developing generators, which is at the heart of our implementation, is discussed in Section 17.6. A use case in the medical domain to explain our results is provided in Section 17.7. Implementing constraints is the subject of Section 17.8. The chapter is summarized in Section 17.9. Figure 17.1 illustrates our approach to implementing the inference controller.

231

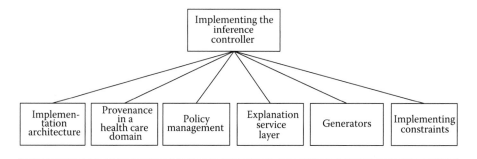

Figure 17.1　Implementing the inference controller.

17.2　Implementation Architecture

Figure 17.2 illustrates the implementation architecture of an inference controller for provenance data. We have designed a modular approach for the inference controller that can be extended and adapted. That is, we can use a plug and play approach to substitute the various modules of the system. In addition, our implementation utilized open source products that facilitates reuse.

The products we have used in our implementation include Jena and Pellet. Our policies and data are represented in RDF. Jena is used to manage the RDF data. Our reasoner is based on Pellet. That is, our inference controller reasons about

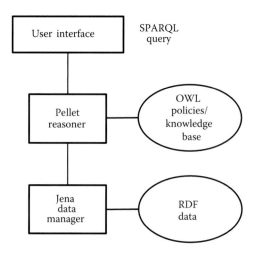

Figure 17.2　Implementation architecture.

the policies and the data utilizing Pellet. We built additional inference strategies utilizing Pellet. When a user poses a query in SPARQL, the inference controller examines the policies, rewrites the query based on the policies, queries the Jena RDF store, and retrieves the data that the user is authorized to see. In the next several sections, we give examples of how our inference controller functions based on health care applications.

17.3 Provenance in a Health Care Domain

The health care domain sees provenance as a critical component of its operations. The provenance can be used to facilitate the communication and coordination between organizations and among members of a medical team. It can be used to provide an integrated view of the execution of treatment processes, to analyze the performance of distributed health care services, and to carry out audits of a system to assess that, for a given patient, the proper decisions were made and the proper procedures were followed (Kifor et al. 2006).

We describe a medical domain with respect to sources available online such as http://www.webmd.com/. Our medical domain is made up of patients, physicians, nurses, technicians, equipment, medical procedures, and so forth. We focus on one example of the medical domain, a fictitious hospital. This is a toy example of a hospital that carries out procedures described at credible websites such as http://www.nlm.nih.gov/ and http://www.mghp.com/services/procedure/. These procedures include heart surgery procedures, hip replacement procedures, and the like. Since the procedures are described by actual documents on the Web, our generated workflow structures typically follow a set of guidelines that are also known to the user. However, the workflows generated by our system may not reflect exactly what goes on in a real hospital. We take into consideration that real hospitals follow guidelines related to a patient's privacy, and therefore, our fictitious hospital generates workflows so that the entities in the provenance graph are known only internally. This ensures that the content of a record (i.e., an artifact), the agent who generated a version of a record, the time when the record was updated, and the workflow processes are only revealed to a user via queries. Furthermore, the laws governing the release of the provenance (i.e., the contents of the generated workflow) are enforced by policies that are implemented by translating them into a suitable format for use internally by our system.

17.3.1 Populating the Provenance Knowledge Base

The provenance knowledge base is updated using a set of generators. There are background generators that are responsible for extracting background information that is normally available online. There is also a workflow generator that produces the actual provenance. The workflow generator produces synthetic provenance data that are not available online. It is these provenance data that have subsets that we must protect. We populate the provenance store by extracting information related to a health care domain. The health care domain is suitable in two ways. First, this domain actually records provenance, and second, data about this domain are partially available online (Kifor et al. 2006).

17.3.2 Generating and Populating the Knowledge Base

We create a set of seeds that consists of a first name, a last name, a state, and a city. Each seed is used to create a query that is issued against the http://www.yellowpages.com/ or the http://www.whitepages.com/ website. These websites are useful for locating businesses and individuals via search terms. In order to extract information from these websites, we employ the services of a Web crawler. A Web crawler is a computer program that browses the World Wide Web in a methodical, automated manner or in an orderly fashion. Web crawlers are sometimes referred to as automatic indexers, bots, ants, harvesters, Web spiders, Web robots, or Web scutters. These crawlers are computer programs that follow the link structure of the World Wide Web and perform some tasks on the Web pages they visit.

After the pages matching our initial query seed are crawled, we store the results in an appropriate format in a text file. Because this process is expensive, we build all our Web crawl routines off-line and load the text file contents into memory during the test cycles of our experimental phase. The first crawl gathers our assumed lists of patients. We use the zip codes of the patients to create queries for hospitals, doctors, and their specialties. The results of these searches are also stored in text files, which have predetermined formats. These predetermined formatted text files allow us to build object classes with properties for entities such as persons, hospitals, doctors, and nurses.

17.3.3 Generating Workflows

For each patient in our toy knowledge base, we initiate workflows that update the records for the patient. The recorded provenance is the only confidential data we assumed in our system. The intent is to give the querying user an opportunity to guess the patient's disease, medications, or tests associated with the record. Provenance data are more interesting than traditional databases because the controller not only has to anticipate inferences involving the users' prior knowledge, but also the inferences associated with the causal relationships among the provenance data objects.

Properties of the workflow. We observe a few properties of the workflows we generated:

- Our provenance workflows are generated using the OPM toolbox (http:// openprovenance.org/). This toolbox captures the skeleton of a workflow generated by using the predicates in V_G^P, where

$$V_G^P = \{Was\ Controlled\ By, Used, Was\ Derived\ From, Was\ Generated\ By, Was\ Triggered\ By\}.$$

That is, the initial workflows we generate are typically not annotated with RDF triples that are related to the entities in our workflow; for example, triples that make assertions about an agent name, address, or age. Therefore, we avoid clutter, which makes it easier to visualize the medical procedures.

- Each entity in our workflow graph, G, can be annotated by RDF triples that make assertions about the entities. Our workflow is typically stored in its full form. That is, we add annotations to each workflow by transforming it into one that has relevant background information corresponding to the entities in the workflow.

- Each entity in G has attributes that were derived from either the yellow pages (http://www.yellowpages.com) or the white pages (http://www.whitepages. com/) websites. These attributes are the ones that are a part of the user background knowledge. We also add other fictitious attributes to the entities in our provenance graph. These fictitious attributes allow us to scale the size and complexity of a provenance graph so that we will have some experimental data about the scalability of our system.

- The workflow graph G contains the private information (i.e., the provenance of the activities performed on a patient's record). This is the information our inference controller is protecting. The primary methods we employ for protecting this information are provided by the reasoning services available in Semantic Web reasoners and policies that operate over G.

17.4 Policy Management

We have already discussed several aspects of policy management in the design; as a review, in this section we repeat some of that information.

Policy screen. A policy screen provides the user with options to load and execute policies against the provenance graph database. The user has the option of executing any policy type; for example, the default ones (access control, redaction, DL rules or policies encoded as SWRL rules) or another policy type. The default policies are provided with a set of parsers that translate them to an internal policy

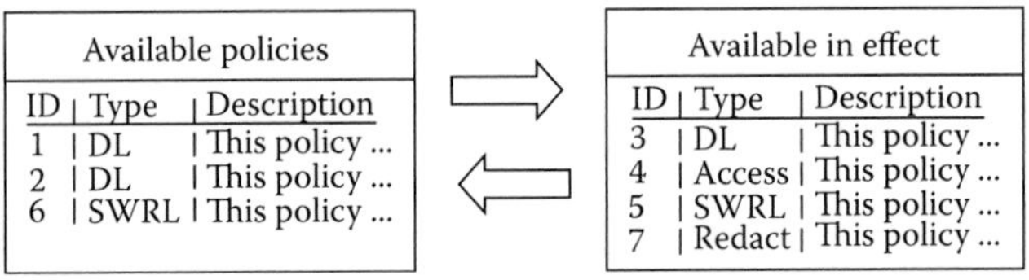

Available policies				Available in effect		
ID	Type	Description		ID	Type	Description
1	DL	This policy ...		3	DL	This policy ...
2	DL	This policy ...		4	Access	This policy ...
6	SWRL	This policy ...		5	SWRL	This policy ...
				7	Redact	This policy ...

Figure 17.3   Policy screen.

representation. New policy types are compatible as long as a suitable parser is provided to translate each policy type to an internal representation. The internal representation can be any technology that operates over an RDF graph; for example, a SPARQL query, DL, or SRWL rule. The policy screen has two panels as shown in Figure 17.3. The left panel displays a list of policies loaded but not in effect, while the right panel displays the list of loaded policies that are in effect.

Parsing process. A high-level policy has to be translated to a suitable format and representation in order to be processed by a provenance inference controller. This often involves the parsing of a high-level policy to a low-level representation. Our design makes use of an extensible language for expressing policies. This language has been used successfully to write access control policies (Moses et al. 2005; Ni et al. 2009). Our policies are written as XML documents that reside on disk until they are requested (Bray et al. 2000). XML is also equipped with features for writing rules (Governatori 2005; Grosof and Poon 2003; Horrocks et al. 2004). In addition, RDF and OWL can be represented in an XML syntax (Bechhofer et al. 2004; Horrocks et al. 2004). Our choice of an XML language allows us to take as input any high-level policy specification and an associated parser that maps it to a low-level policy format. The high-level application user also benefits from our use of an XML language, since XML is an open standard that is widely used and many data exchange formats are based on XML. For the rest of this book, we will refer to the policies as though they are in their XML standard form.

Figure 17.4 provides us with an overview of a policy parsing process. When an XML policy file is loaded, each policy in the policy file is parsed using a compatible parser. The parser is responsible for ensuring that the policies are well-formed. The default policies (i.e., access control, redaction, inference rules) are written in an XML file and the parser evaluates the XML file against an XML schema file. The policies in a successfully parsed XML file are then translated to a low-level representation.

High-level policy translation. In this section, we discuss how a correctly parsed high-level policy is translated to an internal low-level policy. We first discuss two inference assemblers, the SWRL rule assembler and the DL rule assembler, and then discuss two policy assemblers that translate the assess control and redaction high-level policies, respectively.

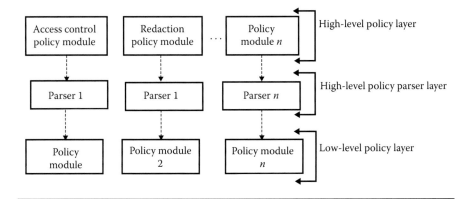

Figure 17.4 Parsing process.

SWRL rule assembler. This module maps a high-level XML file onto a set of SWRL rules. A SWRL rule has a head and a body. The body is used to encode a condition that must be satisfied before the information encoded in the head is applied to the provenance knowledge base.

SWRL policy translation. The following is a policy that states that if a doctor has (or is attending to) a patient, and then that doctor can also read the patient's record.

```
<policies>
<policy ID="1">
<description>...some description....</description>
<body>
<atom>?x rdf:type provac:Doctor</atom>
<atom>?y rdf:type provac:Patient</atom>
<atom>?y provac:patientHasDoctor ?x</atom>
<atom>?y provac:hasRecord ?r</atom>
</body>
<head>
<atom>?x provac:canReadRecord ?r</atom>
</head>
</policy>
</policies>
```

This policy could be represented internally as

$$Doctor(?x) \wedge Patient(?y) \wedge patientHasDoctor(?y, ?x) \wedge hasRecord(?r) \rightarrow canReadRecord(?x, ?r)$$

DL rule assembler. This module maps a high-level XML file onto a set of OWL restrictions. The OWL properties are used to create restrictions that are then used to restrict the individuals that belong to a class. These restrictions can be placed into three main categories:

1. Quantifier restrictions
2. Cardinality restrictions
3. hasValue restrictions

Quantifier restrictions. Quantifier restrictions consist of three parts:

1. A quantifier, which is either the existential quantifier (∃) or the universal quantifier (∀)
2. A property, along which the restriction acts
3. A filler, which is a class description

For a given individual, the quantifier effectively puts constraints on the relationships that the individual participates in. It does this by either specifying that at least one kind of relationship must exist or by specifying the only kinds of relationships that can exist (if they exist). An example of an existential quantifier can be used to define a physician as someone with a medical degree:

$$Physician \sqsubseteq \exists \ has.MedicalDegree.$$

Universal restriction states that if a relationship exists for the property then it must be to individuals that are members of a specific class. An example of a universal quantifier can be used to define a happy physician as one whose patients all have insurance:

$$HappyPhysician \sqsubseteq \forall \ hasPatients.(\exists hasCoverage.Insurer).$$

Cardinality restrictions. OWL cardinality restrictions describe the class of individuals that have at least (≤), at most ≤, or exactly a specified number of relationships with other individuals or datatype values. Let P be a property; then

1. A Minimum Cardinality Restriction specifies the minimum number of P relationships that an individual must participate in
2. A Maximum Cardinality Restriction specifies the maximum number of P relationships that an individual can participate in
3. A Cardinality Restriction specifies the exact number of P relationships that an individual must participate in

hasValue restriction. A hasValue restriction describes the set of individuals that has at least one relationship along a specified property to a specific individual. The hasValue restriction is denoted by the symbol ∈. An example of a hasValue restriction is *hasCountryOfOrigin ∈ Italy* (where Italy is an individual). This describes the set of individuals (the anonymous class of individuals) that has at least one relationship along the hasCountryOfOrigin property to the specific individual Italy.

17.4.1 Supporting Restrictions

We currently supported the following OWL restrictions:

1. **SomeValuesFromRestriction**
   SomeValuesFrom restrictions are existential restrictions that describe the set of individuals that have at least one specific kind of relationship to individuals that are members of a specific class.
2. **AllValuesFromRestriction**
   AllValuesFromRestriction are universal restrictions that constrain the filler for a given property to a specific class.
3. **MinCardinalityRestriction**
   MinCardinalityRestriction are cardinality restrictions that specify the minimum number of relationships that an individual must participate in for a given property. The symbol for a minimum cardinality restriction is the greater than or equal to symbol (≥).
4. **MaxCardinalityRestriction**
   MaxCardinalityRestriction are cardinality restrictions that specify the maximum number of relationships that an individual can participate in for a given property. The symbol for maximum cardinality restrictions is the less than or equal to symbol (≤).
5. **DataRange**
   DataRange is a built-in property that links a property (or some instance of the class rdf:Property) to either a class description or a data range. An rdfs:range axiom asserts that the values of this property must belong to the class extension of the class description or to data values in the specified data range.
6. **Domain**
   Domain is a built-in property that links a property (or some instance of the class rdf:Property) to a class description. An rdfs:domain axiom asserts that the subjects of such property statements must belong to the class extension of the indicated class description.

A DL policy translation. The following is a policy which states that any process that is controlled by a surgeon is a sensitive process:

```
<policies>
<policy ID="1">
<description>...some description....</description>
<rule>
<restriction>AllValuesFromRestriction</restriction>
<property>opm:WasControlledBy</property>
<class>provac:Surgeon</class>
<label>provac:SensitiveProcess</label>
```

```
</rule>
</policy>
</policies>
```

This policy is converted internally as

$$\forall Wascontrolled By. Surgeon \sqsubseteq Sensitive Process.$$

Access control policy assembler. This module maps a high-level access control XML policy file to a low-level access control policy.

An access control policy translation. The following is a policy which states that any user has permission to access Doc_2 if it was generated by a process that was controlled by a surgeon:

```
<policies>
<policy ID="1">
<description>description</description>
<target>
<subject>anyuser</subject>
<record>provac:Doc_2</record>
<restriction>Doc.WasGeneratedBy == opm:Process</restriction>
<restriction>process.WasControlledBy == provac:Surgeon</
restriction>
</target>
<effect>NecessaryPermit</effect>
</policy>
</policies>
```

This policy could be translated to a query that retrieves the part of a provenance graph that this policy is allowing a user to view. A corresponding SPARQL query would then be

```
Select ?x
{
med:Doc1_2 gleen:OnPath("([opm:WasGeneratedBy]/
      [opm:WasControlledBy])" ?x
      ?x rdf:type provac:Surgeon).
}
```

Redaction policy assembler. This module maps a high-level XML redaction policy file to a low-level redaction policy.

A redaction policy translation. The following is a policy which states that if there is a path that starts at Doc_4 and Doc_4 was derived from an artifact that was generated by a process that was controlled by a physician, then we should redact this path from the provenance subgraph containing the path.

```
<policies>
<policy ID="1">
```

```
<description>description</description>
<lhs>
<chain>
<start>provac:Doc_4</start>
<path>
        [opm:WasDerivedFrom]+ artifact AND artifact
[opm:WasGeneratedBy] process AND
        process [opm:WasControlledBy] physician
</path>
</lhs>
<rhs>_:A1</rhs>
<condition>
<application>null</application>
<attribute>null</attribute>
</condition>
<embedding>
<pre>null</pre>
<post>(provac:HeartSurgery_1,opm:Used, _:A1)</post>
</embedding>
</policy>
</policies>
```

This policy would evaluate over a provenance graph, replacing any path that starts with a node labeled Doc_4 and connected to a process via a WasGeneratedBy link, followed by a WasControlledBy link that has an end node labeled as physician (or is of type physician). Each such path would be replaced by a blank label _:A1 and :_A1 would be joined to the original provenance graph to some node labeled provac:HeartSurgery_1 using a link with the label opm:Used.

17.5 Explanation Service Layer

We discussed the explanation service layer when we described the design of our inference controller in Chapter 12. In this section we will repeat some of the information for completeness and also discuss some of the implementation aspects. A good feature to have is one where the reasoner derives new knowledge and then explains how it derived that new knowledge. The Pellet reasoner can explain its inferences by providing the minimal set of facts or other knowledge necessary to justify the inference. For any inference that Pellet computes, we exploit the Pellet inference service, which will explain why that inference holds. The explanation itself is a set of OWL axioms which, taken together, justify or support the inference in question. There may be many (even infinitely many) explanations for an inference; Pellet heuristically attempts to provide a good explanation.

Our provenance inference controller can then provide information about the classification of the knowledge base. For example, we may be interested in why a

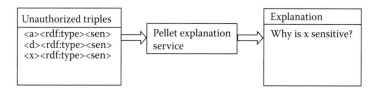

Figure 17.5 Explanation service layer.

set of RDF triples was classified as sensitive or why a concept is considered sensitive. The answers to these questions are left to the explanation service layer. This layer is built on top of Pellet explanation service and displays the set of axioms used to derive the concepts that are subsumed by another class.

The explanation service layer uses Pellet service to provide justifications (also warrants) for each piece of the provenance that is sensitive. The explanation service layer is useful for providing feedback to the application designer. The explanations are displayed using the low-level descriptions and may reveal details of how the internal classification works. This may be a bad feature of the system, since the application user may not understand DL or OWL. Nevertheless, this service provides a desired feature whereby the application designer can view the how his or her policies are interpreted by the low-level inference services. For example, since a high-level description logic rule may be applied differently from what the author intended, the policy designer now has an opportunity to tweak the high-level policies for the desired outcome (Figure 17.5).

17.6 Generators

We now explain the process whereby the knowledge is added to a provenance store. We build a set of generators. There is a set of background generators that are responsible for extracting background information that is normally available online. There is also a set of miscellaneous generators that build synthetic data about diseases, medication, tests, and treatments. The miscellaneous generator uses online sources to guide it in associating the diseases with related tests, treatment, and diseases and thus there is additional background information produced by these miscellaneous generators. Finally, we discuss the workflow generator that produces the actual provenance. The workflow generator produces synthetic provenance data that are not available online. It is these provenance data that have subsets that we must hide.

17.6.1 Selecting Background Information

We use real information that actually exists on current Web pages so that we can demonstrate the effectiveness of the inference controller with respect to a set of prior knowledge of the querying agent. We identify a city and state in the United States.

For this city, we target a set of zip codes. The information is downloaded from freely available websites such as yellow pages and white pages. We crawl these websites and extract the name, address, telephone numbers, age, sex, and relatives of various individuals by setting a seed for a list of popular first and last names. This would allow us to capture similar attribute values for each individual patient in our toy hospital. For the hospitals, we select only those hospitals within the zip codes for the patients. Each hospital has a name, an address, and telephone number. Because many hospitals do not release the names of their staff, we perform searches for doctors and their specialty within the same zip codes. This is normal, since most specialists are affiliated with a particular hospital close to their practice. Some insurance companies do provide a list of the doctors and their affiliation on their websites, but many of these websites require a login ID or different verification code each time it is accessed. Due to these obstacles, we must make do with a less accurate picture of the actual hospital. Also, since our system is user-driven, automation and efficiency become a greater priority. This does not preclude clients from populating the knowledge base with their own data. Generating data this way makes the system more realistic than if we had used complete synthetic data. A querying user can combine the responses from the system with accessible background information to draw inferences. The querying user could then issue new queries to verify his or her guesses about the data in the knowledge base.

17.6.2 Background Generator Module

Figure 17.6 is a diagram of the different background generators. Each generator is built to target specific websites (or pages) that contain some information of interest. For example, http://www.ratemd.com provides structured information about doctors at a specific zip code.

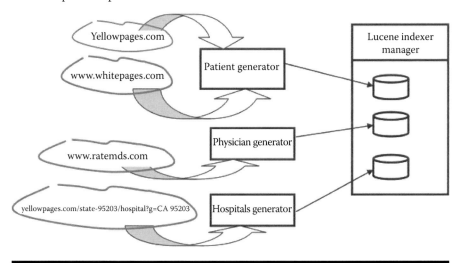

Figure 17.6 Background generator.

Patient generator. The patient generator extracts the attributes of a person from a set of Web pages. Algorithm 17.1 details the job of the patient generator.

Algorithm 17.1: *findPersons*()

1:*baseUri* ← *yellowpages.com*;
2:*uri* ← *baseUri* + *name* + *zip*;
3:*Link*[] ← *Spider*(*uri*);
4:**for all** *r* ∈ *RS* **do**
5:*Contents* ← *Extract*(*Link*[*i*]);
6:*Person* ← *Parse*(*Contents*);
7:*AddToDatabase*(*Person*);
8:***end for***

```
http://www.yellowpages.com/findaperson
?fap_terms%5Bfirst%5D = " fname "
&fap_terms%5Blast%5D = " Lname "
&fap_terms%5Bstate%5D = " State "
&page = 1"
```

Figure 17.7 shows the result when *fname=John, lname=Smith* and *State=CA*. We then extract the address and telephone number from the result page. Figure 17.8 shows the result of executing Algorithm 17.1 when the base URI is http://www.whitepages.com and the parameters are *fname=John, lname=Smith* and *State=CA*. We then extract the address and age from the result page. Figure 17.9 is a list of attributes we collect for each patient in our provenance knowledge base.

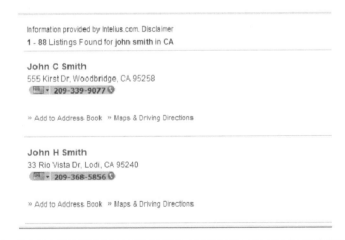

Figure 17.7   Partial page, yellowpages.com.

2 Results for John Smith in Woodbridge, CA
Or search: Last name only | Metro area   See in map »

| You? Claim & edit » | **John C Smith Jr** (Age 45-49) | Kirst Dr Woodbridge, CA | Associated people: Michael A Gillet Kimberly A Gillet + more ... See full listing » |
| You? Claim & edit » | **Wayne E Smith** | N Lower Sacramento Rd Woodbridge, CA | Associated people: unknown See full listing » |

Find more people named John Smith at our sponsors

Figure 17.8   Partial page, whitepages.com.

```
<id> 1 </id>
<firstname> John </firstname>
<lastname> Smith </lastname>
<address> 555 Kirst Dr </address>
<city> Woodbridge </city>
<state> CA </state>
<zip> 95258 </zip>
<telephone> 209-339-9077 </telephone>
<age> 49 </age>
<sex> ? <sex>
```

Figure 17.9   Patient attributes.

Physician generator. The physician generator extracts information as attribute values for a doctor (Figure 17.9). We modify the line 1 of Algorithm 17.1 by replacing the value of the base URI to base rateMd.com. Figures 17.10, 17.11, and 17.12 display the user interface for searching a doctor and the results, respectively.

Find and Rate Doctors and Dentists

Over a million free doctor reviews since 2004

Doctor's **Last** Name: smith
Enter **last** name or last name, first name (include comma)
City or Zip: 95258   State: CA   USA
Specialty: All

Clear   Find Doctors in USA

Figure 17.10   Partial page, ratemd.com.

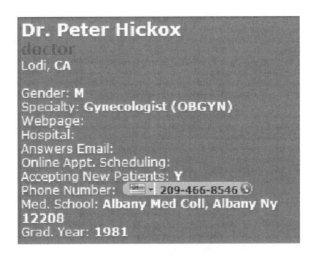

Dr. Peter Hickox
doctor
Lodi, CA

Gender: **M**
Specialty: **Gynecologist (OBGYN)**
Webpage:
Hospital:
Answers Email:
Online Appt. Scheduling:
Accepting New Patients: **Y**
Phone Number: ⊞ ▾ | **209-466-8546** ⟡
Med. School: **Albany Med Coll, Albany Ny 12208**
Grad. Year: **1981**

Figure 17.11   Single result page (obtained from ratemd.com).

Doctor Search Results

Your Search Parameters:

- country = USA
- zip = 95258

Change params & search again

Add a Doctor   Search Again

More than 200 results found; showing the 200 highest-rated.
You may want to go back and search again to constrain your search results.

(Ordered from highest-rated to lowest, weighted by # of ratings)

Name	Sex	Specialty	City	Last Rated	# of Ratings	Average Rating
Sackschewsky, Leslie	F	Gynecologist (OBGYN)	LODI, CA	3/7/11	4	4.8
Kellar, Robert	M	Family / G.P.	LODI, CA	1/23/09	3	5.0
Hickox, Peter	M	Gynecologist (OBGYN)	Lodi, CA	5/16/11	10	4.1
Stammler, Kira A.	F	Family / G.P.	LODI, CA	3/21/10	3	4.8
Duncan, David	M	Family / G.P.	LODI, CA	3/13/09	2	5.0

Figure 17.12   Multiresult page, ratemd.com.

Hospital generator. We also generate hospital information from the *yellowpages. com* website. Figure 17.13 shows the results returned from searching for a hospital. Figure 17.14 is a list of attributes we extracted for each physician in our provenance knowledge base.

Miscellaneous generators. This module uses http://www.webMD.com to determine the relationships between a disease, a medication, a test, and a treatment. Therefore, this allows us to add semantic association among these entities to our

Figure 17.13 Partial page (hospital), yellowpages.com.

```
<id> 3 </id>
<firstname> Peter </firstname>
<lastname> Hickox </lastname>
<address></address>
<city> Lodi </city>
<state> CA </state>
<zip></zip>
<telephone> 20
66-8546 </telephone>
<speciality>Gynecologist</speciality>
<age></age>
<sex> Male <sex>
<school> Albany Med Coll, Albany NY 12208
<school>
<sex> Male <sex>
```

Figure 17.14 Physician attributes.

knowledge base. Since the relationships are background information that is also available to any user, we build rules that take these semantic relationships into consideration when disclosing provenance information.

Workflow generator. We build a set of standard workflows, which are taken from the procedures described at http://www.mghp.com/services/procedure/. Since these procedures are freely available, we build rules to protect some sensitive components in the generated workflows. Furthermore, the relationships among the entities in these workflows can be explicit or implicit. Therefore, our inference controller utilizes a mixture of policies and inference rules to protect the information in these workflows.

17.6.3 Annotating the Workflow

We annotate our workflow using the data produced by the background generator. Therefore, the associations between the attributes of a patient are the ones gathered from www.yellowpages.com and http://www.whitepages.com. Similarly, the hospital and physician attributes are in fact the ones gathered from http://www.yellowpages.com and http://www.ratemd.com.

17.6.4 Generating Workflows

As stated earlier, for each patient in our toy hospital example, we initiate workflows that update the record for the patient. The recorded provenance is the only confidential data we assumed in our system. The intent is to give the querying user an opportunity to guess the patient's disease, medications, or tests associated with the record. Provenance poses more challenges than that of traditional data. The controller not only anticipates inferences involving a user's prior knowledge, but also considers the inferences associated with the causal relationships among the data items as well as the provenance entities (Algorithm 17.2).

Algorithm 17.2: *generateworkflow*()

> *patient* ← getPatient();
> *graph* ← generateOpmGraph();
> *annotateGraph*(*graph*);

17.6.5 Incomplete Information in the Databases

We generated our data from various web pages, each contributing a part to the knowledge base. This represents a classic case of our knowledge base containing partial or incomplete information.

An incomplete database is defined by a set of constraints and a partial database instance. Answering conjunctive queries over incomplete databases is an important computational task that lies at the core of many problems such as information integration, data exchange, and data warehousing. A common example of partial information over a relational database is a view. A view can be defined so as to hide important data in the underlying database and thus restrict access to a user. This is usually done to satisfy some constraints; for example, employees in the accounts department can view the accounting records but not the human resources records. Given a query and an incomplete database, the task is to compute the set of certain answers. The certain answers are tuples that satisfy the query in every database instance that conforms to the partial instances and satisfies the constraints. Answering queries under general constraints is undecidable. Therefore, the expressivity of the constraint language considered is typically restricted in order to achieve decidability. An analogy to incomplete information in databases is an OWL ontology. In an OWL ontology, the TBox can be seen as a conceptual schema containing the set of constraints and the ABox as some partial instances of the schema.

An incomplete database has an important property that an inference controller can use when answering queries over the RDF database. When a query returns a negative response, the user must decide whether the query was attempting to access confidential information or whether the query was not entailed in the RDF database.

17.7 Use Case: Medical Example

In this section we provide examples of provenance queries. These queries can be used to identify resources for a policy or identify the answer for a user query. The examples in this section are based on the provenance graph in Figure 9.4, which we duplicate in Figure 17.15.

The provenance graph in Figure 17.15 shows a workflow that updates a fictitious record for a patient who went through three medical stages at a hospital. In the first phase, the physician performed a checkup on the patient. At checkup, the physician consulted the history in the patient's record, med:Docl_1, and performed the task of recording notes about the patient. At the end of the checkup, the physician then updated the patient's record, which resulted in a newer version, med:Docl_2. In the second phase, the patient returned for a follow-up visit at the physician's request. During this visit, the physician consulted with the patient's record for a review of the patient's history and then performed a series of tests on the patient. At the end of this visit, the physician then updated the patient's record, which results in a newer version, med:Docl_3. In the third phase, the patient returned to undergo heart surgery. This was ordered by the patient's physician and carried out by a resident surgeon. Before the surgeon started the surgery operation, a careful review of the patient's record was performed by both the patient's physician and surgeon. During the surgery process, the surgeon performed the task of recording the results at each

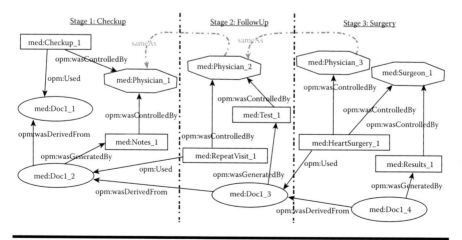

Figure 17.15 Provenance graph.

stage of the heart surgery process. At the end of the surgery, the patient's record was updated by the surgeon, which resulted in a newer version, med:Docl_4.

We assume that a hospital has a standard set of procedures that govern every health care service that the hospital provides. Therefore, each patient that needs to use a health care service will need to go through this set of procedures. We use a fixed set of notations in Figure 17.15 to represent an entity in the provenance graph; for example

```
<med:Checkup_n_1>.
```

The "n" denotes a particular patient who is undergoing a procedure at the hospital. Therefore, n = 1 identifies a patient with id = 1, n = 2 identifies a patient with id = 2, and so on. A larger number in the suffix of each process, agent, and artifact signifies that the particular provenance entity is used at a later stage in a medical procedure. In practice, "n" would be instantiated with an actual patient id; this leads to the following set of RDF triples for a patient with id = 1 at stage 1:

```
<med:Checkup_1_1><opm:WasControlledBy><med:Physician_1_1>
<med:Checkup_1_1><opm:Used><med:Doc_1_1>
<med:Doc_1_2><opm:WasDerivedFrom><med:Doc_1_1>
<med:Doc_1_2><opm:WasGeneratedBy><med:Notes_1_1>
<med:Notes_1_1><opm:WasControlledBy><med:Physician_1_1>
```

The sameAs annotations on the light shaded arrows in Figure 17.15 illustrate that the reference to physician is meant to be the same person in all the three phases.

This is not a complete picture of the provenance graph; it would be further annotated with RDF triples to indicate, for example, location, time, and other contextual information. Each entity in the graph would have a unique set of RDF annotations based on its type. Table 17.1 shows a set of compatible annotations for each type of provenance entity. A usage of these annotations in RDF representation for a physician associated with a patient with id = 1 would be

```
<med:Physician_1_1><med:Name> "John Smith"
<med:Physician_1_1><med:Sex> "M"
<med:Physician_1_1><med:Age> "35"
<med:Physician_1_1><med:Zip> "76543"
```

Table 17.1 RDF Annotations

Entity	RDF annotation
Process	Performed on
Agent	Name, sex, age, and zip code
Artifact	Updated on

17.7.1 Semantic Associations in the Workflow

We identified various semantic associations such as, if X is a heart surgeon who updates patient Y record, then patient Y procedures and medications are related to heart surgery. This would allow the querying user to determine the disease of Y after querying for Y, X, and Y and X on the same path in the provenance for Y's record.

17.8 Implementing Constraints

We describe the encoding of each of the constraints that were described and summarized in the earlier chapters of Section III. Constraints are generally rules, but may have additional conditions as well. The conditions may specify circumstances for applying the rules (e.g., some temporal or location criteria).

One of our approaches is to use regular expressions to write our constraints. Therefore, we could specify the LHS of a rule by using regular expressions so that the constraint is enforced whenever a pattern exists in a provenance graph. We have examined the following approaches to constraint processing. We next discuss the query modification process.

- DL concepts
- Query implementation
- SWRL rules
- Graph grammar/graph rewriting

17.8.1 Query Modification for Enforcing Constraints

We propose two approaches for modifying the graph patterns in a SPARQL query. These approaches use SPARQL filters and property functions. In order to determine the type of triple with respect to a security type (or label), the inference engine would use the domain ontology to determine the concept of each data item found in the subject or object of a triple or the classification of the property found in the TBox. This approach, however, fails when a triple pattern contains only variables and literals. We assume that either the subject, object, or predicate is a URI in any triple in the graph pattern. Special provisions could be made to determine the security type for kinds of literals occurring in the object of a triple; for example, identifying a nine-digit SSN or a 16-digit credit card number.

Query filter. Graph pattern matching produces a solution sequence where each solution has a set of bindings of variables to RDF terms. SPARQL filters restrict solutions to those for which the filter expression evaluates to TRUE. The SPARQL specification (Prud'hommeaux and Seaborne 2006) provides different techniques for modifying a graph pattern.

■ **SPARQL filters can restrict the values of strings with regex**

```
PREFIX dc: <http://purl.org/dc/elements/1.1/>
SELECT ?title
WHERE {?x dc:title ?title
FILTER regex(?title, "^SPARQL")
}
```

■ **SPARQL filters can restrict on arithmetic expressions**

```
PREFIX dc: <http://purl.org/dc/elements/1.1/>
PREFIX ns: <http://example.org/ns#>
SELECT ?title ?price
WHERE {?x ns:price ?price.
       FILTER (?price < 30.5)
       ?x dc:title ?title.}
```

■ **Constraints in optional pattern matching (for example)**

```
PREFIX dc: <http://purl.org/dc/elements/1.1/>
PREFIX ns: <http://example.org/ns#>
SELECT ?title ?price
WHERE {?x dc:title ?title.
       OPTIONAL {?x ns:price ?price. FILTER (?price < 30)}
       }
```

17.9 Summary and Directions

In this chapter we described the implementation of an inference controller for data provenance. The inference controller is built using a modular approach; therefore, it is very flexible in that most of the modules can be extended or replaced by another application module. For example, an application user may substitute the policy parser module that handles the parsing of the high-level policies to a low-level policy object. This substitution would allow the application user to continue using his or her business policies independent of our software implementation of the provenance inference controller. Essentially we have followed a plug-and-play approach for implementing the inference controller. We have used open-source products as much as possible in our implementation.

This implementation is the first of its kind with respect to next generation inference controllers. We have migrated from the relational database approach in the 1980s and 1990s to a Semantic Web-based approach. The reasoning capabilities of the Semantic Web technologies make this approach more powerful. Our next step is to develop even more powerful reasoning strategies using machine-learning techniques. Furthermore, we need to take into consideration the risks of unauthorized disclosure of provenance data. In addition, we can model the inference strategies as games where the players are the inference controller and the user of the system who could also be an adversary. That is, a game is played between the two parties and each party's goal is to win the game. Essentially, the inference controller will try to prevent any unauthorized information from getting into the hands of the adversary while the adversary will attempt to extract as much information as possible from the system. We discuss some of these directions in Section IV.

References

Bechhofer, S., van Harmelen, F., Hendler, J., Horrocks, I., McGuinness, D., Patel-Schneider, P., Stein, L. et al., OWL web ontology language reference, W3C Recommendation 10, 2004.

Bray, T., Paoli, J., Sperberg-McQueen, C., Maler, E. and Yergeau, F., Extensible Markup Language (XML) 1.0., W3C Recommendation 6, 2000.

Governatori, G., Representing business contracts in RuleML, *International Journal of Cooperative Information Systems,* Vol. 14, 2005.

Grosof, B. and Poon, T., SweetDeal: Representing agent contracts with exceptions using XML rules, ontologies, and process descriptions, Proceedings of the 12th International Conference on World Wide Web, 2003.

Horrocks, I., Patel-Schneider, P., Boley, H., Tabet, S., Grosof, B. and Dean, M., SWRL: A Semantic Web rule language combining OWL and RuleML, W3C Member Submission 21, 2004.

http://openprovenance.org/.

Kifor, T., Varga, L. Z., Vazquez-Salceda, J., Alvarez, S., Willmott, S., Miles, S. and Moreau, L., Provenance in agent-mediated healthcare systems, *IEEE Intelligent Systems,* Vol. 21, No. 6, 2006.

Moses, T. et al., Extensible Access Control Markup Language (XACML) Version 2.0, Oasis Standard, 2005.

Ni, Q., Xu, S., Bertino, E., Sandhu, R., and Han, W., An access control language for a general provenance model, Secure Data Management, LNCS 5766, pp. 68–88, Springer-Verlag, Berlin Heidelberg, 2009.

Prud'hommeaux, E. and Seaborne, A., SPARQL query language for RDF, W3C Working Draft, Volume 20, 2006.

CONCLUSION

Section III consisted of seven chapters: 11–17. In Chapter 11 we described an inference controller that operates over a provenance graph and protects important provenance information from unauthorized users. We used RDF as our data model, which supports the interoperability of multiple databases having disparate data schemas. In Chapter 12 we discussed our philosophy of designing an inference controller for provenance with Semantic Web data. The provenance data were represented as RDF graphs, and DL was used to support the inference tasks of our inference controller. In Chapter 13, we investigated different data formats for representing and storing provenance. We preferred a format representation that naturally supports the directed graph structure of provenance and naturally allows path queries of arbitrary lengths.

In Chapter 14, we described the processing of queries with regular path expressions. Our graph matching was based on regular expressions. We identified the patterns in the provenance graph by composing regular path queries in SPARQL. In Chapter 15, we discussed inference control through query modification. In this approach, the inference controller takes a user query and modifies the query according to the policies and gives a sanitized result to the query. In Chapter 16, we discussed inference rules and then we discussed some of the approaches to the inference problem in provenance. Finally, in Chapter 17, we described the implementation of an inference controller for provenance. The inference controller is built using a modular approach, and therefore it is very flexible in that most of the modules can be extended or replaced by another application module.

Now that we have described secure data provenance and inference control, in Section IV we will describe some novel approaches for inference control and also describe a unifying framework.

UNIFYING FRAMEWORK

INTRODUCTION IV

While Section II discussed secure data provenance and Section III discussed inference control, in Section IV we discuss novel models for secure data provenance and inference control. In particular, we will discuss risk models, game theoretic models, and machine-learning models. We also provide a unifying framework that integrated our architectures for secure data provenance and inference control with the novel models.

Section IV consists of Chapters 18–23. Risk and game-based models are discussed in Chapter 18, while novel approaches including game theoretic approaches as well as those based on probabilistic deduction and mathematical programming are discussed in Chapter 19. Cloud-based implementation of our policy engine for information sharing is discussed in Chapter 20. While much of the discussion in this book focuses on confidentiality aspects of the inference problem, the relationship of confidentiality to privacy and trust are discussed in Chapter 21. The inference problem for big data is the subject of Chapter 22. Finally, a unified framework for inference control which integrates policies for confidentiality, privacy, trust, redaction, and information sharing with respect to inference is discussed in Chapter 23.

Chapter 18

Risk and Inference Control

18.1 Overview

The focus of this chapter will be a risk model for inference control. That is, we discuss a formal model that decides a comparable trade-off for releasing both data and their associated provenance while hiding provenance in the case of intolerable losses. In Chapter 19 we discuss some novel approaches for inference control including game theoretic models amd mathematical programming techniques.

All of our security mechanisms explored so far for provenance suffer from what is known as an inference attack. That is, a user may employ different inference strategies in order to arrive at new information using prior knowledge and the answers to queries provided by our framework. When the newly inferred information is sensitive, we say the confidentiality of the system is compromised. To prevent the release of the confidential information, a first step is to identify the possible inference strategies available to the user.

As discussed in Section III, an inference controller is a software device that guards against known inference attacks (Thuraisingham et al. 1993). We have explored different mechanisms for handling these attacks. An inference controller could be an autonomous module that lies between the interface layer and the data layers in our architecture. The Semantic Web offers many technologies that we can use to perform inferences. These include reasoners that support forward and backward chaining, classification, and subsumption reasoning. For example, we can build sophisticated SWRL rules and DL constraints. These new rules and constraints will allow us to detect the implicit knowledge in a knowledge base before

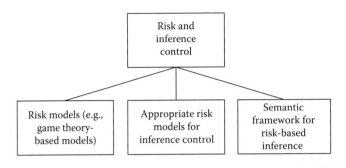

Figure 18.1   Risk and inference control.

any information is released from it. We can also leverage from existing Semantic Web frameworks that allow us to plug in any suitable reasoners. A suitable reasoner is one that implements any of the inference strategies supported by our inference controller.

So far we have made it clear that provenance data contain relationships that can be used to infer highly sensitive data. For example, the provenance data may have an ancestry chain involving nodes of type "Secret Agent" or some top-secret algorithm. Revealing complete provenance, including the chain, may reveal the identity of the sensitive information. In this chapter we propose a new approach that takes both the utility of provenance and the risks of disclosing provenance into account when we are adding provenance to the query answers (Cadenhead et al. 2010). The organization of this chapter is as follows. In Section 18.2 we discuss the risk model and in Section 18.3 we discuss aspects of Semantic Web-based reasoning for building the risk model. The chapter is summarized in Section 18.4. Figure 18.1 illustrates the contents of this chapter. In Chapter 23 we will discuss how the novel models can be incorporated into an inference controller.

18.2   Risk Model

In this section, we present a formal presentation of our model, which is adapted from Ayyub (2003). This model captures the essence of provenance and privacy risk. We first give a diagrammatic overview of the query process in Figure 18.2. This is followed by a formal description of our model and then a discussion of the modules in our system, which is composed of an external user system and an internal knowledge base system. Finally, we present a discussion on how to incorporate provenance into the model by means of utility functions.

Figure 18.2 shows a query as input and a response (or answer) as output. The user system describes the process by which a user combines a subset, C_i, of the entire external collection available as background information with the history of

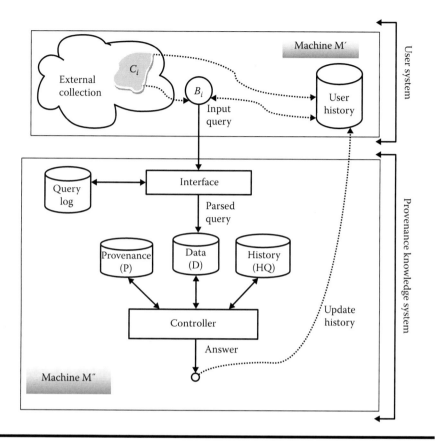

Figure 18.2 Processing a query.

previous answers to formulate a query. The internal system describes the process that ensures a query adheres to the security policies. The security policies are used to ensure that we do not inadvertently release any information that can be classified as sensitive, private, or confidential. We now present the steps composing our model:

1. $\exists B_j i = \{1, 2, 3, \ldots, n\}$ set of most likely backgrounds. Each B_j has a corresponding probability Pr_i that captures the likelihood of an attacker having background information $B_i \in B$, the set of all probable backgrounds.
2. $O_j \in O$ set of outcomes, $j = \{1, 2, 3, \ldots, m\}$.
   For any given query $Q_j \in Q$, all possible query sets.
   Ans: $Q \rightarrow K \subseteq 2°$.
3. $I{:}K \times B \rightarrow 2°$, an inference function.
4. $L{:} 2° \rightarrow R$, a loss function.
   $U{:} 2° \rightarrow R$, a utility function.

$$E[L(O)] = \sum_{i=1}^{n} L(I(O), B_i) \times \Pr(B = B_i)$$

$$E[L(Ans(Q_j))] \geq E[L(\phi)]$$

Prov(*K*), the provenance for *K*.
P_i, a privacy label, $i = \{public, private\}$, $P_i < P_{i+1}$ $\forall i$
$\ell : O \rightarrow P$, maps O_i to labels.

In step 1, we consider the case where a user has some background information associated with a likelihood of occurring. First, this is motivated by the fact that if no information is revealed ($Ans(Q_j) = \phi$) or if only complete noisy data are available after sanitization, then there is no utility. In this case, the privacy of the data is not compromised. Second, if everything is known $B_i \supseteq KB$, then in the worst case we may have total loss of privacy. The first of these is not desirable to achieve any utility in the responses given to a user. The second is an extreme, which may be too pessimistic. In step 2, we take into consideration that when a user queries the knowledge base system, the possibility exists that a user learns a subset of the knowledge base (that is, a user learns K). In step 3, we note that a user could use the background information from step 1 and what is learned in step 2 to draw inferences. Step 4 highlights the fact that what is learned at step 2 may have an associated loss. A background could take on any of the possible subset of backgrounds from step 1. Our model shows the expected loss associated with answering the query as opposed to not answering the query.

We need to estimate the parameters to our model to make it useful. We assume these are provided to the system before a query is answered. That is, *L*, *Pr*, *U*, *L*, and *B* are given by an expert. This is usual when assigning values to unknowns in a system. For *I* we use a Semantic Web framework, which allows us to infer triples from the ones in a knowledge base. The function ℓ maps a set of outputs to a privacy label, which is not limited to the ones we presented here. This is useful in determining whether we can infer private data. This function is used to determine which set of outputs to release to the user and which set we should not. In addition, if we could infer some private information using the labels, the private information that is inferred could be used as a guidance for defining the loss function.

Let $\mathcal{D}$, $\mathcal{P}$ be the set of triples in the data and provenance collections, respectively. Using the privacy labels from our model, we define a partition on $\mathcal{D}(\mathcal{P})$ as a public set and a private set denoted as $\mathcal{D}_V$ ($\mathcal{P}_V$) and $\mathcal{D}_H$ ($\mathcal{P}_H$), respectively. The set of labels is not limited to the ones presented here. The public set is visible to the user and the private set is hidden. We assume a user combines B_i with each $Ans(Q_j)$ to deduce new data not explicit in $\mathcal{D}_V \cup \mathcal{P}_V$.

18.2.1 User's System

A user may use the query history with an auxiliary source of information to build a reservoir of background knowledge. From this reservoir, a user can formulate specific queries that exploit the relationships between the background knowledge and the knowledge from the internal knowledge base system. It is not a trivial process to estimate the knowledge in this reservoir, since, for example, the sheer size of the Web alone is intractable for the knowledge base system. For the user system in Figure 18.2, we assume that the user constrains the background over time as he or she builds a profile of the data from the internal knowledge base system (i.e., the user builds the user history collection). From this profile, the user adapts the background collection (C_i) or the next query. From this background collection and the answer given for the query, the user applies some inferencing techniques to make sense of the answer. It is this inferencing technique that makes it possible to learn some of the private data from the knowledge base system.

18.2.2 Internal Knowledge Base System

The internal knowledge base system is composed of an interface module and a controller module (which implements an inference controller). We will speak of a controller module whenever it is clear that we are talking about the implementation of an inference controller. The interface module parses the query and also keeps a log of all the queries seen so far. We now describe the interface module as follows:

1. Assign the user a privacy P_u
   This could be based on the context, attributes, authentication, credentials, and so forth, of the user.
2. Add Q_J to the query log.
3. Parse the query Q_J.

This is to identify and remove triple patterns with labels above P_u from the query string. This ensures that we do not match the BGPs in the query string against the data in $\mathcal{D}_V$.

18.2.3 Controller

The controller has the responsibility of fulfilling the request of the user. It retrieves the requested information by querying for a subset of $\mathcal{D}_V$ and it also determines the provenance associated with $Ans(Q_J)$ as a subset of the data in $\mathcal{P}_V$. The controller then applies the privacy policies to the current results. Finally, it decides if the query can be answered according to the rules governing the release of data. The controller is described as follows:

1. $KB' = Ans(Q_j) \cup Prov(Ans(Q_j))$

   If answers are available from fulfilling the request of Q_J from the set $\mathcal{D}_V \cup \mathcal{P}_V$, it is added to an empty knowledge base and we continue to the next step. Otherwise, there are no answers for Q_J. This case is most likely when it is not possible to release answers after satisfying the constraints from the privacy policies.

2. $KB' = KB' \cup H_Q$

   The query history is derived from all the queries answered so far (e.g., $(Q_1...Q_{j-1}) \vdash H_Q$. KB' is updated from the history.

3. $R(KB') \rightarrow KB' + Inf(KB')$

   R is a decidable RDFS/OWL reasoner.

   The reasoner performs inferencing over the knowledge base to determine newly inferred triples that are different from those already in the knowledge base.

4. $\ell.Inf(KB') \rightarrow P.$

$$A = \{x | x \in KB', \ell(x) = P_i, P_i > P_u\}$$

   This determines all labels that are higher than that of the user.

5. $Ans(Q_j) = Ans(Q_j) \cup Prov(Ans(Q_j)) - A$

$$H_Q = H_Q \cup Ans(Q_j)$$

   The answer set is then adjusted and the history reflects the new changes.

18.2.4 Adding Provenance

We now discuss when to provide provenance as part of the answer set given to the user. This process is very subjective and is based on the user's utility function, as we show in the following two examples.

Example 18.1

Assume that we are playing a game with the user where we accept monetary payments for the services of the knowledge base system. Each time the system answers the user's query, the user makes a payment commensurate with the utility of the answers.

Example 18.2

Assume we are trying to catch a terrorist. By answering queries, we can facilitate the sharing of information and this sharing of information can be used to capture a terrorist. Therefore, by answering the query, we help some tasks to get done or executed, which results in the capture of a terrorist.

We adapt our model to allow provenance to be part of the answer set for a query. We release provenance data to a user whenever $E[L(O)] + U(O) \geq E[L(\phi)]$. That is, we answer a query based on whether the addition of provenance improves the user's utility value of the answers. In other words, when $U(I(Prov(Ans(Q_j)))) > \phi$.

Our model decides to answer a query as follows:

1. If $E[L(Prov(Ans(Q_j)) \cup Ans(Q_j))]+$

   $U(Prov(Ans(Q_j)) \cup Ans(Q_j)) \geq E[L(\phi)]$, release $Prov(Ans(Q_j)) \cup Ans(Q_j)$

2. If $E[L(Ans(Q_j))] + U(Ans(Q_j)) \geq E[L(\phi)]$, release $Ans(Q_j)$.
3. Else release ϕ

In step 1, we release provenance data if the user's utility increases by adding provenance data. In step 2, we release only the answers, since the utility resulting from integrating the provenance has not improved. If neither step 1 nor step 2 produces an answer, it means that our knowledge base system has no way of answering the user's query without revealing some private information.

18.3 Semantic Framework for Inferences

We now discuss the inference function in our model. This function takes two inputs, the answer for the current query and the background information, and infers new knowledge. We do not know the particular background information available to a user when a query is issued. However, we can conclude that the user has a large pool of data to rely on. The amount of information on the Web grows daily and search engines make it easier to find information about any topic. Furthermore, there are efforts to represent information as RDF, which increases the amount of linked data available to a user (Auer et al. 2007; Bizer et al. 2007; Bizer et al. 2009; W3C SWEO 2010). Therefore, it is becoming increasingly easier for a user to link information in an answer set with any type of background information. We will study the behavior of a user under the assumption that the background knowledge can be encoded as rules. In addition, we limit our analysis to the health care domain, which was discussed in Chapters 9 and 17. The workflow in Chapters 9 and 17 is annotated with RDF triples to indicate contextual information about the patients and other entities; the annotations are a subset of the semistructured information on the Web.

We estimate the inferencing capabilities of the user by allowing the controller in our internal knowledge base system to mimic some basic inferencing strategies. We use a combination of ontology reasoning, rule-based reasoning, and heuristics to estimate the user's background information. For estimating the background knowledge, we make use of the query logs and adapt the rules to anticipate certain types of inferences. The answers provided for a query are composed of different data from different databases in the knowledge base system, as shown in Figure 18.2. The controller combines data from different data stores when formulating responses. Important sources of information are the semistructured data available on the web (e.g., census data). This information can be cleaned and imported, thus allowing the controller to engage in limited record linking (see Winkler 2006 for a background on record linkage methods). Although we cannot know the exact background of a user, we could use heuristics to limit the amount of inferencing by the user. Our controller also tracks the history of the interactions with the user; for example, we are tracking the previous queries and previously released information. In the rest of this section, we discuss the use of ontologies, which can be used to classify data, followed by a discussion on basic inferences by rules, and finally we discuss how we can incorporate query logs as part of the inferencing process.

18.3.1 Ontologies

Tools exist that support RDF and its semantic extensions (e.g., RDF, RDFS, OWL). These tools support reasoners. An example is Jena (Carroll et al. 2004). This is a Java framework for building Semantic Web applications. It provides a programmatic environment for RDF, RDFS, OWL, and SPARQL and includes a rule-based inference engine.

Knowledge representation languages like RDF, RDFS, and OWL are used for creating ontologies. An ontology is a specification that represents knowledge as a set of individuals and a set of property assertions that relate these individuals to each other. It consists of a set of axioms that place constraints on sets of individuals (called classes) and the types of relationships (or properties) permitted between them. Data items are connected to each other and to literal data via properties. A statement in an ontology is of the form of a triple (s p o).

An ontology for provenance would model the data items and processes as instances of a class and the links between them as properties. In this ontology, we could have statements such as

med:CheckUp_1 opm:wasControllrdBy med:Physician_1

An ontology for OPM contains three basic entities: artifact, process, and agent (Moreau 2010; Zhao 2010). The instances of these objects are the nodes in a provenance graph. This model represents an edge as a causal dependency between its source, denoting the effect, and its destination, denoting the cause (Moreau et al. 2011). The semantics of RDF and OWL allow us to define terms so that a reasoner can make logical inferences about the interconnections among the data items and processes in the provenance graph. Given a provenance graph, all of the direct and indirect connections it has to other data items and processes can be inferred and then retrieved by a SPARQL query (Golbeck and Hendler 2008).

18.3.2 Rules

For the inferences that are not captured by modeling the data as an ontology, we add rules to the knowledge base. That is, we add rules to step 3 for the controller module. Rules are of two types: those used to express the privacy policies and those used to improve the inferencing power of the controller. So far we assume a user combines his or her background with the information in the answers to infer new data, which was not explicit in $\mathcal{D}_V \cup \mathcal{P}_V$. We formalize this as an inference rule:

$$\bigwedge_{i}^{n} B_i \wedge \bigwedge_{j=1}^{m} Ans(Q_j) \wedge Prov(Ans(Q_j)) \wedge Ans(Q_{m+1}) \wedge Prov(Ans(Q_{m+1})) \rightarrow \varphi.$$

This rule represents basic implication and is a method for deducing information from existing ones. We also need a way to assign labels to triples in a knowledge base. For example, if there is a person Jack in our knowledge base, and some information about Jack is private, then if the fact that Jack has the flu is private, we must label the triple, (Jack hasDisease flu), as private. In addition, if part of the triple is private, we need to make the entire triple private. For instance, if Jack is private, then revealing any information in triples with Jack as the subject or object would reveal that there is someone named Jack in the knowledge base system.

Definition 18.1: Private Triple

Let t be a triple of subparts s, p, and o and L_u be the privacy label for a user. For any subpart v of t, if $\ell(v) = L$, and $L > L_u$, then $\ell(t) = L$.

The classification of an inferred triple φ using the basic implication rule could be used to collect statistics about a user. By keeping track of how many times φ is labeled private from Definition 19.1 since the last n queries, as well as the total number of times this happens, we can formulate a profile of the background knowledge of the user. This could be used to build new rules or adjust existing ones to enforce the policies under the new estimates of the user's background patterns.

There are different ways we can build our rules. In an association rule, $\alpha \wedge \beta \rightarrow \varphi$, if $(\ell(\alpha) \le L_u) \wedge (\ell(\beta) \le L_u)$ and we already release α, we may want to adjust the label for β to $\ell(\beta) > L_u$. This follows from the fact that both α and β when taken together reveal private information.

18.3.3 Query Logs

Posing queries to a dataset to get answers with high utility is not new. In information retrieval (IR), users pose similar queries against sets of documents, and various literature highlights that these queries have context (Bai et al. 2007; Shen et al. 2005).

The context could determine the user's domain of interest, knowledge, preferences, relevance, judgments, and so forth. These could be used to construct a user profile to reflect the user's domains of interest and background. In IR, the use of previous queries and clickthrough history information has been suggested to improve accuracy of the answers. This is worth considering for our initial model. We could also perform a fine-grained recording of an agent's previous activities in order to examine in more detail the potential threat posed by each query. This would allow us to capture a subset of the background associated with the user's queries. Under our RDF data model, SPARQL is the standard query language. A simple syntax of a SELECT query in SPARQL is

$$\text{SELECT } \vec{V} \text{ FROM } u \text{ WHERE } \{T\},$$

where u is the URL of an RDF graph G, T is a SPARQL graph pattern, and $\vec{V}$ is a tuple of variables appearing in T. For brevity, T is matched against G and bindings are returned for each solution for the variables in T. The SELECT is a projection over the solutions from the bindings. An answer may provide the user with feedback about the matching of T. If the query was matched and we return an answer, the user knows that T exists in the knowledge base (i.e., $T \subseteq KB$). If there is no answer, then the user still knows something about the pattern. However, under the OWA of RDF, there is a probability that $T \subseteq KB$, either it is part of the private section $\mathcal{D}_H \cup \mathcal{P}_H$ or it is not part of the system (i.e., $KB \cap T = \emptyset$). Therefore, keeping query logs could provide useful information about the possible inferencing capabilities and patterns of the user's background.

18.4 Summary and Directions

In this chapter we discussed aspects of a formal model, which decides a comparable trade-off for releasing both data and its associated provenance while hiding provenance in the case of intolerable losses. All of our security mechanisms explored so far for provenance suffer from what is known as an inference attack. That is, a user may employ different inference strategies in order to arrive at new information using prior knowledge and the answers to queries provided by our framework. When the newly inferred information is sensitive, we say the confidentiality of the system is compromised. To prevent the release of the confidential information, a first step is to identify the possible inference strategies available to the user. This was the major focus of this chapter.

Note that the ideas presented in this chapter are preliminary. We need to carry out an in-depth study of risk-based access control and inference control. There has been a lot of recent research on incorporating trust, risk, and cost in security and privacy models. Such research has to incorporate the study of inference control. In the next chapter we will continue to explore some novel models, including those based on machine learning, probabilistic reasoning, and game theory.

References

Auer, S., Bizer, C., Kobilarov, G., Lehmann, J., Cyganiak, R. and Ives, Z., DBpedia: A nucleus for a web of open data, In Proceedings of the Intl. Semantic Web Conference, 2007.

Ayyub, B., *Risk Analysis in Engineering and Economics,* CRC Press, Boca Raton, FL, 2003.

Bai, J., Nie, J., Cao, G. and Bouchard, H., Using query contexts in information retrieval, Proceedings of the 30th Annual International ACM SIGIR Conference on Research and Development in Information Retrieval, 2007.

Bizer, C., Heath, T., Ayers, D. and Raimond, Y., Interlinking open data on the Web, 4th European Semantic Web Conference, http://www.eswc2007.org/pdf/demopdf/LinkingOpenData.pdf, 2007.

Bizer, C., Heath, T. and Berners-Lee, T., Linked data—The story so far, *International Journal on Semantic Web and Information Systems,* Vol. 5, No. 3, 2009.

Cadenhead, T., Kantarcioglu, M. and Thuraisingham, B., An evaluation of privacy, risks and utility with provenance, Proceedings Secure Knowledge Management Workshop (SKM), 2010.

Carroll, J., Dickinson, I., Dollin, C., Reynolds, D., Seaborne, A. and Wilkinson, K., Jena: Implementing the Semantic Web recommendations, Proceedings of the 13th International World Wide Web Conference, Alternate Track Papers and Posters, ACM, 2004.

Golbeck, J. and Hendler, J., A Semantic Web approach to the provenance challenge, *Concurrency and Computation: Practice and Experience,* Vol. 20, No. 5, 2008.

Moreau, L., Open Provenance Model (OPM) OWL Specification, latest version, http://openprovenance.org/model/opmo, 2010.

Moreau, L., Clifford, B., Freire, J., Futrelle, J., Gil, Y., Groth, P., Kwasnikowska, N., Miles, S., Missier, P., Myers, J. et al., The Open Provenance Model Core Specification (v1. 1), *Future Generation Computer Systems,* Vol. 27, No. 6, 2011.

Shen, X., Tan, B. and Zhai, C., Context-sensitive information retrieval using implicit feedback, Proceedings of the 28th Annual International ACM SIGIR Conference on Research and Development in Information Retrieval, ACM, 2005.

Thuraisingham, B., Ford, W., Collins, M. and O'Keeffe, J., Design and implementation of a database inference controller. *Data & Knowledge Engineering,* Vol. 11, No. 3, 1993.

Winkler, W., Overview of record linkage and current research directions, Bureau of the Census, 2006.

W3C SWEO Linking Open Data Community Project, latest version, http://esw.w3.org/topic/SweoIG/TaskForces/CommunityProjects/LinkingOpenData, 2010.

Zhao, J., Open Provenance Model Vocabulary Specification, latest version, http://openbiomed.sourceforge.net/opmv/ns.html, 2010.

Chapter 19

Novel Approaches to Handle the Inference Problem

19.1 Overview

The word "inference" is commonly used to mean "forming a conclusion from premises," where the conclusion is usually formed without expressed or prior approval (i.e., without the knowledge or consent of anyone or any organization that controls or processes the premises or information from which the conclusion is formed). The resulting information that is formed can be innocuously or legitimately used or it can be used for clandestine purposes with sinister overtones threatening the security of the system. The term "information" is broadly defined to include raw data as well as data and collections of data that are transformed into knowledge.

It is possible for users of any database management system to draw inferences from the information that they obtain from the databases. The inferred knowledge could depend only on the data obtained from the database system or it could depend on some prior knowledge possessed by the user in addition to the data obtained from the database system. As stated in Chapter 4, the inference process can be harmful if the inferred knowledge is something that the user is not authorized to acquire. That is, a user acquiring information that he or she is not authorized to know has come to be known as the inference problem in database security.

Much of our previous work on the inference problem has been for a multilevel operating environment based on the relational data model. In such an environment, the users are cleared at different security levels and they access a multilevel database where the data are classified at different sensitivity levels (Thuraisingham et al. 1993). An MLS/DBMS manages a multilevel database where its users cannot access data to which they are not authorized. However, providing a solution to the inference problem, where users issue multiple request and consequently infer unauthorized knowledge, is beyond the capability of currently available MLS/DBMSs.

Unlike our prior work, the work described in this book has focused on the inference problem that utilizes Semantic Web technologies. In particular, we use Semantic Web technologies for expressing policies representing the data as well as reasoning. Our inference controller reasons about the policies and determines what data have to be released to the user. We described our inference controller in Chapter 17. In Chapter 18 we introduced some novel concepts and discussed how risk management can be taken into consideration to operate with the inference controller. That is, the risk manager will determine the risk for disclosing a particular piece of information and determines whether that piece of information has to be released to the user.

In this chapter we continue with our investigation of novel approaches to handle the inference problem. In particular, we discuss four novel approaches that could possibly be used in order to build inference controllers in the long term that mimic certain aspects of human reasoning. These approaches utilize techniques from inductive inference, probabilistic deduction, mathematical programming, and game theory. Much research needs to be done before these approaches can be implemented to develop a viable inference controller. In fact we presented these approaches in 1990 and mentioned that they were nearly impossible problems given the state of the art at that time (Thuraisingham et al. 1990). However, recent developments in artificial intelligence, machine learning, and the applications of game theory to cyber security show much promise for these approaches.

The organization of this chapter is as follows. Motivation for novel approaches is discussed in Section 19.2. The novel approaches based on inductive inference, probabilistic deduction, mathematical programming, and game theory are discussed in Sections 19.3, 19.4, 19.5, and 19.6, respectively. The chapter is summarized in Section 19.7. Figure 19.1 illustrates the novel approaches discussed. Note that the information in this chapter has been taken from Thuraisingham et al. (1990).

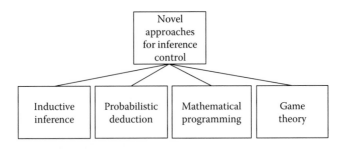

Figure 19.1 Novel approaches.

19.2 Motivation for Novel Approaches

The approaches that have been suggested previously for handling the inference problem focus on handling only two of the strategies that users could utilize to draw inference (Hinke 1988; Morgenstern 1987; Thuraisingham 1987). These strategies are inference by deduction, where new information is deduced from existing information, and inference by association, where inferences are drawn based on the associations between the various entities. In reality, however, there are many other inference strategies, such as inference by induction, inference by default reasoning, inference by analogical reasoning, and inference by heuristic reasoning, which could be utilized by users to draw inferences (Thuraisingham et al. 1990). During the past two decades, various novel reasoning techniques have been investigated by researchers of artificial intelligence in order to make expert systems mimic human reasoning, and this research has indicated that it may be possible for sophisticated inference controllers to be built eventually. Such inference controllers could therefore detect the intentions of the human users and take appropriate measures or actions. We explore the use of four of these reasoning techniques, which are

Inductive inference. Inductive inference techniques enable users to hypothesize rules from the examples observed. In the database security context, the data in the database that is released to the user are the examples. Sensitive data are the rules or hypothesis. If a user can infer sensitive data from the responses that he or she has obtained, then there is a security violation. The inference controller is intended to prevent users from drawing unauthorized inferences using inductive reasoning (note that the inference controller may also use a similar strategy for its reasoning).

Probabilistic deduction. Results from information theory can be used to specify rules to define and quantify inference. The actual computation of the measure of inference could use uncertain reasoning such as probabilistic reasoning. In the database security context, the database is regarded as a probabilistic deductive system. By means of reasoning within such a system the inferences drawn may be quantified. If any sensitive information has a measure of greater than zero, then security violation by inference occurs. The inference controller is intended to prevent users from drawing unauthorized inferences using probabilistic reasoning (note that the inference controller may also use a similar strategy for its reasoning).

Mathematical programming. It has been shown that inferences can be drawn from solution sets to mathematical programming (MP) problems. In the database security context, the constraints to the MP problem are the responses already released into the environment at the querying user's level. The objective function is stated in terms of the new response to be released into that environment. The inference controller first computes the solution set to the MP problem. It then examines the solution set and checks whether it can infer information whose level is dominated by the querying user's level. If so, the response is not released to the user. The inference controller is intended to prevent the user from drawing unauthorized conclusions using nonmonotonic logic-based reasoning.

Game theory. When playing games, the players adopt various game plans. Game theory deals with the formalization of these game plans. In the database security context, the players are (1) the user who poses various queries in order to infer information to which he or she is not authorized, and (2) the inference controller formulates counter game plans to detect the hostile moves of the user and release only certain information that does not result in security violations. That is, the inference controller functions as an expert system. It appears that the heuristic inference strategies could be handled by such an inference controller. The essential point here is to play games with the adversary and the goal is to beat the adversary.

Adapting the four approaches to design inference controllers is by no means a simple task. Nevertheless they appear to be viable approaches that should be explored further to determine their feasibility. In this chapter we explore each of the four approaches and give a preliminary discussion on how the inference problem in database security could be handled using these approaches. We call these approaches novel approaches for want of a better term. The four approaches are discussed in Sections 19.3 through 19.6.

19.3 Inductive Inference

19.3.1 Learning by Examples

In inductive inference, a general rule is hypothesized from examples. For example, given the strings 011, 000111, 000011, 01111, one can hypothesize that each string generated will be a sequence of zeros followed by a sequence of ones. The study of inductive inference originated from Gold's work on language learning (Gold 1967). Since then, many results have been obtained on the theoretical aspects of the problem. Some of the issues that are being researched are

1. Evaluation of inference methods
2. Criteria for comparing hypothesis
3. Formulating theoretical models of inference methods

Recently, efforts at applying inductive inference techniques in artificial intelligence systems have been described. For many artificial intelligence applications, it is often necessary to hypothesize rules from uncertain or incomplete information. An excellent survey on inductive inference is given in Angluin and Smith (1983). Also, recent applications in artificial intelligence are given in Angluin and Smith 1992).

19.3.2 Security Constraints and Inductive Inference

One way of stating the inference problem in database security informally is as follows:

> Given information from the database, if it is possible for a user to infer rules that he or she is not authorized to know, then security violation by inference has occurred.

We explain the above statement with an example. Assume that the security constraints cannot be seen by an unclassified user. It is reasonable to assume this for the following reasons:

> Suppose there is a security constraint which classifies the salaries that are higher than 60K at the secret level. Assume that the employee names are unclassified. An unclassified user can query the database and retrieve all names. If any of these employees earn more than 60K, then their salaries will be secret. Therefore, for certain names, an unclassified user may not be able to retrieve the salaries. If the security constraint that classifies salaries more than 60K at the secret level is itself assigned an unclassified level, then the unclassified user may be able to infer that those employees whose salary values he or she cannot see must have salaries of more than 60K.

Now, when an unclassified user requests for the salaries, he or she will get all salary values that are less than or equal to 60K. From these values he or she may be able to infer that all the salary values more than 60K are Secret. That is, the examples in this case are the salary values released, the hypothesis is the security constraint, and the inference strategy of the user is the learning program that the user implements in his or her mind. One learning program used by the unclassified user could be as follows:

1. Find the least upper bound of all the examples seen so far
2. Hypothesize that any value that is greater than the least upper bound is secret

The inference controller's task is to detect when an unclassified user can infer sensitive rules from the examples that this user has seen. When the inference controller detects that a security violation is about to occur via inference, it should take appropriate steps. That is, the learning program is implemented by the inference controller.

There are many unanswered questions in this area. The first question is, "Is the inference problem in database security as stated in this section a solvable one?" That is, does it belong to a class of functions that is learnable? If it is learnable, then is it computationally feasible to implement a learning algorithm. That is, if is belongs to a class of functions that is learnable in exponentially many steps, then in practice this class will not be learnable.

The results that have been obtained on learning algorithms show the difficulty in computing them. Even in very simple cases that deal with monomial functions, defining plausible learning mechanisms is extremely nontrivial. The main difficulty is in giving a definition of learning that is both realistic and computationally feasible. From a security point of view, this complexity is very desirable. This is because as the complexity of the learning algorithm increases, it will be more difficult for an unclassified user to infer secret rules.

It should be pointed out that the conjectures in cryptography have also strengthened the belief that learnable classes of functions are very limited. As stated in Valiant (1985), one task of cryptography is to find encoding schemes so that an enemy that has access to even a large sample of previous messages and their encodings is unable to replicate the encoding algorithm. The notion of learnability, when restricted to protocols using examples alone, requires the converse property. That is, in learning schemes it is required that the particular function can be easily replicated from the input/output behavior of any member of a class of functions. Furthermore, in encoding schemes, no member of the class should be deducible, while in a learnable class, all of them are expected to be deducible.

19.4 Probabilistic Deduction

In this section we first define and quantify inference based on results from information theory, after which an implementation approach to measure inferences based on probabilistic reasoning is stated. Finally, the application to database security of some results obtained in algorithmic information theory will be stated.

19.4.1 Formulation of the Inference Problem

The inference problem has been formulated using concepts in information theory (Denning and Morgenstern 1986) as follows:

Let $H(X)$ denote the information content of X. Another way of describing $H(X)$ is the amount of uncertainty that is removed when X is known. The lower the probability of X, the higher its information content will be. $H(Y/X)$ is the information content of Y given the information content of X.

■ Y cannot be inferred from X if $H(Y/X) = H(Y)$.
■ Y can be completely inferred from X if $H(:Y/X) = 0$ (that is, once X is known, there is no uncertainty about Y).
■ If $0 < H(Y/X) < H(Y)$, then Y can be partially inferred from X. (The higher the value of $H(Y/X)$ the lower is the probability of Y being inferred from X.)

Information can be measured using probabilities. A common measure of the information content of some information I with probability P is "-LogP."

In the database security context, if a user infers information about some entity Y and the information content of Y is greater than 0 and if the information inferred is sensitive, then security violation by inference occurs.

Investigation of the inference problem using results from information theory has not progressed much from its formulation given above. In the ensuing discussion, we show how probabilistic calculus can be used to measure inferred information. We regard the database as a probabilistic deductive system. We first give some results on probabilistic systems and then illustrate the connection to database security with an example.

19.4.2 Probabilistic Calculus

We extend Maslov's work on probabilistic calculus (Maslov 1987), which will provide a framework for handling the inference problem. The definition of this calculus will be given progressively next.

As stated in Maslov (1987), with the exception of deterministic calculi, deductive systems define a set of potentially derivable objects without predetermining how exactly a particular derivation will develop and consequently which objects will be derived. The notion of probabilistic calculus is based on assigning probabilities for possible derivations.

Let K be a canonical calculus of {A, P, {D}, {R1}, {R2}, ... {Rt}} where A is the alphabet of words, P is the alphabet of variables, D is the initial state, and each Ri is a rule set. (In Maslov's theory only one rule set is assumed.) Each rule set will consist of a finite number of one-premise rules.

Let rule set Ri have j rules, say $\mu1, \mu2, ... \mu j$.

An analyzed derivation in K for rule set, say Ri, is any list Σ of the form

$$D, D_1 <k1,s1>, D_2 <k2, s2>, ... D_n <kn, sn>,$$

where $n >= 0$, D, D_1, D_2, ... D_n are words in A, $0 <= k1 <= 0$, $0 <= k2 <= 1$, ... $0 <= kn <= n - 1$, $1 <= s1 <= j$, $1 <= s2 <= j$, ... $1 <= sm <= j$ for all y ($1 <= y <= n$). D_y is derivable from D_{ky} by one application of some rule μ_{sy}. The list D, D_1, D_2, ... D_n is called the derivation associated with Σ.

A probabilistic calculus is a pair <K,π> where π is an algorithm applicable to any analyzed derivation that assigns to every Σ of the form given above, a matrix {r_{ks}} where ($r_{ks}(\Sigma) >= 0$; $k = 0, 1, ... n$; $s = 1, 2, ... j$) for which SUMMATION $_s$ $r_{ks}(\Sigma) = 1$. Here r_{ks} is interpreted as the probability of continuing Σ by applying μs to D_k. The probability of an analyzed derivation can be defined inductively as follows:

1. If $\Sigma = D$, then p[Σ] = 1
2. If $\Sigma = \Omega$, D <k,s>, then p[Σ] = p[Ω]. $r_{ks}(\Omega)$

To define the probability of a derivation B, let the set of analyzed derivations associated with B be MB. Then, p[B] = SUMMATION$_{\Sigma \in MB}$ p[Σ].

Now to decide whether Y can be derived from X, compute the probability of the derivation Y from X for all the rule sets. The minimum value of these probabilities will be assumed to be the probability of the derivation of Y from X. Let this probability be p$_Y$. The information content of Y given X is then (–log p$_Y$). If Y1, Y2, … Ym are all derived from X and the probabilities of the derivations are p$_{Y1}$, p$_{Y2}$, … p$_{Ym}$, respectively, then the information content of Y1, Y2, … Ym is

$$\text{SUMMATION}_{1<=i<=m} -p_{Yi} \log p_{Yi}.$$

One could also define a formulation for the information content of a database, and furthermore, the information content of databases at different security levels. We will not discuss the details here.

19.4.3 *Probabilistic Calculus and Database Security*

In this section we give an example that illustrates how the concepts on probabilistic calculus and information theory can be used in query processing. Consider a database with names, cities, occupations, and salaries of people. Let us assume that the salaries are secret and everything else is unclassified. We will show how probabilities can be used to infer salaries from names.

Consider the derivation trees shown in Figure 19.2. Each tree corresponds to a rule set. If the name Thatcher is released to a user, then the information that this user can infer includes the following: Thatcher lives in London with probability 0.7, Thatcher lives in Paris with probability 0.2, and Thatcher lives in Rome with probability 0.1. If someone lives in London, then the probability that he or she earns £30K is 0.6, the probability that he or she earns £20K is 0.2, and the probability that he or she earns £10K is 0.2. If someone lives in Paris, the probability that he or she earns £30K is 0.8 and the probability that he or she earns £20K is 0.2.

From the second derivation tree, the user can infer that Thatcher is a prime minister with probability 0.6; Thatcher is a physician with probability 0.2; and Thatcher is a professor with probability 0.2. If someone is a prime minister, then the probability that he or she earns £30K is 0.7; if someone is a physician, the probability that he or she earns £30K is 0.5; and if someone is a professor, the probability that he or she earns £30K is 0.2.

Given that Thatcher is the name of a person according to the first derivation, the probability that there is a salary value of £30K in the database is (0.7*0.6 + 0.2*0.8) = 0.58, and according to the second derivation the probability is (0.6*0.7 + 0.2*0.5 + 0.2*0.2) = 0.56. Therefore, the probability of the derivation "there is salary of £30K" from "Thatcher is a name" is 0.56. Since the probability computed in the second derivation is less than that of the first, the information content of deducing the salary of £30K given the name Thatcher is given by (–log 0.56). That is, the

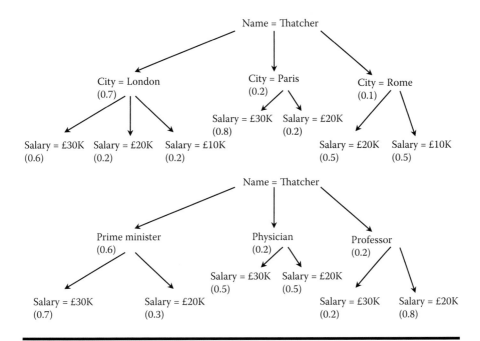

Figure 19.2   Derivation trees.

fact that there is a salary of £30K can be partially inferred from the name Thatcher. Whether one should release the name Thatcher to an unclassified user depends on the value of the information content computed above.

19.4.4 A Note on Algorithmic Information Theory

Algorithmic information theory deals with applying information theory to computational complexity. The fundamental concept is the complexity of a binary string. This complexity is defined to be the shortest program that computes the string. The following are some of the important results obtained on the algorithmic information theory by Chaitin (we have stated the results almost identically to the way they are given in Chaitin 1974):

1. In a formal system with n bits of axioms, it is impossible to prove that a particular string is of complexity greater than n + c (where c is a constant).
2. However, formal systems do exist with n + c bits of axioms in which it is possible to determine each string of complexity less than n and the complexity of each of these strings. Furthermore, it is also possible to exhibit each string of complexity great than or equal to n without being able to know by how much the complexity of each of these strings exceeds n.

We now discuss the relationship between algorithmic information theory and database security. One can view a database as a formal system. The data in the database will constitute the axioms (of some finite length) of this formal system. In the case of a multilevel database, for each security level there is a corresponding formal system. The axioms of the formal system are the data that area classified at the corresponding security level. Queries are represented as binary strings. Therefore the complexity of a query is the length of the shortest proof to derive it (this can also be taken to be the length of the shortest program to compute the query). Security violation by inference occurs, if, say, an unclassified user poses a query to retrieve secret data and the query has a sufficiently small proof in the formal system representing the unclassified database. By "sufficiently small" we mean any length that can be practically computed.

The inference controller component of the database (which prevents security violations via inference) should determine the length of a proof of each query. If this length is acceptable for a query that could result in higher-level information being inferred by a lower-level user, then the response should not be released to the user. Unfortunately, we have shown in Thuraisingham (1990) that in general it is not possible to construct such an inference controller. For example, if the maximum acceptable length of a proof is, say, n, then it is impossible to prove that a query has complexity greater than n + c. That is, it is impossible to prove that a query has complexity greater than n + c. However, we have also shown in Thuraisingham (1990) that for some formal systems one cannot only determine whether a query has complexity less than n, but also be able to compute the complexity of the query if it is less than n. In addition, one can also determine whether the complexity of a query is greater than or equal to n. Therefore, if the database under consideration is such a formal system, then one can build an inference controller.

19.5 Mathematical Programming

19.5.1 Nonmonotonic Reasoning

Yager has developed an approach for inferencing using concepts in mathematical programming (Yager 1988). This approach also has the capability for nonmonotonic reasoning and implementing default rules. An advantage of the MP approach is that all of the knowledge in the knowledge base is considered when making inferences. This facilitates nonmonotonic reasoning where premises may have to be retracted. As stated in Yager (1988), the batch-processing characteristic of MP problem solving provides the holistic environment needed to reason with nonmonotonic logic.

To formalize the inference problem in database security, a form of nonmonotonic reasoning is required. This is because as responses are released to users certain other data become more sensitive. For example, in the case of the context-based constraint that classifies names and salaries at the secret level, once the names are released to an unclassified user, the salaries cannot be released. In other words, the salary values are regarded as secret once the names are released to an unclassified user. Therefore, the previous fact "salary is unclassified" has to be retracted once the names are released. When reasoning with classical logics, facts cannot be retracted. Therefore, in this case a form of nonmonotonic reasoning is required. Based on the results obtained by Yager on MP applications, it appears that such reasoning could show promise for inference detections.

In the next section we give the background information on reasoning in MP environments and then formulate the inference problem within this framework.

19.5.2 Inferencing in an MP Environment

An MP environment consists of the following:

1. A set of variables V1, V2, ... Vn
2. A set of constraints C1, C2, ... Cp, where each constraint is of the form

$$a_{k1}V1 + a_{k2}V2 + \dots a_{kn}Vn \le b_k.$$

3. An objective function usually of the form g1V1 + g2V2 + ... + gnVn
4. A set of allowable values from the set Di for each variable Vi

The structure of the MP problem is the following:
Find the set of values for the variables V1, V2, ... Vn that

1. Satisfies all of the constraints
2. Lies in the respective domains (e.g., value vi for Vi is in domain Di)
3. Maximizes (or minimizes) the objective function

Formally this is represented as follows:
Find values vi of variable Vi ($1 \le i \le n$) such that MAX (or MIN) g1V1 + g2V2 + ... gnVn, C1, C2, ... Cp are satisfied and vi ∈ Di.

Next, we show how the propositions in a knowledge base (or a database) may be represented as constraints of an MP problem. The following rules are used to convert the propositions into constraints:

- If proposition X is true, then it is represented as the constraint $X \ge 1$
- If X is false, it is represented as $X \le 0$
- If X1 or X2 or ... or Xn is true, it is represented as $X1 + X2 + \dots Xn \ge 1$
- If X1 and X2 and ... Xn is true, it is represented as $X1 + X2 + \dots Xn \ge n$
- If X1 implies X2 is true, it is represented as $X1 - X2 \le 0$

Similarly, more complex propositions can be represented as constraints of an MP problem.

Inferences in an MP environment can be drawn as follows:

Let P1, P2, ... Pq be a set of premises involving the atoms X1, X2, ... Xn. These premises can be represented as linear equations discussed earlier. From the well-known result in mathematical logic, if Xk is any atom, then Xk is a logical consequence of the premises if and only if Xk is true in any interpretation that makes all the premises true. Suppose we want to check whether Xk can be inferred from the premises. This can be represented as an MP problem:

Objective function: $Q = \min Xk$
Constraints: P1, P2, ... Pq
$Xi \in \{0, 1\}$ for $i = 0, 1, 2, ..., n$

A solution point to this MP problem consists of an element in the set D1 × D2 × ... × Dn where each $Di = \{0, 1\}$ such that all constraints are satisfied. This means that the solution point is an interpretation that makes all premises true. The solution set to this problem is the set of all solution points. Note that if the solution set is null, then there is no interpretation that makes the premises true. This means that the premises are contradictory and therefore everything can be inferred.

If the solution set is not null, then there is an optimal solution to the MP problem. Let this solution be $X^* = (X1^*, X2^*, ... Xn^*)$. That is, at the point X^*, the objective function Q is minimal. Let the optimal value of Q be Q^*. That is, $Q^* = Xk^*$.

It can be shown that the following holds:

$$Q^* = Cert_p(Xk) = Min_p(Xk)$$

where P indicates the space constrained by the premises and $Cert_p(Xk)$ and $Min_p(Xk)$ are defined as follows:

$Cert_p(Xk) = Min_{d \in P} Xk(d)$ (that is the minimum value of $Xk(d)$ where d is in P)
$Min_p(Xk) = Min_{d \in P} Xk(d)$

Note that if $Cert_p(Xk) = 1$, then Xk is a logical consequence of the premises. Therefore, if the solution $Q^* = 1$, then Xk can be inferred from the premises.

If $Q^* = 0$, then Xk is not provable. This means that either Xk is false (i.e., Xk is not a logical consequence) or Xk is undecidable. To distinguish between the two cases, a second MP problem has to be solved. The objective function of the second problem is $Q' = Max\ Xk$.

The constraints are the same as the first MP problem. Let the optimal solution to this second problem be Q+. It can be shown that the following holds:

$$Q+ = Poss_p(Xk) = Max_p(Xk)$$

where P indicates the space constrained by the premises and $Poss_p(Xk)$ and $Max_p(Xk)$ are defined as follows:

$Poss_p(Xk)$ = Max $_{d \in P}$ Xk(d) (that is the maximum value of Xk(d) where d is in P)
$Max_p(Xk)$ = Max $_{d \in P}$ Xk(d)

- Therefore, if $Q^* = 1$, then Xk can be inferred from the premises
- If $Q^* = 0$, then it is not the case that Xk can be inferred
- If $Q^* = 0$ and $Q+ = 0$, then Xk cannot be inferred
- If $Q^* = 0$ and $Q+ = 1$, then it cannot be decided whether Xk can be inferred

19.5.3 Mathematical Programming and Database Security

In the previous section we stated the essential points on inferencing in an MP environment. The basic concepts can be extended to include nonmonotonic reasoning. For a more detailed discussion on such reasoning we refer the reader to Yager (1988). In this section we briefly discuss a way to formulate the inference problem within this framework.

The MP constraints are the responses that are released into the environment. The security constraints assign security levels to the atoms (or propositions). As new responses are released into the environment, the number of MP constraints increase. The objective functions are of the form "Max or MIN Xk" where Xk is an atom. When a user at level L poses a query, the inference controller should do the following: Insert the response (temporary update) into the environments at level L' that dominate L. The response is then represented as an MP constraint. For an environment L', first formulate objective functions for all Xk so that Xk is classified at a security level that is not dominated by L'. For each such Xk, solve the corresponding MP problem (note that all the responses in E(L') are included as constraints). Then check whether Xk can be deduced. If so, the response is not released. If not, solve the second MP problem. If it is then determined that Xk cannot be deduced, then the response is release. If it is undecidable, then a decision has to be made as to whether the response should be released or not (based on some other criterion such as the real-world knowledge that the user has).

19.6 Game Theory

19.6.1 Noncooperative and Cooperative Games

Game theory is the study of problems of conflict by abstracting the common strategic features of these problems and modeling them (Jones 1980). These features are strategic and not pure chance as they are controlled by the participants of the game. Two types of common games are noncooperative and cooperative. In a non-cooperative game, no preplay communication is permitted between the players. That is, all players are for themselves. In a cooperative game, players have complete freedom of preplay communication. They may either coordinate their strategies or share payoffs.

To handle the inference problem in database security, it appears that modeling the query processing scenario as a noncooperative game is more appropriate. The players are the user and the inference controller. The user's objective is to compromise the system, whereas the inference controller prevents such compromise from occurring. Cooperative games, on the other hand, may have applications in handling covert channels. Here the transmitter and receiver coordinate their strategies in order to force information flow from a higher level to a lower level. Since we are concerned with the inference problem, we focus only on noncooperative games.

19.6.2 Query Processing as a Noncooperative Game

The application of game theory in artificial intelligence has concentrated mainly on noncooperative games. The well-known strategies that have been used include the min-max strategy, alpha-beta pruning. and the A* algorithm (Feigenbaum and Barr 1981). Such strategies can also be applied to the query-processing scenario. In this section we discuss how this scenario may be modeled as a two-person, noncooperative game.

The players of the game are the user and the inference controller. Furthermore, the user is malicious and has the intent of compromising the system. The user also has a specific objective. That is, he or she may know that the value of some entity is sensitive and we want to obtain this value. The inference controller also knows of the user's objective. A move made by a user is a query. A move made by the inference controller is the response to the query. The game continues until the user has achieved his or her objective or the user gets tired of playing the game.

The essential points in a two-person, noncooperative game as stated in Jones (1980) are as follows: The game Ω can be regarded as a graphic theoretic tree of vertices and edges with the following properties:

1. Ω has a distinguished vertex that is its initial state.
2. There is a payoff function that assigns a pair (Q1, Q2) to each of the two players P1 and P2 (Qi ($1 \le i \le 2$) is the payoff to the player Pi).

In our application, the payoff for the user is high if he or she is closer to obtaining the sensitive value. The payoff for the inference controller is high if the response does not reveal anything about the sensitive value.

If the inference controller does not give any output or if it gives erroneous output, then it cannot be regarded as a player. Therefore, the aim here is for the inference controller to participate in the game without giving away sensitive information.

19.6.3 Ehrenfeucht–Fraisse Game

A noncooperative game that has been applied to solve problems in mathematical logic discussed in Ehrenfeucht (1957) and in classifying database queries discussed in Chandra and Harel (1982) is the Ehrenfeucht–Fraisse game (Ehrenfeucht 1961; Fraisse 1952). This game may also have application on handling the inference problem. In this section we attempt a formulation of the inference problem based on the Ehrenfeucht–Fraisse game. Note that the ideas presented are preliminary and much needs to be investigated even before a satisfactory formulation of the inference problem base on this game can be given.

The Ehrenfeucht–Fraisse game is between two noncooperating players. The first player attempts to discern two structures (such as models of databases or languages) and the second player attempts to prevent the first player from doing this. In the application to mathematical logic, the structures are models of certain formalized theories. The objective of the first player is then to find a formula that is true in one model and not true in the other. In the application to classifying queries, the structures are certain databases and the formula is a query. The objective of the first player is to show that there is a query that produces different results when evaluated against two databases.

For our application, the structures are the following:

1. S1—the database and the rules associated with the database at a single security level, say, L (note that the rules are used to deduce a new date)
2. S2—the real world, which operates at level L

The first player is a malicious user operating at security level L whose objective is to obtain some sensitive information. The second player is the inference controller. If the first player can discern between the two structures S1 and S2, then he or she at least knows that the database plus the rules at security level L are not secure and can then analyze the response that he or she has obtained and can, in turn, infer the sensitive information. The aim of the first player is to find a formula that evaluates to true in one structure and false in another structure. The second player is the inference controller and his or her attempt is to stop the first player from discerning the two structures.

19.6.4 Adversarial Mining and Inference

In our more recent work (Zhou et al. 2012), we have developed data mining algorithms that can adapt to the adversary. For example, many learning tasks such as credit card fraud detection face an active adversary that tries to avoid detection. For learning problems that deal with an active adversary, it is important to model the adversary's attack strategy. We have developed a support vector machine-based method that will attempt to thwart the adversary. We can apply a similar approach for handling unauthorized inferences. That is, the adversary will try to learn and defeat the inference controller. The inference engine has to adapt its strategy so that the adversary can be thwarted. We believe with many data mining tools that are available now to the adversary, the inference engine has to employ a variety of adversarial data mining techniques.

19.7 Summary and Directions

In this chapter we have described the inference problem and discussed four novel approaches that could be used to design inference controllers in the long term. These approaches use techniques from inductive inference, probabilistic deduction, mathematical programming, and game theory. They handle various types of inference strategies that the users could utilize to draw inferences. The developments in artificial intelligence, machine learning, and game theory research show much promise in designing inference controllers that mimic some aspects of human reasoning.

In Chapter 20 we will show how the novel approaches as well as risk assessment can be combined together to build powerful inference controllers. That is, we will integrate the access control manager, the redaction manager, and the inference controller discussed in Sections II and III and develop a unified framework that will also include the risk manager and the novel approaches. Ultimately the goal is to be several steps smarter than the adversary and thwart the actions of the adversary. However, we also need to integrate the risks involved in divulging the information to the user. That is, if the value of information is very low, then we need not employ expensive adversarial mining techniques to thwart the adversary. However, if the information to be released is of high value such as highly confidential corporate data or top-secret data, then we need to employ a comprehensive range of strategies to defeat the adversary.

References

Angluin, D. and Smith, C., Inductive inference: Theory and methods, *ACM Computing Surveys*, Vol. 15, 1983, pp. 237–269.

Angluin, D. and Smith, C., Inductive inference, in *Encyclopedia of Artificial Intelligence*, Vol. 1, Shapiro, S. (ed.), John Wiley & Sons, Inc., 1992, pp. 672–682.

Chaitin, G. J., Information-theoretic computational complexity, *IEEE Transactions on Information Theory*, Vol. 20, January 1974, pp. 10–15.

Chandra, A. and Harel, D., Structure and complexity of relational queries, *Journal of Computer and Systems Sciences*, Vol. 25, No. 1, August 1982.

Denning, D. E. and Morgenstern, M., Military database technology study: AI techniques for security and reliability, Final Report, SRI International, Project 1644, Menlo Park, CA, August 1986.

Ehrenfeucht, A., Application of games to some problems of mathematical logic, *Bulletin Academi Polska*, Warsaw, Vol. 5, 1957, pp. 35–37.

Ehrenfeucht, A., Application of games to the completeness problem for formalized theories, *Fundamenta Mathematicae*, Vol. 49, 1961, pp. 129–140.

Feigenbaum, E. and Barr, A., *Handbook of (Heuris Tech Press, no city listed) Artificial Intelligence*, Vol. 1, 1981.

Fraisse, R., Sur les rapports entre la theorie des relations, *Colloque de Logique Mathematique*, Paris, 1952.

Gold, E. M., Language identification in the limit, *Information Control*, Vol. 10, 1967, pp. 447–474.

Hinke, T., Inference aggregation detection in database management systems, Proceedings of the IEEE Symposium on Security and Privacy, Oakland, CA, 1988.

Jones, A. J., *Game Theory: Mathematical Models of Conflict*, Ellis Horwood, Chichester, UK, 1980.

Maslov, M., *Theory of Deductive Systems and its Applications,* The MIT Press, Cambridge, MA, 1987.

Morgenstern, M., Security and inference in multilevel database and knowledge base systems, Proceedings of the ACM SIGMOD Conference, San Francisco, May 1987.

Thuraisingham, B., Security checking in relational database management systems augments with inference engines, *Computers & Security*, Vol. 6, No. 6, 1987.

Thuraisingham, B. et al., Novel approach to handle the inference problem, Proceedings of the 3rd RADC Database Security Workshop, NY, 1990.

Thuraisingham, B., Ford, W., Collins, M. and O'Keeffe, J., Design and implementation of a database inference controller. *Data & Knowledge Engineering*, Vol. 11, No. 3, 1993.

Valiant, L., Deductive learning, in *Mathematical Logic and Programming Languages,* Hoare, C. A. R. and Shepherdson, J. C. (eds.), Prentice Hall, Englewood Cliffs, NJ, 1985.

Yager, R., A mathematical programming approach to inference with capability of implementing default rules, *International Journal of Man-Machine Studies,* Vol. 29, 1988, pp. 685–714.

Zhou, Y., Kantarcioglu, M. and Thuraisingham, B., Adversarial support vector machine learning, Proceedings of ACM KDD, Beijing, China, 2012.

Chapter 20

A Cloud-Based Policy Manager for Assured Information Sharing

20.1 Overview

In the previous chapters we discussed a system for access control for provenance data and inference control. In this chapter we describe our implementation of our Semantic Web-based policy manager in the cloud. This policy layer is essentially a variation of the policy engines we described in Sections II and III. However, while the policy engines described in Sections II and III addressed access control, redaction, and inference control, the policy engine described in this chapter handles information sharing policies. The purpose of this cloud-based system is to facilitate assured information sharing. Essentially, multiple partners in a coalition store the data and policies in a cloud. When a partner queries for the data, the policy manager will reason about the data and give only the data the partner organization is authorized to obtain.

The cloud computing paradigm enables the sharing of large amounts of data securely and efficiently. Furthermore, the advent of *cloud computing* and the continuing movement toward *software as a service* (SaaS) paradigms has posed an increasing need for *assured information sharing* (AIS) as a service in the cloud. In order to satisfy the cloud-centric AIS needs of coalition organization, there is a critical need to develop an AIS framework that operates in the cloud. To our knowledge, no such system currently exists. In particular, we describe the detailed design and implementation of AIS in a semantic cloud. That is, we have used Semantic Web

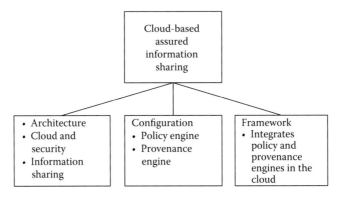

Figure 20.1 Cloud-based AIS.

technologies for providing cloud-based Semantic Web services. These Semantic Web services enable information sharing. Our framework consists of a three-layer architecture that includes a user interface layer, a policy engine layer, and a data connection layer that integrates multiple data sources in the cloud.

The organization of this chapter is as follows. We describe the detailed design and implementation of our system in Section 20.2. In particular, the system architecture, its operations, modules, and usage are discussed. Extension of the policy engine for inference control is discussed in Section 20.3. The chapter is concluded in Section 20.4 with a discussion of future work. To our knowledge this is the first of its kind of an AIS framework that operates in the cloud. Figure 20.1 illustrates cloud-based assured information sharing. Some of our preliminary work on cloud-based assured information sharing was provided in Thuraisingham et al. (2012). Much of the content in this chapter was discussed in Cadenhead et al. (2012a).

20.2 Architecture

20.2.1 Overview

Our policy engine framework is driven by RDF configuration documents that encode the logic of the policy engines and their usage, the user interface layouts and customizable parameters, and the mappings of dereferenceable URIs to the data stores using the available data connections. Our policy engine framework can be used as a key enabler in augmenting security for relational database management systems (RDBMSs) as well as cloud-based systems. RDBMSs are developed with atomicity, concurrency, and durability in mind, but are normally shipped with limited support for access control. A cloud storage layer allows the agencies to store and scale policies with finer levels of control over RDF resources. The cloud was developed with scalability and availability in mind, but security considerations were neglected. Our policy engine can be configured to complement policies in an RDBMS with an entry point for supporting security policies over cloud-based back-ends. We first present an overview of the configuration of the framework, then we define the layers in our architecture, and finally, we provide a description of the novel features of our implementation. Figure 20.2 illustrates our architecture and Figure 20.3 illustrates our configuration framework.

A loosely coupled system provides easy configuration and flexibility to our RDF policy engine framework. Each component is abstracted from the others by employing RDF documents consisting of an agency's preferences for a policy or data connection to a data store. Furthermore, a loosely coupled Web front-end promotes easier maintenance and reusability of the policy framework, since an adapter pattern abstracts the mapping of the Web interfaces (and communications) to the other layers. An abstraction hides the actual implementation and intricacies of the policy engine manager and data managers from the agencies. This therefore allows agencies to specify their policies in any representation languages, such as XML, RDF, or Rei (Kagal 2002); an adapter hides the translation of high-level policy specification to policy implementation.

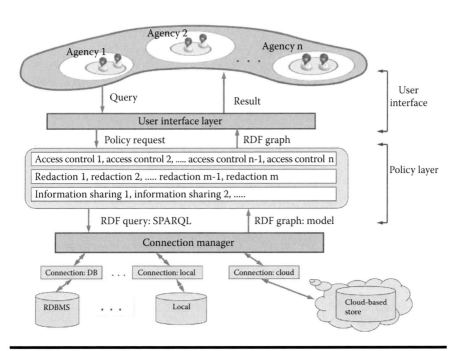

Figure 20.2   Architecture.

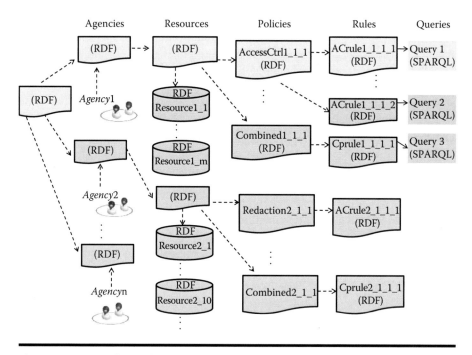

Figure 20.3   Configuration overview.

20.2.2 Modules in Our Architecture

Our system architecture consists of three layers. At the front-end, we have a user interface, the middle layer consists of our policy engine logic, and at the back-end, we have our data stores. We provide a discussion of these modules next.

20.2.2.1 User Interface Layer

To enable a one-to-one interaction with our framework, a Web-based user interface is built on top of the policy layer. Rich client and open source Web technologies simplify the interactions between users, Web pages, and the underlying policy and data layers. This integration has many advantages. The policy framework operates in a distributed environment and has a greater geographical spread; therefore, agencies and users have mobility. The Web interface requires users to create an account (also a registration) and choose unique credentials that will then be used by the users to identify them to the policy framework. A form-based authentication pattern as well as a challenge-response test distinguishes legitimate users from robots (which may pose as normal users). The legitimate users are presented with a querying screen that allows them to compose SPARQL queries once they have been authenticated. Note that SPARQL (Prud'hommeaux and Seaborne 2006) is a query language for RDF and is used for retrieving data from triple stores. The SPARQL queries are validated and then sent to our policy engine layer that in turn returns a resultant RDF graph that is then displayed on a Web page.

User registration. The user registration presents the user the opportunity to register with the system using a Web registration form. The registration form captures the user's name, password, and other metadata about the user. Metadata could be an agency that the user is a part of or data that are used for mapping the user's credentials to a role that is to be performed by the user. The following RDF graph displays contents from a user configuration file. The final triple in the RDF graph contains a dereferenceable URI to another RDF graph, which then contains a list of dereferenceable URIs of the actual resources that the user is allowed to query.

```
<http://policy.org/agency/pol#users>
pol:user <http://policy.org/agency/pol#user1>.
# resources
<http://policy.org/agency/pol#user1>
pol:name "user1" ;
pol:passwd "_:b1" ;
pol:organization <http://policy.org/agency/pol#Agency1> ;
pol:resourcelist <http://example/users/resources/user1>.
```

Agency registration. The agency registration comprises a sequence of Web pages, each being a child page of the previous one. The process commences with an agency registering information to describe itself. First, an agency registers important metadata about itself. These metadata are an RDF document that can be used to introduce one agency to another, and therefore should be self-describing. Some example triples in these metadata could assert an agency's name, address, industry, affiliations, and so forth. Second, an agency records its resources. A resource has a unique URI that is a dereferenceable URI to an agency's RDF document that contains both the sensitive and nonsensitive data for the agency; this is the information that is normally stored in a relational database but has now migrated to the cloud. Third, an agency defines the policies for its resources. An agency may choose among the various policies that are supported at the policy engine layer. Examples of policies are access control, redaction, and information sharing. Fourth, an agency describes various policy rules for a policy. Note that an agency may use access control to protect its resources; however, the agency may need more than one rule for a particular policy choice. For example, one access control rule may specify a positive authorization while another may specify a negative authorization on the same resource. Finally, an agency specifies queries. It is a very popular technique to write policy rules as views (i.e., SPARQL queries) over a data store. An agency may specify in its policy rule configuration document that queries are to be materialized or nonmaterialized. A materialized query may speed up the policy execution, while a nonmaterialized query refreshes the result set in real time.

20.2.2.2 Policy Engines

The *Policy Engine Layer* first evaluates the user queries against the stored data resources (which can be traditional data or provenance metadata). A data resource is characterized by a URI, which connects to an actual RDF graph in the data storage layer. The policy layer uses a factory object to create the underlying policies. The factory exposes a policy through a consistent interface, thus making it easy to extend our policy engine to support other types of policies in the future. We currently support access control, redaction, and information sharing policies. To support traditional policies, we use SPARQL queries to define views over resources, where a view can be associated with positive and negative authorizations or a target in a subgraph replacement procedure. Important metadata are provenance, which records the history of a piece of data item. However, provenance takes on a DAG structure, and as such requires its own policies (Braun et al. 2008). Therefore, we support the use of regular expression SPARQL queries for access control policies (Cadenhead et al. 2011a) as well as redaction policies (Cadenhead et al. 2011b). We have also implemented information sharing policies over data and provenance that allow cooperating agencies to share information based on mutual agreements (Cadenhead et al. 2012b).

An agile environment pushes policy designers to constantly fine-tune or extend their policies to rapidly adapt to ever-changing conditions, thus ensuring that data integrating and combinations do not violate data confidentiality, especially when quick actions are critical (e.g., in intelligence). To meet this demand, our policy engine layer supports many policy engines, while the cloud supports many policy configuration documents.

A policy engine takes as input a user's credential and a dereferenceable URI; it then evaluates the underlying logic of a policy before returning a new RDF graph (or model) to the user interface layer. The dereferenceable URI points to a configuration document which itself contains other dereferenceable URIs to the policies about an agency's resource and to the agency's resource at the data layer. An agency's resource is an RDF document with triples at one or more classification levels; for example, an entire RDF document would be classified as sensitive in case it contains intelligence information or some subset of triples may have actual intelligence information. An agency therefore requires more than one type of policy to achieve fine grain control over its resources. A policy is therefore defined by an interface, which allows the implementation of the logic of each policy. The policy engine evaluates the underlying logic of a policy before returning a new RDF graph (or model) to the user interface layer. By migrating its policies to the cloud, an agency overcomes the restriction on the number of policy definitions previously possible. The following sections summarize various policy types and we discuss the details of the policy engine layer. This layer comprises many policy types, for example, access control, redaction, and information sharing, to name a few. We will also highlight the need for a flexible policy engine by discussing each of these policy types in turn.

Access control policy engine. An access control policy authorizes a set of users to perform a set of actions on a set of resources within an environment. Unless authorized through one or more access control policies, users have no access to any resource of the system. There are different kinds of access control policies that can be grouped into three main classes (Samarati and de Capitani di Vimercati 2001). These policies differ by the constraints they place on the sets of users, actions, and objects (access control models often refer to resources as objects). These classes are (1) RBAC, which restricts access based on roles, (2) DAC, which controls access based on the identity of the user, and (3) MAC, which controls access based on mandated regulations determined by a central authority.

Policies based on RBAC are often used to simplify the management of policy mappings, which is a common feature in the three classes of access control policies. Policy creation and manageability are important in getting finer levels of access control over the shared resources. We use the convention that a permission is a unique pair of (action, resource). Given n resources, m users and a set of only two actions (read, write), we have a maximum of $2 \times n$ possible permissions. This gives $m \times (2 \times n) = c_1 n$ mappings. A further improvement of RBAC is the case where there is at least one role with two or more users assigned to it from a possible set of r roles. Therefore, we have $r \times (2 \times n) = c_2 n$ mappings and we also assume that $c_2 \leq c_1$. However, even with this simplification, the number of policies needed to achieve finer levels of access control in a dynamic and agile community may be intractable. Our cloud-centric policy framework addresses this by providing the agencies the ability to support and scale their access control policies to meet their ever growing security needs.

Redaction policy engine. A redaction policy identifies and removes sensitive information from a document before releasing it to a user. Unlike access control policies, which restrict access, redaction policies encourage sharing of information by ensuring that sensitive or proprietary information is removed (or obscured) before providing the final RDF graph (referred to as a redacted graph) to a user's query. Redaction policies rely on a transformation operation in order to circumvent any identifying or sensitive information. The redaction policy engines currently supported rely on a graph transformation technique that is based on a graph grammar approach that is presented in Ehrig et al. (2006) and Rozenberg (1997). Basically, there are two steps to applying a redaction policy over a directed labeled RDF graph: (1) Identify a resource (or subgraph) in the original RDF graph that we want to protect. This can be done with a graph query (i.e., a query equipped with regular expressions). (2) Apply a redaction policy to this identified resource in the form of a graph transformation rule. An implementation of this graph transformation is used in Cadenhead et al. (2011b) for redacting provenance graphs.

Information sharing policy engine. An information sharing policy allows agencies to determine the context in which their resources are shared or combined with resources from other agencies. An information sharing policy engine has logic for processing a query requesting information on two or more RDF graphs simultaneously. We illustrate this using the following SPARQL query:

SELECT $\vec{B}$ FROM NAMED uri1 FROM NAMED uri2 WHERE P,

where P is a graph pattern, $\vec{B}$ is a tuple of variables appearing in P and uri1 and uri2 are dereferenceable URIs for two resources, R1 and R2. Resources R1 and R2 may be from the same agency in case an agency strictly requires a partitioning of its resources based on confidentiality concerns or they could belong to two agencies, Agency 1 and Agency 2, respectively. Therefore, each of these resources may define individual information sharing policy rules. We define an operator ⊙ so that an information sharing policy is now evaluated over uri1 ⊙ uri2. The operator ⊙ can be implemented as a graph operation over an RDF graph. Note that ⊙ could be one of the following operators: ∩, ∪, or – and can also be applied to an original RDF graph or to a previous one that resulted from the operator, ⊙. In order to execute the operator, ⊙, we define a graph recursively as follows:

- ε is a graph.
- The set of graphs are closed under intersection, union, and set difference. Let G_1 and G_1 be two graphs, then $G_1 \cup G_2$, $G_1 \cap G_2$ and $G_1 - G_2$ are graphs, so that if t ∈ $G_1 \cup G_2$ then t ∈ G_1 or t ∈ G_2; if t ∈ $G_1 \cup G_2$ then t ∈ G_1 and t ∈ G_2; or if t ∈ $G_1 - G_2$ then t ∈ G_1 and $t \notin G_2$.

The following RDF graph lists the triples of a combined policy configuration document containing policies with embedded logic for sharing two resources, R1 and R2, which belong to two agencies, Agency 1 and Agency 2, respectively.

```
# entity
<http://policy.org/entity/pol#Combined1_1_1>
   pol:owner <http://policy.org/entity/pol#Agency1>;
      pol:rule <http://policy.org/entity/pol#Cprule1_1_1_1>.

# mappings
<http://policy.org/entity/pol#Cprule1_1_1_1>
   pol:agency<http://policy.org/entity/pol#Agency2>;
      pol:operator "UNION" ;
      pol:type "combined1".
```

This policy works at the level of the agencies. For example, Agency 1 shares all its resources as a union with all of Agency 2 resources. The policy type allows an agency to have modes of sharing. For example, a type *combined*1 provides sharing at the agency level, while another policy type, *combined*2, could offer a finer level of control in determining how Agency 1 shares each of its resources with a classification of a resource for Agency 2. In other words, information sharing policies can incorporate contextual information about an agency and metadata about each of its resources at the resource level. The following shows two policy types for our information sharing policies:

1. *combined*1. $\forall r1 \in Agency1, \forall r2 \in Agency2$, use r1∪r2. This policy states that Agency 1 shares all its resources with Agency 2 as a union of the resources.
2. *combined*2. Let $r1_1, r1_2, \ldots, r1_n \in$ Agency1, use $r1_1 \cup r2$, $r1_2 \cap r2$, $\forall r2 \in Agency2$. This policy offers a finer level of control.

Provenance policy engines. Sometimes the relationships among the triples in an RDF graph need be taken into consideration when defining policies. The three policy types discussed so far fail to address the cases where sensitive information is implicit in the various paths within an RDF graph. We will explore other policy engines in this section. The focus will be on the definition of policy engines tailored to the execution of access control and redaction policies over a provenance graph. We base the logic of these policy engines on Cadenhead et al. (2011a), which discusses an access control policy language for provenance, and Cadenhead et al. (2012b), which discusses how to perform redaction over provenance. We first give an example of a provenance graph and the type of provenance information that may exist in the example provenance graph. Then we present brief definitions of some of the theories behind executing policies over a provenance graph.

Figure 20.4 shows an intelligence example as a provenance graph using an RDF representation that outlines a flow of a document through a server located in some unfriendly territory (or at another agency posing a potential threat). This document was given to a journalist. The contents of this provenance graph could serve to evaluate the trustworthiness of the servers (i.e., processes in the example graph) from which the document originated. This example provenance graph also shows the base skeleton of the actual provenance, which is usually annotated with RDF triples indicating contextual information (e.g., time and location). Note that the predicates (i.e., arcs) are labeled with the OPM abstract predicate (Moreau et al. 2011) labels and that the final report can be traced back to a Central Intelligence Agency (CIA) agent.

The information embedded in the graph in Figure 20.4 represents a directed RDF graph. A provenance path in Figure 20.4 is defined as follows:

Definition 20.1: Provenance Path

Given a provenance graph, a provenance path (s p o) is a path $s \xrightarrow{p} o$ that is defined over the provenance vocabulary V using regular expressions. ■

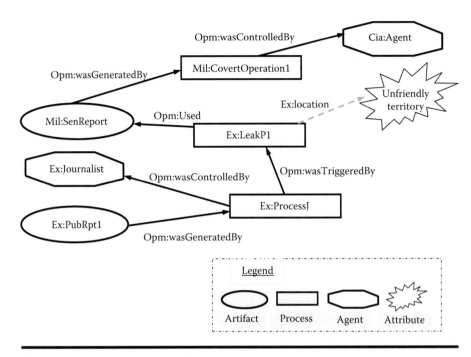

Figure 20.4 Provenance graph.

Definition 20.2: Regular Expressions

Let Σ be an alphabet of terms in V, then the set $RE(\Sigma)$ of regular expressions is inductively defined by ■

- $\forall x \in \Sigma, x \in RE(\Sigma)$
- $\Sigma \in RE(\Sigma)$
- $\varepsilon \in RE(\Sigma)$
- If $A \in RE(\Sigma)$ and $B \in RE(\Sigma)$, then

$$A|B,\ A/B,\ A^*,\ A^+,\ A? \in RE(\Sigma)$$

The symbols | and / are interpreted as logical OR and composition, respectively.

Our intention is to define paths between two nodes by edges equipped with * for paths of arbitrary length, including length 0 or + for paths that have at least length 1. Therefore, for two nodes x, y and predicate name p, $x(\xrightarrow{p})^* y$ and $x(\xrightarrow{p})^+ y$ are paths in G.

A SPARQL query extended with regular expressions (Harris and Seaborne 2010) can define a resource (or subgraph) of the provenance graph in Figure 20.4 as follows:

Example 20.1: Provenance Path Query

Select ?x
{ex:PubRpt1 arq:OnPath("([opm:WasGeneratedBy]/
[opm:WasTriggeredBy]/[ex:location])"?x).}

This query would return the location as a binding to the variable *x* and could be used to pinpoint the origin of a compromise (and leakage) of the original report. This could also serve to alert policy designers to add appropriate policies for reports and servers in their respective agencies.

Policy sequence. The execution of the policies over an agency's resource results in a policy sequence. In particular, a protected resource could employ the services of multiple policy engines and policy types. Each policy type produces a new subgraph of its input RDF graph. It is important to note that the effect of a policy is directly dependent on the RDF graph it receives as input, and furthermore, the effect may be different from the original effect the policy was intended to achieve. A sequence takes the original input graph through a series of transformations until a final RDF graph is returned to the user. Note that the success of a policy rule (which is implemented as a SPARQL query) returning a particular set of RDF triples is dependent on the transformation step at which the rule was applied in a policy sequence. We illustrate this using the following SPARQL query:

CONSTRUCT G WHERE P,

G is a newly constructed graph that contains a set of triples that satisfy condition *P* in the input graph. A policy protecting the following RDF triples,

```
<http://cs.utdallas.edu/semanticweb/Prov-AC/agency#agent_1>
    foaf:name "John brown";
    foaf:projectHomepage <http://www.agency1.gov/>.
```

will fail if either the name or project home page triple was earlier removed or altered by a previous policy rule.

A policy precedence feature in the framework helps an agency determine the ordering of its policies. In the user interface layer, an agency configures the ordering of its policies. The policy sequence is then stored in a RDF sequence file (using the "rdf:seq" feature of the RDF specification). When a query is evaluated, the policy framework will in turn invoke each policy in the intended order.

Rule sequence. In a similar way, a policy may be implemented using a set of rules. For example, to fully redact a shared resource, an agency may need a separate rule to redact each sensitive triple in an RDF graph. Each rule is triggered when a triple (or set of triples) meets some specified criteria in the input graph. Note that each rule transforms the current state of a shared resource. Therefore, each sequencing of the rules will impact the final graph (also called the redacted graph).

20.2.2.3 Data Layer

At the data layer is a connection factory that acts as a facade for creating connection objects. These connection objects expose the same properties (functionally) as public methods to the policy designer. This makes it easier for the policy designer to concentrate on the policy engine design. The policy designer makes a call to an RDF policy factory, which returns an RDF model object. This RDF model object is backed by a connection store that can be a local connection, a relational database connection, or a cloud connection. During the registration process, an agency is given an opportunity to decide where it wants to store its resources and configuration documents. It is recommended that the smaller configuration documents be stored locally on disk (or in a local database) to enable quick access to them. Local connections also consume lower bandwidth, offer real-time access, and enable development before deployment. However, an agency may decide to store them in a private cloud (or on a remote database server) to take advantage of the added protection there.

The connection factory also enables agencies to store their resources in any cloud infrastructure. For example, an agency's resources could reside on a private cloud, a community cloud. or a public cloud. A private cloud deployment provides more control in that agencies could house their own cloud. A community cloud is provisioned for exclusive access by a specific community, thus serving the common interest of cooperating agencies. A public cloud is open to the public and thus susceptible to more vulnerabilities due to the loss of control over the data uploaded onto the public cloud. Agencies may choose to use a mixture of connections and also employ more than one deployment simultaneously (e.g., a hybrid cloud model).

20.2.3 Features of Our Policy Engine Framework

In the sections below, we present some novel features of our policy engine framework.

Policy reciprocity. Policy reciprocity enables agencies to specify policies when knowledge of the other agencies, their resources, or policy specification are available. This is made possible via the registration process, where agencies make metadata available about themselves, their recourses, and associated policies. The following discussion provides scenarios for policy reciprocity.

*Agency*1 wishes to share its resources if *Agency*2 also shares its resources with it. Current access control and redaction policies do not provide for this reciprocity. Our framework provides information sharing policies that allow agents to define policies based on reciprocity and mutual interest amongst cooperating agencies.

We present two sample information sharing policies:

1. $\forall r1 \in Agency1, \forall r2 \in Agency2$, use $r1 \cup r2$.
   This policy states that *Agency*1 shares all its resources with any resource of *Agency*2 as a union of the resources (i.e., $\Theta \in \{\cup\}$).
2. Let $r1_1, r1_2, \ldots, r1_n \in Agency1$. *Agency*1 can use $r1 \cup r2$, $r1_2 \cap r2$, $\forall r2 \in Agency2$.
   This policy offers a finer level of control and defines the combined operator, $\Theta \in \{\cap, \cup\}$.

Conditional policies. A consequence of policy reciprocity is allowing the use of conditional sharing policies. For example, *Agency*1 shares its resources with *Agency*2 if *Agency2* does not share *Agency1*'s resources with *Agency3*. We next present a sample information sharing policy:

$\forall r1 \in$ *Agency1*, $\forall r2 \in$ *Agency2*, *Agency1* defines $r1 \cap r2$. If $\forall r3 \in$ *Agency3*, then

- *Agency2* does not define any sharing policy of the form $r1 \cap r3$
- *Agency2* does not define any sharing policy of the form $r1 \subseteq r2 \odot r3$, where $\odot \in \{\cup, \cap\}$

Policy symmetry. Another consequence of policy reciprocity is to have symmetry in the sharing of policies. For example, *Agency1* shares its resources with *Agency2* with a combined operator, $\odot$, if *Agency2* also shares its resources with *Agency1* using the same combined operator, $\odot$. We present a sample information sharing policy below:

$\forall r1 \in$ *Agency1*, $\forall r2 \in$ *Agency2*, *Agency1* uses $r1 \cup r2$ if *Agency2* also uses $r2 \cup r1$

20.2.3.1 Develop and Scale Policies

To enable freedom of maneuverability across the information environment and to deliver the power of information to ensure mission success, an agency should be able to rapidly develop policies and deploy them as needed. We next discuss the features that are available to an agency during and after development of its policies.

Policy development. Agency1 wishes to simulate a live environment and create test scenarios to visualize the results of each policy configuration. Our policy framework provides three configurations: (1) a stand-alone version for development and testing, (2) a version backed by a relational database, and (3) a cloud-based version that achieves high availability and scalability while maintaining low setup and operation costs.

Sequencing effects. Agency1 wishes to vary the result set to a user's query based on the user's credentials. The policy sequence feature can be used to configure different outcomes by permuting the policies and their respective rules.

Rapid elasticity. Agency1 identifies recent security vulnerabilities in its existing policy configurations and wishes to extend (or grow) its existing policy set with support for policies at a finer granularity. Our policy engine provides a policy interface that should be implemented by all policies; therefore, we can add newer types of policies as needed. In addition, our policy engine gives an agency rapid elasticity whereby the capabilities available by our policy framework appear unlimited.

Location independence. Agency1 wishes to store its resources closer to where it is consumed but with little or no change at the policy layer. Our policy engine provides location independence whereby the policy engine has no control or knowledge over the exact location of the resources, but may be able access the resources through a specified location using the connection manager. Note that an agency's resources can be in any cloud, geographically. The ability to locate any resource by a dereferenceable URE provides much flexibility.

*Deployment models. Agency*1 can take advantage of different deployment models such as a private cloud, a hybrid cloud, a community, or a public cloud. The connection manager allows an agency to choose among a list of connection types based on different risk factors and objectives to protect data confidentiality.

20.2.3.2 Justification of Resources

Provenance makes available an explanation about why information was manipulated and a trace to the source of the information manipulation. This establishes trust among agencies, thus facilitating partnerships for common goals.

*Agency*1 asks *Agency*2 for a justification of resource R2. The current commercial access control policies are mainly designed to protect single data items, while current redaction policies are designed for redacting text and images. Our policy engine allows agents to define policies over provenance; therefore, *Agency*2 can provide the provenance to *Agency*1, but protect it by using access control or redaction policies.

20.2.3.3 Policy Specification and Enforcement

Our architectural design supports a high-level specification of policies, thus separating the business layer from a specific policy implementation.

*Agency*1 wishes to express its policies in a high-level language (e.g., XACML), and would prefer not learning RDF or any of its variations. The framework exposes a Web interface layer between the users and the policy engine layer whereby the users can specify their policies independent of the actual implementation of the policy. A suitable adapter, also known as a data translator, will translate each high-level policy specification into the appropriate RDF representation used by the appropriate policy that protects an agency's resources.

Policies may be specified using more expressive languages than RDF by extending RDF with a formal vocabulary, in particular a sublanguage of OWL. OWL has a formal semantics that is based on DL, a decidable fragment of first-order logic. Thus, by supporting this adapter pattern, our framework is extended to handle semantic policies specified in OWL and high-level policies can be translated into a suitable sublanguage of OWL using existing or custom-built translators.

20.3 Cloud-Based Inference Control

The policy engine described in Section 20.2 essentially addresses assured information sharing. We can, however, follow a similar approach and reimplement the policy engines described in Sections II and III in the cloud. For example, the inferencing process is extremely time consuming due to the vast amounts of data that have to be examined. Therefore, cloud-based inference control is an efficient way to handle the inference problem. Similarly, our access control and redaction-based policy engines can also be reimplemented in the cloud for efficient processing.

With respect to assured information sharing, the coalition partners can also utilize an inference controller to determine whether by sharing the data the partners can infer unauthorized information via inference. That is, the information sharing module is augmented with an inference controller that examines the data to be shared before they are released to the partners. We illustrate this capability in Figure 20.5. We consider the case where organizations A, B, and C are part of a coalition sharing information in the cloud. Each organization stores the data and policies in the cloud. Suppose organization B requests data from A. Then the information sharing module will first examine the policies and determine whether the data are to be shared. It will then consult with the inference controller to determine whether B can infer any unauthorized information with the data shared. If so, then A will not share the data with B.

In the previous paragraph we discussed our preliminary ideas on inference control for information sharing. We need to carry out an in-depth investigation on integrating the inference controller discussed in Section III with the policy engine discussed in this chapter.

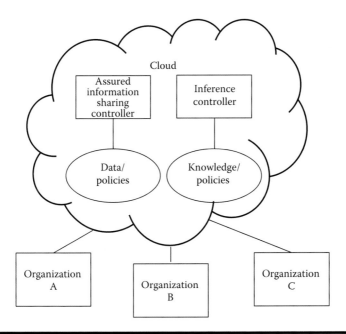

Figure 20.5 Inference control in the cloud.

20.4 Summary and Directions

This chapter has described the design and implementation of the first-of-its-kind AIS framework that operates in the cloud. As stated earlier, the idea is for each organization to store their data and the information sharing policies in a cloud. The information is shared according to the policies. We described a cloud-based information sharing framework that utilized Semantic Web technologies. Our framework consists of a policy engine that reasons about the policies for information sharing purposes and a secure data engine that stores and queries data in the cloud. We also described the operation of our system with example policies. Our framework is flexible so that additional data sources and clouds can be added. Furthermore, by using RDF for a policy engine, we can add more sophisticated policies for information sharing. This is one of the major strengths of our system. Future directions include specifying and reasoning about more sophisticated policies as well as testing our system in a real-world environment.

We have described several extensions to our work on inference control in Section IV. In Chapter 18 we discussed a risk model. Some novel approaches to inference control were discussed in Chapter 19. In this chapter we provided an overview of our implementation of the policy engine in the cloud. In the next chapter (Chapter 20), we examine the relationship between confidentiality and privacy while in Chapter 21 we address the security and privacy issues for big data systems. Finally, in Chapter 22, we integrate all of the concepts discussed in Sections II, III, and IV and describe a unified framework for secure data provenance and inference control.

References

Braun, U., Shinnar, A. and Seltzer, M., Securing provenance, Proceedings of the 3rd Conference on Hot Topics in Security, USENIX Association, 2008.

Cadenhead, T., Kantarcioglu, M., Khadilkar, V. and Thuraisingham, B. M., Design and implementation of a cloud-based assured information sharing system, MMM-ACNS, 2012a, pp. 36–50.

Cadenhead, T., Khadilkar, V., Kantarcioglu, M. and Thuraisingham, B., A language for provenance access control, *Proceedings of the First ACM Conference on Data and Application Security and Privacy*, ACM, 2011a, pp. 133–144.

Cadenhead, T., Khadilkar, V., Kantarcioglu, M. and Thuraisingham, B. M., Transforming provenance using redaction, *Proceedings of the 16th ACM Symposium on Access Control Models and Technologies*, ACM, 2011b, pp. 93–102.

Cadenhead, T., Khadilkar, V., Kantarcioglu, M. and Thuraisingham, B., A cloud-based RDF policy engine for assured information sharing, *Proceedings of the 17th ACM Symposium on Access Control Models and Technologies*, ACM, 2012b, pp. 113–116.

Ehrig, H., Ehrig, K., Prange, U. and Taentzer, G. (eds), *Fundamentals of Algebraic Graph Transformation*, Springer, Berlin, 2006.

Harris, S. and Seaborne, A. SPARQL 1.1 Query Language, W3C Working Draft, 2010.

Kagal, L., Rei: A policy language for the Me-Centric Project, HP Labs. Accessible online at http://www.hpl.hp.com/techreports/2002/HPL-2002-270.html, 2002.

Moreau, L., Clifford, B., Freire, J. et al., The Open Provenance Model core specification (v1. 1), *Future Generation Computer Systems,* Vol. 27, No. 6, 2011, pp. 743–756.

Prud'hommeaux, E. and Seaborne, A., SPARQL query language for RDF, W3C Working Draft 4, 2006.

Rozenberg, G. (ed.), *Handbook of Graph Grammars and Computing by Graph Transformation,* Volume 1, World Scientific Publishing, Singapore, 1997.

Samarati, P. and de Capitani di Vimercati, S., Access control: Policies, models, and mechanisms, in *Foundations of Security Analysis and Design,* Focardi, R. and Gorrieri, R. (eds.), Springer-Verlag, Berlin, 2001, p. 289.

Thuraisingham, B., Khadilkar, V., Rachapalli, J. et al., Cloud-centric assured information sharing. In Proceedings of Pacific Asia Workshop *PAISI*, 2012.

Chapter 21

Security and Privacy with Respect to Inference

21.1 Introduction

Much of this book has discussed access control and inference control. Furthermore, we have focused on provenance data represented by Semantic Web technologies. We have also addressed confidentiality aspects of security. Security also has other dimensions and these include privacy, trust, availability, and dependability among others. Prior to starting the research discussed in this book, we examined confidentiality, privacy, and trust aspects of security and how they relate to each other. Confidentiality is essentially secrecy. Privacy deals with not disclosing sensitive data about the individuals. Trust is about the assurance one can place on the data or on an individual. For example, even though John is authorized to get salary data, can we trust John not to divulge these data to others? Even though the website states that it will not give out SSNs of individuals, can we trust the website? Our prior work has designed a framework called confidentiality, privacy, trust (CPT) utilizing Semantic Web technologies that provides an integrated approach to addressing confidentiality, privacy, and trust (Thuraisingham et al. 2007). In this chapter, we will revisit CPT and discuss how it relates to the work discussed in this book.

The organization of this chapter is as follows. Our definitions of confidentiality, privacy, and trust as well as the current status on administering the Semantic Web will be discussed in Section 21.2. This will be followed by a discussion in Section 21.3 of our proposed framework (mentioned above) for securing the Semantic Web,

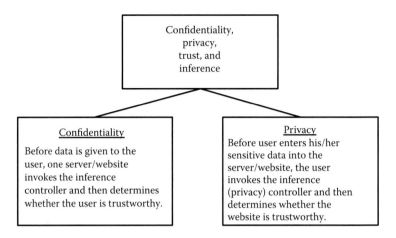

Figure 21.1   Confidentiality, privacy, trust, and inference.

CPT. Next we will take each of the features, confidentiality, privacy, and trust, and discuss various aspects as they relate to the Semantic Web in Sections 21.4, 21.5, and 21.6, respectively. An integrated architecture for CPT as well as inference and privacy control is discussed in Section 21.7. Finally the chapter is summarized and future directions are given in Section 21.8. Figure 21.1 illustrates the concepts of this chapter.

21.2 Trust, Privacy, and Confidentiality

In this section we discuss aspects of the security and privacy relationship to the inference problem. In particular, confidentiality, privacy, trust, integrity, and availability will be briefly defined with an examination of how these issues specifically relate to the trust management and inference control. Confidentiality is preventing the release of unauthorized information. One view of privacy is to consider it to be a subset of confidentiality in that it is the prevention of unauthorized information being released with regard to an individual. However, much of the recent research on privacy, especially relating to data mining, addresses the following aspect: How can we mine and extract useful nuggets about groups of people while keeping the values of the sensitive attributes of an individual private? That is, even though we can make inferences about groups, we want to maintain individual privacy. For example, we want to protect the fact that John has cancer. However, the fact that people who live in Dallas, Texas are more prone to cancer is something we make public. More details on privacy and its relationship to data mining can be found in Agrawal and Srikant (2000) and Kantarcioglu and Clifton (2003).

Integrity of data is the prevention of any modifications made by an unauthorized entity. Availability is the prevention of unauthorized omission of data. Trust is a measure of confidence in data correctness and legitimacy from a particular source. Integrity, availability, and trust are all very closely related in the sense that data quality is of particular importance and all require individuals or entities processing and sending information to not alter the data in an unauthorized manner. If confidentiality, privacy, trust, integrity, and availability are all guaranteed, a system can be considered secure. Thus if the inference problem can be solved so that unauthorized information is not released, the rules of confidentiality, privacy, and trust will not be broken. A technique such as inference can either be used to aid or impair the cause of integrity, availability, and trust. If correctly used, inference can be used to infer trust management policies. Thus inference can be used for good or bad purposes. The intention is to prevent inferred, unauthorized conclusions and to use inference to apply trust management.

21.2.1 Current Successes and Potential Failures

The W3C has proposed encryption techniques for securing XML documents. Furthermore, logic, proof, and trust belong to one of the layers of the Semantic Web. However, trust in that context means whether the Semantic Web can trust the statements such as data and rules. In our definition, by trust we mean to what extent we can believe that the user and the website will enforce the confidentiality and privacy policies as specified. Privacy has been discussed by the Semantic Web community, which has developed the Platform for Privacy Preferences (P3P).

P3P requires the Web developer of the server to create a privacy policy, validate it, and then place it in a specific location on the server as well as write a privacy policy in English. When the user enters the website, the browser will discover the privacy policy and if the privacy policy matches the user's browser security specifications, then the user can simply enter the site. If the policy does not match the user's specifications, then the user will be informed of the site's intentions and the user can then choose to enter or leave.

While this is a great start, it is lacking in certain areas. One concern is the fact that the privacy policy must be placed in a specific location. If a website, for example a student website on a school's server, is to implement P3P and cannot place it in a folder directly from the school's server, then the user's browser will not find the privacy policy.

Another problem with P3P is that it requires the data collector on the server side to follow exactly what is promised in the privacy policy. If the data collections services on the server side decide to abuse the policy and instead do other things not stated in the agreement, then no real consequences occur. The server's privacy policy can simply choose to state that it will correct the problem upon discovery, but if the user never knows it until the data are shared publicly, correcting it to show the data are private will not simply solve the problem. Accountability should be addressed where it is not the server's decision but rather the lawmaker's decision. When someone breaks a law or doesn't abide by contractual agreements, we do not turn to the accused and ask what punishment they deem necessary. Instead we look to the law and apply each law when applicable.

Another point of contention is trust and inference. Before beginning any discussions of privacy, a user and a server must evaluate how much the other party can be trusted. If neither party trusts each other, how can either party expect the other to follow a privacy policy? Currently P3P only uses tags to define actions; it uses no Web rules for inference or specific negotiations regarding confidentiality and privacy. With inference a user can decide if certain information should not be given because it would allow the distrusted server to infer information that the user would prefer to remain private or sensitive.

21.2.2 Motivation for a Framework

While P3P is a great initiative to approaching the privacy problem for users of the Semantic Web, it becomes obvious from the above discussion that more work must be continued on this process. Furthermore, we need to integrate confidentiality and privacy within the context of trust management. A new approach, which we will discuss later, must be used to address these issues so that the user can establish trust, preserve privacy and anonymity, and ensure confidentiality. Once the server and client have negotiated trust, the user can begin to decide what data can be submitted that will not violate his or her privacy. These security policies, one each for trust, privacy, and confidentiality, are described with Web rules. Describing policies with Web rules can allow an inference engine to determine what is in either the client or server's best interest and help advise each party accordingly. As well, with Web rules in place, a user and server can begin to negotiate confidentiality. Thus if a user does not agree with a server's privacy policies but would still like to use some services, a user may begin negotiating confidentiality with the server to determine if the user can still use some services but not all (depending on the final conclusion of the agreement). The goal of this new approach is to simulate real-world negotiations, thus giving semantics to the current Web and providing much-needed security.

21.3 CPT Framework

In this section we discuss a framework for enforcing CPT. We first discuss the basic framework where rules are enforced to ensure confidentiality, privacy, and trust. In the advanced framework, we include inference controllers that will reason about the application and determine whether confidentiality, privacy, and trust violations have occurred.

21.3.1 Role of the Server

In the previous section, focus was placed on the client's needs; we now discuss the server's needs in this process. The first obvious need is that the server must be able to evaluate the client in order to grant specific resources. Therefore, the primary goal is to establish trust regarding the client's identity and based on this identity grant various permissions to specific data. Not only must the server be able to evaluate the client, but also be able to evaluate its own ability to grant permission with standards and metrics. As well, the server needs to be able to grant or deny a request appropriately without giving away classified information, or instead of giving away classified information, the server may desire to give a cover story. Either scenario, a cover story or protecting classified resources, must be completed within the guidelines of a stated privacy policy in order to guarantee a client's confidentiality. One other key aspect is that all of these events must occur in a timely manner so that security is not compromised.

21.3.2 CPT Process

Now that the needs of the client and server have been discussed, focus will be placed on the actual process of our system CPT. First, a general overview of the process is presented. After the reader has garnered a simple overview, this chapter continues to discuss two systems, advanced CPT and basic CPT, based on the general process previously discussed. The general process of CPT is to first establish a relationship of trust and then negotiate privacy and confidentiality policies. Figure 21.2 shows the general process.

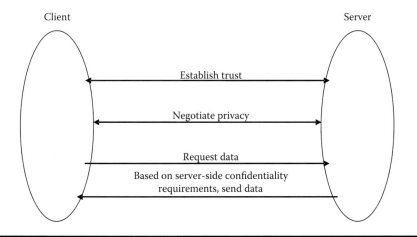

Figure 21.2   Basic framework for CPT.

Notice that both parties partake in establishing trust. The client must determine the degree to which it can trust the server in order to decide how much trust to place in the resources supplied by the server and also to negotiate privacy policies. The server must determine the degree to which it can trust the client in order to determine what privileges and resources it can allow the client to access as well as how to present the data. The server and client will base their decisions of trust on credentials of each other. Once trust is established, the client and server must come to an agreement of privacy policies to be applied to the data that the client provides the server. Privacy must follow trust because the degree to which the client trusts the server will affect the privacy degree. The privacy degree affects what data the client chooses to send. Once the client is comfortable with the privacy policies negotiated, the client will then begin requesting data. Based on the initial trust agreement, the server will determine what and when the client views these

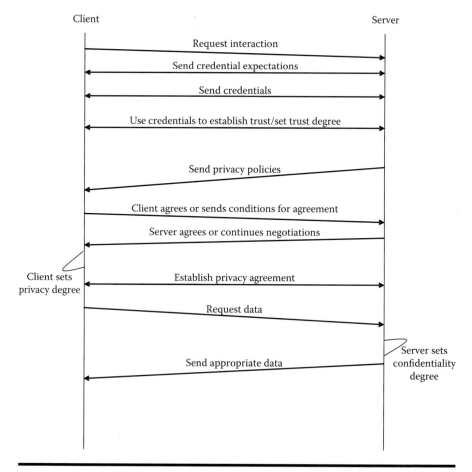

Figure 21.3   Communication between the components for basic CPT.

resources. The client will make decisions regarding confidentiality and what data can be given to the user based on its own confidentiality requirements and confidentiality degree. It is also important to note that the server and client must make these decisions and then configure the system to act on these decisions. The basic CPT system will not advise the client or server in any way regarding outcomes of any decisions. Figure 21.3 illustrates the communication between the different components.

21.3.3 Advanced CPT

The previous section discussed the basic CPT system; the advanced CPT system is an extension of the basic system. The advanced CPT system is outlined in Figure 21.4, which incorporates three new entities not found in the basic system. These three new entities are the trust inference engine (TIE), the privacy inference engine (PIE), and the confidentiality inference engine (CIE). The first step of sending

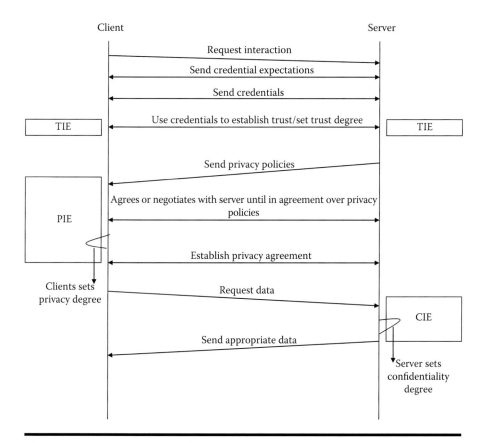

Figure 21.4 Communication between components for advanced CPT.

credentials and establishing trust is the same as the basic system except that both parties consult with their own TIE. Once each party makes a decision, the client receives the privacy policies from the server and then uses these policies in configuration with PIE to agree, disagree, or negotiate. Once the client and server have come to an agreement about the client's privacy, the clients send a request for various resources. Based on the degree of trust that the server has assigned to a particular client, the server determines what resources it can give to the client. However, in this step the server will consult the CIE to determine what data are preferable to give to the client and what data, if given, could have disastrous consequences. Once the server has made a conclusion regarding data the client can receive, it can then begin transmitting data over the network.

21.3.4 Trust, Privacy, and Confidentiality Inference Engines

With regard to trust, the server must realize that if it chooses to assign a certain percentage of trust, then this implies the client will have access to the specific privileged resources and can possibly infer other data from granted permissions. Thus, the primary responsibility of the trust inference engine is to determine what information can be inferred and whether this behavior is acceptable. Likewise, the client must realize the percentage of trust it assigns to the server will affect permissions of viewing the site as well as affecting how data given to the client will be processed. The inference engine in the client's scenario will guide the client regarding what can or will occur based on the trust assignment given to the server.

Once trust is established, the privacy inference engine will continue the inference process. Note that the privacy inference engine only resides on the client side. The server will have its own privacy policies but these policies may not be acceptable to the client. It is impossible for the server to evaluate each client and determine how to implement an individual privacy policy without first consulting the client. Thus the privacy inference engine is unnecessary on the server's side. The privacy inference engine must guide the client in negotiating privacy policies. In order to guide the client through negotiations, the inference engine must be able to determine how the server will use data the client gives it as well as who else will have access to the submitted data. Once this is determined, the inference engine must evaluate the data given by the client to the server. If the inference engine determines that these data can be used to infer other data that the client would prefer to remain private, the inference engine must warn the client and then allow the client to choose the next appropriate measure of either sending or not sending the data.

Once the client and server have agreed on the privacy policies to be implemented, the client will naturally begin requesting data and the server will have to determine what data to send based on confidentiality requirements. Note that the confidentiality inference engine is located only on the server side. The client has already negotiated its personal privacy issues and is ready to view the data, thus leaving the server to decide what the next appropriate action is. The confidentiality inference engine must first determine what data will be currently available to the client based on the current trust assignment. Once the inference engine has determined this, the inference engine must explore what policies or data can be potentially inferred if the data are given to the client. The primary objective of the confidentiality inference engine is to ponder how the client might be able to use the information given to it and then guide the server through the process of deciding a client's access to resources.

21.4 Confidentiality Management

While much of our previous work focused on security control in relational databases, our work discussed in this book focuses on extending this approach to the Semantic Web. The Semantic Web is augmented by an inference controller that examines the policies specified as ontologies and rules and utilizes the inference engine embedded in the Web rules language, reasons about the applications, and deduces the security violations via inference. In particular we focus on the design and implementation of an inference controller where the data are represented as RDF documents.

Prior to the work discussed in this book, we designed and developed a preliminary confidentiality controller in 2005. There, we utilized two popular Semantic Web technologies in our prototype called Intellidimension RDF Gateway and Jena (see Intellidimension, the RDF Gateway, http://www.intellidimension.com/, and Jena, http://jena.sourceforge.net/). RDF Gateway is a database and integrated Web server utilizing RDF, and is built from the group up rather than on top of existing Web servers or databases (RDF Primer, http://www.w3.org/TR/rdf-primer/). It functions as a data repository for RDF data and also as an interface to various data sources, external or internal, that can be queried. Jena is a Java application programming package to create, modify, store, query, and perform other processing tasks on RDF/XML documents from Java programs. RDF documents can be created from scratch or preformatted documents can be read into memory to explore various parts. The node-arc-node feature of RDF closely resembles how Jena accesses an RDF document. It also has a built-in query engine designed on top of RDF Query Language (RDFQL) that allows querying documents using standard RDFQL query statements. Our initial prototype utilized RDFQL while our current work focuses on SPARQL queries.

Using these technologies we specify the confidentiality policies. The confidentiality engine ensures that the policies are enforced correctly. If we assume the basic framework, then the confidentiality engine will enforce the policies and will not examine security violations via inference. In the advanced approach, the confidentiality engine will include what we call an inference controller. Figure 21.5 illustrates an inference/confidentiality controller for the Semantic Web that has been the basis of this book.

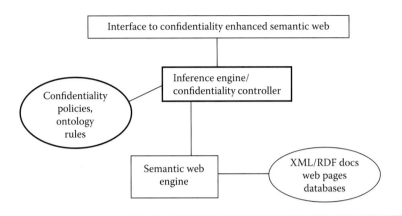

Figure 21.5　Confidentiality controller for the Semantic Web.

21.5　Privacy Management

As discussed in Chapter 4, privacy is about protecting information about individuals. Furthermore, an individual can specify, say to a Web service provider, the information that can be released about him or her. Privacy has been discussed a great deal in the past, especially when it relates to protecting medical information about patients. Social scientists as well as technologists have always worked on privacy issues; however, privacy has received enormous attention recently. This is mainly because of the advent of the Web, the Semantic Web, counterterrorism, and national security. For example, in order to extract information about various individuals and perhaps prevent and/or detect potential terrorist attacks, data mining tools are currently being examined. As stated previously, we have heard much about national security versus privacy in the media. This is mainly due to the fact that people are now realizing that to handle terrorism, the government may need to collect data about individuals and mine the data to extract information. Data may be in relational databases or it may be text, video, and images. This is causing a major concern with various civil liberties unions (Thuraisingham 2003).

　　From a technology policy of view, a privacy controller could be considered to be identical to the confidentiality controller we have designed and developed in this book; however, it is implemented at the client side. The privacy controller is illustrated in Figure 21.6. Before the client gives out information to a website, it will check whether the website can divulge aggregated information to the third party and subsequently result in privacy violations. For example, the website may give out medical records without the identity so that the third party can study the patterns of flu or other infectious diseases. Furthermore, at some other time the website may give out the names. However, if the website gives out the link between the names and diseases, then there could be privacy violations. The inference engine will make such deductions and determine whether the client should give out personal data to the website.

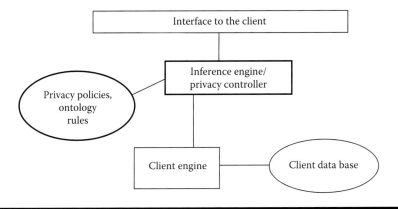

Figure 21.6   Privacy controller for the Semantic Web.

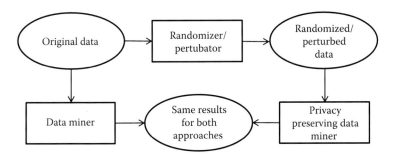

Figure 21.7   Privacy control for data mining and analysis.

As we have stated earlier, privacy violations could also result due to data mining and analysis. In this case the challenge is to protect the values of the sensitive attributes of an individual and make public the results of the mining or analysis. This aspect of privacy is illustrated in Figure 21.7. A CPT framework should handle both aspects of privacy.

21.6 Trust Management

Researchers are working on protocols for trust management. Languages for specifying trust management constructs are also being developed and there is also research on the foundations of trust management. For example, if A trusts B and B trusts C, then can A trust C? How do you share the data and information on the Semantic Web and still maintain autonomy? How do you propagate trust? For example, if A trusts B 50% of the time and B trusts C 30% of the time, then what value do you assign for A trusting C? How do you incorporate trust into semantic interoperability? What are the quality of service primitives for trust and negotiation? That is, for certain situations one may need 100% trust while for certain other situations, 50% trust may suffice (Yu and Winslett 2003).

Another topic that is being investigated is trust propagation and propagating privileges. For example, if you grant privileges to A, what privileges can A transfer to B? How can you compose privileges? Is there an algebra and/or calculus for the composition of privileges? Much research still needs to be done here. One of the layers of the Semantic Web is logic, proof, and trust. Essentially this layer deals with trust management and negotiation between different agents and examining the foundations and developing logics for trust management. Some interesting work has been carried out by Finin et al. (Denker et al. 2003; Finin and Joshi 2002; Kagal et al. 2003). For example, if given data A and B can someone deduce classified data X (i.e., A + B → X)? The inference engines will also use an inverse inference module to determine if classified information can be inferred if a user employs inverse resolution techniques. For example, if given data A and the user wants to guarantee that data X remains classified, the user can determine that B, which combined with A implies X, must remain classified as well (i.e., A + ? → X; the question mark results with B). Once the expert system has received the results from the inference engines, it can conclude a recommendation and then pass this recommendation to the client or server who will have the option to either accept or reject the suggestion.

21.7 Integrated System

In order to establish trust, privacy, and confidentiality, it is necessary to have an intelligent system that can evaluate the user's preferences. The system will be designed as an expert system to store trust, privacy, and confidentiality policies. These policies can be written using a Web rules language with foundations of first-order logic. Traditional theorem provers can then be applied to the rules to check for inconsistencies and alert the user (Antoniou and Harmelen 2008). Once the user approves of all the policies, the system can take action and properly apply these policies during any transaction occurring on a site. Also the user can place percentages next to the policies in order to apply probabilistic scenarios. Figure 21.8 gives an example of a probabilistic scenario occurring with a trust policy.

Trust degree = 59%
90 Policy1
75 Policy2
70 Policy3
60 Policy4
50 Policy5
35 Policy6
10 Policy7
0 Policy8

Figure 21.8   Trust probabilities.

In Figure 21.8, the user sets the trust degree to 59%. Because the user trusts another person 59%, only policies 5–8 will be applied. Figure 21.9 shows some example policies. These example policies will be converted into a Web rules language such as the Semantics Web Rules Language (SWRL) and enforced by the trust engine. Figure 21.10 illustrates an integrated architecture for ensuring confidentiality, privacy, and trust for the Semantic Web. The Web server as well as the client have trust management modules. The Web server has a confidentiality engine, whereas the client has a privacy engine. The inference controller described in this book is the first toward an integrated CPT system with XML, RDF, and Web rules technologies. Details of the modules are illustrated in Figure 21.11.

In Figure 21.11, ontologies, CPT policies, and credentials are given to the expert system so that the expert system can advise the client or server who should receive access to what particular resource and how these resources should further be regulated. The expert system will send the policies to the Web rules, credentials, ontologies, and policies (WCOP) parser to check for syntax errors and validate the inputs.

Policy1:	if A then B else C
Policy2:	not A or B
Policy3:	A or C
Policy4:	A or C or D or not E
Policy5:	not (A or C)

Figure 21.9   Example policies.

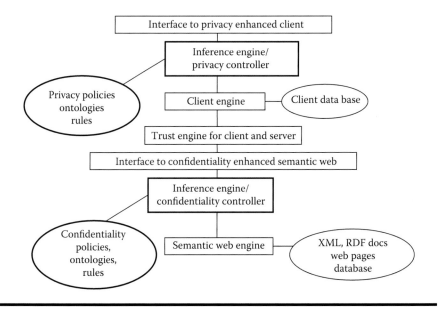

Figure 21.10   Integrated architecture for confidentiality, privacy, and trust.

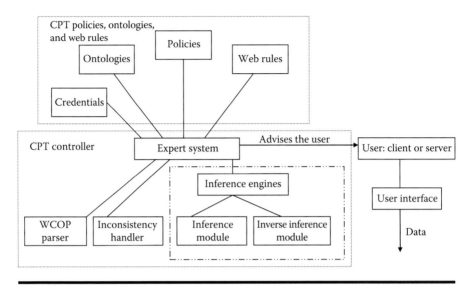

Figure 21.11 Modules of CPT controller.

The information contained within the dashed box is a part of the system that is only included in the advanced TPC system. The inference engines (e.g., TIE, PIE, and CIE) will use an inference module to determine if classified information can be inferred.

21.8 Summary and Directions

This chapter has provided an overview of security and privacy considerations with respect to inference. We first discussed a framework for enforcing confidentiality, privacy, and trust for the Semantic Web. Next we described our approach to confidentiality and inference control and then we discussed privacy for the Semantic Web. Finally, we discussed trust management as well as an integrated framework for CPT.

While this chapter has provided a high-level discussion of CPT with Semantic Web technologies, the overall focus in this book has been on one aspect, which is confidentiality. There are many directions for future work. We need to continue with research on confidentiality and privacy as well as trust management and subsequently develop an integrated framework for CPT. Finally, we need to formalize the notions of CPT and build a security model. One very productive area of research would be to enhance our framework for secure data provenance and inference control, which has mainly focused on confidentiality, and incorporate both privacy and trust models into this framework. We will discuss this further when we present a unifying framework in Chapter 23. In the next chapter we will examine security and privacy issues for big data technologies and explore inference control.

References

Agrawal, R. and Srikant, R., Privacy-preserving data mining, SIGMOD Conference, pp. 439–450, 2000.

Antoniou, G. and Harmelen, F V., *A Semantic Web Primer*, The MIT Press, Cambridge, MA, 2008.

Denker, G. et al., Security for DAML Web services: Annotation and matchmaking, Proceedings of the International Semantic Web Conference, Sanibel Island, FL, 2003.

Finin T. and Joshi, A., Agents, trust, and information access on the Semantic Web, *ACM Sigmod Record*, Vol. 31, No. 4, December 2002, pp. 30–35.

Intellidimension, the RDF Gateway, http://www.intellidimension.com/.

Jena, http://jena.sourceforge.net/.

Kagal, L, Finin, T. and Joshi, A., A policy based approach to security for the Semantic Web, Proceedings of the International Semantic Web Conference, Sanibel Island, FL, 2003.

Kantarcioglu, M. and Clifton, C., Assuring privacy when big brother is watching, In Proceedings of DMKD (Data Mining Knowledge Discovery), 2003, pp. 88–93.

RDF Primer, http://www.w3.org/TR/rdf-primer/.

SWRL, Semantic Web Rules Language, 2004, http://www.w3.org/Submission/SWRL/.

Thuraisingham, B., Data mining, national security and privacy, *ACM SIGKDD*, January 2003.

Thuraisingham, B. M., Tsybulnik, N. and Alam, A., Administering the Semantic Web: Confidentiality, privacy, and trust management. *IJISP1*, Vol. 1, 2007, pp. 18–34.

Yu, T. and Winslett, M., A unified scheme for resource protection in automated trust negotiation, Proceedings of IEEE Symposium on Security and Privacy, Oakland, CA, 2003.

Chapter 22

Big Data Analytics and Inference Control

22.1 Overview

As stated in Appendix A, due to the explosion of Web-based services, unstructured data management, and social media and mobile computing, the amount of data to be handled has increased from terabytes to petabytes and zettabytes in just two decades. Such vast amounts of complex data have come to be known as big data. Not only does big data have to be managed efficiently, such data also have to be analyzed to extract useful nuggets to enhance businesses as well as improve society. This has come to be known as big data analytics. However, as data grow exponentially and the analytics tools are becoming more powerful, there is also greater potential for violating the inference (and privacy) problem. In other words, storage, management, and analysis of large quantities of data also result in security and privacy violations. Therefore as we make progress on big data analytics, we also need to investigate security (i.e., confidentiality) and privacy issues.

Often data have to be retained for various reasons including for regulatory compliance. The data retained may have sensitive information and could violate user privacy. Furthermore, manipulating such big data, such as combining sets of different types of data, could result in security and privacy violations. For example, while the raw data remove personally identifiable information, the derived data may contain private and sensitive information. The raw data about a person may be combined with the person's address, which may be sufficient to identify the person.

Different communities are working on the big data challenge. For example, the systems community is developing technologies for massive storage of big data. The

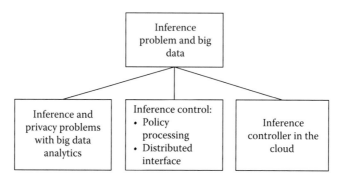

Figure 22.1   Inference problem and big data.

network community is developing solutions for managing very large networked data. The data community is developing solutions for efficiently managing and analyzing large sets of data. Big data research and development is being carried out in academia, industry, and government research labs. However, little attention has been given to security and privacy considerations for big data. Security cuts across multiple areas including systems, data, and networks. We need these multiple communities to come together to develop solutions for big data security and privacy and subsequently investigate the inference (and privacy) problem for big data.

In this chapter we discuss security and privacy issues for big data with emphasis on the inference problem. In Section 22.2 we provide a brief overview of big data management and analysis. Security and privacy challenges for big data are discussed in Section 22.3. Inference control is discussed in Section 22.4. The chapter is concluded in Section 22.5. Figure 22.1 illustrates the topics addressed in this chapter.

22.2 Big Data Management and Analytics

Big data management and analytics research is proceeding in three directions:

1. Building infrastructure and high-performance computing techniques for the storage of big data
2. Data management techniques such as integrating multiple data sources (both big and small) and indexing and querying big data
3. Data analytics techniques that manipulate and analyze big data to extract nuggets

We briefly review the progress made in each of the areas. With respect to building infrastructures, technologies such as Hadoop and MapReduce as well as Storm are being developed for managing large amounts of data in the cloud. In addition, main memory data management techniques have advanced so that a few terabytes of data can

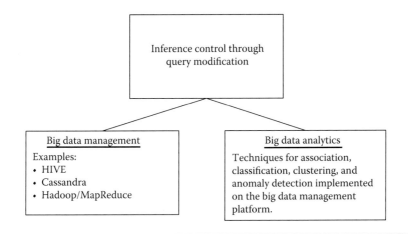

Figure 22.2 Big data management and analytics.

be managed in main memory. Furthermore, systems such as HIVE and Cassandra as well as NoSQL databases have been developed for managing petabytes of data.

With respect to data management, traditional data management techniques such as query processing and optimization strategies are being examined for handling petabytes of data. Furthermore, graph data management techniques are being developed for the storage and management of very large networked data.

With respect to data analytics, various data mining algorithms are being implemented on Hadoop- and MapReduce-based infrastructures. Additionally, data reduction techniques are being explored to reduce the massive amounts of data into manageable chunks while still maintaining the semantics of the data.

In summary, big data management and analytics techniques include extending current data management and mining techniques to handle massive amounts of data as well as developing new approaches, including graph data management and mining techniques, for maintaining and analyzing large networked data. Figure 22.2 illustrates the big data management and analysis challenges.

22.3 Security and Privacy for Big Data

The collection, storage, manipulation, and retention of massive amounts of data have resulted in serious security and privacy considerations. Various regulations are being proposed to handle big data so that the privacy of the individuals is not violated. For example, even if personally identifiable information is removed from the data, when data are combined with other data, an individual can be identified. This is essentially the inference and aggregation problem that data security researchers have been exploring for the past four decades. This problem is exacerbated with the management of big data as different sources of data now exist that are related to various individuals.

In some cases, regulations may cause privacy to be violated. For example, data that are collected (e.g., e-mail data) have to be retained for a certain period of time (usually 5 years). As long as one keeps such data, there is a potential for privacy violations. Too many regulations can also stifle innovation. For example, if there is a regulation that raw data have to be kept as is and not manipulated or models cannot be built out of the data, then corporations cannot analyze the data in innovative ways to enhance their business. This way innovation may be stifled.

Therefore, one of the main challenges for ensuring security and privacy when dealing with big data is to come up with a balanced approach toward regulations and analytics. That is, how can an organization carry out useful analytics and still ensure the privacy of individuals? Numerous techniques for privacy-preserving data mining, privacy-preserving data integration, and privacy-preserving information retrieval have been developed. The challenge is to extend these techniques for handling massive amounts of often networked data.

Another security challenge for big data management and analytics is to secure the infrastructures. Many of the technologies that have been developed including Hadoop, MapReduce, HIVE, Cassandra, PigLatin, Mahout, and Storm do not have adequate security protections. The question is, how can these technologies be secured and at the same time ensure high-performance computing?

Next, big data management strategies such as access methods and indexing and query processing have to be secure. So the question is, how can policies for different types of data such as structured, semistructured, unstructured, and graph data be integrated? Since big data may result from combining data from numerous sources, how can one ensure the quality of the data?

Finally, the entire area of security, privacy, integrity, data quality, and trust policies have to be examined within the context of big data security. What are the appropriate policies for big data? How can these policies be handled without affecting performance? How can these policies be made consistent and complete?

This section has listed just some of the challenges with respect to security and privacy for big data. We need a comprehensive research program that will identify the challenges and develop solutions for big data security and privacy. Security cannot be an afterthought. That is, we cannot incorporate security into each and every big data technology that is being developed. We need to have a comprehensive strategy so that security can be incorporated while the technology is being developed. We also need to determine the appropriate types of policies and regulations to enforce before big data technologies are employed by an organization. This means researchers in multiple disciplines have to come together to determine what the problems are and explore solutions. These disciplines include high-performance computing, data management and analytics, network science, and policy management.

While the above challenges deal with securing big data and ensuring the privacy of individuals, big data management and analytics techniques can be

Figure 22.3   Big data security and privacy.

used to solve security problems. For example, an organization can outsource activities such as identity management, e-mail filtering, and intrusion detection to the cloud. This is because massive amounts of data are being collected for such applications and these data have to be analyzed. Cloud data management is just one example of big data management. The question is, how can the developments in big data management and analytic techniques be used to solve security problems?

Recently a few workshops and panels were held on big data security. Examples include the ACM CCS workshop on big data security, ACM SACMAT, and IEEE Big Data Conference panels. These workshops and panels have been influenced by different communities of researchers. For example, the ACM CCS workshop series focused on big data for security applications while the IEEE Big Data Conference focused on cloud security issues. Furthermore, these workshops and panels mainly address a limited number of the technical issues surrounding big data security. For example, the ACM CCS workshop does not appear to address the privacy issues dealing with regulations or the security violations resulting from data analytics.

To address the above limitations, we need a workshop consisting of interdisciplinary researchers in the fields of higher-performance computing, systems, data management and analytics, cyber security, network science and policy, and social sciences to come together and determine the strategic direction for big data security and privacy. The topics that need to get addressed include policy management for big data, security and privacy for big data management and analytics, secure infrastructures and storage for big data, securing and analyzing massive networks, and big data analytics for security problems. Figure 22.3 illustrates the challenges for big data security and privacy. More details on big data security and privacy challenges can be found in ACM Conference on Computer and Communications Security Workshop on Big Data Security (2012), *Computer* (2013), ACM SACMAT (2013), and IEEE Services Congress Conference on Big Data (2013). Note also that the CPT framework discussed in Chapter 21 has to be extended to handle massive amounts of data.

22.4 Inference Control for Big Data

Due to the fact that big data result from the combinations, associations, and manipulations of massive amounts of multiple sets of data, big data management exacerbates the inference problem. Data are emanating from numerous sources. Even though the personally identifiable data may be removed from the individual data stores, the combination of the sources may result in highly private and sensitive data. Therefore, we need inference controllers that operate on such big data and control unauthorized inferences.

Due to the nature of big data and the fact that big data may not reside in a single location, we may need some form of distributed inference control. That is, while each data source may have its own inference control, the multiple data sets, when combined, need to be checked for unauthorized inferences. We illustrate distributed inference control in Figure 22.4.

One solution to big data inference control is to implement inference control in the cloud. That is, the inference controller could take advantage of the computational power and the virtual machines offered by a cloud. This does not mean that we simply port the inference controller to the cloud. We need to take advantage of the resources offered by the cloud and reimplement the inference controller. Our initial step toward such an implementation is discussed in Chapter 20. That is, while we have not yet fully implemented the inference controller in the cloud, we have implemented our policy manager in the cloud to facilitate information sharing. Figure 22.5 illustrates inference control in the cloud.

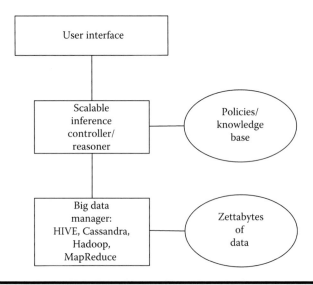

Figure 22.4   Distributed inference control.

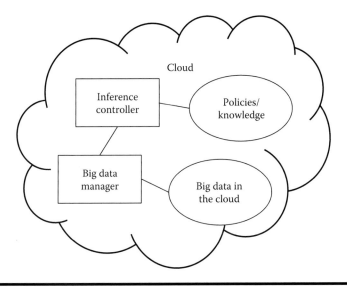

Figure 22.5 Inference control in the cloud.

22.5 Summary and Directions

This chapter discussed the challenges for big data security and privacy. We argue that big data are everywhere, from social network data to mobile and sensor data. Scientific communities have to manage and manipulate massive amounts of data. These data have grown from a few terabytes to multiple petabytes and even zettabytes in just 20 years. Organizations are analyzing massive amounts of data to improve business and to provide better quality of life. Such analysis of data may result in highly sensitive data being divulged to the public. As a result, privacy of the individuals may be compromised. This exacerbates the inference problem as data are combined in unauthorized ways.

The challenge is to formulate appropriate policies and regulations that will ensure the privacy of individuals but at the same time encourage innovation. This is a daunting challenge. One solution is to implement inference controls in the cloud so that we can get the performance needed and yet maintain security and privacy. We discussed our approach to cloud-based implementation of a policy manager for information sharing purposes in Chapter 20. Integrating confidentiality privacy and trust management with respect to inference control was discussed in Chapter 21. We now need to develop a unified framework that will include the various security, privacy, and trust models. Such a framework will be presented in the next chapter.

References

ACM Conference on Computer and Communications Security Workshop on Big Data Security, Raleigh, NC, October 2012.

ACM SACMAT, panel on big data security, Amsterdam, Holland, June 2013.

Computer, Special Issue on Big Data, June 2013.

IEEE Services Congress Conference on Big Data, panel on big data security, Santa Clara, CA, June 2013.

Chapter 23

Unifying Framework

23.1 Overview

In this chapter, we integrate the various parts of the system into an automatic framework for provenance. In particular, we integrate the access control framework discussed in Section II with the inference control framework discussed in Section III. We preserve features such as scalability, efficiency, and interoperability in developing this framework. This framework can be used to execute various policies, including access control policies and redaction policies (which were subjects of Section II) and inference strategies (which was the subject of Section III). Our framework can also be used as a test bed for evaluating different policy sets over a provenance graph and their outcomes graphically. Our recent work in Cadenhead et al. (2011) proposes new mechanisms for extending our framework. One of them includes comparing the words described by regular expression queries to determine equivalence and subsumption of policies. Hence, we will be able to compare and write more compact policies as well as eliminate redundancies and inefficiencies.

The framework we present in this chapter is in the design stages. Specifically, we give guidelines for policy processing for provenance data both for access control and inference control as well as information sharing. We can integrate features such as risk-based access control and inference control discussed in Chapters 18 and 19 into such a framework. Our ultimate goal is to develop an inference controller that not only carries out access control and inference control but also information sharing, privacy management, and risk-based policy processing.

The organization of this chapter is as follows. In Section 23.2 we discuss our framework. Aspects of what we call our global inference controller are discussed in Section 23.3. Such an inference controller will handle unauthorized inference during access control as well as during data sharing. In addition, such an inference

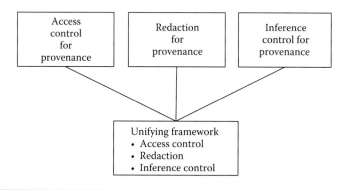

Figure 23.1 Unifying framework.

controller should handle the privacy issues discussed in Chapter 21 and the big data challenges discussed in Chapter 22. The chapter is summarized in Section 23.4. Figure 23.1 illustrates the contents in this chapter.

23.2 Design of Our Framework

The final architecture for our provenance manager is extended to include an inference controller as well as a data sharing manager and a risk manager. This enables us to add the risk-based mechanism discussed in Chapter 19 into our framework. Our architecture takes a user's input query and returns a response that has been pruned using a set of user-defined policy constraints. We assume that a user could interact with our system to obtain both traditional data and provenance. In our design we will assume that the available information is divided into two parts: the actual data and provenance. Both the data and provenance are represented as RDF graphs, but they are not limited to any data format since tools can map existing formats to RDF (Bizer 2003).

The architecture is built using a modular approach and therefore it is very flexible in that most of the modules can be extended or replaced by another application module. For example, an application user may substitute a policy parser module that handles the parsing of high-level business policies to low-level policy objects or replace or extend one policy layer without changing the inner workings of the other policy layer modules. This substitution or replacement of modules would allow the application user to continue using high-level business policies independent of our software implementation.

A user application can submit a query for access to the data and their associated provenance or vice versa. Figure 23.2 shows the design of our framework. All of the modules that comprise this framework make up our inference controller. We call this the global inference controller as it handles inference control for access control as well as for information sharing. We now present a description of these modules

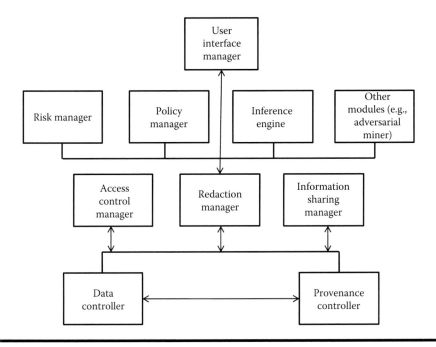

Figure 23.2 Integrated architecture for inference controller.

in Figure 23.2. Some aspects of our global inference controller will be discussed in Section 23.3. Next we discuss the components of the framework.

Data controller. The data controller is a suite of software programs that store and manage access to data. The data could be stored in any format such as in a relational database, in XML files, or in an RDF store. The controller accepts requests for information from the policy manager (and/or the inference engine layer) if a policy allows the requesting user access to the data item. This layer then executes the request over the stored data and returns results back to the policy layer (and/or the inference engine layer) where it is reevaluated based on a set of policies.

Provenance controller. The provenance controller is used to store and manage provenance information that is associated with data items that are present in the data controller. In the case when we select a graph representation of provenance, the provenance controller stores information in the form of logical graph structures in any appropriate data representation format. This controller also records the ongoing activities associated with the data items stored in the data controller. This controller takes as input a graph query and evaluates it over the provenance information. This query evaluation returns a subgraph back to the inference controller layer where it is reexamined using a set of policies.

User interface manager. The user interface manager module provides a layer of abstraction that allows a user to interact with the system. The user interacts with the system via a user interface layer. This layer accepts a user's credentials and authenticates the user. Our interface module hides the actual internal representation of our system from a user by providing a simple question-answer mechanism. This mechanism allows the user to pose standard provenance queries such as why a data item was created, where in the provenance graph it was generated, how the data item was generated, and when and from what location it was created. This layer also returns results after they have been examined against a set of policies.

Essentially, the user interface manager is responsible for processing the user's requests, authenticating the user, and providing suitable responses back to the user. The interface manager also provides an abstraction layer that allows a user to interact with the system. A user can therefore pose either a data query or a provenance query to this layer. The user interface manager also determines whether the query should be evaluated against the traditional data or provenance.

Policy manager. The policy manager module is responsible for enforcing any high-level policy defined by a high-level application user or administrator. The policies are not restricted to any particular security policy definition, model, or mechanism. In fact, we can support different access control policies, for example RBAC, access control based on context such as time (TRBAC), location (LBAC), and so forth. Besides the traditional and well-established security models built on top of access control mechanisms, we also support redaction policies that are based on sharing data for the ongoing mutual relationships among businesses and stakeholders. The policy layer also interacts with any reasoners in the inference layer that offer further protection against inference attacks. The inference layer enforces policies that are in the form of DL constraints, OWL restrictions, or SWRL rules. We also observe that some of the access control policies can be expressed as inference rules or queries via query rewrite or views. Our policy module therefore has many layers equipped with security features, thus ensuring we are enforcing the maximal protection over the underlying provenance store. The policy module also handles the information sharing policies.

Essentially, the policy manager is responsible for ensuring that the querying user is authorized to use the system. It evaluates the policies against a user's query and associated query results to ensure that no confidential information is released to unauthorized users. The policy manager may enforce the policies against the traditional data or against the provenance data. Each data type may have its own policy manager; for example, the traditional data may be stored in a different format from the provenance data. Hence, we may require different implementations for each policy manager.

Inference engine. The inference engine is the heart of the inference controller described in Section III. The engine is equipped to use a variety of inference strategies that are supported by a particular reasoner. Since there are many implementations of reasoners available, our inference controller offers an added feature of flexibility whereby we can select from among any reasoning tool for each reasoning task. We can improve the efficiency of the inference controller since each inference strategy (or a combination of strategies) could be executed on a separate processor.

An inference engine typically uses software programs that have the capability of reasoning over some data representation; for example, a relational data model or an RDF graph model representation. The inference controller is an implementation of the function $I: K \times B \rightarrow 2^\circ$ that was introduced in Section III. Basically, the inference controller is used to address the inference problem.

The inference problem is an open problem and a lot of research has been pivoted around its implementations based on traditional databases (Hinke et al. 1997; Marks 1996). However, since provenance has a logical graph structure, it can also be represented and stored in a graph data model and therefore it is not limited to any particular data format. Although our focus in this chapter is on building an inference controller over the directed graph representation of provenance, our inference controller could be used to protect the case when provenance is represented and stored in a traditional relational database model. Also, the use of an RDF data model does not overburden our implementation with restrictions, since other data formats are well served by an RDF data model. Furthermore, there are tools to convert, say relational data into RDF, and vice versa (see for example D2RQ: Accessing Relational Databases as Virtual RDF Graphs, http://d2rq.org/).

Query manager. The query processing manager module is responsible for accepting a user's query, parsing it, and submitting it to the provenance knowledge base. After the query results are evaluated against a set of policies, it is returned to the user via the user interface layer. The query processing module can accept any standard provenance query as well as any query written in the SPARQL format. The querying user is allowed to view the errors that are due to the syntax of a query as well as the responses constructed by the underlying processes of the inference controller.

Information sharing manager. The information sharing manager module will implement the information sharing policies. For example, if an organization A wants to share data with organization B, then the information sharing controller will examine the policies via the policy manager, determine whether there are any unauthorized inferences by communicating with the inference engine, and determine whether data are to be given to organization B.

Access control manager. This access control manager module is responsible for determining whether the user can access the data. The access control policies are obtained via the policy manager. The inference engine will determine whether any unauthorized information will be released by carrying out reasoning. The results are given to the user via the user interface manager.

Redaction manager. This manager module will determine which data have to be redacted before they are given to the user. It operates in conjunction with the access control manager. It also examines the information that has been released previously and determines whether the new information obtained as a result of executing the query should be given to the user.

Risk manager. The risk manager module will compute the risks for releasing the information and makes a determination whether the information should be released to the user. It interacts with other modules, such as the access control manager, the redaction manager, and the information sharing manager, in making this determination. The results of the risk manager are then given to the access control manager, the redaction manager, and the information snaring manager to execute the results.

The adversarial data miner. This module will implement the strategies we have discussed in Chapter 19. In particular, it will determine how to thwart the adversary as well as apply game theoretics, mathematical programming, and probabilistic deduction in determining what information is to be released to the user. It will work jointly with the inference engine.

23.3 The Global Inference Controller

Our global inference controller should determine unauthorized inference during access control, redaction, and information sharing. It has to compute the risks in disclosing the information as well as apply novel strategies such as adversarial mining to be ahead of the adversary. In addition it also has to protect individual privacy. In this section we discuss some of the key points of such an inference controller.

In Chapter 18, we presented a model that can be used to determine the expected risk of releasing provenance. We further extend this model in order to determine whether the addition of provenance improves the user's utility when interacting with our system. The extended model formally describes what we hope to accomplish by incorporating inference tools into our architecture. In other words, we release provenance data to a user whenever $E[L(O)] + U(O) \geq E[L(\phi)]$. By carefully adjusting $E[L(\phi)]$, we can adjust how much provenance we release based on the identity of a querying user. This is important, for example, in research whereby some provenance is released for the advancement of science. Our inference controller is aware of these special cases and has features for supporting multilevel users. Recall that our model supports different labels; therefore we could label the different users, for example, $l = \{provider, researcher, pharmacist, intern, physician\}$ $P_l < P_{l+1}$ $\forall l$.

We can also use our inference controller to provide feedback so that a high-level domain user can reconfigure the business rules (or high-level policy set).

23.3.1 Inference Tools

Newly published data, when combined with existing public knowledge, allow for complex and sometimes unintended inferences. Therefore, we need semiautomated tools for detecting these inferences prior to releasing provenance information. These tools should give data owners a fuller understanding of the implications of releasing the provenance information as well as help them to adjust the amount of information they release in order to avoid unwanted inferences (Staddon et al. 2007).

The inference controller is a tool that implements some of the inference strategies that a user may use to infer confidential information that is encoded into a provenance graph. Our inference controller leverages from existing software tools that perform inferencing, for example, Pellet (Sirin et al. 2007), Fact++ (Tsarkov and Horrocks 2006), Racer (Haarslev and Möller 2001), Hermit (Shearer et al. 2008), and CWM (Closed World Machine, http://www.w3.org/2001/sw/wiki/CWM). Therefore, we can add more expressive power by replacing the default base engine of our inference controller with a more powerful reasoner. Furthermore, since there is a trade-off of expressivity and decidability, an application user has more flexibility in selecting the most appropriate reasoner for his/her application domain.

For our default reasoner, we employ the services of Pellet (Sirin et al. 2007). Pellet has support for OWL-DL (SHOIN(D)) and is also extended to support OWL 2 specification (SROIQ(D)). The OWL 2 specification adds the following language constructs:

- Qualified cardinality restrictions
- Complex subproperty axioms (between a property chain and a property)
- Local reflexivity restrictions
- Reflexive, irreflexive, symmetric, and antisymmetric properties
- Disjoint properties
- Negative property assertions
- Vocabulary sharing (punning) between individuals, classes, and properties
- User-defined data ranges

In addition, Pellet provides all the standard inference services that are traditionally provided by DL reasoners. These are

- *Consistency checking,* which ensures that an ontology does not contain any contradictory facts. The OWL 2 Direct Semantics provide the formal definition of ontology consistency used by Pellet.
- *Concept satisfiability,* which determines whether it is possible for a class to have any instances. If a class is unsatisfiable, then defining an instance of that class will cause the whole ontology to be inconsistent.
- *Classification,* which computes the subclass relations between every named class to create the complete class hierarchy. The class hierarchy can be used to answer queries such as getting all or only the direct subclasses of a class (Sirin et al. 2007).
- *Realization,* which finds the most specific classes that an individual belongs to (i.e., realization computes the direct types for each of the individuals). Realization can only be performed after classification since direct types are defined with respect to a class hierarchy (Sirin et al. 2007). Using the classification hierarchy, it is also possible to get all the types for each individual.

The global inference controller has to reason with big data, its operation has to be timely, and it has to handle data privacy. Therefore, we propose a cloud-based

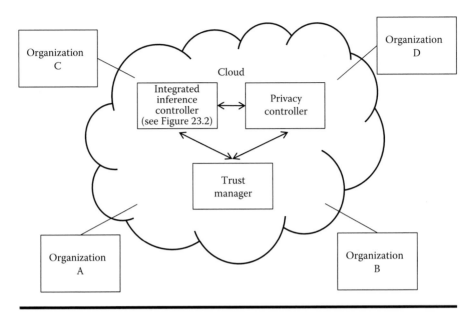

Figure 23.3 Global inference controller.

implementation of such an inference controller. In Chapter 20 we discussed our initial implementation of policy-based information sharing in a cloud. Our ultimate goal is to implement the entire inference controller in the cloud. Figure 23.3 illustrates such a global inferenve controller.

23.4 Summary and Directions

This chapter has essentially integrated much of the design and implementation of the systems discussed in Sections II and III as well as some of the novel methods discussed in Sections IV, and has also described a unifying framework. The framework includes components both for access control and inference control as well as information sharing control. Our framework can also include the modules for risk and game theoretic approaches for access and inference control. We discussed the modules of the framework as well as building of the global inference controller.

Our framework is in the design stages. We have provided guidelines toward implementating such a framework. We can essentially plug and play various modules in order to develop such a framework. We believe that a cloud-based implementation of such a framework can provide scalability and efficiency. Our ultimate goal is to develop our global inference controller in the cloud so that it can handle inferences for big data.

References

Bizer, C., D2R MAP-A database to RDF mapping language, WWW posters, 2003.

Cadenhead, T., Khadilkar, V., Kantarcioglu, K. and Thuraisingham, B. M., A language for provenance access control, CODASPY '11, Proceedings of the First ACM Conference on Data and Application Security and Privacy, 2011, pp. 133–144.

Closed World Machine, http://www.w3.org/2001/sw/wiki/CWM.

D2RQ: Accessing Relational Databases as Virtual RDF Graphs, http://d2rq.org/.

Haarslev, V. and Möller, R., RACER system description, *IJCAR*, 2001, pp. 701–706.

Hinke, T. H., Delugach, H. S. and Wolf, R. P., Protecting databases from inference attacks, *Computers & Security*, Vol. 16, No. 8, 1997, pp. 687–708.

Marks, D. G., Inference in MLS database systems, *IEEE Transactions on Knowledge and Data Engineering*, Vol. 8, No. 1, 1996, pp. 46–55.

Shearer, R., Motik, B. and Horrocks, I., HermiT, a highly-efficient OWL reasoner, *OWLED*, Vol. 432, 2008.

Sirin, E., Parsia, B., Grau, B. C., Kalyanpur, A. and Katz, Y., Pellet: A practical OWL-DL reasoner, *Web Semantics*, Vol. 5, No. 2, 2007.

Staddon, J., Golle, P., Zimny, B., Web-based inference detection, In Proceedings of 16th USENIX Security Symposium, 2007.

Tsarkov, D. and Horrocks, I., FaCT++ description logic reasoner: System description, *IJCAR*, 2006, pp. 292–297.

CONCLUSION IV

Section IV consisted of six chapters: 18, 19, 20, 21, 22, and 23. In Chapter 18, we discussed aspects of a formal model, which decides a comparable trade-off for releasing both data and their associated provenance while hiding provenance in the case of intolerable losses. In particular, we incorporated risk modeling into our work on inference control. In Chapter 19, we described the inference problem and discussed four novel approaches that could be used to design inference controllers in the long term. These approaches use techniques from inductive inference, probabilistic deduction, mathematical programming, and game theory.

In Chapter 20, we described the design and implementation of the first of its kind assured information sharing framework that operates in the cloud. Our framework consists of a policy engine that is an extension of the policy engine we discussed in Sections II and III that reasons about the policies for information sharing purposes and a secure data engine that stores and queries data in the cloud. Chapter 21 discussed a framework for not only considering confidentiality but also privacy and trust aspects for inference control. Chapter 22 discussed the challenges for big data security and privacy and its relationship to the inference problem. Finally, in Chapter 23 we described the integration of the design and implementation of the systems discussed in Sections II and III as well as some of the novel methods discussed in Section IV and described a unifying framework. The framework includes components both for access control and inference control as well as information sharing control. Our framework can also include the modules for risk and game theoretic approaches for access and inference control. We discussed the modules of the framework as well as building of the global inference controller.

Chapter 24

Summary and Directions

24.1 About This Chapter

This chapter brings us to the ending of this book. We discussed several aspects including access control for provenance, redaction for provenance, as well as the design and implementation of an inference controller. Our provenance data and the policies were expressed using Semantic Web technologies. The topics discussed included access control, provenance, redaction, Semantic Web, cloud computing, inference problem, inference controller design and implementation, risk-based inference, game theoretic models for inference, and cloud-based policy management. The experimental systems are the ones that we have developed at The University of Texas at Dallas and include secure data provenance as well as inference control with Semantic Web technologies.

The organization of this chapter is as follows. In Section 24.2 we give a summary of the book. This summary has been taken from the summaries of each chapter. In Section 24.3, we discuss directions for secure data provenance and inference control. In Section 24.4, we give suggestions as to where to go from here. Figure 24.1 illustrates the organization of this chapter.

24.2 Summary of the Book

We summarize the contents of each chapter essentially taken from the "Summary and Directions" section of each chapter. Chapter 1 provided an introduction to the book that included a discussion of our motivation and the contributions we have made in this book. Our framework is a four-layer framework and each layer was addressed in one part of the book. This framework was illustrated in Figure 1.4. We replicate this framework in Figure 24.2.

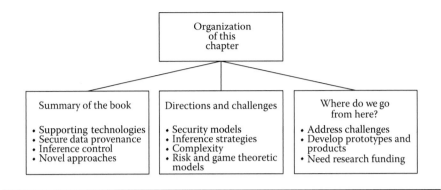

Figure 24.1   Organization of this chapter.

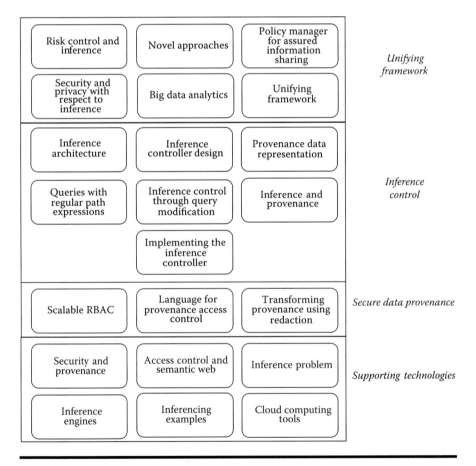

Figure 24.2   Framework for the book.

The book was divided into four sections. Section I, which described supporting technologies, consisted of six chapters: 2, 3, 4, 5, 6, and 7. Chapter 2 provided some background information on provenance relevant to our work. First, we discussed scalability issues for a secure provenance framework. Then we discussed aspects of an access control language for provenance, and finally, we discussed graph operations on provenance. Chapter 3 provided the foundations needed to understand the contents of this book, which were access control and the Semantic Web. We first provided an overview of access control models and then discussed RBAC. This was followed by a discussion of the technologies for the Semantic Web including XML, RDF, ontologies, and OWL. Finally, we discussed security issues for the Semantic Web. Chapter 4 provided details about the inference problem and inference controllers. First we discussed the inference problem. In particular, we defined the inference problem and discussed the inference strategies. We also defined various types of security constraints, which are also known as security policies. Then we discussed our approach to developing an inference controller. Chapter 5 provided an overview of the various inference engines that have been developed. These included Jena, Sesame, and the Inference Web. These inference engines reason with Semantic Web data. We have utilized some of these systems in our work and they form the foundations of the next generation inference controllers. Chapter 6 elaborated on the notion of inference. We first defined inference functions and then we discussed aspects of classifying knowledge bases. This was followed by a detailed discussion of inference strategies and examples for each strategy. For example, strategies such as inference by deduction, inference by induction, and inference by analogical reasoning were discussed. Finally, aspects of inference and provenance were discussed. Chapter 7 discussed cloud computing. Provenance data represent the history of the data. They are collected to answer questions such as, Where did the data originate from? Who accessed the data? Who owns the data? When were the data created? When were the data updated? We have represented provenance data as a graph structure. Over time the graphs structures could become massive. We need scalable solutions to manage large amounts of provenance data. Cloud computing offers a solution to the problem.

Section II, which described secure data provenance, consisted of three chapters: 8, 9, and 10. In Chapter 8 we discussed the drawbacks of using the current access control policies in a heterogeneous environment. These heterogeneous environments can contain either relational data or semistructured data. We began this chapter discussing RBAC systems. We identified the key drawbacks of access control over provenance. Then we discussed the reasons why we need flexible policies, which are both dynamic and interoperable. We then presented a Semantic Web approach for overcoming these challenges. Essentially, we argued that traditional access control does not extend over RDF graph data. We proposed an approach to handle policies on the Semantic Web. In Chapter 9, we defined an access control policy language for provenance. We also described a prototype using Semantic Web technologies that allows a user to query for data and provenance based on access control policies defined using our policy language. Essentially we argued that traditional access control policies do not extend over provenance data. We proposed a language that can be used to express access control over provenance that takes the form of a directed graph. In Chapter 10 we applied a graph grammar technique to perform redaction over provenance. In addition, we provided an architectural design that allows a high-level specification of policies, thus separating the business layer from a specific software implementation. We also implemented a prototype of the architecture based on open-source Semantic Web technologies.

Section III consisted of seven chapters: 11, 12, 13, 14, 15, 16, and 17. In Chapter 11 we described an inference controller that operates over a provenance graph and protects important provenance information from unauthorized users. We used RDF as our data model, which supports the interoperability of multiple databases having disparate data schemas. In addition, we expressed policies and rules in terms of Semantic Web rules and constraints, and we classified data items and relationships between them using Semantic Web software tools. In Chapter 12 we discussed our philosophy of designing an inference controller for provenance with Semantic Web data. The provenance data were represented as RDF graphs, and DL was used to support the inference tasks of our inference controller. In Chapter 13, we investigated different data formats for representing and storing provenance. We preferred a format representation that naturally supports the directed graph structure of provenance and naturally allows path queries of arbitrary lengths. We argued for a separate store for provenance in order to allow existing systems to continue supporting traditional data. This serves the purpose of decoupling the traditional data layer from the provenance data layer that operates on the provenance. In Chapter 14, we described the processing of queries with regular path expressions. Our graph matching was based on regular expressions. We identified the patterns in the provenance graph by composing regular path queries in SPARQL. In Chapter 15, we discussed inference control through query modification. In this approach the inference controller takes a user query and modifies the query according to the policies and gives a sanitized result to the query. We provided background information on query modification for relational data as well as aspects of modifying SPARQL queries. In Chapter 16, we discussed inference rules and then discussed some of the approaches to the inference problem for provenance data. Next, we discussed inferences and the implicit information in a provenance graph, and finally we discussed how a user query log can be used to reveal a user's intent. In Chapter 17, we described the implementation of an inference controller for provenance. The inference controller is built using a modular approach; therefore, it is very flexible in that most of the modules can be extended or replaced by another application module. Essentially we have followed a plug-and-play approach for implementing the inference controller. We have used open-source products as much as possible in our implementation.

Section IV consists of six chapters: 18, 19, 20, 21, 22, and 23. In Chapter 18, we discussed aspects of a formal model that decides a comparable trade-off for releasing both data and their associated provenance while hiding provenance in the case of intolerable losses. In particular, we incorporated risk modeling into our work on inference control. In Chapter 19, we described the inference problem and discussed four novel approaches that could be used to design inference controllers in the long term. These approaches use techniques from inductive inference, probabilistic deduction, mathematical programming, and game theory, and they handle various types of inference strategies on which the users could draw inferences. In Chapter 20, we described the design and implementation of the first of its kind assured information sharing framework that operates in the cloud. Our framework consists of a policy engine that is an extension of the policy engine we discussed in Sections II and III that reasons about the policies for information sharing purposes and a secure data engine that stores and queries data in the cloud. Chapter 21 discussed a framework for not only considering confidentiality but also privacy and trust aspects for inference control. Chapter 22 discussed the challenges for big data security and privacy and their relationship to inference control. We argued that big data are everywhere, from social network data to mobile and sensor data. Organizations are analyzing massive amounts of data to improve business and to provide a better quality of life. Such analysis of data may result in highly sensitive data being divulged to the public. As a result, privacy of the individuals may be compromised. This exacerbates the inference problem as data are combined in unauthorized ways. Chapter 23 essentially integrated much of the design and implementation of the systems discussed in Sections II and III as well as some of the novel methods discussed in Section IV and described a unifying framework. The framework includes components both for access control and inference control as well as for information sharing control. Our framework can also include the modules for risk and game theoretic approaches for access and inference control. We discussed the modules of the framework as well as building of the global inference controller.

This book has several appendices. In Appendix A, we provide a broad picture of how all the books we have written relate to one another. In Appendix B, we discuss database management and security aspects. In Appendix C, we provide a historical perspective of the inference problem. Finally, in Appendix D, we discuss the design and implementation of one of the earliest inference controllers.

As we have stressed, there are many developments in the field and it is impossible for us to list all of them. We have provided a broad but fairly comprehensive overview of the field. The book is intended for researchers and developers as well as technologists who want to get a broad understanding of the field. It is also intended for students who wish to pursue research in data and applications security in general and secure cloud computing in particular.

24.3 Directions for Secure Data Provenance and Inference Control

There are many directions for secure data provenance and inference control. We discuss some of them for each topic addressed in this book. Figure 24.3 illustrates the directions and challenges.

With respect to the discussion in Section II, the major challenges include developing appropriate security models for provenance data. Our focus was mainly on RBAC. Furthermore, the provenance data were represented as RDF graphs. The questions that need to be addressed include, What are the most suitable security models? Should we explore more generalized graphs to represent provenance? What are the reasoning strategies that can be used to analyze provenance? How can powerful machine learning techniques be applied to analyze provenance? How can privacy models be applied to provenance?

With respect to the discussion in Section III, the major challenges include building inference controllers that can handle a variety of inference strategies including inference by deduction, induction, abduction, and analogical reasoning. Another important consideration is developing privacy controllers for provenance. Corporations are gathering a lot of data. Regulations mandate that such data (e.g., e-mail data) have to be stored for a certain number of years. As a result, privacy could be violated. Users can also apply various data mining tools and obtain highly private and sensitive data. The challenge is to develop privacy preserving technologies for provenance and incorporate them into the inference controllers.

With respect to the discussion in Section IV, the major challenges include coming up with appropriate risk models as well as developing novel approaches such as those based on game theory and probabilistic reasoning. For example, if there is no risk for inference, then we need not develop expensive inference controllers

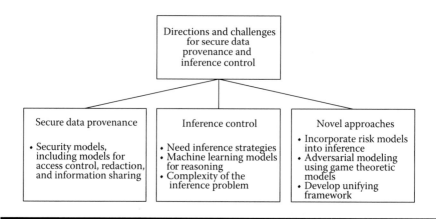

Figure 24.3 Directions and challenges in cloud computing and secure cloud computing.

for provenance data. What would be desirable is to develop adaptive inference controllers that can adapt to the risks involved. Game theoretic models are being explored for privacy controllers. For example, the defender of the data and the attacker who wants to probe and extract sensitive data are essentially playing a game. Both have incentives to win the game. The challenge is to thwart the adversary (i.e., the attacker) so that the defender wins the game. Winning the game for the defender amounts to not giving away any secrets. Winning the game for the attacker amounts to extracting secrets from the provenance data. We also need to integrate privacy and trust models into the inference controller. Another major challenge is securing big data as well as ensuring that the privacy of individuals is not compromised due to big data analytics. We also need scalable solutions to inference control and the cloud is showing some promise.

There are numerous challenges both for theoreticians and practitioners. For example, as we have stated before, we have proved back in 1990 that the inference problem was unsolvable. Dr. John Campbell in the National Security Agency has mentioned that this was one of the more significant developments in data security at that time. What is needed now is to analyze the complexity of the inference problem. That is, what are the complexity classes for this problem? Are there classes of the inference problem for which we can provide decidable solutions? For example, much of our current work has utilized reasons based on DL that is decidable. What are the limits of other logics? These are some interesting questions that need answers. There are also many opportunities for practitioners. Many new technologies are emerging for cloud computing, security, privacy, machine learning, and big data analysis. We need to take advantage of these tools to develop inference and privacy controllers for provenance data. For example, can we use data management systems such HBase, Cassandra, and Hive to store and manage large quantities of data? How can tools such as Pellet be extended to reason with the vast quantities of data? The emerging developments in social networking give us opportunities to test the emerging tools for vast quantities of data.

24.4 Where Do We Go from Here?

This book has focused on secure data provenance and inference control. We have stated many challenges in this field in Section 24.3. We need to continue with research and development efforts if we are to make progress in this very important area.

The question is, Where do we go from here? First, those who wish to work in this area must have a good knowledge of the supporting technologies including Semantic Web, information security data information, and knowledge management. For example, it is important to understand the technologies that comprise the data provenance and inference control. These include data management, Semantic Web, social networking, machine learning, and cloud computing as well as security and privacy.

Next, since the field is expanding rapidly and there are many developments happening within, the reader has to stay current, which includes reading about the commercial products and prototypes. Finally, we encourage the reader to experiment with the products and also develop security tools. This is the best way to get familiar with a particular field. That is, work on hands-on problems and provide solutions to get a better understanding. The developers should be familiar with technologies such as Hadoop/MapReduce, Hive, Hbase, Pellet, Jena, and Cassandra, among others. The cloud will continue to have a major impact on handling massive amounts of data and processing and therefore security for the cloud will be important for secure data provenance and inference control.

Considerable research and development support has been received for research in data security from the United States federal government, including the Department of Defense and the National Science Foundation. We still need substantial research and development support to address the numerous challenges for secure data provenance and inference control. Agencies such as the National Science Foundation, National Security Agency, the US Army, Navy, and Air Force, the Defense Advanced Research Projects Agency, the Intelligence Advanced Research Projects Activity, and the Department of Homeland Security are funding research in security. The Air Force is focusing a great deal on securing the cloud and NSF is funding many efforts on secure data provenance and privacy. It's critical that such research funding continues. We also need commercial corporations to invest research and development funds so that progress can be made in industrial research as well as to be able to transfer the research to commercial products. We also need to collaborate with the international research community to solve problems and promote standards that are not only of national interest but also of international interest. In summary, we need public/private/academic partnerships to develop breakthrough technologies in the very important area of secure data provenance and inference control.

Appendix A: Data Management Systems, Developments, and Trends

A.1 Overview

The main purpose of this appendix is to set the context of the series of books we have written in data management, data mining, and data security. Our series started back in 1997 with our book *Data Management Systems: Evolution and Interoperation* (Thuraisingham 1997). Our subsequent books have evolved from this first book. We have essentially repeated Chapter 1 of our first book in Appendix A of our subsequent books. The purpose of this appendix is to provide an overview of data management systems as well as to show how the field has evolved over the years: from data to information to knowledge and now to big data. We will then discuss the relationships between the books we have written.

As stated in our series of books, the developments in information systems technologies have resulted in computerizing many applications in various business areas. Data have become a critical resource in many organizations, and therefore, efficient access to data, sharing the data, extracting information from the data, and making use of the information, have become urgent needs. As a result, there have been several efforts on integrating the various data sources scattered across several sites. These data sources may be databases managed by database management systems or they could simply be files. To provide the interoperability between the multiple data sources and systems, various tools are being developed. These tools enable users of one system to access other systems in an efficient and transparent manner.

We define data management systems to be systems that manage the data, extract meaningful information from the data, and make use of the information extracted. Therefore, data management systems include database systems, data warehouses, and data mining systems. Data could be structured data such as that found in relational databases or they could be unstructured such as text, voice, imagery, and video. There have been numerous discussions in the past to distinguish between data, information, and knowledge. We do not attempt to clarify these terms. For our purposes, data could be just bits and bytes or they could convey some meaningful information to the user. We will, however, distinguish between database systems and database management systems. A database management system is that component that manages the database containing persistent data. A database system consists of both the database and the database management system.

A key component to the evolution and interoperation of data management systems is the interoperability of heterogeneous database systems. Efforts on the interoperability between database systems have been reported since the late 1970s. However, it is only recently that we are seeing commercial developments in heterogeneous database systems. Major database system vendors are now providing interoperability between their products and other systems. Furthermore, many of the database system vendors are migrating toward an architecture called the client-server architecture, which facilitates distributed data management capabilities. In addition to efforts on the interoperability between different database systems and client-server environments, work is also directed toward handling autonomous and federated environments.

The organization of this appendix is as follows. Since database systems are a key component of data management systems, we first provide an overview of the developments in database systems. These developments are discussed in Section A.2. Then we provide a vision for data management systems in Section A.3. Our framework for data management systems is discussed in Section A.4. Note that data mining and warehousing as well as Web data management are components of this framework. Building information systems from our framework with special instantiations is discussed in Section A.5. The recent development in data management including big data is discussed in Section A.6. Note that this is a new section that we have added here. The relationship between the various texts that we have written (or are writing) for CRC Press is discussed in Section A.7. This appendix is summarized in Section A.8.

A.2 Developments in Database Systems

Figure A.1 provides an overview of the developments in database systems technology. While the early work in the 1960s focused on developing products based on the network and hierarchical data models, much of the developments in database systems took place after the seminal paper by Codd describing the relational model (Codd 1970) (see also Date 1990). Research and development work on relational database systems was carried out during the early 1970s and several prototypes were developed throughout the 1970s. Notable efforts include International Business Machine Corporation's (IBM) System R and University of California at Berkeley's INGRES. During the 1980s, many relational database system products were being

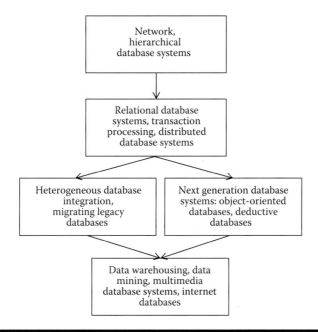

Figure A.1   Developments in database systems technology.

marketed (notable among these products are those of Oracle Corporation, Sybase Inc., Informix Corporation, INGRES Corporation, IBM, Digital Equipment Corporation, and Hewlett Packard Company). During the 1990s, products from other vendors emerged (e.g., Microsoft Corporation). In fact, to date, numerous relational database system products have been marketed. However, Codd has stated that many of the systems that are being marketed as relational systems are not really relational (see, for example, the discussion in Date 1990). He then discussed various criteria that a system must satisfy to be qualified as a relational database system. While the early work focused on issues such as data model, normalization theory, query processing and optimization strategies, query languages, and access strategies and indexes, later the focus shifted toward supporting a multiuser environment. In particular, concurrency control and recovery techniques were developed. Support for transaction processing was also provided.

Research on relational database systems as well as on transaction management was followed by research on distributed database systems around the mid-1970s. Several distributed database system prototype development efforts also began around the late 1970s. Notable among these efforts include IBM's System R*, Distributed Database Testbed System (DDTS) by Honeywell Inc., SDD-I and Multibase by Computer Corporation of America (CCA), and Mermaid by System Development Corporation (SDC). Furthermore, many of these systems (e.g., DDTS, Multibase, Mermaid) function in a heterogeneous environment. During the early 1990s, several database system vendors (such as Oracle Corporation, Sybase Inc., and Informix Corporation) provided data distribution capabilities for their systems. Most of the distributed relational database system products are based on client-server architectures. The idea is to have the client of vendor A communicate with the server database system of vendor B. In other words, the client-server computing paradigm facilitates a heterogeneous computing environment. Interoperability between relational and nonrelational commercial database systems is also possible. The database systems community is also involved in standardization efforts. Notable among the standardization efforts are the ANSI/SPARC 3-level schema architecture, the Information Resource Dictionary System (IRDS) standard for Data Dictionary Systems, the relational query language Structured Query Language (SQL), and the Remote Database Access (RDA) protocol for remote database access.

Another significant development in database technology is the advent of object-oriented database management systems. Active work on developing such systems began in the mid-1980s and they are now commercially available (notable among them include the products of Object Design Inc., Ontos Inc., Gemstone Systems Inc., and Versant Object Technology). It was felt that new generation applications such as multimedia, office information systems, computer-aided design and computer-aided manufacturing (CAD/CAM), process control, and software engineering have different requirements. Such applications utilize complex data structures. Tighter integration between the programming language and the data model is also desired. Object-oriented database systems satisfy most of the requirements of these new generation applications (Cattell 1991).

According to the Lagunita report published as a result of a National Science Foundation (NSF) workshop in 1990 (see Kim 1990; Silberschatz et al. 1990), relational database systems, transaction processing, and distributed (relational) database systems are stated as mature technologies. Furthermore, vendors are marketing object-oriented database systems and demonstrating the interoperability between different database systems. The report goes on to state that as applications are getting increasingly complex, more sophisticated database systems are needed. Furthermore, since many organizations now use database systems, in many cases of different types, the database systems need to be integrated. Although work has begun to address these issues and commercial products are available, several issues still need to be resolved. Therefore, challenges faced by the database systems researchers in the early 1990s were in two areas. One was next generation database systems and the other was heterogeneous database systems.

Next generation database systems include object-oriented database systems, functional database systems, special parallel architectures to enhance the performance of database system functions, high-performance database systems, real-time database systems, scientific database systems, temporal database systems, database systems that handle incomplete and uncertain information, and intelligent database systems (also sometimes called logic or deductive database systems). Ideally, a database system should provide the support for high-performance transaction processing, model complex applications, represent new kinds of data, and make intelligent deductions. While significant progress has been made during the late 1980s and early 1990s, there is much to be done before such a database system can be developed.

Heterogeneous database systems have been receiving considerable attention during the past decade (March 1990). The major issues include handling different data models, different query processing strategies, different transaction processing algorithms, and different query languages. Should a uniform view be provided to the entire system or should the users of the individual systems maintain their own views of the entire system? These are questions that have yet to be answered satisfactorily. It is also envisaged that a complete solution to heterogeneous database management systems is a generation away. While research should be directed toward finding such a solution, work should also be carried out to handle limited forms of heterogeneity to satisfy the customer needs. Another type of database system that has received some attention lately is a federated database system. Note that some have used the terms heterogeneous database system and federated database system interchangeably. While heterogeneous database systems can be part of a federation, a federation can also include homogeneous database systems.

The explosion of users on the Web as well as developments in interface technologies has resulted in even more challenges for data management researchers. A second workshop was sponsored by NSF in 1995, and several emerging technologies have been identified to be important as we proceed through the twenty-first century (Widom 1995). These include digital libraries, managing very large databases, data administration issues, multimedia databases, data warehousing, data mining, data management for collaborative computing environments, and security and privacy. Another significant development in the 1990s was the development of object-relational systems. Such systems combine the advantages of both object-oriented database systems and relational database systems. Many corporations are now focusing on integrating their data management products with Web technologies. Finally, for many organizations there is an increasing need to migrate some of the legacy databases and applications to newer architectures and systems such as client-server architectures and relational database systems. We believe there is no end to data management systems. As new technologies are developed, there are new opportunities for data management research and development.

A comprehensive view of all data management technologies is illustrated in Figure A.2. As shown, traditional technologies include database design, transaction processing, and benchmarking. Then there are database systems based on data models such as relational and object-oriented. Database systems may depend on the features they provide such as security and real time. These database systems may be relational or object-oriented. There are also database systems based on multiple sites or processors such as distributed and heterogeneous database systems, parallel systems, and systems being migrated. Finally, there are the emerging technologies such as data warehousing and mining, collaboration, and the Web. Any

Traditional technologies: • Data modeling and database design • Enterprise/business modeling and application design • DBMS design • Query, metadata transactions, • Integrity and data quality • Benchmarking and performance • Data administration, auditing, database administration • Standards	Database systems based on data models: • Hierarchical • Network • Relational • Functional • Object-oriented • Deductive (logic-based) • Object-relational **Multisite/processor-based systems:** • Distribution • Interoperability • Federated • Client-server • Migration • Parallel/high performance	Database systems based on features: • Secure database • Real-time database • Fault-tolerance database • Multimedia database • Active database • Temporal database • Fuzzy database **Emerging technologies:** • Data warehousing • Data mining • Internet • Collaboration • Mobile computing

Figure A.2 Comprehensive view of data management systems.

comprehensive text on data management systems should address all of these technologies. We have selected some of the relevant technologies and put them in a framework. This framework is described in Section A.5.

A.3 Status, Vision, and Issues

Significant progress has been made on data management systems. However, many of the technologies are still stand-alone technologies, as illustrated in Figure A.3. For example, multimedia systems are yet to be successfully integrated with warehousing and mining technologies. The ultimate goal is to integrate multiple technologies so that accurate data, as well as information, are produced at the right time and distributed to the user in a timely manner. Our vision for data and information management is illustrated in Figure A.4.

The work discussed in Thuraisingham (1997) addressed many of the challenges necessary to accomplish this vision. In particular, integration of heterogeneous databases, as well as the use of distributed object technology for interoperability, has been discussed. While much progress has been made on the system aspects of interoperability, semantic issues still remain a challenge. Different databases have different representations. Furthermore, the same data entity may be interpreted differently at different sites. Addressing these semantic differences and extracting

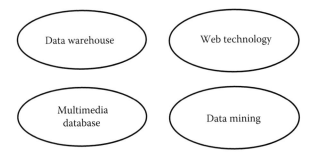

Figure A.3   Stand-alone systems.

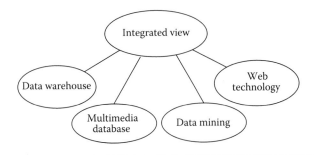

Figure A.4   Vision.

useful information from the heterogeneous and possibly multimedia data sources are major challenges.

A.4 Data Management Systems Framework

For the successful development of evolvable interoperable data management systems, heterogeneous database systems integration is a major component. However, there are other technologies that have to be successfully integrated with each other to develop techniques for efficient access and sharing of data as well as for the extraction of information from the data. To facilitate the development of data management systems to meet the requirements of various applications in fields such as medical, financial, manufacturing, and military, we have proposed a framework, which can be regarded as a reference model, for data management systems. Various components from this framework have to be integrated to develop data management systems to support the various applications.

Figure A.5 illustrates our framework that can be regarded as a model for data management systems. This framework consists of three layers. One can think of the component technologies, which we will also refer to as components, belonging

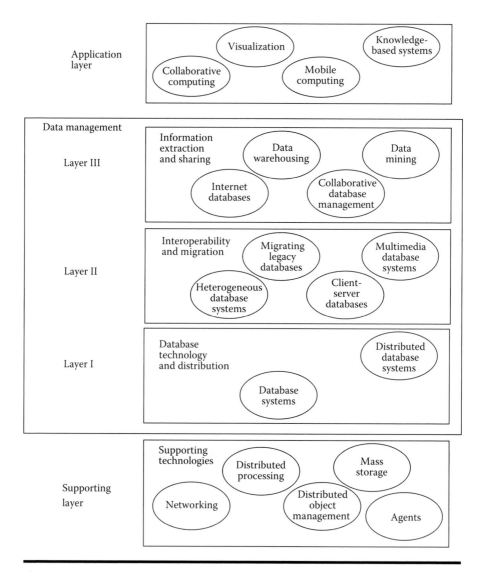

Figure A.5   Data management systems framework.

to a particular layer to be more or less built upon the technologies provided by the lower layer. Layer I is the database technology and distribution layer. This layer consists of database systems and distributed database systems technologies. Layer II is the interoperability and migration layer. This layer consists of technologies such as heterogeneous database integration, client-server databases, and multimedia database systems to handle heterogeneous data types and migrating legacy databases. Layer III is the information extraction and sharing layer. This layer essentially consists of technologies for some of the newer services supported by data management systems. These include data warehousing, data mining (Thuraisingham 1998), Web databases, and database support for collaborative applications. Data management systems may utilize lower-level technologies such as networking, distributed processing, and mass storage. We have grouped these technologies into a layer called the supporting technologies layer. This supporting layer does not belong to the data management systems framework. This supporting layer also consists of some higher-level technologies such as distributed object management and agents. Also shown in Figure A.5 is the application technologies layer. Systems such as collaborative computing systems and knowledge-based systems that belong to the application technologies layer may utilize data management systems. Note that the application technologies layer is also outside of the data management systems framework.

The technologies that constitute the data management systems framework can be regarded to be some of the core technologies in data management. However, features like security, integrity, real-time processing, fault tolerance, and high-performance computing are needed for many applications utilizing data management technologies. Applications utilizing data management technologies may be medical, financial, or military, among others. We illustrate this in Figure A.6, where a three-dimensional view relating data management technologies with features and applications is given. For example, one could develop a secure distributed database management system for medical applications or a fault-tolerant multimedia database management system for financial applications.

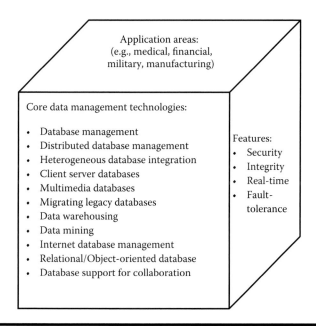

Figure A.6   A three-dimensional view of data management.

Integrating the components belonging to the various layers is important to developing efficient data management systems. In addition, data management technologies have to be integrated with the application technologies to develop successful information systems. However, at present, there is limited integration between these various components. Our previous book, *Data Management Systems: Evolution and Interoperation,* focused mainly on the concepts, developments, and trends belonging to each of the components shown in the framework. Furthermore, our book on Web data management, which we also refer to as Web data management, focuses on the Web database component of layer 3 of the framework of Figure A.5.

Note that security cuts across all the layers. Security is needed for the supporting layers such as agents and distributed systems. Security is needed for all of the layers in the framework including database security, distributed database security, warehousing security, Web database security, and collaborative data management security.

A.5 Building Information Systems from the Framework

Figure A.5 illustrates a framework for data management systems. As shown in that figure, the technologies for data management include database systems, distributed database systems, heterogeneous database systems, migrating legacy databases, multimedia database systems, data warehousing, data mining, Web databases, and database support for collaboration. Furthermore, data management systems take advantage of supporting technologies such as distributed processing and agents. Similarly, application technologies such as collaborative computing, visualization, expert systems, and mobile computing also take advantage of data management systems.

Many of us have heard of the term "information systems" on numerous occasions. These systems have sometimes been used interchangeably with data management systems. In our terminology, information systems are much broader than data management systems, but they do include data management systems. In fact, a framework for information systems will include not only the data management system layers, but also the supporting technologies layer as well as the application technologies layer. That is, information systems encompass all kinds of computing systems. It can be regarded as the finished product that can be used for various applications. That is, while hardware is at the lowest end of the spectrum, applications are at the highest end.

We can combine the technologies of Figure A.5 to put together information systems. For example, at the application technology level, one may need collaboration and visualization technologies so that analysts can collaboratively carry out some tasks. At the data management level, one may need both multimedia and distributed database technologies. At the supporting level, one may need mass storage as well as some distributed processing capability. This special framework is illustrated in Figure A.7. Another example is a special framework for interoperability. One may need some visualization technology to display the integrated information

Collaboration, visualization
Multimedia database, distributed database systems
Mass storage, distributed processing

Figure A.7   Framework for multimedia data management for collaboration.

from the heterogeneous databases. At the data management level, we have heterogeneous database systems technology. At the supporting technology level, one may use distributed object management technology to encapsulate the heterogeneous databases. This special framework is illustrated in Figure A.8.

Finally, let us illustrate the concepts that we have described above by using a specific example. Suppose a group of physicians/surgeons want a system where they can collaborate and make decisions about various patients. This could be a medical video teleconferencing application. That is, at the highest level, the application is a medical application, and more specifically, a medical video teleconferencing application. At the application technology level, one needs a variety of technologies including collaboration and teleconferencing. These application technologies will make use of data management technologies such as distributed database systems and multimedia database systems. That is, one may need to support multimedia data such as audio and video. The data management technologies in turn draw upon lower-level technologies such as distributed processing and networking. We illustrate this in Figure A.9.

In summary, information systems include data management systems as well as application layer systems such as collaborative computing systems and supporting layer systems such as distributed object management systems.

While application technologies make use of data management technologies and data management technologies make use of supporting technologies, the ultimate user of the information system is the application itself. Today numerous applications make use of information systems. These applications are from multiple domains such as medical, financial, manufacturing, telecommunications, and defense. Specific applications include signal processing, electronic commerce, patient monitoring, and situation assessment. Figure A.10 illustrates the relationship between the application and the information system.

Visualization
Heterogeneous database integration
Distributed object management

Figure A.8   Framework for heterogeneous database interoperability.

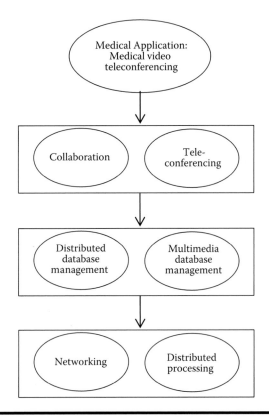

Figure A.9   Specific example using a medical application.

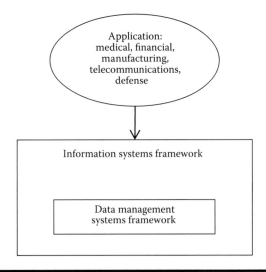

Figure A.10   Application-framework relationship.

A.6 From Data to Big Data

Due to the explosion of Web-based services, unstructured data management, social media, and mobile computing, the amount of data to be handled has increased from terabytes to petabytes and zettabytes in just two decades. Such vast amounts of complex data have come to be known as big data. Not only does big data have to be managed efficiently, such data also have to be analyzed to extract useful nuggets to enhance businesses as well as improve society. This has come to be known as big data analytics.

Different communities are working on the big data challenge. For example, the systems community is developing technologies for massive storage of big data. The network community is developing solutions for managing very large networked data. The data community is developing solutions for efficiently managing and analyzing large sets of data. Big data management and analytics research is proceeding in three directions:

1. Building infrastructure and high-performance computing techniques for the storage of big data
2. Data management techniques such as integrating multiple data sources (both big and small) and indexing and querying big data
3. Data analytics techniques that manipulate and analyze big data to extract nuggets

We will briefly review the progress made in each of the areas. With respect to building infrastructures, technologies such as Hadoop and MapReduce as well as Storm are being developed for managing large amounts of data in the cloud. In addition, main memory data management techniques have advanced so that a few terabytes of data can be managed in main memory. Furthermore, systems such as HIVE and Cassandra as well as NoSQL databases have been developed for managing petabytes of data.

With respect to data management, traditional data management techniques such as query processing and optimization strategies are being examined for handling petabytes of data. Furthermore, graph data management techniques are being developed for the storage and management of very large networked data.

With respect to data analytics, the various data mining algorithms are being implemented on Hadoop- and MapReduce-based infrastructures. Additionally, data reduction techniques are being explored to reduce the massive amounts of data into manageable chunks while still maintaining the semantics of the data.

In summary, big data management and analytics techniques include extending current data management and mining techniques to handle massive amounts of data as well as developing new approaches including graph data management and mining techniques for maintaining and analyzing large networked data. Figure A.11 describes the evolution from data management to big data management.

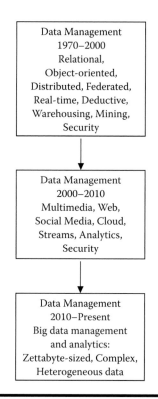

Figure A.11 From data to big data.

A.7 Relationship between the Texts

We have published two book series. The first series is mainly for technical managers while the second series is for researchers and developers. Our books in this series are *Data Management Systems: Evolution and Interoperation* (Thuraisingham 1997), *Data Mining: Technologies, Techniques, Tools, and Trends* (Thuraisingham 1998), *Web Data Management and Electronic Commerce* (Thuraisingham 2000), *Managing and Mining Multimedia Databases for the Electronic Enterprise* (Thuraisingham 2001), *XML Databases and the Semantic Web* (Thuraisingham 2002), *Web Data Mining and Applications in Business Intelligence and Counter-Terrorism* (Thuraisingham 2003), *Database and Applications Security: Integrating Data Management and Information Security* (Thuraisingham 2005), *Building Trustworthy Semantic Webs* (Thuraisingham 2007), and *Secure Semantic Service-Oriented Systems* (Thuraisingham 2010). Our last book in this series, *Developing and Securing the Cloud* (Thuraisingham 2013), has evolved from our book, *Secure Semantic Service-Oriented Systems*. All of these books have evolved from the framework that we illustrated in this appendix and address different parts of the framework. The connection between these texts is illustrated in Figure A.12.

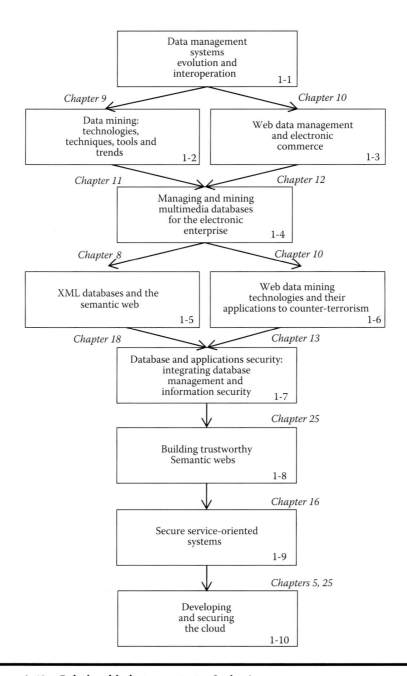

Figure A.12   Relationship between texts: Series I.

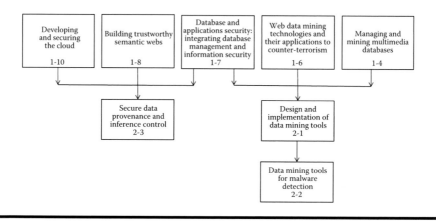

Figure A.13 Relationship between texts: Series II.

We have published three books in the second series. The first is *Design and Implementation of Data Mining Tools* (Awad et al. 2009) and the second is *Data Mining Tools for Malware Detection* (Masud et al. 2011). Our book *Access Control and Inference for Secure Data Provenance* (Cadenhead et al. 2013) is the third in this series. The relationship between these books as well as with our previous books is illustrated in Figure A.13.

A.8 Summary and Directions

In this appendix, we have provided an overview of data management. We first discussed the developments in data management and then provided a vision for data management. Then we illustrated a framework for data management. This framework consists of three layers: a database systems layer, interoperability layer, and information extraction layer. Web data management belongs to layer 3. We then showed how information systems could be built from the technologies of the framework. Finally we discussed the evolution from data to big data.

We believe that data management is essential to many information technologies including data mining, multimedia information processing, interoperability, and collaboration and knowledge management. This appendix focused on data management. However, data security is the foundation for inference control. Therefore we will provide some background information on data security as well as database management in Appendix B. A perspective of the inference problem will be discussed in Appendix C. Our previous approach to developing an inference controller will be discussed in Appendix D.

References

Awad, M., Khan, L., Thuraisingham, B. and Wang, L., *Design and Implementation of Data Mining Tools,* CRC Press, Boca Raton, FL, 2009.

Cadenhead, T., Thuraisingham, B., Kantarcioglu, M. and Khadilkar, V., *Secure Data Provenance and Inference Control with Semantic Web,* CRC Press, 2013.

Cattell, R., *Object Data Management: Object-Oriented and Extended,* Addison-Wesley Longman Publishing Co., Boston, 1991.

Codd, E. F., A relational model of data for large shared data banks, *Commun. ACM,* Vol. 13, No. 6, June 1970, pp. 377–387.

Date, C. J., *An Introduction to Database Management Systems,* Addison-Wesley, Reading, MA, 1990 (6th edition published in 1995 by Addison-Wesley).

Kim, W. (ed.), Directions for future database research & development, *ACM SIGMOD Record,* Vol. 19, No. 4, December 1990.

March, S. T. (ed.), Special Issue on Heterogeneous Database Systems, *ACM Computing Surveys,* Vol. 22, No. 3, September 1990.

Masud, M., Thuraisingham, B. and Khan, L., *Data Mining Tools for Malware Detection,* CRC Press, Boca Raton, FL, 2011.

Silberschatz, A., Stonebraker, M. and Ullman, J. D. (eds.), Database systems: Achievements and opportunities, The "Lagunita" Report of the NSF Invitational Workshop on the Future of Database Systems Research, February 22–23, Palo Alto, CA (TR-90-22), Department of Computer Sciences, University of Texas at Austin, Austin, TX, 1990 (also in *ACM SIGMOD Record,* December 1990).

Thuraisingham, B., *Data Management Systems: Evolution and Interoperation,* CRC Press, Boca Raton, FL, 1997.

Thuraisingham, B., *Data Mining: Technologies, Techniques, Tools, and Trends,* CRC Press, Boca Raton, FL, 1998.

Thuraisingham, B., *Web Data Management and Electronic Commerce*, CRC Press, Boca Raton, FL, 2000.

Thuraisingham, B., *Managing and Mining Multimedia Databases for the Electronic Enterprise,* CRC Press, Boca Raton, FL, 2001.

Thuraisingham, B., *XML Databases and the Semantic Web,* CRC Press, Boca Raton, FL, 2002.

Thuraisingham, B., *Web Data Mining Applications in Business Intelligence and Counter-Terrorism*, CRC Press, Boca Raton, FL, 2003.

Thuraisingham, B., *Database and Applications Security: Integrating Data Management and Information Security,* CRC Press, Boca Raton, FL, 2005.

Thuraisingham, B., *Building Trustworthy Semantic Webs,* CRC Press, Boca Raton, FL, 2007.

Thuraisingham, B., *Secure Semantic Service-Oriented Systems,* CRC Press, Boca Raton, FL, 2010.

Thuraisingham, B., *Developing and Securing the Cloud,* CRC Press, Boca Raton, FL, 2013.

Widom, J. (ed.), Proceedings of the Database Systems Workshop, report published by the National Science Foundation, 1995 (also in *ACM SIGMOD Record,* March 1996, Vol. 25, No. 1), Database Research: Achievements and Opportunities into the 21st Century.

Appendix B: Database Management and Security

B.1 Overview

While the chapters of our book have focused on access control and inference for provenance data represented using Semantic Web technologies, our research has underpinnings in database management and database security. For example, in this book we have described query modification techniques for SPARQL queries. Such queries are posed against Semantic Web data. However, query modification was first developed for relational databases in the mid-1970s and for multilevel databases in the mid-1980s. Therefore, an understanding of database management technologies including query processing and metadata is essential for our current work.

Another topic that is vital to our current research is database security. This is because while our research has focused on access control including role-based access control, the inference problem has been studied extensively within the context of multilevel secure database systems. Therefore, in addition to discussions of access control models and authorization policies, an understanding of multilevel secure data management and data security is also desirable to get a better understanding of the contents of this book.

Due to the reasons discussed above, in this appendix we provide an overview of database system technologies and database security technologies. In particular, topics such as data models, database functions, and architectures as well as access control policies, authorization policies, and multilevel secure data management are discussed. Since the inference problem is the cornerstone of our book, a historical perspective of this problem as well as our prior research is discussed in Appendixes C and D.

The organization of this appendix is as follows. Database management is discussed in Section B.2. Discretionary security within the context of database security is discussed in Section B.3. Mandatory security, which includes a discussion of multilevel secure data management, is provided in Section B.4. The appendix is concluded in Section B.5. Figure B.1 illustrates the contents of this chapter.

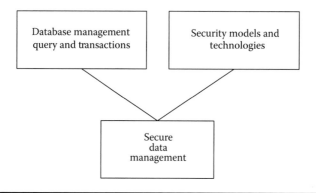

Figure B.1 Database management and security.

B.2 Database Management

B.2.1 Overview

Database systems technology has advanced a great deal during the past four decades from the legacy systems based on network and hierarchical models to relational and object-oriented database systems based on client-server architectures. We consider a database system to include both the DBMS and the database (see also the discussion in Date 1990). The DBMS component of the database system manages the database. The database contains persistent data. That is, the data are permanent even if the application programs go away.

While we have studied access control and inference has been studied within the context of Semantic Web and provenance, our approaches have roots in database systems and security technologies. Therefore, in this section we provide an overview of database systems and in Sections B.3 and B.4 we provide an overview of security technologies. The database systems technologies we discuss in this section are based on the relational model. Therefore, our discussion of database systems is focused mainly in relational databases.

The organization of this section is as follows. In Section B.2.1 we discuss some of the essential points of a relational data model. Database system functions are discussed in Section B.2.2. These functions include query processing, transaction management, metadata management, storage management, and maintaining integrity. Distributed database systems are the subject of Section B.2.3.

B.2.2 Relational Data Model

With the relational model (Codd 1970), the database is viewed as a collection of relations. Each relation has attributes and rows. For example, Figure B.2 illustrates a database with two relations, EMP and DEPT. EMP has four attributes: SS#,

EMP

SS#	Ename	Salary	D#
1	John	20K	10
2	Paul	30K	20
3	Mary	40K	20

DEPT

D#	Dname	Mgr
10	Math	Smith
20	Physics	Jones

Figure B.2   Relational database.

Ename, Salary, and D#. DEPT has three attributes: D#, Dname, and Mgr. EMP has three rows, also called tuples, and DEPT has two rows. Each row is uniquely identified by its primary key. For example, SS# could be the primary key for EMP and D# for DEPT. Another key feature of the relational model is that each element in the relation is an atomic value such as an integer or a string. That is, complex values such as lists are not supported.

Various operations are performed on relations. The SELECT operation selects a subset of rows satisfying certain conditions. For example, in the relation EMP, one may select tuples where the salary is more than 20K. The PROJECT operation projects the relation onto some attributes. For example, in the relation EMP one may project onto the attributes Ename and Salary. The JOIN operation joins two relations over some common attributes. A detailed discussion of these operations is given in Date (1990) and Ullman (1988).

Various languages to manipulate the relations have been proposed. Notable among these languages is the ANSI Standard SQL. This language is used to access and manipulate data in relational databases (SQL3 1992). There is wide acceptance of this standard among database management system vendors and users. It supports schema definition, retrieval, data manipulation, schema manipulation, transaction management, integrity, and security. Other languages include the relational calculus first proposed in the INGRES project at the University of California at Berkeley (Date 1990). Another important concept in relational databases is the notion of a view. A view is essentially a virtual relation and is formed from the relations in the database.

B.2.3 Database Management Functions

This section describes the major functions of database systems. These include query processing, transaction management, storage management, metadata management, and integrity management. Functional architecture for a database system is illustrated in Figure B.3.

Query processor	Transaction processor
Metadata manager	Storage manager
Integrity manager	Security manager

Figure B.3   Functional architecture for a DBMS.

B.2.3.1 Query Processing

Query operation is the most commonly used function in a DBMS. It should be possible for users to query the database and obtain answers to their queries. There are several aspects to query processing. First, a good query language is needed. Languages such as SQL are popular for relational databases. Such languages are being extended for other types of databases. The second aspect is techniques for query processing. Numerous algorithms have been proposed for query processing in general and for the JOIN operation in particular. Also, different strategies are possible to execute a particular query. The costs for the various strategies are computed and the one with the least cost is usually selected for processing. This process is called query optimization. Cost is generally determined by the disk access. The goal is to minimize disk access in processing a query.

Users pose a query using a language. The constructs of the language have to be transformed into the constructs understood by the database system. This process is called query transformation. Query transformation is carried out in stages based on the various schemas. For example, a query based on the external schema is transformed into a query on the conceptual schema. This is then transformed into a query on the physical schema. In general, rules used in the transformation process include the factoring of common subexpressions and pushing selections and projections down in the query tree as much as possible. If selections and projections are performed before the joins, then the cost of the joins can be reduced by a considerable amount.

Figure B.4 illustrates the modules in query processing. The user interface manager accepts queries, parses the queries, and then gives them to the query transformer. The query transformer and query optimizer communicate with each other to produce an execution strategy. The database is accessed through the storage manager. The response manager gives responses to the user.

B.2.3.2 Transaction Management

A transaction is a program unit that must be executed in its entirety or not executed at all. If transactions are executed serially, then there is a performance bottleneck.

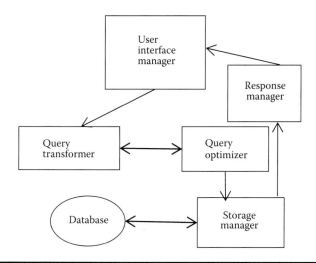

Figure B.4 Query processor.

Therefore, transactions are executed concurrently. Appropriate techniques must ensure that the database is consistent when multiple transactions update the database. That is, transactions must satisfy the atomicity, consistency, isolation, and durability (ACID) properties. Major aspects of transaction management are serializability, concurrency control, and recovery. We discuss them briefly in this section. For a detailed discussion of transaction management we refer to Bernstein et al. (1987) and Korth and Silberschatz (1986).

Serializability. A schedule is a sequence of operations performed by multiple transactions. Two schedules are equivalent if their outcomes are the same. A serial schedule is a schedule where no two transactions execute concurrently. An objective in transaction management is to ensure that any schedule is equivalent to a serial schedule. Such a schedule is called a serializable schedule. Various conditions for testing the serializability of a schedule have been formulated for a DBMS.

Concurrency control. Concurrency control techniques ensure that the database is in a consistent state when multiple transactions update the database. Three popular concurrency control techniques that ensure the serializability of schedules are locking, time-stamping, and validation (which is also called optimistic concurrency control).

Recovery. If a transaction aborts due to some failure, then the database must be brought to a consistent state. This is transaction recovery. One solution to handling transaction failure is to maintain log files. The transaction's actions are recorded in the log file. So, if a transaction aborts, then the database is brought back to a consistent state by undoing the actions of the transaction. The information for the undo operation is found in the log file. Another solution is to record the actions of

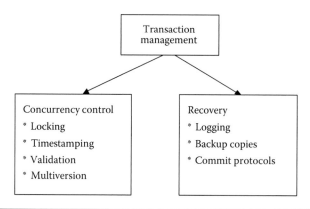

Figure B.5 Some aspects of transaction management.

a transaction but not make any changes to the database. Only if a transaction commits should the database be updated. This means that the log files have to be kept in stable storage. Various modifications to the above techniques have been proposed to handle the different situations.

When transactions are executed at multiple data sources, then a protocol called two-phase commit is used to ensure that the multiple data sources are consistent. Figure B.5 illustrates the various aspects of transaction management.

B.2.3.3 Storage Management

The storage manager is responsible for accessing the database. To improve the efficiency of query and update algorithms, appropriate access methods and index strategies have to be enforced. That is, the access methods and index strategies that are used need to be taken into consideration in generating strategies for executing query and update requests. The access methods used to access the database would depend on the indexing methods. Therefore, creating and maintaining an appropriate index file is a major issue in database management systems. By using an appropriate indexing mechanism, the query processing algorithms may not have to search the entire database. Instead, the data to be retrieved could be accessed directly. Consequently, the retrieval algorithms are more efficient. Figure B.6 illustrates an example of an indexing strategy where the database is indexed by projects.

Much research has been carried out on developing appropriate access methods and index strategies for relational database systems. Some examples of index strategies are B-trees and hashing (Date 1990). Current research is focusing on developing such mechanisms for object-oriented database systems with support for multimedia data as well as for Web database systems, among others.

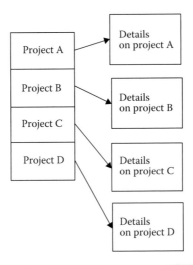

Figure B.6   An example index on projects.

B.2.3.4 Metadata Management

Metadata describe the data in the database. For example, in the case of the relational database illustrated in Figure B.2, metadata would include the following information: the database has two relations, EMP and DEPT; EMP has four attributes and DEPT has three attributes; and so forth. One of the main issues is developing a data model for metadata. In our example, one could use a relational model to also model the metadata. The metadata relation REL shown in Figure B.7 consists of information about relations and attributes.

Relation REL

Relation	Attribute
EMP	SS#
EMP	Ename
EMP	Salary
EMP	D#
DEPT	D#
DEPT	Dname
DEPT	Mgr

Figure B.7   Metadata relation.

In addition to information about the data in the database, metadata also include information on access methods, index strategies, security constraints, and integrity constraints. One could also include policies and procedures as part of the metadata. In other words, there is no standard definition for metadata. There are, however, efforts to standardize metadata (see, for example, the IEEE Mass Storage Systems Technical and Technology Committee efforts as well as IEEE Conferences on Metadata [MASS]). Metadata continue to evolve as database systems evolve into multimedia database systems and Web database systems.

Once the metadata are defined, the issues include managing the metadata. What are the techniques for querying and updating the metadata? Since all of the other DBMS components need to access the metadata for processing, what are the interfaces between the metadata manager and the other components? Metadata management is fairly well understood for relational database systems. The current challenge is in managing the metadata for more complex systems such as digital libraries and Web database systems.

B.2.3.5 Database Integrity

Concurrency control and recovery techniques maintain the integrity of the database. In addition, there is another type of database integrity: enforcing integrity constraints. There are two types of integrity constraints enforced in database systems. These are application-independent integrity constraints and application-specific integrity constraints. Integrity mechanisms also include techniques for determining the quality of the data. For example, what is the accuracy of the data and that of the source? What are the mechanisms for maintaining the quality of the data? How accurate are the data on output? For a discussion of integrity based on data quality, we refer to MIT Total Data Quality Management Program (http://web.mit.edu/tdqm/www/index.shtml). Data provenance is closely related to data integrity. That is, to determine whether data have been corrupted it is important to maintain the history of the data.

Application independent integrity constraints include the primary key constraint, the entity integrity rule, referential integrity constraint, and the various functional dependencies involved in the normalization process (see the discussion in Date [1990]). Application specific integrity constraints are those constraints that are specific to an application. Examples include "an employee's salary cannot decrease" and "no manager can manage more than two departments." Various techniques have been proposed to enforce application-specific integrity constraints. For example, when the database is updated, these constraints are checked and the data are validated. Aspects of database integrity are illustrated in Figure B.8.

B.2.4 Distributed Data Management

Although many definitions of a distributed database system have been given, there is no standard definition. Our discussion of distributed database system concepts

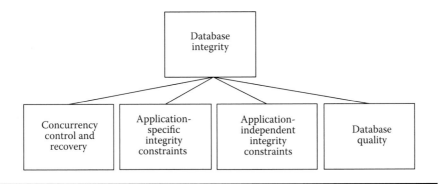

Figure B.8 Aspects of database integrity.

and issues has been influenced by the discussion in Ceri and Pelagatti (1984). A distributed database system includes a DDBMS, a distributed database, and a network for interconnection. The DDBMS manages the distributed database. A distributed database is data that are distributed across multiple databases. Our choice architecture for a distributed database system is a multidatabase architecture that is tightly coupled. This architecture is illustrated in Figure B.9. We have chosen such an architecture because we can explain the concepts for both homogeneous and heterogeneous systems based on this approach. In this architecture, the nodes are connected via a communication subsystem and local applications are handled by the local DBMS. In addition, each node is also involved in at least one global application so there is no centralized control in this architecture. The DBMSs are connected through a component called the distributed processor (DP). In a homogeneous environment, the local DBMSs are homogeneous while in a heterogeneous environment, the local DBMSs may be heterogeneous.

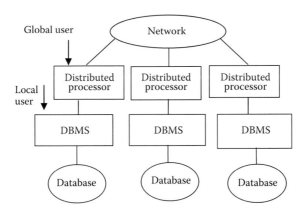

Figure B.9 An architecture for a DDBMS.

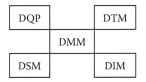

Figure B.10 Modules of the DP.

Distributed database system functions include distributed query processing, distributed transaction management, distributed metadata management, and enforcing security and integrity across the multiple nodes. The DP is an essential component of the DDBMS. It is this module that connects the different local DBMSs. That is, each local DBMS is augmented by a DP. The modules of the DP are illustrated in Figure B.10. The components are the distributed metadata manager (DMM), the distributed processor (DQP), the distributed transaction manager (DTM), the distributed security manager (DSM), and the distributed integrity manager (DIM). DMM manages the global metadata. The global metadata include information on the schemas, which describe the relations in the distributed database, the way the relations are fragmented, the locations of the fragments, and the constraints enforced. DQP is responsible for distributed query processing, DTM is responsible for distributed transaction management, DSM is responsible for enforcing global security constraints, and DIM is responsible for maintaining integrity at the global level. Note that the modules of DP communicate with their peers at the remote nodes. For example, the DQP at node 1 communicates with the DQP at node 2 for handling distributed queries.

B.3 Discretionary Security

B.3.1 Overview

Before one designs a secure system, the first question that must be answered is, What is the security policy to be enforced by the system? Security policy is essentially a set of rules that enforce security. Security policies include mandatory security policies and discretionary security policies. Mandatory security policies are the policies that are mandatory in nature and should not be bypassed. Discretionary security policies are policies that are specified by the administrator or anyone who is responsible for the environment in which the system will operate.

The most popular discretionary security policy is the access control policy. Access control policies were studied for operating systems back in the 1960s and then for database systems in the 1970s. The two prominent database systems, System R and INGRES, were two of the first to investigate access control for database systems (see Griffiths and Wade 1976; Stonebraker and Wong 1974). Since then several variations of access control policies have been reported. Other discretionary policies include administration policies. We also discuss identification and authentication under discretionary policies. Note that much of the discussion in this section focuses on discretionary security in relational database systems.

The organization of this section is as follows. In Section B.3.2 we provide an overview of access control policies. Administration policies are discussed in Section B.3.3. Issues on identification and authentication are discussed in Section B.3.4. Auditing a database management system is discussed in Section B.3.5. Views as security objects are discussed in Section B.3.6. The appendix is concluded in Section B.3.7. Various components of discretionary security policies are discussed in Ferrari and Thuraisingham (2000).

B.3.2 Access Control Policies

B.3.2.1 Authorization Policies

Many of the access control policies are based on authorization policies. Essentially what this means is that users are granted access to data based on authorization rules. In this section we discuss various types of authorization rules. Note that in the book by Ferrari and Thuraisingham (2000) a detailed discussion of authorization policies are discussed. Figure B.11 illustrates authorization policies.

Positive authorization. Early systems focused on what is now called positive authorization rules. Here, user John is granted access to relation EMP or user Jane is granted access to relation DEPT. These are access control rules on relations. One can also grant access to other entities such as attributes and tuples. For example, John has read access to attribute Salary and write access to attribute Name in relation EMP. Write access could include append, modify, or delete access.

Negative authorization. The question here is if John's access to an object is not specified, does this mean John does not have access to that object? In some systems any authorization rule that is not specified is implicitly taken to be a negative authorization while in other systems negative authorizations are explicitly specified. For example, we could enforce rules such as, "John does not have access to relation EMP" or "Jane does not have access to relation DEPT."

Authorization Rules:

- John has read access to employee relation

- John does not have write access to department relation

- Jane has read access to name values in employee relation

- Jane does not have read access to department relation

Figure B.11   Authorization rules.

Conflict resolutions. When we have rules that are conflicting, how do we resolve the conflicts? For example, we could have a rule that grants John read access to relation EMP. However we can also have a rule that does not grant John read access to the salary attribute in EMP. This is a conflict. Usually a system enforces the least privilege rule in which case John has access to EMP except for the salary values.

Strong and weak authorization. Systems also enforce strong and weak authorizations. In the case of strong authorization the rule holds regardless of conflicts. In the case of weak authorizations, the rule does not hold in case of conflict. For example, if John is granted access to EMP and it is a strong authorization rule and the rule where John is not granted access to salary attribute is a weak authorization, there is a conflict. This means the strong authorization will hold.

Propagation of authorization rules. The question here is how do the rules get propagated? For example, if John has read access to relation EMP, does it automatically mean that John has read access to every element in EMP? Usually this is the case unless we have a rule that prohibits automatic propagation of an authorization rule. If we have a rule prohibiting the automatic propagation of a rule then we must explicitly enforce authorization rules that specify the objects that John has access to.

Special rules. In our work on mandatory policies, we have explored extensively the enforcement of content and context-based constraints. Note that security constraints are essentially the security rules. Content and context-based rule are rules where access is granted depending on the content of the data or the context in which the data are displayed. Such rules can also be enforced for discretionary security. For example, in the case of content-based constraints, John has read access to tuples only in DEPT D100. In the case of context- or association-based constraints, John does not have read access to names and salaries taken together; however, he can have access to individual names and salaries. In the case of event-based constraints, after the election, John has access to all elements in relation EMP.

Consistency and completeness of rules. One of the challenges here is ensuring the consistency and completeness of constraints. That is, if the constraints or rules are inconsistent then do we have conflict resolution rules that will resolve the conflicts? How can we ensure that all of the entities (such as attributes, relations, elements, etc.) are specified in access control rules for a user? Essentially what this means is, are the rules complete? If not, what assumptions do we make about entities that do not have either positive or negative authorizations specified on them for a particular user or a class of users?

B.3.2.2 RBAC Policies

RBAC has become one of more popular access control methods (see Sandhu 1996). This method has been implemented in commercial systems including Trusted Oracle. The idea here is to grant access to users depending on their roles and functions.

The essential idea behind RBAC is as follows: Users need access to data depending on their roles. For example, a president may have access to information about his or her vice presidents and the members of the board while the chief financial officer may have access to the financial information and information on those who report to him or her. A director may have access to information about those working in his or her division while the human resources director will have information on personal data about the employees of the corporation. Essentially role-based access control is a type of authorization policy that depends on the user role and the activities that go with the role.

Various research efforts on role hierarchies have been discussed in the literature. There is also a conference series, Symposium on Access Control Models and Technologies (SACMAT), which evolved from RBAC research efforts. For example, how does access get propagated? Can one role subsume another? Consider the role hierarchy illustrated in Figure B.12. This means that if we grant access to a node in the hierarchy, does the access propagate upward? That is, if a department manager has access to certain project information does that access get propagated to the parent node, which is a director node? If a section leader has access to employee information in his or her section does the access propagate to the department manager who is the parent in the role hierarchy? What happens to the child nodes? That is, does access propagate downward? For example, if a department manager has access to certain information, then do his or her subordinates have access to that information? Are there cases where the subordinates have access to data that the department manager does not have? What happens if an employee has to report to two supervisors, a department manager and a project manager? What happens when the department manager is working on a project and has to report to the project leader who also works for him or her?

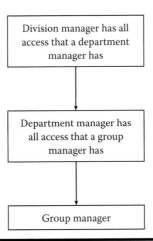

Figure B.12   Role hierarchy.

RBAC has been examined for relational systems, object systems, distributed systems, and now for some of the emerging technologies such as data warehouses, knowledge management systems, Semantic Web, e-commerce systems, and digital libraries. Furthermore, object models have been used to represent roles and activities (see, for example, Proceedings of the IFIP Database Security Conference Series). This is an area that will continue to be discussed and the ACM SACMAT is a venue for publishing high-quality papers on this topic.

More recently, Sandhu et al. have developed yet another access-control-like model: the usage control model, which they refer to as UCON (see, for example, the work reported in Park and Sandhu 2004). The UCON model attempts to integrate three policies: (1) trust management, (2) access control, and (3) rights management. The idea is to provide control on the usage of objects. While the ideas are somewhat preliminary, this model shows a lot of promise.

B.3.3 Administration Policies

While access control policies specify access that specific users have to the data, administration policies specify who is to administer the data. Administration duties would include keeping the data current, making sure the metadata are updated whenever the data are updated, and ensuring recovery from failures and related activities.

Typically the database administer (DBA) is responsible for updating the metadata, the index, and access methods and also ensuring that the access control rules are properly enforced. The system security officer (SSO) may also have a role. That is, the DBA and SSO may share the duties between them. Security-related issues might be the responsibility of the SSO while data-related issues might be the responsibility of the DBA. Some other administration policies being considered include assigning caretakers. Usually owners have control of the data that they create and may manage the data for its duration. In some cases owners may not be available to manage the data, in which case they may assign caretakers.

Administration policies get more complicated in distributed environments especially in a Web environment. For example, in Web environments there may be multiple parties involved in distributing documents including the owner, the publisher, and the users requesting the data. Who owns the data? Is it the owner or the publisher? Once the data have left the owner and arrived at the publisher, does the publisher take control of the data?

There are many interesting questions that need to be answered as we migrate from a relational database environment to a distributed and perhaps a Web environment. These also include managing copyright issues, data quality, data provenance, and governance. Many interesting papers have appeared in recent conferences on administration policies. Figure B.13 illustrates various administration policies.

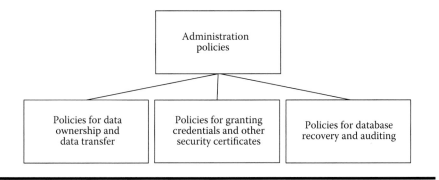

Figure B.13   Administration policies.

B.3.4 SQL Extensions for Security

This section discusses policy specification and the focus will be on SQL extensions for security policy specification. Note that SQL was developed for data definition and data manipulation for relational systems. Various versions of SQL have been developed including SQL for objects, SQL for multimedia, and SQL for the Web. That is, SQL has influenced data manipulation and data definition a great deal over the past 20 years (see SQL3 1992).

As we have stated, SQL is a data definition and data manipulation language. Security policies could be specified during data definition. SQL has GRANT and REVOKE constructs for specifying grant and revoke access to users. That is, if a user John has read access to relation EMP, then one could use SQL and specify something like "GRANT JOHN EMP READ" and if the access is to be revoked, and then we need something like "REVOKE JOHN EMP READ." SQL has also been extended with more complex constraints such as granting John read access to a tuple in a relation and granting Jane write access to an element in a relation.

In Thuraisingham and Stachour (1989) we specified SQL extensions for security assertions. These assertions were for multilevel security. We could use similar reasoning for specifying discretionary security policies. For example, consider the situation where John does not have read access to names and salaries in EMP taken together, but he can read names and salaries separately. One could specify this in SQL-like language as follows:

```
GRANT JOHN READ
EMP.SALARY
GRANT JOHN READ
EMP.NAME
NOT GRANT JOHN READ
Together (EMP.NAME, EMP.SALARY).
```

If we are to grant John read access to the employees who earn less than 30K, then this assertion is specified as follows:

```
GRANT JOHN READ
EMP
Where EMP.SALARY < 30K
```

Note that the assertions we have specified are not standard assertions. These are some of our ideas. We need to explore ways of incorporating these assertions into the standards. SQL extensions have also been proposed for RBAC. In fact, products such as Oracle's Trusted database enforce RBAC. The access control rules are specified in an SQL-like language.

B.3.5 Query Modification

Query modification was first proposed in the INGRES project at the University of California at Berkeley (see Stonebraker and Wong 1974). The idea is to modify the query based on the constraints. We have successfully designed and implemented query modification for mandatory security (see Dwyer et al. 1987; Thuraisingham 1987; Thuraisingham et al. 1993). However, much of the discussion in this section will be on query modification based on discretionary security constraints. We illustrate the essential points with some examples.

Consider a query by John to retrieve all tuples from EMP. Suppose that John only has read access to all the tuples where the salary is less than 30K and the employee is not in the security department. Then the query

```
Select * from EMP
Will be modified to
Select * from EMP
Where salary < 30K
And Dept is not Security
```

where we assume that the attributes of EMP are, for example, Name, Salary, Age, and Department.

Essentially what happens is that the "where" clause of the query has all the constraints associated with the relation. We can also have constraints that span across multiple relations. For example, we could have two relations EMP and DEPT joined by Dept #. Then the query is modified as follows:

```
Select * from EMP
Where EMP.Salary < 30K
And EMP.D# = DEPT.D#
And DEPT.Name is not Security
```

We have used some simple examples for query modification. The detailed algorithms can be found in Dwyer et al. (1987) and Stonebraker and Wong (1974).

B.3.6 Other Aspects

B.3.6.1 Identification and Authentication

For the sake of completion we discuss identification and authentication as part of our discussion on discretionary security. By identification we mean users must identify themselves with their user ID and password. Authentication means the system must then match the user ID with the password to ensure that this is indeed the person he or she is purporting to be. A user may also have multiple identities depending on his or her roles. Identity management has received a lot of attention recently (see Bhargav-Spantzel et al. 2005).

Numerous problems have been reported with the password-based scheme. One is that hackers can break into the system and get the passwords of users and then masquerade as the user. In a centralized system, the problems are not as complicated as in a distributed environment. Now, with the World Wide Web and e-commerce applications, financial organizations are losing billions of dollars when hackers masquerade as legitimate users.

More recently, biometrics techniques are being applied. These include face recognition and voice recognition techniques to authenticate the user. These techniques are showing a lot of promise and are already being used. We can expect widespread use of biometric techniques as face recognition technologies advance.

B.3.6.2 Auditing a Database System

Databases are audited for multiple purposes. For example, they may be audited to keep track of the number of queries posed, the number of updates made, the number of transaction executed, and the number of times the secondary storage is accessed so that the system can be designed more efficiently. Databases can also be audited for security purposes. For example, have any of the access control rules been bypassed by releasing information to the users? Has the inference problem occurred? Has privacy been violated? Have there been unauthorized intrusions?

Audits create a trail and the audit data may be stored in a database. This database may be mined to detect any abnormal patterns or behaviors. Audit trail analysis is especially important these days with e-commerce transactions on the Web. An organization should have the capability to conduct an analysis and determine problems like credit card fraud and identity theft.

B.3.6.3 Views for Security

Views as a mechanism for security have been studied a great deal both for discretionary security and mandatory security. For example, one may not want to grant access to an entire relation, especially if it has, for example, 25 attributes such as health care records, salary, travel information, and personal data. Therefore, the

DBA could form views and grant access to the views. Similarly, in the case of mandatory security, views could be assigned security levels (Thuraisingham 2005).

Views have problems associated with them, including the view update problem (see Date 1990). That is, if the view is updated, we need to ensure that the base relations are also updated. Therefore, if a view is updated by John and John does not have access to the base relation, then can the base relation still be updated? That is, do we create different views for different users and then the DBA merges the updates on views as updates on base relations?

B.4 MAC

B.4.1 Overview

This section describes MAC models that have been developed for DBMSs. While DBMSs must deal with many of the same security concerns as trusted operating systems (identification and authentication, access control, auditing), there are characteristics of DBMSs that introduce additional security challenges. For example, objects in DBMSs tend to be of varying sizes and can be of fine granularity such as relations, attributes, and elements. This contrasts with operating systems where the granularity tends to be coarse, such as files or segments. Because of the fine granularity in MLS/DBMSs, also often called trusted database management systems (TDBMS), the objects on which MAC and DAC are performed may differ. In MLS operating systems, also called trusted operating systems, MAC and DAC are usually performed on the same object such as a file.

There are also some functional differences between operating systems and DBMSs. Operating systems tend to deal with subjects attempting to access some object. DBMSs are employed for sharing data between users and to provide users with a means to relate different data objects. Also, DBMSs are generally dependent on operating systems to provide resources such as interprocess communication and memory management. Therefore, trusted DBMS designs often must take into account how the operating systems deal with security.

The differences between DBMSs and the operating systems discussed above mean that the traditional approaches utilized to developing secure systems need to be adapted for trusted DBMSs. Currently there is no standard architectural approach in the development of MLS/DBMSs. A variety of approaches to designing and building MLS/DBMSs have been proposed. Taxonomies for MAC have been proposed by Hinke and Graubart, among others (see Graubart 1989; Hinke 1989). Details of the various designs are given in Thuraisingham (2005).

Of particular interest to us is the inference problem. This problem was studied extensively in statistical databases for several years before it became a very popular topic for MLS/DBMSs. Inference is the process of posing queries and deducing information from the legitimate response received. It becomes a problem if the information deduced is something that a user is not authorized to know. For example, if one deduces, for example, secret information from unclassified pieces of data, then the inference problem has occurred. We will provide an overview of the inference problem in Appendix C. An implementation of an inference controller is discussed in Appendix D.

B.4.2 MAC Policies

MAC policies specify access that subjects have to objects. Many of the commercial DBMSs are based on the Bell and LaPadula (1973) policy specified for operating systems. Therefore, we first state this policy and then discuss how this policy has been adapted for DBMSs. Note that other mandatory policies include the noninterference policy by Goguen and Messeguer (1982). However, these policies are yet to be investigated fully for DBMSs, although the LOCK Data Views project did some preliminary investigation (see Stachour and Thuraisingham 1990).

In the Bell and LaPadula policy, subjects are assigned clearance levels and they can operate a level up to and including their clearance levels. Objects are assigned sensitivity levels. The clearance levels as well as the sensitivity levels are called security levels. The set of security levels forms a partially ordered lattice with Unclassified < Confidential < Secret < TopSecret. The following are the two rules of the policy:

> *Simple security property:* A subject has read access to an object if its security level dominates the level of the object
> **-Property (read star property):* A subject has write access to an object if the subject's security level is dominated by that of an object

These properties apply for database systems also. However, for database systems, the *-property is usually modified to read as follows:

A subject has write access to an object if the subject's level is that of the object
This means a subject can modify relations at its level.

An important aspect now considered to be part of the security policy for database systems is polyinstantiation (Denning et al. 1987). That is, the same object can have different interpretation and values at different levels. For example, at the unclassified level an employee's salary may be $30,000 and at the secret level the salary may be $70,000. With multilevel relational models one can have both entries but with their security levels as an additional attribute. One of the main motivations toward handling polyinstantiation is to avoid what is called covert channels. For example, if there is an entry at the secret level that John's salary is $70K and if an unclassified subject wants to enter that John's salary is $30K, if the update is not permitted there could be a signaling channel from a higher level to a lower level. Over time this could become a covert channel. Many discussions and debates have taken place on polyinstantiation in the early 1990s (for example, the panel at the

Computer Security Foundations Workshop in Franconia, NH, in 1991). No consensus has been reached. Various systems have implemented multilevel relational data models in different ways.

B.4.3 Granularity of Classification

The granularity of classification in a relational database system could be at the database level, attribute level, tuple level, or even at the element level. Furthermore, one could also assign security levels to views as well as to collections of attributes. Essentially, security levels are assigned based on what we have called security constraints and these constraints classify data based on content, context, association, and events. We discuss security constraints in more detail when we discuss the inference problem in Part V. In this appendix we discuss classifying databases, relational, tuples, attributes, and elements, which are the components of the relational data model.

Figure B.14 illustrates how a database D consisting of relations EMP and DEPT is classified at the secret level. This means that all of the contents of the relations EMP and DEPT are assigned the level secret. It does not mean that the existence of the relations is classified. We discuss metadata classification later on in this section.

The next level of classification is classifying relations. Figure B.15 shows how relation EMP is classified at the level secret while the relation DEPT is assigned the level unclassified. This means the contents of EMP are secret while the contents of DEPT are unclassified. Note that here again we are not classifying the existence of the relations.

Figure B.16 illustrates the classification of attributes. Here the attributes Ename and D# in EMP are unclassified while the attributes SS# and Salary in EMP are secret. This means all the names and department numbers in EMP are unclassified while the salaries and social security numbers are secret. Note that we have also classified some of the attributes in DEPT. We can apply security constraints to classify collections of attributes.

DATABASE D: Level = Secret

EMP

SS#	Ename	Salary	D#
1	John	20K	10
2	Paul	30K	20
3	Mary	40K	30

DEPT

D#	Dname	Mgr
10	Math	Smith
20	Physics	Jones

Figure B.14   Classifying databases.

EMP: Level = Secret

SS#	Ename	Salary	D#
1	John	20K	10
2	Paul	30K	20
3	Mary	40K	30

DEPT: Level = Unclassified

D#	Dname	Mgr
10	Math	Smith
20	Physics	Jones

Figure B.15   Classifying relations.

EMP

SS#: S	Ename: U	Salary: S	D#: U
1	John	20K	10
2	Paul	30K	20
3	Mary	40K	20

DEPT

D#: U	Dname: U	Mgr: S
10	Math	Smith
20	Physics	Jones

U = Unclassified

S = Secret

Figure B.16   Classifying attributes.

Figure B.17 illustrates the classification of tuples. Here the tuples relating to John are unclassified while the tuples relating to Paul are secret. Furthermore the tuples relating to Mary are top secret. Note that we have also assigned tuple level labeling to the relation DEPT. Here again we can classify collections of tuples taken together at say the top secret level.

Figure B.18 illustrates element level classification. This is the finest level of granularity. For example, we classify the salary of John at the confidential level while the

EMP

SS#	Ename	Salary	D#	Level
1	John	20K	10	U
2	Paul	30K	20	S
3	Mary	40K	20	TS

DEPT

D#	Dname	Mgr	Level
10	Math	Smith	U
20	Physics	Jones	C

U = Unclassified

C = Confidential

S = Secret

TS = TopSecret

Figure B.17   Classifying tuples.

EMP

SS#:	Ename:	Salary	D#:
1, S	John, U	20K, C	10, U
2, S	Paul, U	30K, S	20, U
3, S	Mary. U	40K, S	20, U

DEPT

D#:U	Dname: U	Mgr: S
10, U	Math, U	Smith, C
20, U	Physics, U	Jones, S

U = Unclassified

C = Confidential

S = Secret

Figure B.18 Classifying elements.

salaries of Paul and Mary are secret. Note that each element in EMP and DEPT are assigned a label that is its security level. Here again we may use constraints to assign the classification levels.

In Figure B.19 we illustrate the classification of views. Here we have formed two views from relation EMP. One view consists of all those who work in department number 20 and this view is classified at the secret level. The other view is all those who work in department number 10 and this view is classified at the unclassified level. Here again we may use constraints to classify the views and these constraints will be discussed in Section IV. Note also when we classify views there are some issues to be considered. That is, if we classify the view that consists of all those who work in department number 20 at the secret level, then do we still classify all those who work in department number 20 in the base relation EMP at the secret level? If we are to ensure consistency as well as not leak classified information from the base relations, we have to assign the secret level to all those work in department number 20 in the relation EMP.

Finally, we discuss the classification of the existence of relations, attributes, and tuples. This is essentially classifying the metadata. For example, the relation EMP could be secret, but its existence could be confidential. This means while all the contents of EMP are secret, the fact that there is a relation called EMP is confidential. Figure B.20 illustrates the classification of metadata. Here we have a relation called REL, which is unclassified, but the existence of certain attributes such as Salary in EMP and Mgr in DEPT are confidential and the existence is SS# in EMP is secret. Note that one cannot have the existence of the relation be secret while its contents are unclassified. That is, one cannot classify the existence of relation EMP as secret while the contents of EMP are unclassified. This means the security level of the existence of EMP must be dominated by the security levels of the contents of EMP. Various multilevel relational data models such as SeaView and LOCK Data Views have studied security properties for metadata (see Stachour and Thuraisingham 1990).

EMP

SS#	Ename	Salary	D#
1	John	20K	10
2	Paul	30K	20
3	Mary	40K	20
4	Jane	20K	20
5	Bill	20K	10
6	Larry	20K	10
1	Michelle	30K	20

SECRET VIEW EMP (D# = 20)

SS#	Ename	Salary
2	Paul	30K
3	Mary	40K
4	Jane	20K
1	Michelle	30K

UNCLASSIFIED VIEW EMP (D# = 10)

SS#	Ename	Salary
1	John	20K
5	Bill	20K
6	Larry	20K

Figure B.19   Classifying views.

The discussion in this section has illustrated how classification levels, which we also refer to as security levels, may be assigned to the data in a relational database. As we have stated, more complex classification policies will be discussed in Section IV when we discuss the inference problem. In the next section we review a concept that has been discussed at length in the definition of multilevel relational data models. This concept is called polyinstantiation. This is the situation where users cleared at different levels have different views of the same data. This causes inconsistencies in a database. However, if we do not have polyinstantiation, then there is a potential for signaling channels.

Relation REL

Relation	Attribute	Level
EMP	SS#	Secret
EMP	Ename	Unclassified
EMP	Salary	Confidential
EMP	D#	Unclassified
DEPT	D#	Unclassified
DEPT	Dname	Unclassified
DEPT	Mgr	Confidential

Figure B.20 Classifying metadata.

B.5 Summary and Directions

We first provided an overview of database systems technologies. We began with a discussion of relational data model. We then provided an overview of the various functions of database systems. These include query processing, transaction management, storage management, metadata management, integrity, and fault tolerance. We also briefly discussed distributed database systems.

Next, we provided an overview of discretionary security policies in database systems. We started with a discussion of access control policies including authorization policies and RBAC. Then we discussed administration policies. We briefly discussed identification and authentication. We also discussed auditing issues as well as views for security.

Next, we discussed policy enforcement issues including policy specification, policy implementation, and policy visualization. We discussed SQL extensions for specifying policies as well as provided an overview of query modification. We also briefly discussed how policy visualization might be used to integrate multiple policies.

Next, we provided an overview of MAC and policies for MLS/DBMSs as well as described a taxonomy for the designs of MLS/DBMSs. We first described the differences between access control in operating systems and access control in DBMSs. Then we provided an overview of the Bell and La Padula security policy and its adaptation for MLS/DBMSs. Finally, we provided an overview of classifying data in a database system.

There is still a lot of work to be done. For example, much work is still needed on RBAC for emerging technologies such as cloud computing and the Semantic Web. We need administration policies to manage multiparty transactions in a Web environment. We also need biometric technologies for authenticating users. Security policy enforcement is a topic that will continue to evolve as new technologies emerge. We have advanced from relational to object to multimedia to Web-based data management systems. Each system has some unique features that are incorporated into the security policies. Enforcing policies for the various systems will continue to be a major research focus.

References

Bell, D. and LaPadula, L., Secure computer systems: Mathematical foundations and model, M74-244, The MITRE Corporation, Bedford, MA, 1973.

Bernstein, P., Hadzilacos, V. and Goodman, N., *Concurrency Control and Recovery in Database Systems,* Addison-Wesley, MA, 1987.

Bhargav-Spantzel, A., Cinzia Squicciarini, A. and Bertino, E., Establishing and protecting digital identity in federation systems, In Proceedings of the 2005 Workshop on Digital Identity Management, Fairfax, VA, 2005, pp. 11–19.

Ceri, S. and Pelagatti, G., *Distributed Databases: Principles & Systems,* McGraw-Hill, New York, 1984.

Codd, E. F., A Relational Model of Data for Large Shared Data Banks, *Commun. ACM,* Vol. 13, No. 6, 1970.

Date, C., *An Introduction to Database Systems,* Addison-Wesley, Reading, MA, 1990.

Denning, D. E., Akl, S. G., Heckman, M., Lunt, T. F., Morgenstern, M., Neumann, P. G. and Schell, R. R., Views for multilevel database security, *IEEE Trans. Software Eng.,* Vol. 13, No. 2, 1987, pp. 129–140.

Dwyer, P. et al., Multilevel security in relational database systems, *Computers & Security,* Vol. 6, No. 3, 1987, pp. 252–260.

Ferrari, E. and Thuraisingham, B., Secure database systems, in *Advanced Database Technology and Design,* M. Piattini and O. Diaz (eds.), Artech House, Norwood, MA, 2000.

Goguen, J. and Meseguer, J., Security policies and security models, Proceedings of the IEEE Symposium on Security and Privacy, Oakland, CA, April 1982.

Graubart, R., A comparison of three secure DBMS architectures, Proceedings of the IFIP Database Security Conference, Monterey, CA, 1989 (proceedings published by North Holland, 1989).

Griffiths P. and Wade, B., An authorization mechanism for a relational database system, *ACM Transactions on Database Systems,* Vol. 1, No. 3, 1976.

Hinke, T., DBMS trusted computing base taxonomy, Proceedings of the IFIP Database Security Conference, Monterey, CA, 1989 (proceedings published by North Holland, 1989).

Korth, H. and Silberschatz, A., *Database System Concepts,* McGraw Hill, New York, 1986.

MASS, IEEE Mass Storage Systems Technical and Technology Committee, http://www.msstc.org (see also http://www.csee.umbc.edu/csee/research/kqml/events/ieee-metadata.html).

MIT Total Data Quality Management Program, http://web.mit.edu/tdqm/www/index.shtml.

Park, J. and Sandhu, R., The UCON usage control model, *ACM Transactions on Information and Systems Security,* Vol. 7, No. 1, 2004.

Sandhu, R., Coyne, E. J. Feinstein, H. L. and Youman, C. E., Role-based access control models, *Computer,* Vol. 29, No. 2, 1996.

SQL3, American National Standards Institute, draft, 1992.

Stachour, P. and Thuraisingham, B., Design of LDV: A multilevel secure relational database management system, *IEEE Transactions on Knowledge and Data Engineering,* Vol. 2, No. 2, 1990.

Stonebraker, M. and Wong, E., Access control in a relational data base management system by query modification, Proceedings of the ACM Annual Conference, ACM Press, New York, 1974.

Thuraisingham, B., Security checking in relational database management systems augmented with inference engines, *Computers & Security,* Vol. 6, No. 6, 1987.

Thuraisingham, B., *Database and Applications Security: Integrating Information Security and Data Management*, CRC Press, Boca Raton, FL, 2005.

Thuraisingham, B., Ford, W. and Collins, M., Design and implementation of a database inference controller, *Data and Knowledge Engineering Journal*, Vol. 11, No. 3, 1993.

Thuraisingham, B. and Stachour, P., SQL extensions for security assertions, *Computer Standards and Interface Journal*, Vol. 11, No. 1, 1989.

Ullman, J. D., *Principles of Database and Knowledge Base Management Systems,* Volumes I and II, Computer Science Press, Rockville, MD, 1988.

Appendix C: A Perspective of the Inference Problem

C.1 Overview

The inference problem was studied extensively in statistical databases for several years before it became a very popular topic for MLS/DBMSs. Inference is the process of posing queries and deducing information from the legitimate response received. It becomes a problem if the information deduced is something that a user is not authorized to know. For example, if one deduces secret information from unclassified pieces of data, then the inference problem has occurred.

In the case of statistical databases, Dorothy Denning and others were the first to study the problem extensively (see *IEEE Computer Magazine* 1983). Here the idea is to give out, for example, averages and sums while protecting the individual pieces of data. The census bureau also studied the inference problem in collecting and maintaining census data. However, it was not until the late 1980s when there were many activities on MLS/DBMSs that the inference problem was investigated extensively. Morgernstern at SRI International (Morgenstern 1987), Thuraisingham at Honeywell (Thuraisingham 1987), and Hinke at TRW (Hinke 1988) developed the early solutions. Later, Thuraisingham at MITRE carried out extensive work on the problem together with Ford, Rubinovitz, and Collins (see Thuraisingham 1989; Thuraisingham et al. 1993; Thuraisingham and Ford 1995). Since then, many efforts have been reported, including those by Marks, Farkas, and others (see Farkas et al. 2001; Marks 1996). Today, the inference problem is resurfacing due to data warehousing and data mining because these technologies exacerbate the inference problem and also contribute toward privacy violations via inference.

In this appendix we give a perspective of the inference problem. In Section C.2 we discuss statistical databases. In Section C.3 we discuss the various approaches proposed to handle the inference problem. Complexity of the inference problem, which was examined by Thuraisingham in 1990, is discussed in Section C.4. Summary and directions are provided in Section C.5. Figure C.1 illustrates the process where users infer unauthorized information from the legitimate responses. Figure C.2 illustrates the early approaches to handling the inference problem by Morgenstern, Thuraisingham, and Hinke. Figure C.3 illustrates the various types of inferences such as inference by deduction, induction, and other inference strategies. Figure C.4 illustrates the inference problem in various information systems.

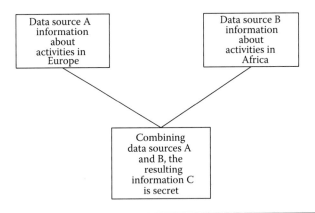

Figure C.1   Inference problem.

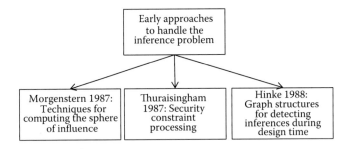

Figure C.2   Early approaches.

```
Types of Inferences:

Inference by deduction
Inference by induction
Inference by abduction
Inference by association
Inference by aggregation
```

Figure C.3   Types of inference problems.

> Inference problem in different
> information systems:
>
> Inference problem in relational databases
> Inference problem in object databases
> Inference problem in distributed databases
> Inference problem in heterogeneous databases
> Inference problem in multimedia databases

Figure C.4 Inference problem in different information systems.

C.2 Statistical Database Inference

As we have stated, the inference problem was studied in statistical databases especially by the Census Bureau. Statistical databases are used by various organizations starting from the census bureau to marketing organizations that want to study the behavior patterns of a population. Statistical databases essentially give out values such as sums, averages, mean, deviation, and so forth that are useful for studying the population in terms of the numbers or their behavior patterns (Denning 1979). More recently, with applications such as e-commerce, organizations carry out targeted marketing based on salaries, property owned, purchase patterns, and other somewhat personal information. With such information, organizations can then focus on the population that would be most suitable to market a product. For example, expensive jewelry could be marketed to wealthy women earning more than 200K while clothes such as blue jeans could be marketed to teenaged girls.

Dorothy Denning and others have studied various types of statistical databases and the inference problem that arises in such databases. This problem is called the statistical inference problem. For example, one could give out average salaries while protecting the individual salaries. Another example would be that one could give out health care information about a particular county while protecting the individual health care records of the people in that county. The question is, Can an adversary infer the individual salaries by posing queries to obtain the average salary of 10 people, then 9 people, then 8 people, and so on?

Another practice with statistical databases is not to use all of the values in the databases but work with sample values. That is, averages and mean are computed from a representative sample. From the sample values, it would be probably more difficult to divulge the individual sensitive information. Here again the question is, Can one infer sensitive data from the averages and sums computed from the sample records? Figure C.5 illustrates the approaches to handling the statistical inference problem.

While statistical inference has been explored extensively for the past several decades, more recently it has gained a lot of prominence especially with emerging technologies such as data warehousing and data mining. For example, data warehouses have been developed to give out specific information for decision makers, including sums and averages. Therefore, while the warehouse data may be

```
Statistical inference techniques:

Computing averages, Mean, Mode, Standard deviation;
Sampling;
Estimation;
Hypothesis testing.
```

Figure C.5   Statistical inference.

unclassified, there could be sensitive information residing in the back-end databases. That is, based on the information the warehouse gives out, can one determine the sensitive data in the back-end databases? Note also that statistical inference emerged as a machine-learning method and is being used extensively for machine learning and data mining in order to extract information previously unknown from large collections of data (see Mitchell 1997).

Data mining has also resulted in much interest in statistical databases. Data mining gives out information not previously known using various reasoning techniques such as statistical inference. Therefore, the challenge is by mining can one uncover sensitive or private information? Essentially the inference problem is exacerbated by data mining. More recently there is also much concern about the privacy problem. Clifton et al. (see Clifton 2000) and many others are now working on what is called privacy-preserving data mining. The idea is to maintain privacy and at the same time give out information perhaps slightly perturbed. The same techniques can be used to handle the inference problem. We discuss privacy-preserving data mining in a later section.

In summary, statistical databases and statistical inference will continue to be studied as new technologies emerge. That is, not only is the Census Bureau interested in statistical databases and statistical inference, various organizations including those involved in marketing, sales, health care, finance, and manufacturing, are also interested in using statistical reasoning techniques to get as much information as possible through mining. This causes major concerns regarding both the inference and privacy problems.

C.3 Approaches to Handling the Inference Problem in an MLS/DBMS

In the previous section we discussed statistical inference. In this section we discuss the approaches that have been developed to handle the inference problem. The approaches can essentially be divided into two groups; one is based on security constraints and the other that is based on conceptual structures. Appendix D will elaborate on the security-constraint-based approach since much of the work discussed in this book has its origins in this approach.

Security constraints are essentially rules that assign security levels to the data. The approach was first introduced by Thuraisingham et al. in 1987 as a result of the LOCK Data Views effort (see Stachour and Thuraisingham 1990; Thuraisingham 1987). In this approach, some security constraints are handled during query processing. That is, during the query operation, the constraints are examined and the query is modified. Furthermore, before the release operation the constraints are examined to determine which information can be released. The approach also allows for some constraints to be processed during database updates. That is, the constraints are examined during the update operation and the data are assigned appropriate security levels. Finally, some constraints are handled during the database design where the metadata or schemas are assigned security levels. In Appendix D we will give more details on security constraint processing, including a discussion of architectures and algorithms. Note that more recently Wiederhold (2000) and Jajodia (2003) have developed an approach where constraints are examined only after the data are released. This approach is called release control. Figure C.6 illustrates aspects of constraint processing.

In the second set of approaches, conceptual structures are used to represent the application and reason about the application. If there are potential security violations via inference then they are detected during application design time. Hinke was the first to examine graphs for representing and reasoning about applications (Hinke 1988). Later, a more extensive investigation was carried out by Thuraisingham using conceptual structures such as semantic nets and conceptual

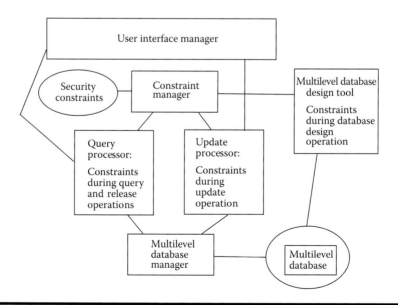

Figure C.6   Security constraint processing.

graphs (see Thuraisingham 1992). Following this, Hinke and Delugach carried out an extensive investigation on the use of conceptual graphs (see Delugach and Hinke 1992). Around the mid- to late 1990s, Thuraisingham, Binns, Marks, and Collins explored various other conceptual structures such as hypersemantic data models (see Marks et al. 1994) and deductive object models (see Collins et al. 1996). Figure C.7 briefly illustrates the use of conceptual structures.

Another direction worth mentioning is Thuraisingham's work on multilevel deductive databases and the logic called nonmonotonic typed multilevel logic (NTML). The idea here is to develop an MLS/DBMS based on logic so that the resulting deductive MLS/DBMSs could also handle the inference problem while carrying out other functions (see Thuraisingham 1991, 1992). This approach shows a lot of promise and should be examined now for the privacy problem. However, it should be noted that deductive databases have not resulted in much commercial interest. Therefore, there have been some questions as to whether we need to invest in deductive MLS/DBMSs. We provided a brief overview of such systems in Appendix B. Figure C.8 illustrates logic database systems for handing the inference problem.

In addition to the work of Morgenstern, Hinke, and Thuraisingham, other notable efforts have been reported on the inference problem. Meadows showed how the Chinese wall policy model of Brewer and Nash (see Brewer and Nash 1989) could be applied to the inference problem (see Meadows 1990). Lin (2002) refuted some of the concepts of applying the Chinese wall policy model. Lin (1992) also pursued some early work on the inference problem and applied fuzzy logic. Lunt (1989) published an interesting paper discussing the facts and fallacies of the inference problem. In addition to the inference problem, researchers also examined the aggregation problem where collections of elements taken together are classified while the individual pieces are unclassified (see also Lunt 1989).

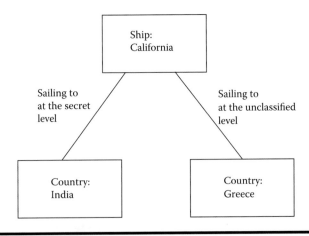

Figure C.7   Conceptual structures.

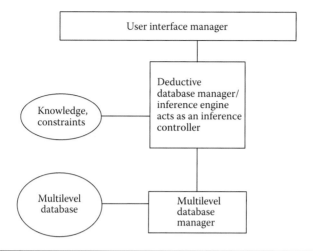

Figure C.8   Deductive databases for the inference problem.

C.4 Complexity of the Inference Problem

While many of the efforts have focused on approaches to handle the inference problem, Thuraisingham examined the complexity of the inference problem in Thuraisingham (1990). This work was quoted by Dr. John Campbell as one of the major developments in secure databases in 1990 in Proceedings of the 1990 National Computer Systems Security Conference (Campbell 1990).

In Thuraisingham (1990), we examined the recursion theoretic complexity of the inference problem. Our ultimate goal is to obtain a complete characterization of the inference problem and investigate measures of complexity. Such an investigation could usefully begin with aspects of recursive functions theory. This is because recursive function theory from which the notion of computability is derived (see Rogers 1967) has provided the basis from which other abstract theories such as computational complexity (see Blum 1967) and Kolmograv complexity theory (see Kolmogorov 1965) has evolved. Moreover the work of Rosza Peter (see Peter 1981) has shown the practical significance of recursive function theory in computer science and provided the basis for possible exploitation of such results. Therefore, the study of the foundations of the inference problem could usefully begin with aspects of recursive function theory. We have investigated the recursion theoretic properties of the inference problem associated with database design. We gave a formulation of the inference problem as a database design problem and investigated the recursion theoretic properties of this problem. Our research is influenced by our work on security constraints.

The essence of our work is as follows. We defined a set X(L) corresponding to each security level L. This set consists of all databases D that are not secure with

Complexity of the inference problem:

Unsolvability of the inference problem:
Analyzing the recursion theoretic properties
of the inference problem

Complexity of the inference problem:
Computational complexity theories for the
inference problem

Logic: Special logics for MLS/DBMSs
(example: NTML, nonmonotonic typed
multilevel logic)

Figure C.9   Complexity of the inference problem.

respect to security level L. The inference problem with respect to level L would then be the membership problem for the set X(L). That is, given a database D, if it can be effectively decided whether D belongs to X(L), then one can decide whether the design of the database D is secure with respect to level L. By a secure database at a level L we mean that all information that should be labeled at security level L is correctly labeled at level L. We proved properties of the set X(L). For more details of this work we refer to Thuraisingham (1990). Note that more recently we are applying the techniques explored for the inference problem to the privacy problem. Furthermore, there is a lot of research that needs to be done on the computational complexity of both the inference and privacy problems. Figure C.9 illustrates our view of the complexity of the inference problem.

C.5 Summary and Directions

In this appendix we described the early approaches to handle the inference problem. In particular, we discussed statistical inference, security constraint processing, and the use of conceptual structures. We also briefly discussed deductive MLS/DBMSs as well as the complexity of the inference problem.

As new technologies emerge, the inference problem continues to receive attention. This is especially the case for data warehousing, data mining, and Web data management. Furthermore, applications such as medical informatics are also examining the inference problem. Finally, research on the privacy problem is following along the lines of research on the inference problem. In summary, while much progress has been made, there is still a lot of research to carry out on the inference problem not only for MLS/DBMSs but also for DBMSs that enforce discretionary security. The inference problem also needs to be examined for the emerging database systems and applications including for Semantic Web technologies. This is one of our main motivations to carry out the research on secure data provenance and inference control with Semantic Web technologies discussed in this book.

References

Blum, M., A machine independent theory of the complexity of recursive functions, *Journal of the Association for Computing Machinery,* Vol. 14, 1967.

Brewer, D. and Nash, M., The Chinese wall security policy, Proceedings of the IEEE Symposium on Security and Privacy, Oakland, CA, April 1989.

Campbell, J., Progress in database security, Proceedings of the National Computer Security Conference, Washington, DC, October 1990.

Clifton, C., Using sample size to limit exposure to data mining, *Journal of Computer Security,* Vol. 8, No. 4, 2000.

Collins, M. et al., Deductive object-oriented data model for handling the inference problem, Proceedings of the AFCEA Database Colloquium, San Diego, CA, August 1996.

Delugach, H. S. and Hinke, T., AERIE: Database inference modeling and detection using conceptual graphs, Workshop on Conceptual Graphs, 1992.

Denning, D., The tracker: A threat to statistical database security, *ACM Transactions in Database Systems,* Vol. 4, No. 2, 1979.

Farkas, C. et al., The inference problem and updates in relational databases, Proceedings of the IFIP Database Security Conference, Lake Niagara, Canada, 2001 (proceedings published by Kluwer, 2002).

Hinke, T., Inference aggregation detection in database management systems, Proceedings of the IEEE Symposium on Security and Privacy, Oakland, CA, April 1988.

Jajodia, S., Release control for XML documents, Proceedings IFIP Conference in Integrity and Control, Lausanne, Switzerland, November 2003 (proceedings published by Kluwer, 2004).

Kolmogorov, A., Three approaches for defining the concept of information quantity, *Problemy Peredaci Informacii,* Vol. 1, No. 1, 1965.

Lin, T. Y., Inference secure multilevel databases, Proceedings of the IFIP Database Security Conference, Vancouver, Canada, 1992 (proceedings published by North Holland, 1993).

Lin, T. Y., Placing the Chinese walls on the boundary of conflicts analysis of symmetric binary relations, Proceedings of the IEEE COMPSAC Conference, Oxford, UK, August 2002.

Lunt, T., Inference and aggregation, facts and fallacies, Proceedings of the IEEE Symposium on Security and Privacy, Oakland, CA, April 1989.

Marks, D. et al., Hypersemantic data modeling for inference analysis, Proceedings of the IFIP Database Security Conference, Hildesheim, Germany, 1994 (proceedings published by North Holland, 1995).

Marks, D., Inference in MLS database system, *IEEE Transactions on Knowledge and Data Engineering,* Vol. 8, No. 1, 1996.

Meadows, C., Extending the Brewer-Nash model to a multilevel context, Proceedings of the IEEE Symposium on Security and Privacy, Oakland, CA, May 1990.

Mitchell, T., *Machine Learning,* WCB McGraw-Hill, Boston, 1997.

Morgenstern, M., Security and inference in multilevel database and knowledge base systems, Proceedings of the ACM SIGM CD Conference, San Francisco, May 1987.

Peter, R., *Recursive Functions in Computer Theory,* Ellis Horwood, Chichester, UK, 1981.

Rogers, H., Jr., *Theory of Recursive Functions and Effective Computability,* McGraw-Hill, New York, 1967.

Special Issue in Computer Security, *IEEE Computer Magazine,* Vol. 16, No. 7, 1983.

Stachour, P. and Thuraisingham, B., Design of LDV: A multilevel secure relational database management system, *IEEE Transactions on Knowledge and Data Engineering*, Vol. 2, No. 2, June 1990.

Thuraisingham, B., Security checking in relational database management systems augmented with inference engines, *Computers & Security*, Vol. 6, No. 6, 1987.

Thuraisingham, B., Secure query processing in intelligent database systems, Proceedings of the Computer Security Applications Conference, Tucson, AZ, December 1989.

Thuraisingham, B., Recursion theoretic properties of the inference problem, presented at the IEEE Computer Security Foundations Workshop, Franconia, NH, June 1990 (also available as MITRE Technical Paper MTP291, June 1990).

Thuraisingham, B., The use of conceptual structures to handle the inference problem, Proceedings of the IFIP Database Security Conference, Shepherdstown, WV (proceedings published by North Holland, 1992).

Thuraisingham, B., Recursion theoretic properties of the inference problem, *IEEE CIPHER*, Winter 1991.

Thuraisingham, B. and Ford, W., Security constraint processing in a multilevel distributed database management system, *IEEE Transactions on Knowledge and Data Engineering*, Vol. 7, No. 2, 1995.

Thuraisingham, B., Ford, W., and Collins, M., Design and implementation of a database inference controller, *Data and Knowledge Engineering Journal*, Vol. 11, No. 3, 1993.

Wiederhold, G., Release control in database systems, Proceedings IFIP Database Security Conference, Amsterdam, August 2000 (proceedings published by North Holland, 2001).

Appendix D: Design and Implementation of a Database Inference Controller

D.1 Overview

This book has focused on secure data provenance and inference control with Semantic Web technologies. We have used the reasoning power of the Semantic Web technologies to deduce whether there are security violations through inference. Our approach utilized SPARQL query modification. It has origins in query modification in multilevel relational database systems. In this appendix we discuss the early approaches based on query modification to handle the inference problem. These early approaches carry out query modification based on security policies, often called security constraints in the 1980s and 1990s, to handle the inference problem.

Back in 1987 we introduced the notion of security constraints, which are rules that assign security levels to the data (see Dwyer et al. 1987). We also designed and developed architecture for a database management system augmented with inference engines to handle the inference problem by processing the security constraints. Our initial work on the inference problem was published in Thuraisingham (1987) and elaborated on in Thuraisingham (1990). This work spawned several activities on the inference problem and security constraint processing (see also Thuraisingham et al. 1993; Thuraisingham and Ford 1995). This appendix essentially summarizes our prior work on security constraint processing carried out in the 1990s that was the motivation for much of the current work discussed here.

The organization of this appendix is as follows. In Section D.2 we provide some background on security constraints. In Section D.3 we describe the various types of security constraints that we have considered. In Section D.4 we

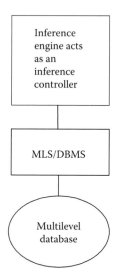

Figure D.1   Inference engine approach.

provide a high-level overview of our approach to handling the security constraints. Constraint generation aspects are discussed in Section D.5. In Section D.6 we discuss the design of the query processor. In our design, a MLS/DBMS is augmented with an inference engine (which we also call a security engine). The inference engine has the capability of processing all of the security constraints in such a way that certain security violations via inference cannot occur. In Section D.7 we describe the design of a database update processor, which is responsible for processing certain constraints during database updates. That is, appropriate security levels to the data are assigned based on the constraints during the update operation. In Section D.8 we describe algorithms that could be utilized by the SSO in order to design the schema of the database. These algorithms handle certain security constraints. Handling release information is briefly discussed in Section D.9. Handling security constraints for distributed inference control is discussed in Section D.10. Section D.11 gives summary and directions. Figure D.1 illustrates the inference engine approach.

D.2 Background

The security constraints that we have identified include those that classify data based on content, context, aggregation, and time. The work reported in Thuraisingham (1987) and Keefe et al. (1989) suggest ways of handling security constraints during query processing in such a way that certain security violations via inference do not occur. The work reported in Hinke (1988) and Morgenstern (1987) focuses on handling constraints during database design where suggestions for database design tools are given. They expect that security constraints during database design to be handled in such a way that security violations cannot occur. We describe the design techniques for processing security constraints. We believe that appropriate handling of security constraints is essential for developing a useful MLS/DBMS.

From an analysis of the various types of security constraints, we believe that they are a form of integrity constraints enforced in a MLS/DBMS. This is because in a multilevel database one can regard the security level of an entity to be part of the value of that entity. Therefore, security constraints specify permissible values that an entity can take. Since a security constraint can be regarded as a form of integrity constraint, many of the techniques developed for handling integrity constraints in non-MLS relational database systems by the logic programming researchers could be used for handling security constraints in a MLS/DBMS. In these techniques, some integrity constraints, which are called derivation rules, are handled during query processing, some integrity constraints known as integrity rules are handled during database updates, and some integrity constraints known as schema rules are handled during database design (see Gallaire and Minker 1978). Our approach to handling security constraints has been influenced by the approach taken to process integrity constraints by the logic programming researchers (Lloyd 1987).

Before designing a constraint processor, a question that must be answered is whether a constraint should be processed during query processing, during database updates, or during database design. When constraints are handled during query processing, they are treated as a form of derivation rules. That is, they are used to assign security levels to the data already in the database before it is released. In other words, new information (e.g., the security labels) is deduced from information already in the database. When the security constraints are handled during update processing, they are treated as a form of integrity rules. That is, they are constraints that must be satisfied by the data in the multilevel database. When the constraints are handled during database design, then they must be satisfied by the database schema in the same way functional and multivalued dependency constraints must be satisfied by the schema of a relational database.

We believe that it is essential for the query processor to have the capability of processing the security constraints. This is because most users usually build their reservoir of knowledge from responses that they receive by querying the database. It is from this reservoir of knowledge that they infer secret information. Moreover, no matter how well the database has been designed with respect to security or the data in the database accurately labeled with security labels, users could eventually violate security by inference because they are continuously updating their reservoir of knowledge as the world evolves. It is not feasible to have to redesign the database or to reclassify the data continuously. It should, however, be noted that processing a large number of security constraints could have an impact on the performance of the query processing algorithms. Therefore, it is desirable to process as many constraints as possible during database updates and during database design. This is because, in general, the database design and the update operation are performed less frequently than the query operation. Therefore, when the database is designed initially, the security constraints should be examined and the schema should be generated. Whenever the data are updated, the constraints are examined and the security levels are assigned or reassigned to the affected data. Periodically the SSO should examine the security constraints and redesign the database and/or reclassify the data. If the application is static and if the data in the database are consistent with the security constraints, the query processor need not examine the constraints handled by the update processor and the database designer. If there is some change that has occurred in the real world that makes the database or the schema inconsistent, then the query processor should be triggered so that it can process the relevant constraints during its operation. This way, much of the burden placed on the query processor is alleviated.

D.3 Security Constraints

We have defined various types of security constraints. They include the following:

1. Constraints that classify a database, relation, or an attribute. These constraints are called simple constraints.
2. Constraints that classify any part of the database depending on the value of some data. These constraints are called content-based constraints.
3. Constraints that classify any part of the database depending on the occurrence of some real-world event. These constraints are called event-based constraints.
4. Constraints that classify associations between data (such as tuples, attributes, elements, etc.). These constraints are called association-based constraints.
5. Constraints that classify any part of the database depending on the information that has been previously released. These constraints are called release-based constraints. We have identified two types of release-based constraints. One is the general release constraint, which classifies an entire attribute depending on whether any value of another attribute has been released. The other is the individual release constraint, which classifies a value of an attribute depending on whether a value of another attribute has been released.
6. Constraints that classify collections of data. These constraints are called aggregate constraints.
7. Constraints that specify implications. These are called logical constraints.
8. Constraints that have conditions attached to them. These are called constraints with conditions.
9. Constraints that classify any part of the database depending on the security level of some data. These constraints are called level-based constraints.
10. Constraints that assign fuzzy values to their classifications. These are called fuzzy constraints.

We will give examples of constraints belonging to each category. In our examples, we assume that the database consists of two relations, SHIP and MISSION, where SHIP has attributes S#, SNAME, CAPTAIN, and M# (with S# as the key), and MISSION has attributes M#, MNAME, and LOCATION (with M# as the key). Note that M# in SHIP and M# in MISSION take values from the same domain. The constraints may be expressed as some form of logical rules. We have chosen horn clauses to represent the constraints. This way we could eventually take advantage of the techniques that have been developed for logic programs.

Simple constraints:

```
R(Al, A2,...An)- > Level(Ail, Ai2,...Ait) = Secret
```

{Each attribute Ai1, Ai2,... Ait of relation R is Secret)

```
Example: SHIP(S#, SNAME, CAPTAIN, M#)- >
Level(CAPTAIN) = Secret.
```

Content-based constraints:

```
R(Al, A2,... An) AND COND(Value(Bl, B2,... Bm))- > Level(Ail,
Ai2,... Ait) = Secret
```

{Each attribute Ai1, Ai2,... Ait of relation R is Secret if some specific condition is enforced on the values of some data specified by B1, B2,... Bm)

```
Example: SHIP(S#, SNAME, CAPTAIN, M#) AND (Value(SNAME) =
Washington)- >
Level(CAPTAIN) = Secret.
```

Association-based constraints (also called context or together constraints):

```
R(Al, A2,... An)- > Level(Together(Ail, Ai2,... Ait)) = Secret
```

(The attributes Ai1, Ai2,... Ait of relation R taken together is Secret)

```
Example: SHIP (S#, SNAME, CAPTAIN, M#)- >
Level(Together(SNAME, CAPTAIN)) = Secret.
```

Event-based constraints:

```
R(Al, A2,... An) AND Event(E)- > Level(Ail, Ai2,... Ait) = Secret
```

(Each attribute Ai1, Ai2,... Ait of relation R is Secret if event E has occurred)

```
Example: SHIP(S#, SNAME, CAPTAIN, M#) AND Event(Change of
President)- >
Level(CAPTAIN, M#) = Secret.
```

General release-based constraints:

```
R(Al, A2,... An) AND Release(Ai, Unclassified)- > Level(Aj) =
Secret
```

(The attribute Aj of relation R is Secret if the attribute Ai has been released at the Unclassified level)

```
Example: SHIP(S#, SNAME, CAPTAIN, M#) AND Release(SNAME,
Unclassified)- >
Level(CAPTAIN) = Secret.
```

Individual release-based constraints:

```
R(Al, A2,... An) AND Individual-Release(Ai, Unclassified)- >
Level(Aj) = Secret.
```

The individual release-based constraints classify elements of an attribute at a particular level after the corresponding elements of another attribute have been released. They are more difficult to implement than the general release-based constraints. In our design, the individual release-based constraints are handled after the response is assembled while all of the other constraints are handled before the response is generated.

Aggregate constraints:

Aggregate constraints classify collections of tuples taken together at a level higher than the individual levels of the tuples in the collection. There could be some semantic association between the tuples. We specify these tuples in the following form:

```
R(Al, A2,... An) AND Set(S, R) AND Satisfy(S, P)- > Level(S) =
Secret
```

This means that if R is a relation and S is a set containing tuples of R and S satisfies some property P, then S is classified at the Secret level. Note that P could be any property such as "number of elements is greater than 10."

Logical constraints:

Logical constraints are rules which are used to derive new data from the data in the database. The derived data could be classified using one of the other constraints. Logical constraints are of the form: Ai = > Aj; where Ai and Aj are attributes of either a database relation or a real-world relation. Note that logical constraints are not really security constraints. That is, they do not assign security levels to the data. They are in fact integrity constraints. In particular, they can be regarded as integrity constraints that are treated as derivation rules.

Constraints with conditions:

An example of a constraint with a condition is a condition-based constraint. Other constraints such as association-based constraints and logical constraints can also be specified with conditions.

Consider the following example: Ai = > Aj if condition C holds.
This constraint can be instantiated as follows:

```
The LOCATION of a MISSION implies its MNAME if the
LOCATION = Atlantic Ocean
```

Other constraints:

There are several other types of constraints that could be incorporated into our design fairly easily. These include level-based constraints and fuzzy constraints. We describe them below.

Level-based constraints:

```
R(Al, A2,... An) AND Level(Ai) = Unclassified— > Level(Aj) =
Secret
```

(The attribute Aj of relation R is Secret if the attribute Ai is Unclassified)

```
Example: SHIP(S#, SNAME, CAPTAIN, M#) AND Level(SNAME) =
Unclassified— >
Level(CAPTAIN) = Secret
```

Fuzzy constraints:

Fuzzy constraints are constraints which use fuzzy values. They can be associated with any of the other types of constraints. An example of a fuzzy constraint that is associated with a content-based constraint is given below.

```
R(Al, A2,... An) AND COND(Value(Bl, B2,... Bm))— > Level(Ail,
Ai2,... Ait) = Secret and Fuzzyvalue = r
```

(Each attribute Ai1, Ai2,... Ait of relation R is Secret with a fuzzy value of r if some specific condition is enforced on the values of some data specified by B1, B2,... Bm)

```
Example: SHIP(S#, SNAME, CAPTAIN, M#) AND (Value(SNAME) =
Washington)— >
Level(CAPTAIN) = Secret and Fuzzyvalue = 0.8.
```

Complex constraints:

The examples of constraints that we have given above are enforced on a single relation only. Note that constraints can also be enforced across relations. We call such constraints complex constraints. An example is given below:

```
Rl(Al,A2 An)&R2(Bl,B2 Bm)&Rl.Ai = R2.Bj →
Level(Together(Ak, Bp)) = Secret
```

This constraint states that a pair of values involving the kth attribute of R1 and the pth attribute of R2 are Secret provided the corresponding values (i.e., in the same row) of the ith attribute of R1 and the jth attribute of R2 are equal.

This constraint may be instantiated as follows:

```
SHIP(S#, SNAME, CAPTAIN, M#) & MISSION(M#, MNAME LOCATION) &
SHIP.M# = MISSION.M# — > Level(Together(SNAME, MNAME) = Secret
```

D.4 Approach to Security Constraint Processing

As stated in Section D.1, security constraints enforce a security policy. Therefore, it is essential that constraints be manipulated only by an authorized individual. In our approach constraints are maintained by the SSO. That is, constraints are protected from ordinary users. We assume that constraints themselves could be classified at multiple security levels. However, they are stored at the system-high level. The constraint manager, which is trusted, will ensure that a user can read the constraints classified only at or below his or her level. Our approach to security constraint processing is to handle certain constraints during query processing, certain constraints during database updates, and certain constraints during database design.

Below we briefly illustrate the architectures for processing constraints during the query, update, and database design operations. The architecture for query processing is shown in Figure D.2. This architecture can be regarded as a loose coupling between an MLS/DBMS and a deductive manager. The deductive manager is what we have called the query processor. It has to operate online. The architecture for update processing is shown in Figure D.3. This architecture can also be regarded as

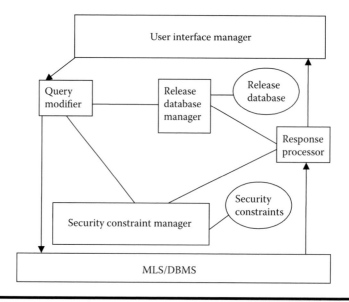

Figure D.2   Query processor.

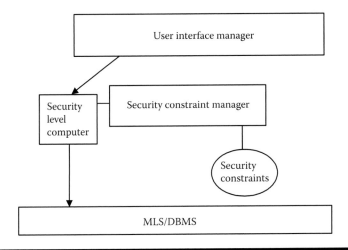

Figure D.3   Update processor.

a loose coupling between an MLS/RDBMS and a deductive manager. The deductive manager is what we have called the update processor. It could be used online where the security levels of the data are determined during database inserts and updates, or it could be used offline as a tool that ensures that data entered via bulk data loads and bulk data updates are accurately labeled. If the tool is used offline, however, it may be difficult to recompute the levels of the data already in the database if these levels are affected by the new data that are being inserted. The tool, which handles security constraints during database design and is illustrated in Figure D.4, can be used by the SSO to design the schema. The input to the tool is the set of security constraints that should be handled during database design and the schema. The output of the tool is the modified schema and the constraints.

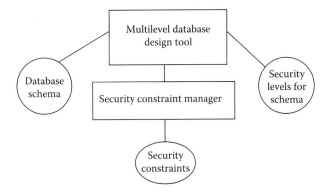

Figure D.4   Database design tool.

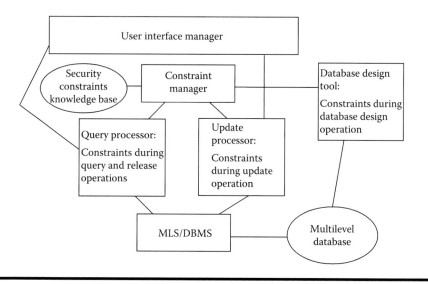

Figure D.5   Integrated architecture.

Although the query processor, the update processor, and the database design tool are separate modules, they all constitute the solution to constraint processing in multilevel relational databases. That is, they provide an integrated solution to security constraint processing in a multilevel environment.

Figure D.5 illustrates the integrated architecture. In this architecture, the constraints and schema that are produced by the constraint generator are processed further by the database design tool. The modified constraints are given to the constraint updater in order to update the constraint database. The schema is given to the constraint generator. The constraints in the constraint database are used by the query and update processors. We assume that there is a trusted constraint manager processor that manages the constraints. In a dynamic environment where the data and the constraints are changing, the query processor will examine all the relevant constraints and ensure that users do not obtain unauthorized data.

D.5 Consistency and Completeness of the Constraints

In Section D.2 we described the two tasks involved in constraint handling—constraint generation and constraint enforcement. While our main focus is on constraint enforcement, the relationship between the two tasks is illustrated in Figure D.6. That is, the constraint generator takes the specification of the multilevel application and outputs the initial schema and the constraints that must be enforced. The database design tool takes this output as its input and designs the database.

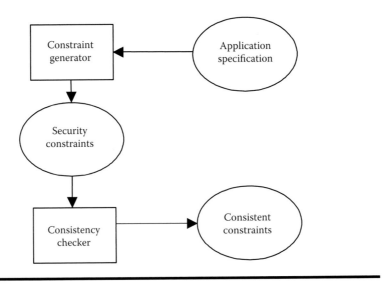

Figure D.6   Constraint generation.

The update processor and the query processor use the constraints and schema produced by the database design tool. Generating the initial set of constraints remains a challenge. We need to examine the use of conceptual structures and semantic data models to see if we can specify the application and subsequently generate the security constraints. Algorithm A checks for the consistency and completeness of the security constraints.

Algorithm A: Consistency and Completeness Checker

Input: Set of security constraints
Output: Set of consistent and complete security constraints

  Step 1: For each relation and attribute compute the security level of the relation and attribute
  Step 2: If there are constraints that assign multiple security levels to a relation or attribute then delete/modify the constraint that assigns the lower security level; the constraint is modified if that constraint assigns security levels to other attributes and relations
  Step 3: If there is some relation or attribute that is not assigned a security level by the constraints, then create a constraint that will assign the lowest security level to the relation or attribute
  Step 4: The resulting set of constraints is the output

D.6 Design of the Query Processor

We first describe a security policy for handling inferences during query processing and then discuss our design approach.

D.6.1 Security Policy

A security policy for query processing that we propose extends the simple security property in Bell and LaPadula (1973) to handle inference violations. This policy is stated below.

Given a security level L, E(L) is the knowledge base associated with L. That is, E(L) will consist of all responses that have been released at security level L over a certain time period and the real-world information at security level L.

Let a user U at security level L pose a query. Then the response R to the query will be released to this user if the following condition is satisfied:

For all security levels L* where L* dominates L, if (E(L*) UNION R) = = > X (for any X) then L* dominates Level(X).

Where A = = > B means B can be inferred from A using any of the inference strategies and Level(X) is the security level of X.

We assume that any response that is released into a knowledge base at level L is also released into the knowledge bases at level L* > = L. The policy states that whenever a response is released to a user at level L, it must be ensured that any user at level L* > = L cannot infer information classified at a level L+ > = L from the response together with the knowledge that he or she has already acquired. Note that while we consider only hierarchical levels in specifying the policy, it can also be extended to include nonhierarchical levels.

D.6.2 Functionality of the Query Processor

The strength of the query processor depends on the type of inference strategies that it can handle. In our design we consider only a limited set of inference strategies such as inference through association and deduction. In this section, we discuss the techniques that we have used to implement the security policy, which are query modification and response processing. Each technique is described below. Note that much of the code of the query modification module and the response processing module has to be trusted because they perform security critical functions. Detailed discussion of the trusted modules is given in Thuraisingham et al. (1993).

D.6.2.1 Query Modification

Query modification technique has been used in the past to handle discretionary security and views (Stonebraker and Wong 1974). This technique has been extended to include mandatory security in Dwyer et al. (1987). In our design of the query processor, this technique is used by the inference engine to modify the query depending on the security constraints, the previous responses released, and real-world information. When the modified query is posed, the response generated will not violate security.

Consider the architecture for query processing illustrated in Figure D.2. The inference engine has access to the knowledge base that includes security constraints, previously released responses, and real-world information. Conceptually one can think of the database as part of the knowledge base. We illustrate the query modification technique with examples. The actual implementation of this technique could adapt any of the proposals given in Gallaire and Minker (1978) for deductive query processing.

Consider a database that consists of relations SHIP and MISSION where the attributes of SHIP are S#, SNAME, CAPTAIN, and M# with S# as the key, and the attributes of MISSION are Mt#, MNAME, and LOCATION with M# as the key. Suppose the knowledge base consists of the following rules:

1. SHIP(X,Y,Z,A) and Z = Smith— > Level(Y,Secret)
2. SHIP(X,Y,Z,A) and A = 10— > Level(Y,TopSecret)
3. SHIP(X,Y,Z,A)— > Level(Together(Y,Z), Secret)
4. SHIP(X,Y,Z,A) and Release(Z,Unclassified)— > Level(Y,Secret)
5. SHIP(X,Y,Z,A) and Release(Y,Unclassified)— > Level(Z,Secret)
6. NOT(Level(X,Secret) or Level(X,TopSecret))— > Level(X,Unclassified)

The first rule is a content-based constraint that classifies a ship name whose captain is Smith at the Secret level. Similarly, the second rule is also a content-based constraint that classifies a ship name whose M# number is 10 at the TopSecret level. The third rule is an association-based constraint that classifies ship names and captains taken together at the Secret level. The fourth and fifth rules are additional restrictions that are enforced as a result of the context-based constraint specified in rule 3. The sixth rule states that the default classification level of a data item is Unclassified.

Suppose an unclassified user requests the ship names in SHIP. This query is represented as follows:

```
SHIP (X,Y,Z,D)
```

Since a ship name is classified at the Secret level if either the captain is "Smith" or the captain name is already released at the Unclassified level, and it is classified at the TopSecret level if the M# is "10", assuming that the captain names are not yet released to a unclassified user, the query is modified to the following:

```
SHIP(X,Y,Z,D) and NOT (Z = Smith and D = 10).
```

Note that since query modification is performed in real time, it will have some impact on the performance of the query processing algorithm. However, several techniques for semantic query optimization have been proposed for intelligent query processing (see, for example, Hinke 1988). These techniques could be adapted for query processing in a multilevel environment in order to improve the performance.

D.6.2.2 Response Processing

For many applications, in addition to query modification, some further processing of the response such as response sanitization may need to be performed. We will illustrate this point with examples.

Example D.1

Consider the following release constraints:

1. All ship names whose corresponding captain names are already released to unclassified users are secret
2. All captain names whose corresponding ship names are already released to unclassified users are secret

Suppose an unclassified user requests the ship names first. Depending on the other constraints imposed, let us assume that only certain names are released to the user. Then the ship names released have to be recorded into the knowledge base. Later, suppose an unclassified user (who does not necessarily have to be the same one) asks for captain names. The captain name values (some or all) are then assembled in the response. Before the response is released, the ship names that are already released to the unclassified user need to be examined. Then the captain name value which corresponds to a ship name value that is already released is suppressed from the response. Note that there has to be a way of correlating the ship names with the captains. This means the primary key values (which is the S#) should also be retrieved with the captain names as well as be stored with the ship names in the release database.

Example D.2

Consider the following aggregate constraint:
A collection of 10 or more tuples in the relation SHIP is secret.
Suppose a unclassified user requests the tuples in SHIP. The response is assembled and then examined to see if it has more than 10 tuples. If so, it is suppressed.
There are some problems associated with maintaining the release information. As more and more relevant release information gets inserted, the knowledge base could grow at a rapid rate. Therefore, efficient techniques for processing the knowledge base need to be developed. This would also have an impact on the performance of the query processing algorithms. Therefore, one solution would be to include only certain crucial release information in the knowledge base. The rest of the information can be stored with the audit data, which can then be used by the SSO for analysis.

D.7 Design of the Update Processor

We first discuss the security policy for database updates and then describe the design approach.

D.7.1 Security Policy

MLS/DBMSs ensure the assignment of a security level to data as data are inserted or modified. The security level assigned to the data, however, is generally assumed to be the login security level of the user entering the data. A more powerful and dynamic approach to assigning security levels to data is through the utilization of security constraints during update operations.

The security policy of the update processor is formulated from the simple security property in Bell and LaPadula (1973) and from a security policy provided by the underlying MLS/DBMS. This policy is as follows:

1. All users are granted a maximum clearance level with respect to security levels. A user may log in at any level that is dominated by his or her maximum clearance level. Subjects act on behalf of users at the user's login security level.
2. Objects are the rows, tables, and databases, and every object is assigned a security level upon creation.
3. A subject has read access to an object if the security level of the subject dominates the security level of the object.
4. A subject has write access to an object if the security level of the object dominates the security level of the subject.

Statements 3 and 4 of the policy presented above are the simple and * -property of the Bell and La Padula policy.

D.7.2 Functionality of the Update Processor

The update processor utilizes simple and content-dependent security constraints as guidance in determining the security level of the data being updated. The use of security constraints can thereby protect against users incorrectly labeling data as a result of logging in at the wrong level, against data being incorrectly labeled when it is imported from systems of different modes of operation such as a system high, and against database inconsistencies as a consequence of the security label of data in the database being affected by data being entered into the database.

The security level of an update request is determined by the update processor as follows. The simple and content-dependent security constraints associated with the relation being updated and with a security label greater than the user login security level are retrieved and examined for applicability. If multiple constraints apply, the security level is determined by the constraint that specifies the highest classification level; if no constraints apply, the update level is the login security level of the user. The update processor, therefore, does not determine the security level of the data solely from the security constraints but utilizes the constraints as guidance in determining the level of the input data. The following examples illustrate the functionality of the update processor.

Consider a database that consists of a relation SHIP whose attributes are ship number, name, class, date, and MISSION, with mission number as its primary key. The content-based constraint that classifies all SHIP values with the name Josephine as secret is expressed as

```
SHIP.sname = "Josephine"— — > Secret.
```

A user at login security level of, for example, Confidential enters the following data to insert a tuple into the SHIP relation:

```
Insert SHIP values ("SSN 729", "James","Thomsen","MR1800").
```

That is, the ship number for James is SSN729, his captain is Thomsen, and his mission record number is MR1800.

The update processor will receive this insert and retrieve the constraints associated with the SHIP relation that specify a level greater than the user level, which is Confidential, and whose level is less than or equal to the user level. The content-based constraint stated above is retrieved. Since the data entered for the name field is not "Josephine," the security constraint associated with the SHIP relation will not affect the classification level of the insert and the update processor will determine the insert level to be the user level, which is Confidential.

Suppose a user at login security level Confidential then enters the following: Insert SHIP values ("SSN 730," "Josephine," "Jane," "MR2100"). The update processor will again retrieve the content-based constraint associated with the SHIP relation, which specifies a level greater than the user level and whose level is less than or equal to the user level. Since the data for the name field is "Josephine," the update processor will determine the insert level to be Secret. If, however, the user entered this insert at login security level TopSecret, the update processor would perform the insert at the user level since the user level is higher than the level specified by the security constraint.

The update operation of the update processor functions similarly to the insert operation. As an example, suppose a user at the Confidential level enters the following: Update SHIP set Sname = "Josephine" where captain = "Thomsen." The update processor will retrieve the security constraints associated with the SHIP relation that specify a level greater than the user level and whose level is less than or equal to the user level. The content-dependent constraint stated above will be retrieved, and the update processor will determine the update level to be Secret since the name field is being modified to "Josephine." The tuple with a primary key of "SSN 729" as defined above will then be updated at the secret level, and the original tuple will be deleted.

In addition to describing the functionality of the update processor, the examples above illustrate the potential signaling channels that exist when operating with the update processor. A signaling channel is a form of covert channel that occurs when the actions of a high-security-level user or subject interfere with a low-security-level user or subject in a visible manner. Potential signaling channels occur when data are entered at a level higher than the user level and the user attempts to retrieve the data that he or she has entered, or when the update processor attempts to enter data at a higher level but cannot since a tuple with the same primary key already exists at this level. More details on the design of the update processor and the trusted components are discussed in Thuraisingham et al. (1993).

D.8 Handling Security Constraints during Database Design

D.8.1 Overview

The main focus of this section is a discussion on how security constraints could be handled during database design. We then briefly discuss how simple constraints as well as logical constraints could be handled.

An association-based constraint classifies a collection of attributes taken together at a particular security level. What is interesting about the association-based constraint is that it can generate several relationships between the various attributes. For example, if there is a relation SHIP whose attributes are S#, SNAME, and CAPTAIN, and if an association-based constraint classifies the SNAME and CAPTAIN taken together at the Secret level, then one of the pairs (S#, SNAME), (S#, CAPTAIN) should also be classified at the Secret level. Otherwise, an unclassified user can obtain the (S#, SNAME) and the (S#, CAPTAIN) pairs and infer the secret association (SNAME, CAPTAIN).

We have designed an algorithm that processes a given set of association-based constraints and outputs the schema for the multilevel database (see Thuraisingham et al. 1993; Thuraisingham and Ford 1995). Given a set of association-based constraints and an initial schema, the algorithm will output clusters of attributes and the security level of each cluster. We then prove that the attributes within a cluster can be stored securely at the corresponding level. A tool based on this algorithm can help the SSO design the multilevel database. The algorithm that we have designed does not necessarily have to be executed only during database design; it can also be executed during query processing. That is, the query processor can examine the attributes in the various clusters generated by the algorithm and then determine which information has to be released to the users. For example, if the algorithm places the attributes A1, A2 in cluster 1 at level L, and the attributes A3, A4 in cluster 2 at level L, then, after an attribute in cluster 1 has been released to a user at level L, none of the attributes in cluster 2 can be released to users at level L.

Since simple constraints can be regarded as a special form of association-based constraints where only one attribute is classified, we feel that such constraints could also be handled during database design. Another constraint that could be handled during database design is the logical constraint. For example, if attribute A implies an attribute B, and if attribute B is classified at the Secret level, then attribute A must be classified at least at the Secret level. Note that if any of the constraints have conditions attached to them, then handling them during database design time would be difficult. For example, consider the following constraint: "SNAME and LOCATION taken together are Secret if LOCATION is from company X." Such a constraint depends on data values. Therefore, they are best handled during either query or update processing.

We will first elaborate on the processing of association-based constraints. The input to this algorithm is a set of association-based constraints and a set of attributes. The output of this algorithm is a set of clusters for each security level. Each cluster for a security level L will have a collection of attributes that can be safely classified at the level L. That is, if A1, A2, and A3 are attributes in a cluster C at level Secret, then the attributes A1, A2, and A3 can be classified together safely at the security level Secret without violating security. The clusters are formed depending on the association-based constraints that are input to the program. Once the clusters are formed, then the database can be defined according to the functional and multivalued dependencies that are enforced.

Next let us consider the simple constraints. Since simple constraints classify individual attributes at a certain security level, they could also be handled during database design. Note that when an attribute A in relation R is classified at level L, then all elements that belong to A is also classified at level L. Therefore, we can store A itself at level L.

The algorithm that handles simple constraint is straightforward. Each attribute that is classified by a simple constraint is stored at the level specified in the constraint. Once the algorithm for processing simple constraints is applied and the corresponding schema is obtained, then this schema is given as input to the algorithm handling association-based constraints. The association-based constraints are then applied and the final schema is obtained.

Logical constraints are rules that can be used to deduce new data from existing data. If a security constraint classifies the new data at a level that is higher than that of the existing data, then the existing data must be reclassified. Logical constraints could be straightforward, such as $Ai => Aj$, or they could be more complex, such as $A1 \& A2 \& A3 \& An => Am$. If Aj is classified at the Secret level then Ai must be classified at least at the Secret level. If Am is classified at the Secret level, then at least one of $A1, A2,...$ An must be classified at least at the Secret level. Further details of the algorithms on processing constraints during database design are given in Thuraisingham et al. (1993) and Thuraisingham and Ford (1995).

D.9 Security Control Processing and Release Control

Until now we have discussed an integrated architecture mainly for a centralized environment where constraints are examined during query, database update, and database design time. That is, in the case of the query operation much of the work is carried out before the query is sent to the MLS/DBMS. Once the query is executed, then we examine certain release constraints to see what has been released before.

Recently there has been some work on processing constraints only after the response is released by the DBMS but before the response is given to the user. These approaches can be found in Jajodia (2003) and Wiederhold (2000). The idea behind this approach is that it may not be feasible to modify the query, especially if there are many constraints. Therefore, rather than doing the work before the query is executed, why not do all of the processing after the response is released by the DBMS?

This approach does have some disadvantages. That is, after the response is released, one has to examine all of the security constraints and determine what information to release to the user. Essentially many of the operations carried out by the DBMS will now have to be carried out by the release control manager (RCM). That is, the RCM will have to carry out selections, projects, joins, and so forth to obtain the final result. However, the advantage with this approach is that if there are many constraints, the complex query modification process is avoided.

Note that the DBMS will produce the result at the user's security level. The RCM will then examine the result and the constraints and determine whether all of the data could be released. Suppose there is a constraint that states that LOCATION values in MISSION are secret and the user's level is Unclassified. The release data will have all of the information in the relation MISSION. RCM will apply the constraint and only give out the mission names and not the location values. Figure D.7 illustrates the RCM.

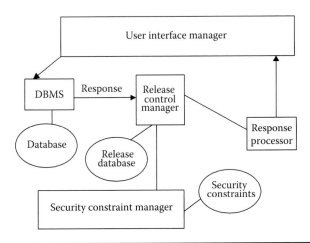

Figure D.7   RCM.

D.10 Distributed Inference Control

Much of the work has focused on the inference problem in a centralized environment. Data distribution exacerbates the problem as users from different sites can retrieve information and make associations. An investigation of the inference problem for distributed database systems began around 1992. This approach was based on processing security constraints in a multilevel secure distributed database system. The first step was to design a multilevel secure distributed data management system and then augment such a system with constraint processors. Details of this work are reported in Thuraisingham and Rubinovitz (1993) and Thuraisingham and Ford (1995).

Figure D.8 illustrates a distributed inference controller. The distributed constraint processor examines the constraints at the global level, communicates with its peer distributed constraint processors, and determines whether security violations via inference can occur. The techniques are similar to the ones we have discussed in the earlier sections except that the constraints are now enforced across the nodes. We will explain with an example. Suppose we have a constraint that classified ship's mission at the Secret level after the location has been released at the Unclassified level. An unclassified user can pose a query at site A to retrieve the location and

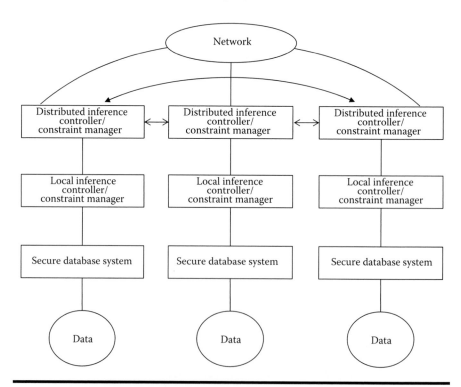

Figure D.8   Distributed inference controller/constraint processor.

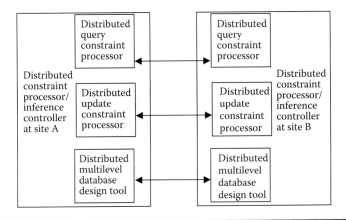

Figure D.9   Modules of the distributed constraint processor.

pose a query at site B to retrieve the mission and this violates security. Therefore, the fact that the location has been released at site A has to be recorded and made available to all the distributed constraint processors. We have also designed techniques for handling security constraints during distributed update processing and during multilevel distributed database design. Modules of the distributed constraint processor are illustrated in Figure D.9. Details of our algorithms can be found in Thuraisingham and Ford (1995).

D.11 Summary and Directions

In this appendix we first defined various types of security constraints. Security constraints are rules that assign security levels to the data. Then we described an integrated approach to constraint processing. That is, some constraints are handled during query processing, some during database updates, and some during database design. We then described the design of a system that processes constraints during query and update operations. We also described the design of a database design tool. Finally, we discussed an alternative approach to security constraint processing, called release processing, as well as distributed inference control.

Future work includes examining the release control approach further. In addition, we need to conduct research on security control algorithms for federated environments. Some initial directions for distributed environments are given in Thuraisingham (2005). We also need to develop techniques for generating constraints. For example, we may need to examine the use of semantic models and conceptual structures to specify the application and reason about the application and detect security violations during design time. We also need to examine the enforcement of more complex constraints. In other words, there is lot of research to be done on security constraint processing. The information in this book can be considered the first step toward developing next generation inference controllers.

References

Bell, D. and LaPadula, L., Secure computer systems: Mathematical foundations and model, M74-244, The MITRE Corporation, Bedford, MA, 1973.

Dwyer, P. et al., Multilevel security for relational database systems, *Computers & Security,* Vol. 6, No. 3, 1987.

Gallaire, H. and Minker, J. (eds.), *Logic and Databases,* Plenum Press, New York, 1978.

Hinke, T., Inference and aggregation detection in database management systems, Proceedings of the 1988 Conference on Security and Privacy, Oakland, CA, April 1988.

Jajodia, S., Release control for XML documents, Proceedings IFIP Conference in Integrity and Control, Lausanne, Switzerland, November 2003 (proceedings published by Kluwer, 2004).

Keefe, T. et al., Secure query processing strategies, *IEEE Computer,* Vol. 22, No. 3, 1989.

Lloyd, J., *Foundations of Logic Programming,* Springer-Verlag, Berlin, 1987.

Morgenstern, M., Security and inference in multilevel database and knowledge base systems, Proceedings of the ACM SIGM CD Conference, San Francisco, May 1987.

Stonebraker, M. and Wong, E., Access control in a relational data base management system by query modification, Proceedings of the ACM Annual Conference, ACM Press, New York, 1974.

Thuraisingham, B., Security checking in relational database management systems augmented with inference engines, *Computers & Security,* Vol. 6, No. 6, 1987.

Thuraisingham, B., Towards the design of secure database and knowledge base management system, *Data and Knowledge Engineering Journal,* Vol. 5, No. 1, 1990.

Thuraisingham, B., *Database and Applications Security*, Auerbach Publications, Boca Raton, FL, 2005.

Thuraisingham, B. and Ford, W., Security constraint processing in a multilevel distributed database management system, *IEEE Transactions on Knowledge and Data Engineering,* Vol. 7, No. 2, 1995.

Thuraisingham, B., Ford, W. and Collins, M., Design and implementation of a database inference controller, *Data and Knowledge Engineering Journal,* Vol. 11, No. 3, 1993.

Thuraisingham, B. and Rubinovitz, H., Design and implementation of a distributed query processor for a trusted distributed database management systems, *Journal of Systems and Software*, April 1993.

Wiederhold, G., Release control in database systems, Proceedings IFIP Database Security Conference, Amsterdam, August 2000 (proceedings published by Kluwer, 2001).

Index

Page numbers followed by f and t indicate figures and tables, respectively.